2-cylinder Owners Workshop Manual

I M Coomber

Models covered
Citroën 2CV, 2CV4 and 2CV6
Citroën Ami 6 and 8; Saloon and Estate
Citroën Dyane 4 and 6
425 cc, 435 cc & 602 cc

Does not cover Visa or Ami Super
Does not fully cover 2CV van or Fourgonette

ISBN 0 85696 972 9

ABCDE
FGHIJ
KLM

Printed in England *(196-2K1)*

Haynes THE BOOK ®

HAYNES PUBLISHING GROUP
SPARKFORD YEOVIL SOMERSET BA22 7JJ ENGLAND

distributed in the USA by
HAYNES PUBLICATIONS INC
861 LAWRENCE DRIVE
NEWBURY PARK
CALIFORNIA 91320
USA

Acknowledgements

Thanks are due to Citroën Cars Ltd for the supply of technical information and for the use of certain illustrations. John Richards of the Citroën Car Club gave valuable specialist advice. The Champion Sparking Plug Company supplied the illustrations showing the various spark plug conditions. Castrol Limited supplied the lubrication data. Special thanks are due to all those people at Sparkford who helped in the production of this manual.

About this manual

Its aim

The aim of this manual is to help you get the best value from your car. It can do so in several ways. It can help you decide what work must be done (even should you choose to get it done by a garage), provide information on routine maintenance and servicing, and give a logical course of action and diagnosis when random faults occur. However, it is hoped that you will use the manual by tackling the work yourself. On simpler jobs it may even be quicker than booking the car into a garage and going there twice to leave and collect it. Perhaps most important, a lot of money can be saved by avoiding the costs the garage must charge to cover its labour and overheads.

The manual has drawings and descriptions to show the function of the various compoents so that their layout can be understood. Then the tasks are described and photographed in a step-by-step sequence so that even a novice can do the work.

Its arrangement

The manual is divided into twelve Chapters, each covering a logical sub-division of the vehicle. The Chapters are each divided into Sections, numbered with single figures, eg 5; and the Sections into paragraphs (or sub-sections), with decimal numbers following on from the Section they are in, eg 5.1, 5.2, 5.3 etc.

It is freely illustrated, especially in those parts where there is a detailed sequence of operations to be carried out. There are two forms of illustration: figures and photographs. The figures are numbered in sequence with decimal numbers, according to their position in the Chapter – eg Fig. 6.4 is the fourth drawing/illustration in Chapter 6. Photographs carry the same number (either individually or in related groups) as the Section or sub-section to which they relate.

There is an alphabetical Index at the back of the manual as well as a contents list at the front. Each Chapter is also preceded by its own individual contents list.

References to the 'left' or 'right' of the vehicle are in the sense of a person in the driver's seat facing forwards.

Unless otherwise stated, nuts and bolts are removed by turning anti-clockwise, and tightened by turning clockwise.

Vehicle manufacturers continually make changes to specifications and recommendations, and these, when notified, are incorporated into our manuals at the earliest opportunity.

Whilst every care is taken to ensure that the information in this manual is correct, no liability can be accepted by the authors or publishers for loss, damage or injury caused by any errors in, or omissions from the information given.

Introduction to the Citroën 2CV

Although the Citroën 2CV was first marketed in 1948, it was originally designed and the first prototypes produced in the late 1930s. The original ambition was cheap, go anywhere, practical family transport. The original power unit was a 375cc flat twin, but this was subsequently changed to 425 or 435cc and later 602cc. This apart, the model has changed very little over the years, having just the occasional facelift or refinement added, the basic concept remaining unchanged.

As well as being an economical vehicle, the 2CV has several unique features which allow it reliability, good handling and a surprising amount of comfort for four people. The principal features are front wheel drive and independent front and rear suspension. Standard equipment also includes a facia gear change and a roll back sunshine roof, and on some models a 'trafficlutch' is also fitted. This last mentioned device eliminates the need to use the clutch pedal in the lower gears below certain engine speeds and is most beneficial in heavy traffic, especially for a novice driver.

The engine is a very simple unit, being air-cooled from the large front mounted fan. Lubricant to the valvegear is supplied via an oil cooler and this enables the engine to be driven hard for prolonged periods without harm.

All body panels are removable, being bolted in position, and this is essential in some operations to gain access to certain components.

Other models derived from the 2CV include the Dyane 4 and 6 and the Ami 6 and 8. The Dyane is a refined version of the 2CV with a 'hatchback', whilst the Ami has a completely different body style but is still distinctively Citroën. All versions have also been produced with a van body and the Ami was at one time available in Saloon or Estate form.

Over the many years of production, the 2CV and derivatives have proved to be among the most successful 'economy' vehicles ever made and when treated with a modicum of respect will serve very well.

Contents

Citroën 2CV

Citroën Ami 8

Citroën Dyane

Buying spare parts and vehicle identification numbers

Buying spare parts

Spare parts are available from many sources, for example, Citroën garages, other garages and accessory shops, and motor factors. Our advice regarding spare parts is as follows.

Officially appointed Citroën garages. This is the best source of parts which are peculiar to your car and otherwise not generally available (eg complete cylinder heads, internal gearbox components badges, interior trim etc). It is also the only place at which you should buy parts if your car is still under warranty; non-Citroën parts may invalidate the warranty. To be sure of obtaining the correct parts it will always be necessary to give the storeman your car's engine and chassis number, and if possible, to take the old part along for positive identification. Many parts are available under a factory exchange scheme; any parts returned should always be clean. It obviously makes good sense to go straight to the specialists on your car for this type of part for they are best equipped to supply you.

Other garages and accessory shops. These are often very good places to buy material and components needed for the maintenance of your car, (eg oil filters, spark plugs, bulbs, belts, oils and grease, touch-up paint, filler paste etc). They also sell general accessories, usually have convenient opening hours, charge lower prices and can often be found not far from home.

Motor factors. Good factors stock all the more important components which wear out relatively quickly (eg clutch components, pistons and cylinders, valves, exhaust systems, brake pipes/seals and pads, etc). Motor factors will often provide new or reconditioned components on a part exchange basis – this can save a considerable amount of money.

Vehicle identification numbers

Modifications are a continuing and unpublicised process in vehicle manufacture quite apart from major model changes. Spare parts manuals and lists are compiled upon a numerical basis, the individual vehicle numbers being essential for correct identification of the component required.

There are considerable specification differences between the models covered by this manual. Always use the correct Citroën model number when describing your car to a storeman.

The vehicle identification plate is located in the engine compartment. On the 2CV and Dyane models the plate is situated on the right-hand side of the scuttle panel, or on the chassis under the right-hand driveshaft (photo). On the Ami it is under the gear lever control.

The engine number plate on all models is on the engine housing on the right-hand side. The engine code is shown on this plate.

A stamped identification number is also to be found on the platform under the front seat.

The paint colour code appears on a disc attached to the scuttle panel.

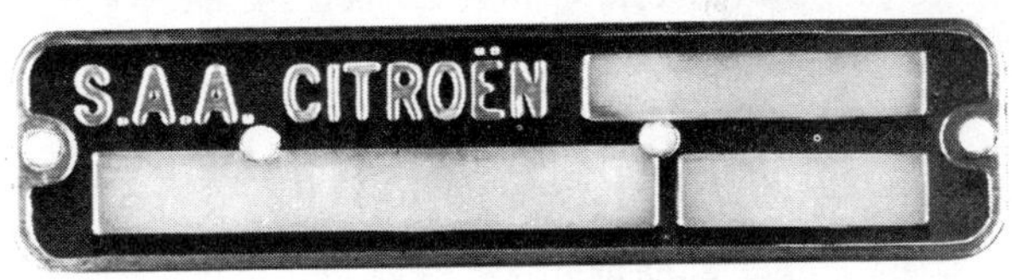

Engine number plate

The vehicle identification plate

Tools and working facilities

Introduction

A selection of good tools is a fundamental requirement for anyone contemplating the maintenance and repair of a motor vehicle. For the owner who does not possess any, their purchase will prove a considerable expense, offsetting some of the savings made by doing-it-yourself. However, provided that the tools purchased are of good quality, they will last for many years and prove an extremely worthwhile investment.

To help the average owner to decide which tools are needed to carry out the various tasks detailed in this manual, we have compiled three lists of tools under the following headings: *Maintenance and minor repair, Repair and overhaul,* and *Special.* The newcomer to practical mechanics should start off with the *Maintenance and minor repair* tool kit and confine himself to the simpler jobs around the vehicle. Then, as his confidence and experience grow, he can undertake more difficult tasks, buying extra tools as, and when, they are needed. In this way, a *Maintenance and minor repair* tool kit can be built-up into a *Repair and overhaul* tool kit over a considerable period of time without any major cash outlays. The experienced do-it-yourselfer will have a tool kit good enough for most repair and overhaul procedures and will add tools from the *Special* category when he feels the expense is justified by the amount of use these tools will be put to.

It is obviously not possible to cover the subject of tools fully here. For those who wish to learn more about tools and their use there is a book entitled *How to Choose and Use Car Tools* available from the publishers of this manual.

Maintenance and minor repair tool kit

The tools given in this list should be considered as a minimum requirement if routine maintenance, servicing and minor repair operations are to be undertaken. We recommend the purchase of combination spanners (ring one end, open-ended the other); although more expensive than open-ended ones, they do give the advantages of both types of spanner.

Combination spanners - 8, 9, 10, 11, 12, 13, 14, 15 16 and 19 mm
Box spanners – 8, 12, 14, (long) and 21 mm
Adjustable spanner - 9 inch
Spark plug spanner (with rubber insert)
Spark plug gap adjustment tool
Set of feeler gauges
Plug/points file
Brake bleed nipple spanner
Screwdriver - 4 in long x $\frac{1}{4}$ in dia (flat blade)
Screwdriver - 4 in long x $\frac{1}{4}$ in dia (cross blade)
Combination pliers - 6 inch
Hacksaw, junior
Tyre pump
Tyre pressure gauge
Grease gun
Oil can
Fine emery cloth (1 sheet)
Wire brush (small)
Funnel (medium size)

Repair and overhaul tool kit

These tools are virtually essential for anyone undertaking any major repairs to a motor vehicle, and are additional to those given in the *Maintenance and minor repair* list. Included in this list is a comprehensive set of sockets. Although these are expensive they will be found invaluable as they are so versatile - particularly if various drives are included in the set. We recommend the $\frac{1}{2}$ in square-drive type, as this can be used with most proprietary torque spanners. If you cannot afford a socket set, even bought piecemeal, then inexpensive tubular box wrenches are a useful alternative.

The tools in this list will occasionally need to be supplemented by tools from the *Special* list.

Sockets (or box spanners) to cover range in previous list, and $\frac{3}{4}$ in square drive 32 mm ($1\frac{1}{4}$ in AF) and 44 mm
Reversible ratchet drive (for use with sockets)
Extension piece, 10 inch (for use with sockets)
Universal joint (for use with sockets)
Torque wrench (for use with sockets)
Mole wrench - 8 inch
Ball pein hammer
Soft-faced hammer, plastic or rubber
Screwdriver - 6 in long x $\frac{5}{16}$ in dia (flat blade)
Screwdriver - 2 in long x $\frac{5}{16}$ in square (flat blade)
Screwdriver - $1\frac{1}{2}$ in long x $\frac{1}{4}$ in dia (cross blade)
Screwdriver - 3 in long x $\frac{1}{8}$ in dia (electricians)
Pliers - electricians side cutters
Pliers - needle nosed
Pliers - circlip (internal and external)
Cold chisel - $\frac{1}{2}$ inch
Scriber (this can be made by grinding the end of a broken hacksaw blade)
Scraper (this can be made by flattening and sharpening one end of a piece of copper pipe)
Centre punch
Pin punch
Hacksaw
Valve grinding tool
Steel rule/straight edge
Allen keys
Selection of files
Wire brush (large)
Axle-stands
Jack (strong scissor or hydraulic type)

Special tools

The tools in this list are those which are not used regularly, are expensive to buy, or which need to be used in accordance with their manufacturers' instructions. Unless relatively difficult mechanical jobs are undertaken frequently, it will not be economic to buy many of these tools. Where this is the case, you could consider clubbing together with friends (or a motorists' club) to make a joint purchase, or borrowing the tools against a deposit from a local garage or tool hire specialist.

The following list contains only those tools and instruments freely available to the public, and not those special tools produced by the vehicle manufacturer specifically for its dealer network. You will find occasional references to these manufacturers' special tools in the text of this manual. Generally, an alternative method of doing the job without the vehicle manufacturers' special tool is given. However, sometimes, there is no alternative to using them. Where this is the case and the relevant tool cannot be bought or borrowed you will have to entrust the work to a franchised garage.

Valve spring compressor (where applicable)
Piston ring compressor
Balljoint separator
Universal hub/bearing puller
Impact screwdriver
Micrometer and/or vernier gauge
Dial gauge
Stroboscopic timing light
Dwell angle meter/tachometer
Universal electrical multi-meter
Cylinder compression gauge
Lifting tackle (photo)
Trolley jack
Light with extension lead

Buying tools

For practically all tools, a tool dealer is the best source since he will have a very comprehensive range compared with the average garage or accessory shop. Having said that, accessory shops often offer excellent quality tools at discount prices, so it pays to shop around.

Remember, you don't have to buy the most expensive items on the shelf, but it is always advisable to steer clear of the very cheap tools. There are plenty of good tools around at reasonable prices, so ask the proprietor or manager of the shop for advice before making a purchase.

Care and maintenance of tools

Having purchased a reasonable tool kit, it is necessary to keep the tools in a clean serviceable condition. After use, always wipe off any dirt, grease and metal particles using a clean, dry cloth, before putting the tools away. Never leave them lying around after they have been used. A simple tool rack on the garage or workshop wall, for items such as screwdrivers and pliers is a good idea. Store all normal spanners and sockets in a metal box. Any measuring instruments, gauges, meters, etc, must be carefully stored where they cannot be damaged or become rusty.

Take a little care when tools are used. Hammer heads inevitably become marked and screwdrivers lose the keen edge on their blades from time to time. A little timely attention with emery cloth or a file will soon restore items like this to a good serviceable finish.

Working facilities

Not to be forgotten when discussing tools, is the workshop itself. If anything more than routine maintenance is to be carried out, some form of suitable working area becomes essential.

It is appreciated that many an owner mechanic is forced by circumstances to remove an engine or similar item, without the benefit of a garage or workshop. Having done this, any repairs should always be done under the cover of a roof.

Wherever possible, any dismantling should be done on a clean flat workbench or table at a suitable working height.

Any workbench needs a vise: one with a jaw opening of 4 in (100 mm) is suitable for most jobs. As mentioned previously, some clean dry storage space is also required for tools, as well as the lubricants, cleaning fluids, touch-up paints and so on which become necessary.

Another item which may be required, and which has a much more general usage, is an electric drill with a chuck capacity of at least $\frac{5}{16}$ in (8 mm). This, together with a good range of twist drills, is virtually essential for fitting accessories such as wing mirrors and reversing lights.

Last, but not least, always keep a supply of old newspapers and clean, lint-free rags available, and try to keep any working area as clean as possible.

Jaw gap (in)	Spanner size
0.250	$\frac{1}{4}$ in AF
0.276	7 mm
0.313	$\frac{5}{16}$ in AF
0.315	8 mm
0.344	$\frac{11}{32}$ in AF; $\frac{1}{8}$ in Whitworth
0.354	9 mm
0.375	$\frac{3}{8}$ in AF
0.394	10 mm
0.433	11 mm
0.438	$\frac{7}{16}$ in AF
0.445	$\frac{3}{16}$ in Whitworth; $\frac{1}{4}$ in BSF
0.472	12 mm
0.500	$\frac{1}{2}$ in AF
0.512	13 mm
0.525	$\frac{1}{4}$ in Whitworth; $\frac{5}{16}$ in BSF
0.551	14 mm
0.562	$\frac{9}{16}$ in AF
0.591	15 mm
0.600	$\frac{5}{16}$ in Whitworth; $\frac{3}{8}$ in BSF
0.625	$\frac{5}{8}$ in AF
0.630	16 mm
0.669	17 mm
0.686	$\frac{11}{16}$ in AF
0.709	18 mm
0.710	$\frac{3}{8}$ in Whitworth, $\frac{7}{16}$ in BSF
0.748	19 mm
0.750	$\frac{3}{4}$ in AF
0.813	$\frac{13}{16}$ in AF
0.820	$\frac{7}{16}$ in Whitworth; $\frac{1}{2}$ in BSF
0.866	22 mm
0.875	$\frac{7}{8}$ in AF
0.920	$\frac{1}{2}$ in Whitworth; $\frac{9}{16}$ in BSF
0.937	$\frac{15}{16}$ in AF
0.945	24 mm
1.000	1 in AF
1.010	$\frac{9}{16}$ in Whitworth; $\frac{5}{8}$ in BSF
1.024	26 mm
1.063	$1\frac{1}{16}$ in AF; 27 mm
1.100	$\frac{5}{8}$ in Whitworth; $\frac{11}{16}$ in BSF
1.125	$1\frac{1}{8}$ in AF
1.181	30 mm
1.200	$\frac{11}{16}$ in Whitworth; $\frac{3}{4}$ in BSF
1.250	$1\frac{1}{4}$ in AF
1.260	32 mm
1.300	$\frac{3}{4}$ in Whitworth; $\frac{7}{8}$ in BSF
1.313	$1\frac{5}{16}$ in AF
1.390	$\frac{13}{16}$ in Whitworth; $\frac{15}{16}$ in BSF
1.417	36 mm
1.438	$1\frac{7}{16}$ in AF
1.480	$\frac{7}{8}$ in Whitworth; 1 in BSF
1.500	$1\frac{1}{2}$ in AF
1.575	40 mm; $\frac{15}{16}$ in Whitworth
1.614	41 mm
1.625	$1\frac{5}{8}$ in AF
1.670	1 in Whitworth; $1\frac{1}{8}$ in BSF
1.688	$1\frac{11}{16}$ in AF
1.811	46 mm
1.813	$\frac{13}{16}$ in AF
1.860	$1\frac{1}{8}$ in Whitworth; $1\frac{1}{4}$ in BSF
1.875	$1\frac{7}{8}$ in AF
1.969	50 mm
2.000	2 in AF
2.050	$1\frac{1}{4}$ in Whitworth; $1\frac{3}{8}$ in BSF
2.165	55 mm
2.362	60 mm

A Haltrac hoist and gantry in use during a typical engine removal sequence

Jacking and towing

Before carrying out any servicing or repair operations, make sure that you know where to position the jack and axle stands. It is most important to use only the specified points on the front and rear ends of the box-section side-members in order to prevent accidents and damage to the vehicle itself.

If the vehicle breaks down or becomes bogged down, front-mounted towing hooks are provided to which a tow rope may be attached. Rear towing eyes are fitted to the outer sides of the chassis side-members. Always attach a tow-rope to both towing eyes. On vehicles fitted with a steering lock, always release the lock before being towed.

Do not try to start vehicles equipped with a centrifugal clutch (trafficlutch) by pushing or towing – it can't be done and damage may result. It should not be necessary anyway as a starting handle is provided.

The jack supplied is designed only to enable you to change a wheel in the event of a puncture. It is not to be relied on to carry out any maintenance or repair tasks under the vehicle. Always support the vehicle on axle/chassis stands or suitable blocks whenever you have to work under the vehicle. Apply the handbrake and chock the wheels before jacking up the car to prevent it rolling off the jack when raised. Try to jack up on firm level ground whenever possible.

The spare wheel is carried in the boot in the 2CV, whilst the Ami and Dyane models keep it in the engine compartment. Check the air pressure in the spare regularly. The wheelbrace also serves as the jack winding handle and the starting handle.

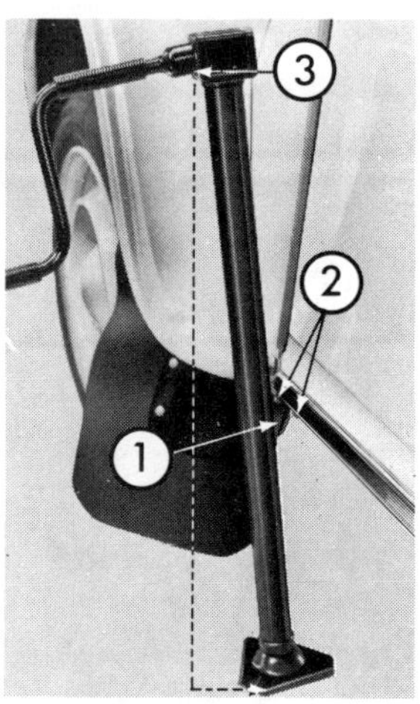

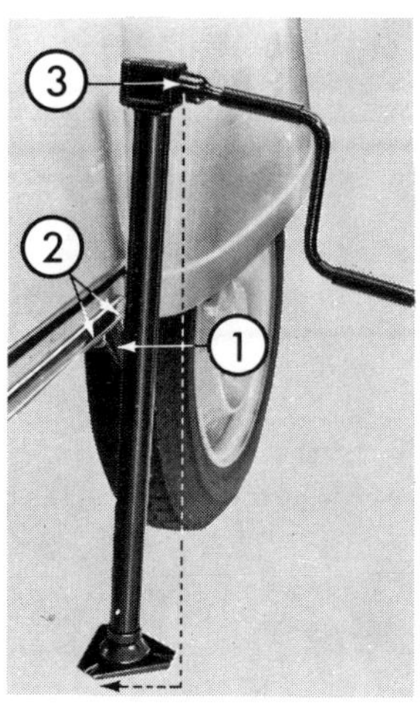

Jacking up at the front and rear (2CV and Dyane)

1 Jack lift arm
2 Chassis support
3 Jack winder/wheelbrace engaged in jack

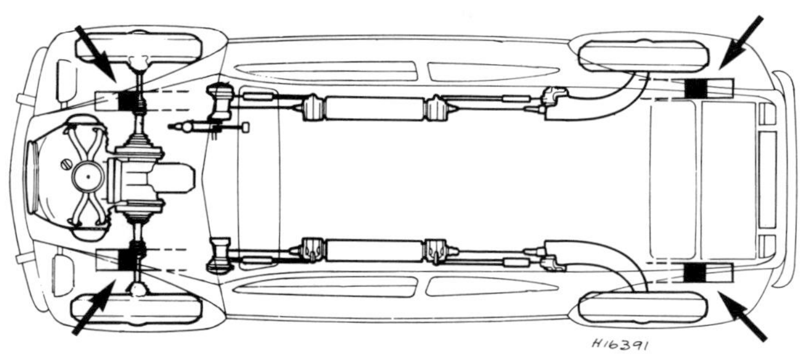

Main jacking points or axle stand locations

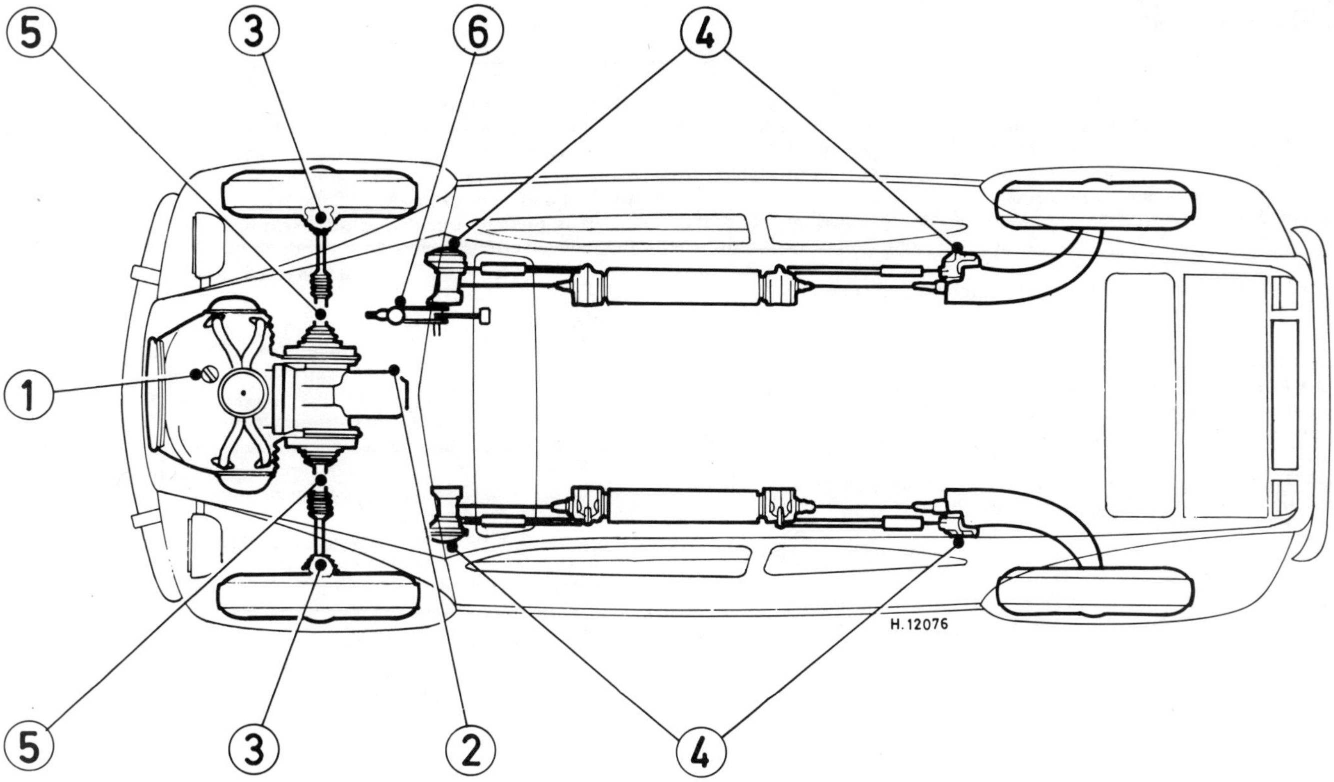

Recommended lubricants and fluids

Component or system	Lubricant type or specification	Castrol product
1 Engine	Multigrade engine oil SAE 20W/50	Castrol GTX
2 Gearbox	EP 80 gear oil	Castrol Hypoy light
3 Kingpin	Multi-purpose grease	Castrol LM
4 Suspension rod knife edges	Multi-purpose grease	Castrol LM
5 Driveshaft sliding joints and CV joints	Molybdenum grease	Castrol MS3
6A Brake hydraulic reservoir (models with drum brakes)	Brake fluid to SAE J1703	Castrol Girling Universal Brake and Clutch Fluid
6B Brake hydraulic reservoir (models with disc brakes)	LHM hydraulic fluid	Castrol LHM

Safety First!

Professional motor mechanics are trained in safe working procedures. However enthusiastic you may be about getting on with the job in hand, do take the time to ensure that your safety is not put at risk. A moment's lack of attention can result in an accident, as can failure to observe certain elementary precautions.

There will always be new ways of having accidents, and the following points do not pretend to be a comprehensive list of all dangers; they are intended rather to make you aware of the risks and to encourage a safety-conscious approach to all work you carry out on your vehicle.

Essential DOs and DON'Ts

DON'T rely on a single jack when working underneath the vehicle. Always use reliable additional means of support, such as axle stands, securely placed under a part of the vehicle that you know will not give way.

DON'T attempt to loosen or tighten high-torque nuts (e.g. wheel hub nuts) while the vehicle is on a jack; it may be pulled off.

DON'T start the engine without first ascertaining that the transmission is in neutral (or 'Park' where applicable) and the parking brake applied.

DON'T suddenly remove the filler cap from a hot cooling system – cover it with a cloth and release the pressure gradually first, or you may get scalded by escaping coolant.

DON'T attempt to drain oil until you are sure it has cooled sufficiently to avoid scalding you.

DON'T grasp any part of the engine, exhaust or catalytic converter without first ascertaining that it is sufficiently cool to avoid burning you.

DON'T syphon toxic liquids such as fuel, brake fluid or antifreeze by mouth, or allow them to remain on your skin.

DON'T inhale brake lining dust – it is injurious to health

DON'T allow any spilt oil or grease to remain on the floor – wipe it up straight away, before someone slips on it.

DON'T use ill-fitting spanners or other tools which may slip and cause injury.

DON'T attempt to lift a heavy component which may be beyond your capability – get assistance.

DON'T rush to finish a job, or take unverified short cuts.

DON'T allow children or animals in or around an unattended vehicle.

DO wear eye protection when using power tools such as drill, sander, bench grinder etc, and when working under the vehicle.

DO use a barrier cream on your hands prior to undertaking dirty jobs – it will protect your skin from infection as well as making the dirt easier to remove afterwards; but make sure your hands aren't left slippery.

DO keep loose clothing (cuffs, tie etc) and long hair well out of the way of moving mechanical parts.

DO remove rings, wristwatch etc, before working on the vehicle – especially the electrical system.

DO ensure that any lifting tackle used has a safe working load rating adequate for the job.

DO keep your work area tidy – it is only too easy to fall over articles left lying around.

DO get someone to check periodically that all is well, when working alone on the vehicle.

DO carry out work in a logical sequence and check that everything is correctly assembled and tightened afterwards.

DO remember that your vehicle's safety affects that of yourself and others. If in doubt on any point, get specialist advice.

IF, in spite of following these precautions, you are unfortunate enough to injure yourself, seek medical attention as soon as possible.

Fire

Remember at all times that petrol (gasoline) is highly flammable. Never smoke, or have any kind of naked flame around, when working on the vehicle. But the risk does not end there – a spark caused by an electrical short-circuit, by two metal surfaces contacting each other, or even by static electricity built up in your body under certain conditions, can ignite petrol vapour, which in a confined space is highly explosive.

Always disconnect the battery earth (ground) terminal before working on any part of the fuel system, and never risk spilling fuel on to a hot engine or exhaust.

It is recommended that a fire extinguisher of a type suitable for fuel and electrical fires is kept handy in the garage or workplace at all times. Never try to extinguish a fuel or electrical fire with water.

Fumes

Certain fumes are highly toxic and can quickly cause unconsciousness and even death if inhaled to any extent. Petrol (gasoline) vapour comes into this category, as do the vapours from certain solvents such as trichloroethylene. Any draining or pouring of such volatile fluids should be done in a well ventilated area.

When using cleaning fluids and solvents, read the instructions carefully. Never use materials from unmarked containers – they may give off poisonous vapours.

Never run the engine of a motor vehicle in an enclosed space such as a garage. Exhaust fumes contain carbon monoxide which is extremely poisonous; if you need to run the engine, always do so in the open air or at least have the rear of the vehicle outside the workplace.

If you are fortunate enough to have the use of an inspection pit, never drain or pour petrol, and never run the engine, while the vehicle is standing over it; the fumes, being heavier than air, will concentrate in the pit with possibly lethal results.

The battery

Never cause a spark, or allow a naked light, near the vehicle's battery. It will normally be giving off a certain amount of hydrogen gas, which is highly explosive.

Always disconnect the battery earth (ground) terminal before working on the fuel or electrical systems.

If possible, loosen the filler plugs or cover when charging the battery from an external source. Do not charge at an excessive rate or the battery may burst.

Take care when topping up and when carrying the battery. The acid electrolyte, even when diluted, is very corrosive and should not be allowed to contact the eyes or skin.

If you ever need to prepare electrolyte yourself, always add the acid slowly to the water, and never the other way round. Protect against splashes by wearing rubber gloves and goggles.

When jump starting a car using a booster battery, for negative earth (ground) vehicles, connect the jump leads in the following sequence: First connect one jump lead between the positive (+) terminals of the two batteries. Then connect the other jump lead first to the negative (–) terminal of the booster battery, and then to a good earthing (ground) point on the vehicle to be started, at least 18 in (45 cm) from the battery if possible. Ensure that hands and jump leads are clear of any moving parts, and that the two vehicles do not touch. Disconnect the leads in the reverse order.

Mains electricity

When using an electric power tool, inspection light etc which works from the mains, always ensure that the appliance is correctly connected to its plug and that, where necessary, it is properly earthed (grounded). Do not use such appliances in damp conditions and, again, beware of creating a spark or applying excessive heat in the vicinity of fuel or fuel vapour.

Ignition HT voltage

A severe electric shock can result from touching certain parts of the ignition system, such as the HT leads, when the engine is running or being cranked, particularly if components are damp or the insulation is defective. Where an electronic ignition system is fitted, the HT voltage is much higher and could prove fatal.

Routine maintenance

Maintenance is essential for ensuring safety, and desirable for the purpose of getting the best in terms of performance and economy from the vehicle. Over the years the need for periodic lubrication – oiling, greasing and so on – has been drastically reduced if not totally eliminated. This has unfortunately tended to lead some owners to think that because no such action is required, the items either no longer exist or will last for ever. This is a serious delusion. It follows therefore that the largest initial element of maintenance is visual examination. This may lead to repairs or renewal. Road test the vehicle after any maintenance has been carried out.

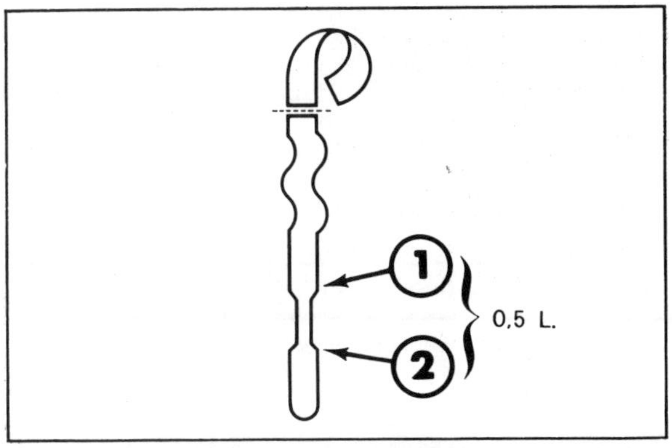

The dipstick oil level marks

1 Maximum level *2 Minimum level*

Weekly or every 250 miles (400 km) – whichever comes first

Check engine oil and top up if necessary
Check battery electrolyte and top up if necessary.
Check brake fluid reservoir and top up if necessary (photo) using only the correct fluid – see Chapter 6.
Top up the windscreen washer reservoir.
Check tyre pressures (including spare).
Check correct operation of electrical equipment (lights, windscreen wipers, horn etc).

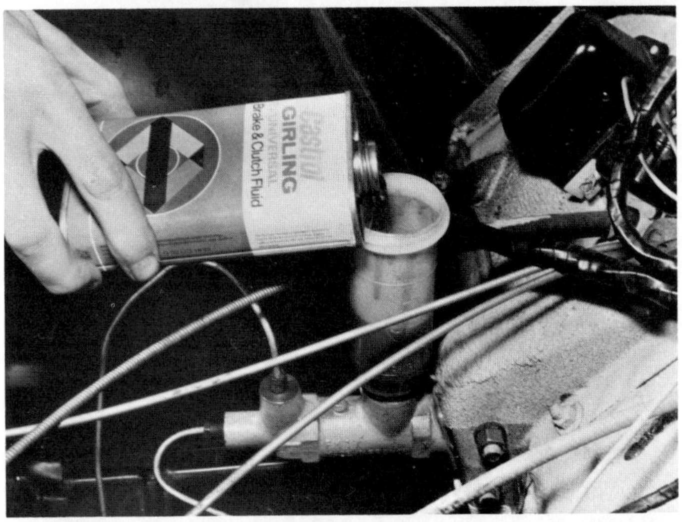

Top up master cylinder level. See Chapter 6 for correct fluid type for your model

Three-monthly or every 3000 miles (5000 km)

Drain engine oil when hot and refill with specified grade and quantity of oil.
Clean battery terminals and smear with petroleum jelly.
Raise and support front of car. Check steering and suspension joints for wear; grease kingpins and check condition of driveshaft gaiters (photo).
Lubricate driveshaft sliding joints.
Lubricate suspension rod knife edges.
Lubricate cables, linkages, locks, hinges etc.
Check gearbox oil level with engine cold and car on level ground and top up if necessary (photo). Allow to drip for ten minutes, clean and refit level plug.
Remove, clean and gap spark plugs (photo).
On models equipped with disc brakes, inspect pads for wear and renew if necessary.

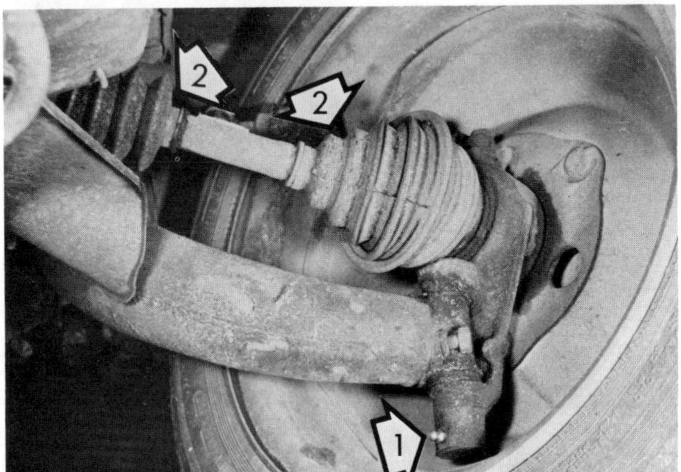

Grease the kingpin at nipple (1) and check driveshaft gaiters (2)

Six-monthly or every 6000 miles (10 000 km)

Renew oil filter (on models so equipped) when changing engine oil (photo).
Check valve-to-rocker arm clearances and adjust if necessary (first 6000-mile service only, thereafter every 18 000 miles).
Remove and clean the air filter element (photo). Spray the clean element with oil or a mixture of oil and petrol, according to the instructions on the filter cover.
Remove and clean the carburettor fuel filter.
Clean the oil cooler fins.
Renew spark plugs if necessary.
Check generator drivebelt tension and condition. Retension or renew if necessary.
Adjust carburettor idle settings if necessary (engine at normal running temperature).
Check clutch pedal free play and adjust if necessary.
Check brake pipes for security and freedom from corrosion.
Adjust drum brakes as necessary.
Check handbrake travel and adjust if necessary.
Check headlight beam alignment and adjust if necessary.
Inspect windscreen wiper arms and blades and renew if necessary.
Check exhaust system for security and leakage.

Yearly or every 12 000 miles (20 000 km)

Drain gearbox oil after a run, clean and refit drain plug securely and refill with specified quantity and grade of oil. Allow to drip for ten minutes before refitting level plug.
Check ignition timing and adjust if necessary.
Have the crankcase vacuum tested by a Citroën dealer.
Remove one front brake drum (if applicable) and inspect linings; renew on *both* sides if necessary.
Check front and rear wheel alignment and suspension heights front and rear.
Grease speedometer cable at the gearbox end.

Every 18 months or 18 000 miles (30 000 km)

Lubricate central suspension cylinder
Drain and renew, brake fluid (not disc brake models). Renew flexible brake lines (if fitted) if perished.

3-yearly or every 36 000 miles (60 000 km)

Check condition of drum brake wheel cylinders and renew if showing signs of leakage.

Seasonal maintenance

The cooling grille muff should be fitted in Autumn (when the temperature drops below 10°C (50°F) and removed again in Spring (temperature above 15°C (60°F)).

Top up the gearbox oil level

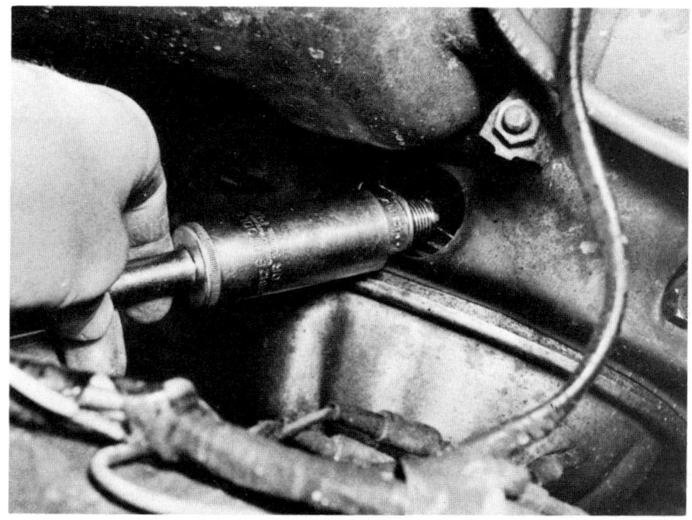

Remove, clean and check the spark plugs

Renew the oil filter (later models)

Remove and clean the air filter element

Fault diagnosis

Introduction

The car owner who does his or her own maintenance according to the recommended schedules should not have to use this section of the manual very often. Modern component reliability is such that, provided those items subject to wear or deterioration are inspected or renewed at the specified intervals, sudden failure is comparatively rare. Faults do not usually just happen as a result of sudden failure, but develop over a period of time. Major mechanical failures in particular are usually preceded by characteristic symptoms over hundreds or even thousands of miles. Those components which do occasionally fail without warning are often small and easily carried in the car.

With any fault finding, the first step is to decide where to begin investigations. Sometimes this is obvious, but on other occasions a little detective work will be necessary. The owner who makes half a dozen haphazard adjustments or replacements may be successful in curing a fault (or its symptoms), but he will be none the wiser if the fault recurs and he may well have spent more time and money than was necessary. A calm and logical approach will be found to be more satisfactory in the long run. Always take into account any warning signs or abnormalities that may have been noticed in the period preceding the fault – power loss, high or low gauge readings, unusual noises or smells, etc – and remember that failure of components such as fuses or spark plugs may only be pointers to some underlying fault.

The pages which follow here are intended to help in cases of failure to start or breakdown on the road. There is also a Fault Diagnosis Section at the end of each Chapter which should be consulted if the preliminary checks prove unfruitful. Whatever the fault, certain basic principles apply. These are as follows:

Verify the fault. This is simply a matter of being sure that you know what the symptoms are before starting work. This is particularly important if you are investigating a fault for someone else who may not have described it very accurately.

Don't overlook the obvious: For example, if the car won't start, is there petrol in the tank? (Don't take anyone else's word on this particular point, and don't trust the fuel gauge either!) If an electrical fault is indicated, look for loose or broken wires before digging out the test gear.

Cure the disease, not the symptom. Substituting a flat battery with a fully charged one will get you off the hard shoulder, but if the underlying cause is not attended to, the new battery will go the same way. Similarly, changing oil-fouled spark plugs for a new set will get you moving again, but remember that the reason for the fouling (if it wasn't simply an incorrect grade of plug) will have to be established and corrected.

Don't take anything for granted. Particularly, don't forget that a 'new' component may itself be defective (especially if it's been rattling round in the boot for months), and don't leave components out of a fault diagnosis sequence just because they are new or recently fitted. When you do finally diagnose a difficult fault, you'll probably realise that all the evidence was there from the start.

Electrical faults

Electrical faults can be more puzzling than straightforward mechanical failures, but they are no less susceptible to logical analysis if the basic principles of operation are understood. Car electrical wiring exists in extremely unfavourable conditions – heat, vibration and chemical attack – and the first things to look for are loose or corroded connections, and broken or chafed wires, especially where the wires pass through holes in the bodywork or are subject to vibration.

All metal-bodied cars in current production have one pole of the battery 'earthed', ie connected to the car bodywork, and in nearly all modern cars it is the negative (–) terminal. The various electrical components – motors, bulb holders etc – are also connected to earth, either by means of a lead or directly by their mountings. Electric current flows through the component and then back to the battery via the car bodywork. If the component mounting is loose or corroded, or if a good path back to the battery is not available, the circuit will be incomplete and malfunction will result. The engine and/or gearbox are also earthed by means of flexble metal straps to the body or subframe; if these straps are loose or missing, starter motor, generator and ignition trouble may result.

Assuming the earth return to be satisfactory, electrical faults wil be due either to component malfunction or to defects in the current supply. Individual components are dealt with in Chapter 10. If supply wires are broken or cracked internally this results in an open-circuit, and the easiest way to check for this is to bypass the suspect wire temporarily with a length of wire having a crocodile clip or suitable connector at each end. Alternatively, a 12V test lamp can be used to verify the presence of supply voltage at various points along the wire and the break can be thus isolated.

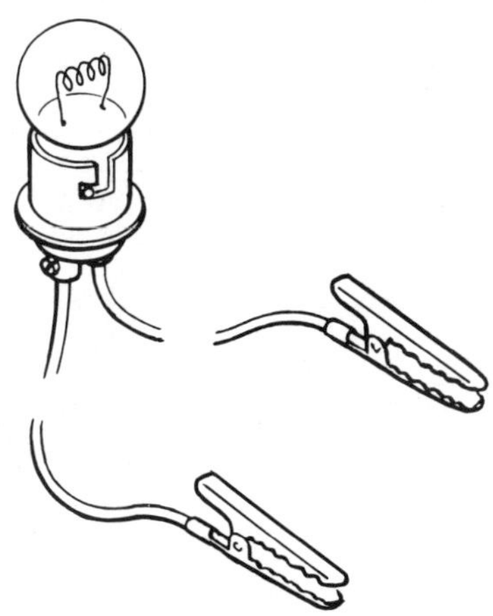

A simple test lamp is useful for tracing electrical faults

If a bare portion of a live wire touches the car bodywork or other earthed metal part the electricity will take the low-resistance path thus formed back to the battery: this is known as a short-circuit. Hopefully, a short-circuit will blow a fuse, but otherwise it may cause burning of the insulation (and possibly further short-circuits) or even a fire. This is why it is inadvisable to bypass persistently blowing fuses with silver foil or wire.

Spares and tool kit

Most cars are only supplied with sufficient tools for wheel changing; the *Maintenance and minor repair* tool kit detailed in *Tools and working facilities,* with the addition of a hammer, is probably sufficient for those repairs that most motorists would consider attempting at the roadside. In addition, a few items which can be fitted without too much trouble in the event of breakdown should be carried. Experience and available space will modify the list below, but the following may save having to call on professional assistance:

Spark plugs, clean and correctly gapped
HT lead and plug cap
Condenser and contact breaker points
Drivebelt – emergency type may suffice
Spare fuses
Set of principal light bulbs
Exhaust bandage
Roll of insulating tape
Length of soft iron wire
Length of electrical flex
Torch or inspection lamp (can double as test lamp)
Battery jump leads
Tow-rope
Water-repellant aerosol
Litre of engine oil
Sealed can of hydraulic fluid
Emergency windscreen

If spare fuel is carried, a can designed for the purpose should be used to minimise risks of leakage and collision damage. A first aid kit, a fire extinguisher and a warning triangle, whilst not at present compulsory in the UK, are obviously sensible items to carry in addition to the above.

When touring abroad, it may be advisable to carry additional spares which, even if you cannot fit them yourself, could save having to wait while parts are obtained. The items below may be worth considering:

Clutch and throttle cables
Alternator fuse
Dynamo or alternator brushes
Fuel pump repair kit
Tyre valve core

One of the motoring organisations will be able to advise on availability of fuel etc in foreign countries.

Engine will not start

Engine fails to turn when starter operated

Flat battery (recharge, use jump leads, use starter handle or push start)
Battery terminals loose or corroded
Battery earth to body defective
Engine earth strap loose or broken
Starter motor (or solenoid) wiring loose or broken
Ignition/starter switch faulty
Major mechanical failure (seizure) or long disuse (piston rings rusted to bores)
Starter or solenoid internal fault (see Chapter 10)

Starter motor turns engine slowly

Partially discharged battery (recharge, use jump leads, use starting handle or push start, but not with a centrifugal clutch)
Battery terminals loose or corroded
Battery earth to body defective
Engine earth strap loose
Starter motor (or solenoid) wiring loose
Starter motor internal fault (see Chapter 10)

Starter motor spins without turning engine

Solenoid or engagement mechanism faulty
Starter motor pinion sticking on sleeve
Flywheel gear teeth damaged or worn
Starter motor mounting bolts loose

Engine turns normally but fails to start

Damp or dirty HT leads (crank engine and check for spark)
No fuel in tank (check for delivery at carburettor)
Excessive choke (hot engine) or insufficient choke (cold engine)
Fouled or incorrectly gapped spark plugs (remove, clean and regap)
Dirty or incorrectly gapped contact breaker joints
Other ignition system fault (see Chapter 3)
Other fuel system fault (see Chapter 2)
Poor compression (see Chapter 1)
Major mechanical failure (eg camshaft drive)

Engine fires but will not run

Insufficient choke (cold engine)
Air leaks at carburettor or inlet manifold
Fuel starvation (see Chapter 2)
Loose connections or other ignition fault (see Chapter 3)

Engine cuts out and will not restart

Engine cuts out suddenly – ignition fault

Loose or disconnected LT wires
Wet HT leads or coil (after traversing water splash)
Coil or condenser failure (check for spark)
Other ignition fault (see Chapter 3)

Engine misfires before cutting out – fuel fault

Fuel tank empty
Fuel pump defective or filter block (check for delivery)
Fuel tank filter vent block (suction will be evident on releasing cap)
Carburettor needle valve sticking
Carburettor jets blocked (fuel contaminated)
Other fuel system fault (see Chapter 2)

Engine cuts out – other causes

Serious overheating
Major mechanical failure (eg camshaft drive)

Engine overheats

Low oil level or incorrect grade
Oil cooler clogged
Engine cowling loose or missing
Ignition timing incorrect or automatic advance malfunctioning
Brakes binding
Mixture too weak

Low engine oil pressure

Warning light illuminated with engine running

Oil level low or incorrect grade
Defective sender unit
Wire to sender unit earthed
Engine overheating
Oil filter clogged or bypass valve defective
Oil pressure relief valve defective
Oil pick-up strainer clogged

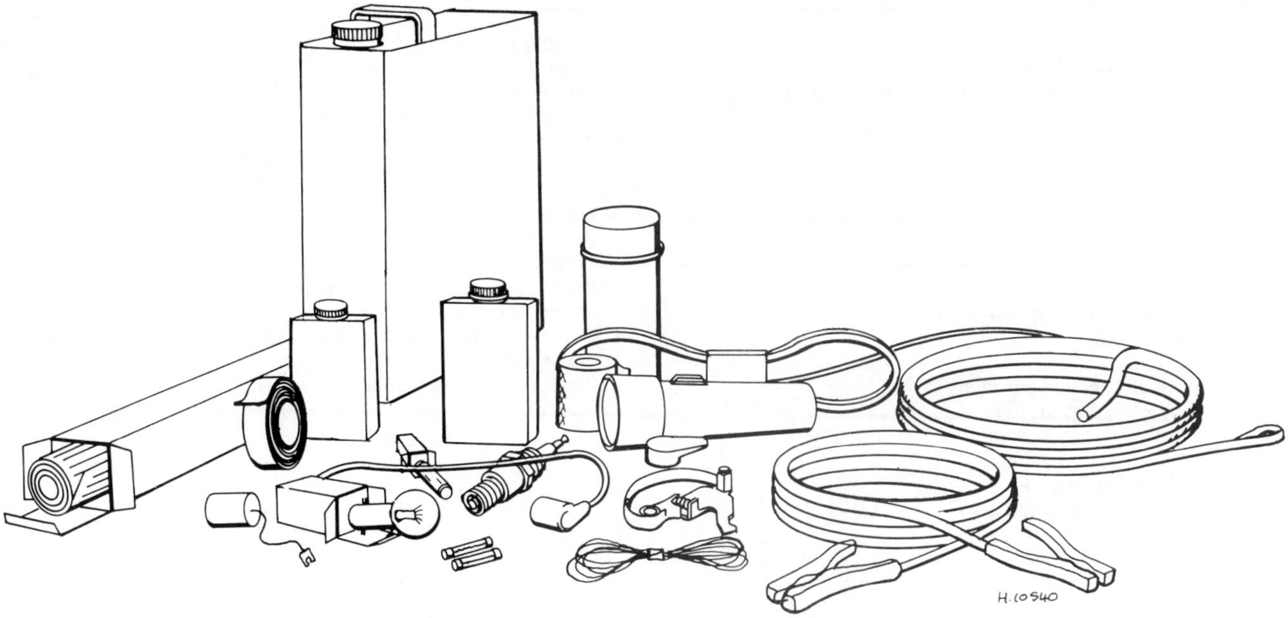

A few spares carried in the car can save you a long walk

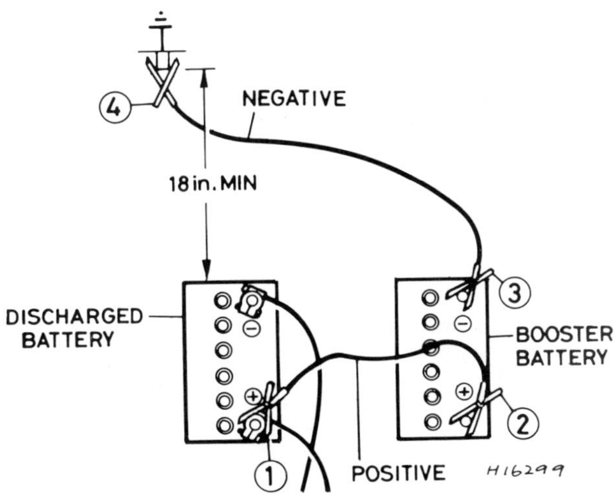

Jump start lead connections for negative earth vehicles – connect leads in the order shown

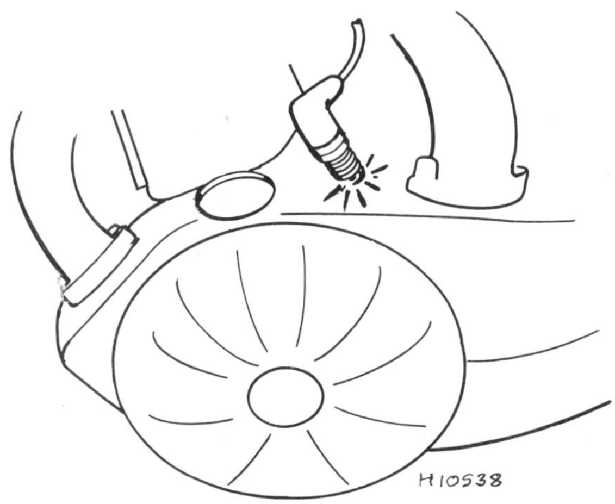

Crank engine and check for spark. Hold plug cap with insulated tool or rubber glove!

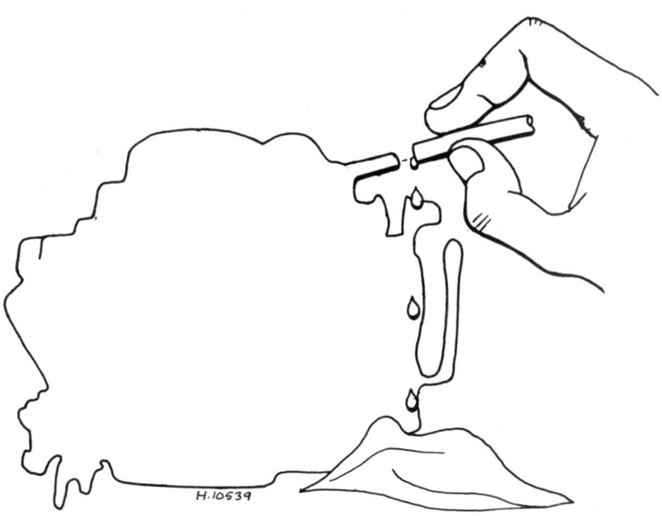

Remove fuel pipe at carburettor and check for delivery

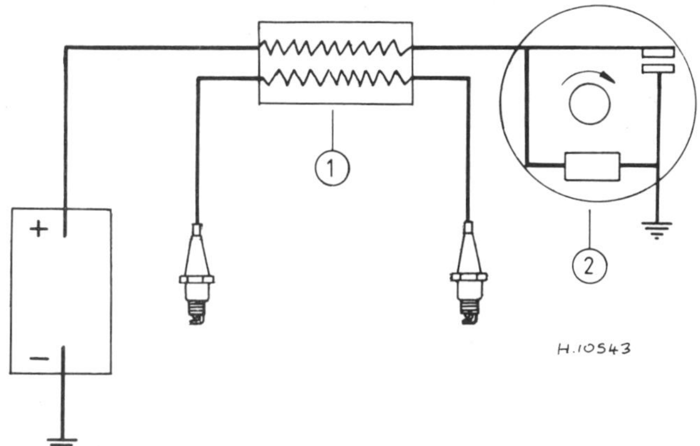

Ignition system schematic diagram. Note that there is no distributor!

1 Coil

2 Points box (behind fan)

Oil pump worn
Worn main or big-end bearings

Note: *Low oil pressure in a high-mleage engine at tickover is not necessarily a cause for concern. Sudden pressure loss at speed is far more significant. In any event, check the warning light sender before condemning the engine.*

Engine noises

Pre-ignition (pinking) on acceleration

Incorrect grade of fuel
Ignition timing incorrect
Automatic advance mechanism faulty
Worn or maladjusted carburettor
Excessive carbon build-up in engine

Whistling or wheezing noises

Leaking carburettor or manifold gasket
Leaking crankcase oil seals

Tapping or rattling

Incorrect valve clearances
Worn valve gear
Broken piston ring (ticking noise)
Worn oil pressure relief valve

Knocking or thumping

Unintentional mechanical contact (eg fan blades)
Worn fanbelt
Peripheral component fault (generator etc)
Worn big-end bearings (regular heavy knocking, perhaps less under load
Worn main bearing (rumbling and knocking, perhaps worsening under load)
Piston slap (most noticeable when cold)

Chapter 1 Engine

For modifications, and information applicable to later models, see Supplement at end of manual

Contents

Specifications

Engine (general)

Type	4-stroke air-cooled horizontally opposed twin, pushrod-operated overhead valves	
Application:		
All models	See Supplement at end of manual	
Bore x stroke:		
425cc	66 x 62 mm	(2.598 x 2.441 in)
435cc	68.5 x 59.0 mm	(2.696 x 2.322 in)
602cc	74.0 x 70.0 mm	(2.913 x 2.755 in)
Compression ratio:		
A53	7.5 : 1	
A79/0 and M4	7.75 : 2	
A79/1 and M28/1	8.5 : 1	
M28	9.0 : 1	
Power output (bhp SAE):		
A79/0	21 @ 5450 rpm	
A79/1	26 @ 6750 rpm	
M4	28 @ 5000 rpm	
M28/1	33 @ 5750 rpm	
M28	35 @ 5750 rpm	

Valves

Valve to rocker arm clearances (inlet and exhaust, engine cold)	0.15 to 0.20 mm (0.006 to 0.008 in)
Valve seat angle:	
Inlet	120°
Exhaust	90°

Camshaft

Drive	Direct by gear from crankshaft
Number of bearings	2
Endfloat	0.04 to 0.09 mm (0.001 to 0.003 in)

Crankshaft and connecting rod assembly

Type	Steel forged crankshaft with two main bearing and two crankpin journals. Supplied pre-assembled with connecting rods and bearings
Main journal diameters:	
Front	48 mm (1.889 in)
Rear	52 mm (2.047 in)
Big-end journal diameter	39 mm (1.535 in)
Crankshaft endfloat	0.07 to 0.14 mm (0.003 to 0.005 in)
Connecting rod endfloat	0.08 to 0.13 mm (0.003 to 0.005 in)
Bearing shell diametrical clearance	0.055 to 0.111 mm (0.002 to 0.004 in)

Pistons

Type	Light alloy
Piston rings	3 (2 compression, 1 oil control)
Clearance in bore	0.05 to 0.07 mm (0.002 to 0.003 in)
Ring gaps:	
Top and middle rings	0.20 to 0.35 mm (0.008 to 0.014 in)
Bottom (oil control) ring:	
Standard type	0.15 to 0.30 mm (0.006 to 0.012 in)
U-Flex type	Zero

Lubrication system

Type	Pressure feed, gear or rotor type oil pump driven from camshaft
Oil filter	Sump strainer (early models), external cartridge filter (later models)
Oil pressure:	
A79/0 and M4	35.5 to 44 lbf/in^2 @ 4000 rpm
A79/1	57 to 71 lbf/in^2 @ 6000 rpm
M28 and M28/1	78 to 92 lbf/in^2 @ 6000 rpm
Oil pump rotor end clearance	0.10 mm (0.004 in) maximum
Oil capacity (drain and refill)*:	
A53	2.0 litres (3.5 pints)
A79/0 and A79/1	2.3 litres (4.0 pints)
M28 and M28/1	2.4 litres (4.2 pints)
M4	2.5 litres (4.4 pints)

** Add 0.3 litres (0.5 pint) approx if rocker covers are removed, 0.2 litres (0.4 pint) approx if filter cartridge (where applicable) is renewed*

Torque wrench settings

	lbf ft	kgf m
Crankcase bolts:		
7 mm	14	1.9
10mm (including main bearing stud nuts	32	4.5
Cylinder head nuts:		
A79/0 and M4 engines (hot):		
Initial tightening	10	1.5
Final tightening	15	2.3
A79/1, M28 and M28/1 engines (cold):		
Initial tightening	7	1
Final tightening	18	2.5
Cylinder head studs to crankcase	3.5	0.5
Manifold fixings	14	1.9
Fan fixing bolt	36	5
Oil cooler bolts	10 to 14	1.4 to 1.9
Oil cooler union nuts	7 to 9	1 to 1.2
Oil strainer	3.5	0.5
Flywheel bolts*	30	4.2
Rocker cover nut	3 to 5	0.5 to 0.7
Oil relief valve plug	29 to 32	4 to 4.5
Cylinder head oil unions	10	1.3
Oil pump cover screws	10	1.3
Front support screws	43	6.0
Sump drain plug	25	3.5

** Use new bolts each time the flywheel is removed*

1 General description

The engine used in the Citroën two-cylinder range over the years of production has remained basically the same, being increased in capacity from the original 375cc to 425cc, 435cc and currently 602cc.

The engine is an air-cooled, horizontally opposed four-stroke twin, with overhead valves. The crankcase and cylinder head are manufactured in aluminium, the crankcase comprising two halves which enclose both the crankshaft and camshaft. An unusual feature of the camshaft is that the oil pump is located on its rear end and the contact breaker cam and centrifugal weight assembly are mounted on the front end. The camshaft drive from the crankshaft is by means of helical gears.

The crankshaft and connecting rod assembly is a factory assembled unit and it is not possible to dismantle them as with a conventional engine. Failure of the big-end or main bearings necessitates renewal of the complete unit.

Each cylinder barrel is mounted separately and has its own cylinder head. A conventional overhead valve and rocker assembly is used in each head. The cylinder heads and barrels are secured to the crankcase by three long studs. The stud nuts and washers tighten against the head which in turn secures the cylinder barrel. No gaskets are used. The aluminium pistons have two compression and one oil control ring fitted. When the cylinder barrels are renewed, they are supplied together with new pistons and not separately.

The lubrication system comprises a rotor type oil pump and according to engine type will have an oil pressure relief valve and an internal or external oil filter (except earlier engines). Oil is transported to each cylinder head by external pipes. An oil cooler is also fitted and mounted at the front of the engine.

The engine cooling fan is mounted on the front of the crankshaft and is secured by the starting handle dog. Air is directed around the engine by cooling cowls.

The maintenance procedures given at the start of this manual must be regularly carried out if your Citroën is to give you reliable and lengthy service. Because of its long production run it is essential to quote the engine number and year of manufacture when ordering spare parts.

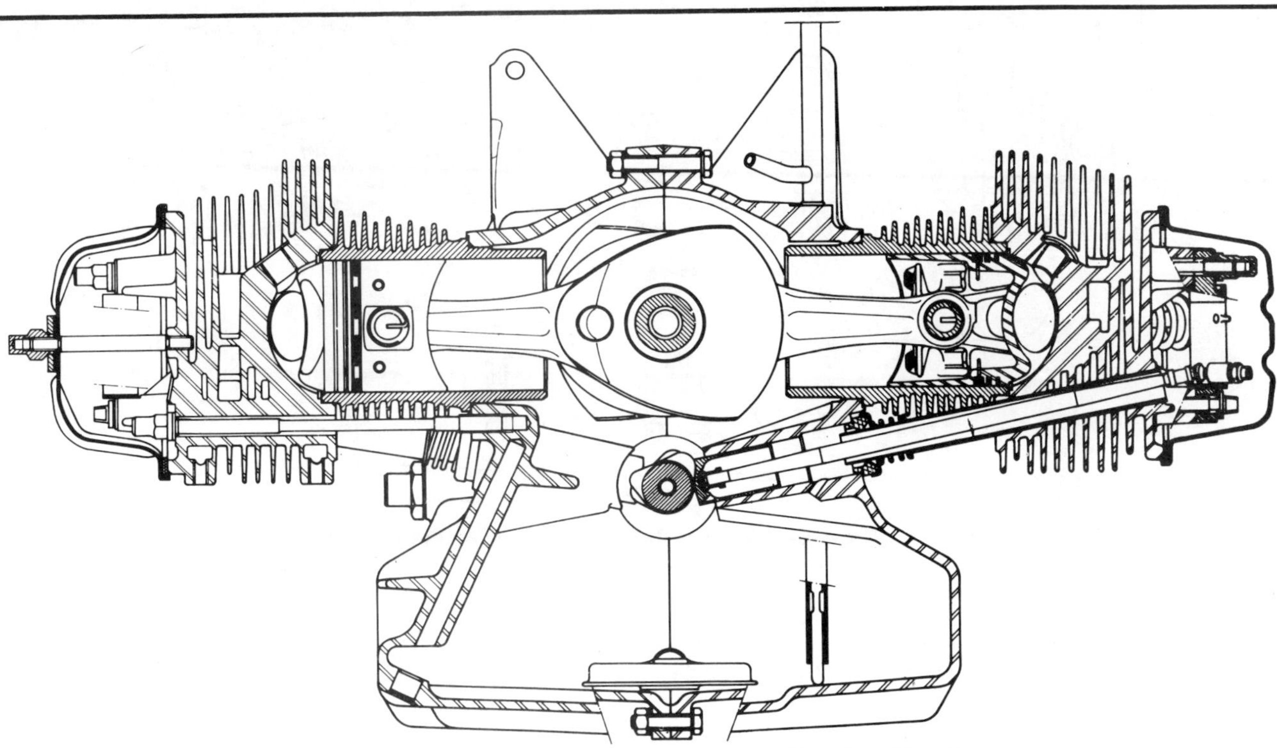

Fig. 1.1 Cross-section of early (pre-1970) engines (Sec 1)

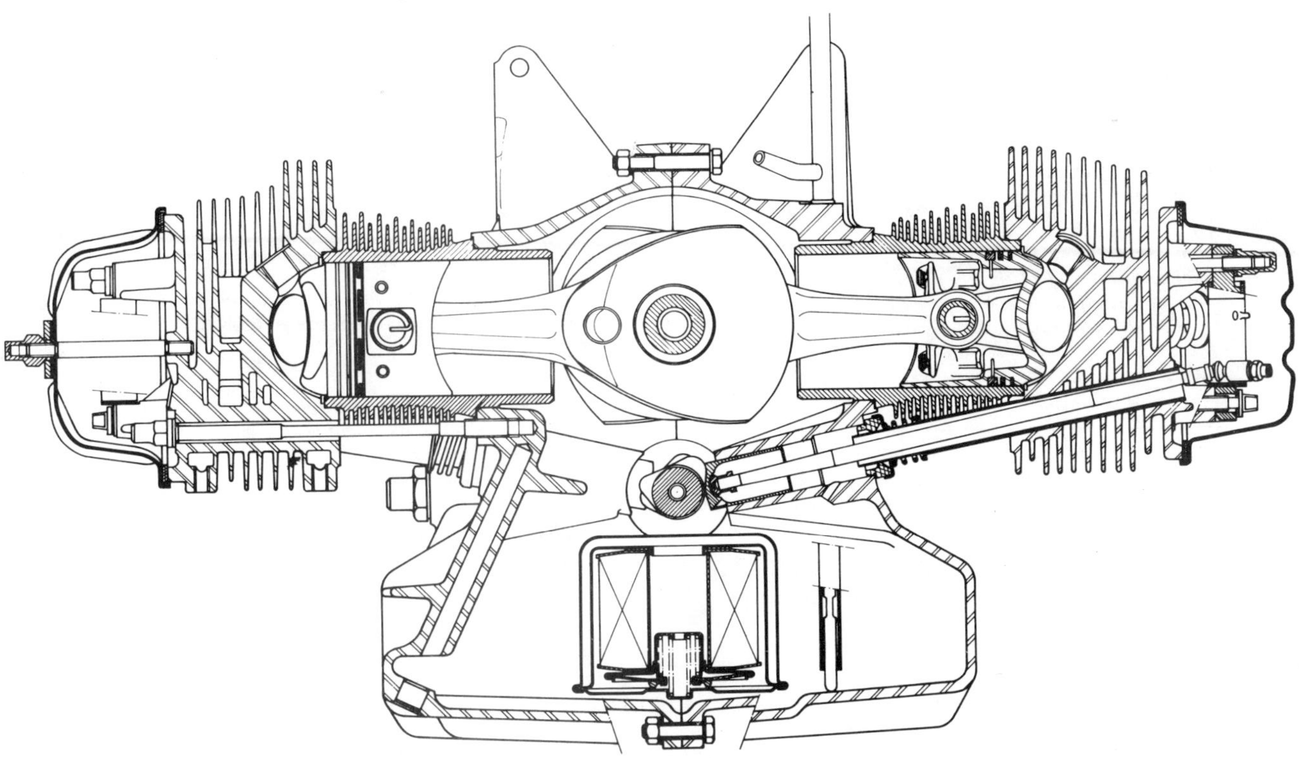

Fig. 1.2 Cross-section of engine with internal oil filter, used from December 1969 to November 1970 (Sec 1)

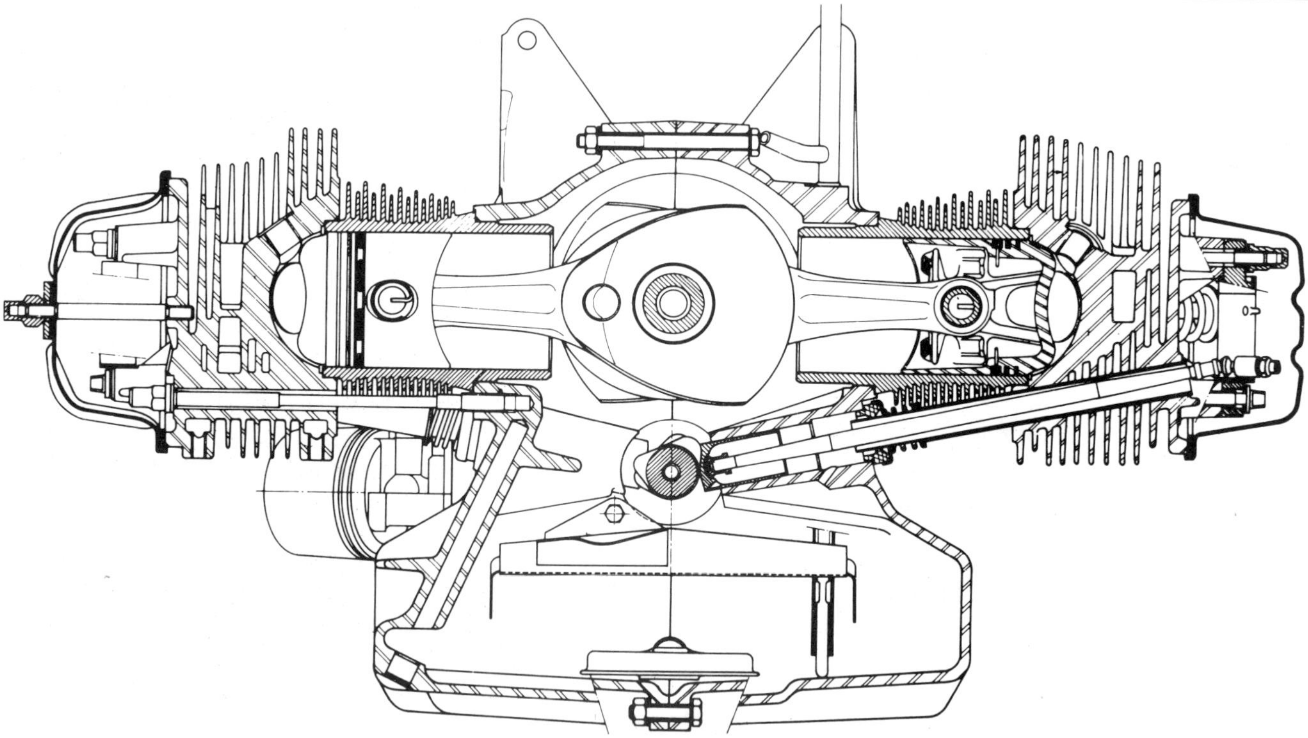

Fig. 1.3 Cross-section of engine with external oil filter, used since November 1970 (Sec 1)

2 Major operations possible with engine in vehicle

The following operations can be carried out without removing the engine from the car:

(a) Removal and refitting of the cylinder heads
(b) Removal and refitting of the barrels and pistons
(c) Removal and refitting of the oil cooler
(d) Renewal of the crankshaft front oil seal

3 Major operations requiring engine removal

Before the following operations can be undertaken, the engine must be extracted from the vehicle:

(a) Removal and refitting of the crankshaft/connecting rod assembly
(b) Removal and refitting of the flywheel
(c) Removal and refitting of the oil pump
(d) Removal and refitting of the camshaft
(e) Renewal of the crankshaft rear oil seal

4 Engine removal – general

1 On all models the engine can be removed either alone or complete with the gearbox. Both methods are described below.
2 Lifting tackle is not essential when removing the engine alone if the services of an able-bodied assistant are available.
3 Whichever method is adopted, it will first be necessary to remove the undershield (if fitted) to gain access to the engine and transmission (photo). On later models the undershield is not detachable, but incorporates a large access hole.

5 Engine and gearbox – removal procedure

1 Removal of the engine and gearbox assembly necessitates the use of a lifting hoist and an engine sling or strong rope.
2 Raise the bonnet and either support it by tying it back, or remove it completely and place it safely out of the way. If tying the bonnet back, pass the string over the roof of the vehicle and fasten at the rear. Place some cloth between the windscreen and bonnet to cushion it. Detach the bonnet stay.
3 Disconnect the battery. It is sensible to remove the battery altogether so that tools are not placed on it, causing short circuits.
4 Remove the spare wheel and its carrier frame (photo).

2CV models

5 Unbolt and remove the front wings and side panels, disconnecting electrical connectors as necessary.
6 Detach the headlight lead connectors, the spark plug leads and coil wires (note which way round they are connected), the headlight adjustment control, the bonnet stay and the headlight securing bracket. Remove the headlight bracket unit complete with coil and control assembly.

All models

7 Loosen the air cleaner nuts and hose clamps, then withdraw the air cleaner unit (photo).
8 Disconnect the following wiring connections if not already done, noting connections for correct reassembly:

(a) Headlights (including earth lead)
(b) Horn
(c) Indicator lights and sidelights
(d) Alternator leads (including earth lead in the fan housing)
(e) Starter motor leads
(f) Spark plug leads
(g) Coil LT leads

9 Disconnect the headlight adjuster cables from the scuttle control, unscrewing the control knob to free the cable ends. Free the cables from their clips and lay them to one side.
10 Disconnect the wiring harness from the front panel, placing it out of the way.
11 Remove the heater ducting, which is secured by rubber straps and/or clips.
12 Disconnect the bonnet release cable from the lock and place the cable out of the way.
13 On 2CV models, detach the earth cable from the bracket on the gearchange lever, and remove the wiring harness from the air inlet manifold and from the horn bracket lug. Lay the wiring around the bonnet surround rim.

4.3 View of the engine and transmission with the undershield removed

5.4 Remove the spare wheel carrier

5.7 The air cleaner retaining clamp at the front. Note the accelerator return spring adjuster

5.14 Removing the front grille panel and bumpers (Dyane)

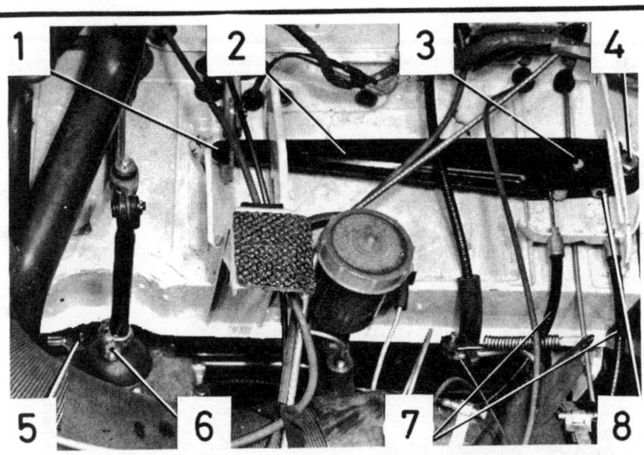

Fig. 1.4 The handbrake return lever (disc brake models) and associated components (Sec 5)

1 Clevis pin
2 Return lever
3 Clevis pin
4 Pivot bolt
5 Earth cable attachment to gearbox
6 Gear lever/selector retaining bolt
7 Handbrake cables to calipers
8 Return roller

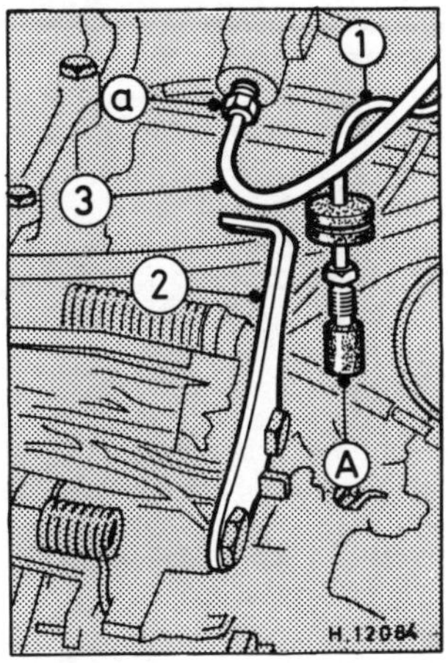

Fig. 1.5 On disc brake models, disconnect brake pipe (1) from left-hand brake unit (Sec 5)

a Master cylinder union
A Pipe plug
2 Bracket
3 Pipe from master cylinder

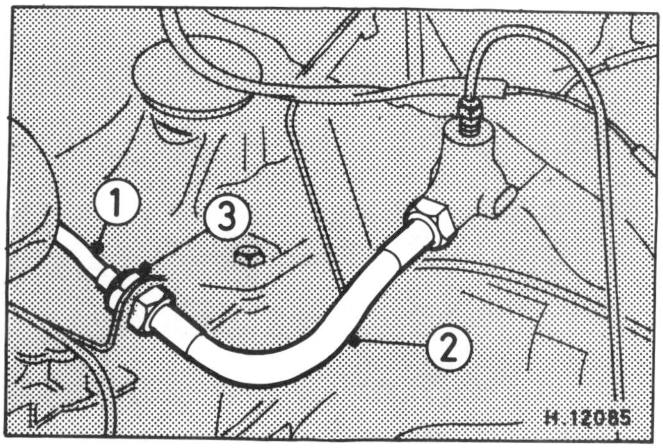

Fig. 1.6 On drum brake models disconnect brake pipe (1) and flexible pipe (2) at the bracket junction (3) (Sec 5)

14 On Ami and Dyane models the front panel is now removed. Unscrew the retaining screws to the wing on each side, to the chassis front side member and the inner wing panels. Before removing the panel unit complete with bumper (photo), check that all fastenings and associate fittings are disconnected. Take care not to scratch the panel during removal and place it out of the way until needed again.

15 Disconnect and detach the choke and throttle cables from the carburettor. Extract the split pin and withdraw the clevis pin to free the tension control. Remove the rear retaining nuts and detach the support, but leave it connected to the cable adjuster sleeve.

16 Remove the heater hoses as follows. Detach the half collars retaining the ducting and expansion chamber. On disc brake models, detach the protective shield on the left-hand side. Withdraw the right-hand side flexible heating duct from its exchanger, then disconnect the exchangers and lay them out of the way on the scuttle and nearside inner wing panel. It is not necessary to detach the outlet ducts or the flexible controls.

17 Loosen the exhaust pipe clamp half collars from the transverse expansion box pipe and detach the expansion box (photo).

18 Disconnect the feed pipe to the petrol pump. Plug the pipe end to prevent leakage.

19 Disconnect the clutch cable by unscrewing the adjustment nuts and unhooking the cable from the pedal. Refer to Chapter 4 if necessary.

20 Unscrew the speedometer cable retaining bolt and detach the speedometer cable from the transmission housing.

21 Unscrew and remove the driveshaft bolts on each side.

22 Unscrew and remove the gear selector lever-to-fork control attachment bolt immediately above the gearbox (photo). Also detach the earth cable from its connection point on top of the gearbox.

Disc brake models

23 Release the handbrake and disconnect the cable by extracting the split pin and withdrawing the clevis pin from the end of the return lever. Unscrew and remove the return lever bolt to release the lever. Detach the cable clevis and return roller to free the cables from the lower bulkhead.

24 Unscrew and detach the hydraulic pipe to the left-hand side brake unit and carefully detach it from the supporting bracket. Plug the pipe to prevent fluid leakage and the ingress of dirt. Also plug the brake unit inlet union in a similar manner. Unscrew and detach the hydraulic pipe from the end of the master cylinder and plug both the pipe and the end of the cylinder to prevent fluid leakage.

Drum brake models

25 Unscrew and detach the brake pipe from its flexible hose connection (when fitted), which is attached to the bracket on top of the gearbox. When detached, plug both steel and flexible pipe ends to prevent fluid leakage and the ingress of dirt.

26 The flexible hose must now be detached from the bracket on top

5.17 Unscrew and remove the exhaust pipe clamp half collars

5.22 Detach the gear lever from the selector control

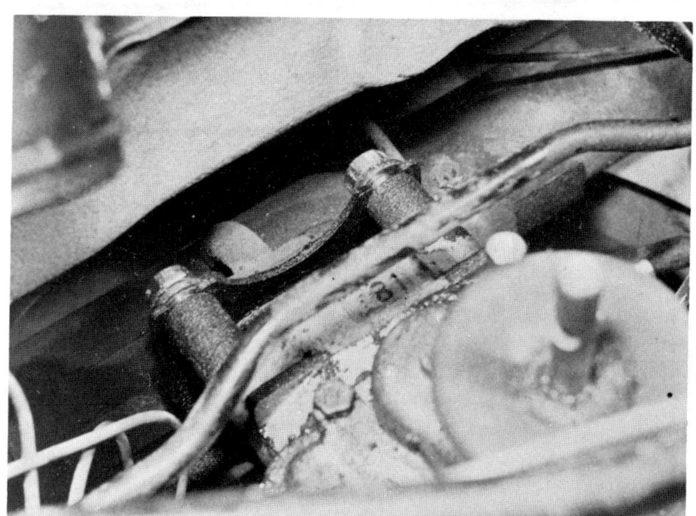

5.27 The transmission mounting at the rear

5.30 The lifting slings in position

5.31 Lifting the engine and transmission clear using a mobile hoist

of the gearbox. Support the pipe endpiece on the reservoir side of the bracket and unscrew the locknut on the other side. When the locknut is unscrewed, withdraw the flexible pipe from the bracket and loosely relocate the locknut. Tie the hose back out of the way.

All models

27 Support the transmission. Unscrew and remove the transmission rear mounting nuts (photo). On some models accessibility is made easier by removing the rubber plugs from the floor panel in front of the control pedals and removing the nuts via the apertures in the floor.

28 The bolts which secure the front crossmember flexible mounting are now removed. They are retained in position by tab washers which must be prised back to enable the bolts to be unscrewed.

29 The engine and transmission units should now be ready for removal from the vehicle. Make a check to ensure that all fittings and attachments between the power unit and body are disconnected.

30 Locate the engine lifting sling, keeping it as short as possible (photo).

31 Lift the engine and gearbox unit to allow the rear end to clear the support. Continue moving the unit forwards and upwards to enable the sump to pass over the crossmember at the front (photo). On models fitted with drum brakes, release the handbrake cables from the crossmember.

32 Once clear of the vehicle the power unit can be cleaned and removed to the work area for further dismantling as necessary. Unscrew the engine-to-gearbox retaining bolts to separate the two units if necessary.

6 Engine only – removal procedure

1 Carry out the operations described in Section 5, paragraphs 1 to 18 inclusive, as applicable.

2 Bend back the lockwasher tabs from the bolts securing the flexible mounting to the front crossmember. Unscrew and remove the bolts.

3 On disc brake models, detach the cooling ducts to the brake units.

4 Place a jack or blocks underneath the gearbox to support it.

5 Unscrew and remove the engine-to-gearbox nuts. On later models the lower nuts can only be reached from above and are accessible if the engine is raised as far as possible.

6 Check that all engine-to-bodywork and associated component fittings are disconnected.

7 The engine can be removed either by attaching a lifting sling or with the aid of an assistant. If a lifting sling is used it must only support the weight of the engine during withdrawal from the gearbox. Pull the engine forwards to separate it from the gearbox input shaft. Under no circumstances allow the weight of the engine to rest on the input shaft during removal.

7 Engine dismantling – general

1 It is best to mount the engine on a dismantling stand, but if this is not available, stand the engine on a strong bench at a comfortable working height. Failing this, it will have to be stripped down on the floor.

2 During the dismantling process, the greatest care should be taken to keep the exposed parts free from dirt. As an aid to achieving this, thoroughly clean down the outside of the engine, first removing all traces of oil and congealed dirt.

3 A good grease solvent will make the job much easier, for after the solvent has been applied and allowed to stand for a time, a vigorous jet of water will wash off the solvent and grease with it. If the dirt is thick and deeply embedded, work the solvent into it with a strong stiff brush.

4 Finally wipe down the exterior of the engine with a rag and only then, when it is quite clean, should the dismantling process begin. As the engine is stripped, clean each part in a bath of paraffin or petrol.

5 Never immerse parts with oilways in paraffin, eg the crankshaft. To clean these parts, wipe down carefully with a petrol-dampened rag. Oilways can be cleaned out with wire. If an airline is available, all parts can be blown dry and the oilways blown through as an added precaution.

6 Re-use of old gaskets is false economy. To avoid the possibility of trouble after the engine has been reassembled always use new gaskets throughout.

7 Do not throw away the old gaskets, for sometimes it happens that an immediate replacement cannot be found and the old gasket is then very useful as a template. Hang up the gaskets as they are removed.

8 Retain unserviceable items until the replacements parts are obtained so that the new parts can be checked against the old part to ensure that the correct components have been supplied.

8 Engine ancillaries – removal

1 Although most of the items concerned in this Section can be removed with the engine in the car (see relevant Chapters, it is more practical to remove them once the engine is out of the vehicle when extensive dismantling is to be carried out.

2 Remove the carburettor and fuel pump (Chapter 2).

3 Remove the alternator/dynamo (Chapter 10).

4 Remove the cooling fan retaining bolt (photo). To prevent the engine from turning over, wedge a screwdriver between the flywheel starter ring teeth and the starter motor mounting. A 14 mm socket or box spanner is needed to unscrew the fan retaining bolt. A sharp blow on the tommy bar or socket handle may be necessary to free the bolt.

5 Should the starting handle dog and fan prove difficult to remove, a suitable bar can be inserted into the central housing of the dog (photo) and this can then be tapped upwards to dislodge the tapered fitting. Alternatively, if the dog is in good condition you could try

8.4 Unscrew the cooling fan retaining bolt

8.5 Using a bar to assist disengagement of the fan from the crankshaft

8.8 Detach the cooling panels

8.9 Remove the fan cowling

8.11 Carefully detach and remove the oil cooler

8.12 Withdraw the front shield panel

inserting the starting handle and turning the engine over whilst the flywheel is locked in position. An assistant will have to support the engine (if removed from the vehicle).
6 Withdraw the fan and extract the alternator drivebelt.
7 Unbolt and remove the inlet and exhaust manifolds.
8 Unbolt and remove the cylinder cooling panels (photo).
9 Unbolt and remove the fan cowling (photo), carefully passing the LT wires through the cowling grommet.
10 Unbolt and remove the oil filler tube on top of the crankcase.
11 Unscrew the oil cooler pipes and remove the cooler from the front of the crankcase (photo). Note the distance pieces as the cooler is removed.
12 Remove the retaining screws and remove the front panel (photo) and the ignition box rubber cover.
13 Support the flywheel and unscrew the clutch unit retaining bolts. Make an alignment mark between the clutch cover and the flywheel to ensure correct repositioning during reassembly.
14 Unscrew and remove the oil filter cartridge.
15 The engine ancillary items are now dismantled and can be placed to one side ready for cleaning and inspection prior to assembly.

9 Engine – dismantling

1 The extent of further engine dismantling is obviously dependant on the particular problem at hand. We have therefore subtitled the various operations in order as the engine is stripped.

Cylinder head assemblies

2 Unscrew the cylinder head lubrication tube union from the crankcase and cylinder head (photo). Detach the tube retaining clip on the crankcase and remove the tube. When removing the tube be careful not to twist or distort it.
3 Unscrew and remove the cylinder head rocker cover.
4 Remove the three domed nuts from the studs and note the washers. The cylinder head can then be pulled free (photo), together with the pushrod guide tube assemblies. Note that if both cylinder heads are being removed then they must be kept separate and preferably marked, together with their respective cylinders, to avoid confusion when reassembling. A punch or file mark on the outer edge of a cooling fin will do, but check that they are not already so marked.
5 Extract the pushrods and cam followers, keeping them in order for correct refitting.

Cylinder barrels and pistons – removal

6 The cylinder/s can now be withdrawn over the three head studs (photo). If required, the cylinder head studs can be removed using either a suitable stud extractor or by screwing two nuts onto the stud and locking the nuts against each other. Apply a spanner to the bottom nut and unscrew it to remove the stud. On removal the stud can be held in a vice and the two nuts loosened and removed from the stud. Take care not to distort the studs during removal.
7 If the piston rings only are to be renewed, then it is not necessary to remove the piston from the connecting rod. However if, as is probable, the ring grooves in the piston are worn, damaged or need decarbonising then the piston will need to be removed for cleaning, machining or renewal.
8 If the pistons are being removed from the connecting rods (the connecting rods cannot be separated from the crankshaft), clean them off and check that they are marked with a 'D' or 'G' which indicates that they are fitted on the right (droit) or left (gauche) side respectively. There should also be an arrow mark on the piston crown to indicate the front face. Dot mark the piston crown if these marks are vague or if you are uncertain, to ensure that they are correctly reassembled. The piston and cylinder are matched during production and they are not interchangeable.
9 The piston is located on the connecting rod by a fully floating gudgeon pin and this is retained by circlips, although in earlier engines the gudgeon pin was an interference fit in the piston. For the latter type you will need a special gudgeon pin extractor tool, although it may be possible to press the pin out if the piston is heated slightly and supported, whilst the pin is removed using a long bolt and suitable distance pieces. It is essential to support the piston when removing the gudgeon pin, otherwise it is possible for the connecting rod to become

9.2 Disconnect the oil feed pipe

9.4 Removing a cylinder head

9.6 Withdraw the cylinder

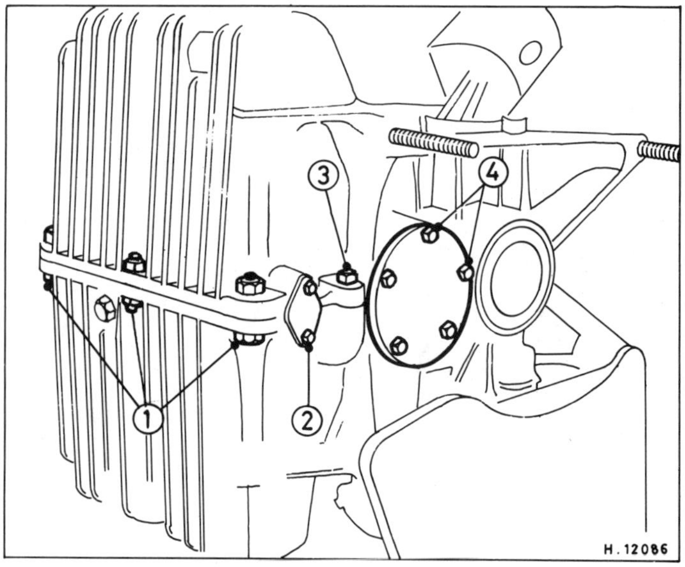

Fig. 1.7A Half housing attachment bolts at bottom of engine (Sec 9)

1 *Flange bolts*
2 *Oil strainer bolts*
3 *Stud nut*
4 *Oil pump cover nuts*

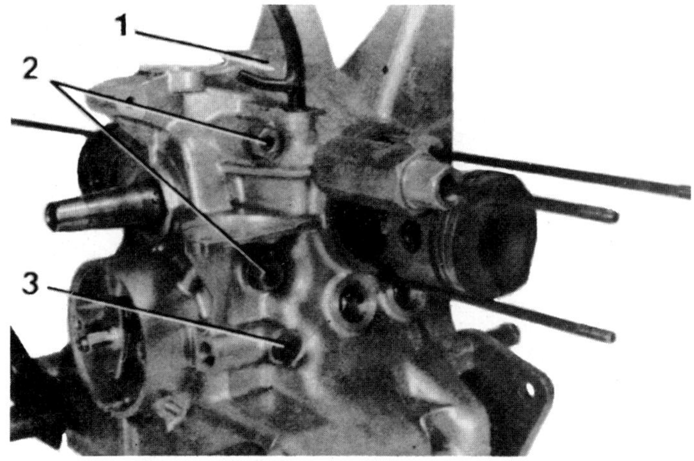

Fig. 1.7B Half housing attachments at top of engine (Sec 9)

1 *Bolt*
2 *Nuts*
3 *Oil pressure relief valve plug*

misaligned. On the later type pistons, use suitable pliers to extract the circlips and press out the gudgeon pin (photos). Keep the gudgeon pins with their respective pistons if they are to be used again.

Flywheel removal

10 Extract the needle bearing and seal from the centre of the crankshaft.
11 Unscrew the five retaining bolts and remove the flywheel from the crankshaft.

Ignition box removal

12 The ignition box can be withdrawn from the front of the crankcase after the two retaining screws have been removed. Mark the location for accurate refitting. See Chapter 3 for details.

Crankcase separation

13 Unscrew and remove the oil pump cover retaining bolts and detach the cover.
14 Unscrew and remove the two nuts and washers from the front face of both halves of the crankcase. Position the engine with its right-hand side downwards.
15 Unscrew and remove the oil strainer/filter bolts (photo), and also remove the casing flange stud nuts and bolts from around the half casing joint.
16 Rotate the crankshaft so that the pistons or connecting rods are at the top dead centre position, then lift clear the left-hand side crankcase housing.

Crankshaft and camshaft removal

17 From the right-hand half casing remove the oil strainer unit.
18 Lift out the camshaft and oil pump unit.
19 Extract the crankshaft and connecting rod assemblies.
20 Remove the front and rear end seals. Take care not to damage the microscopic turbine markings on the crankshaft sealing faces.

Crankcase half housings – final dismantling

21 Remove the oil drain plug.
22 Remove the oil pressure relief valve with its copper gasket.
23 Remove the oil pressure warning switch (where fitted) or plug.
24 On post-1970 models remove the anti-emulsion shield (filter screen) and the oil filter cartridge bracket with its O-ring.

9.9a Extract the circlip ...

9.9b ... press the gudgeon pin through and remove the piston

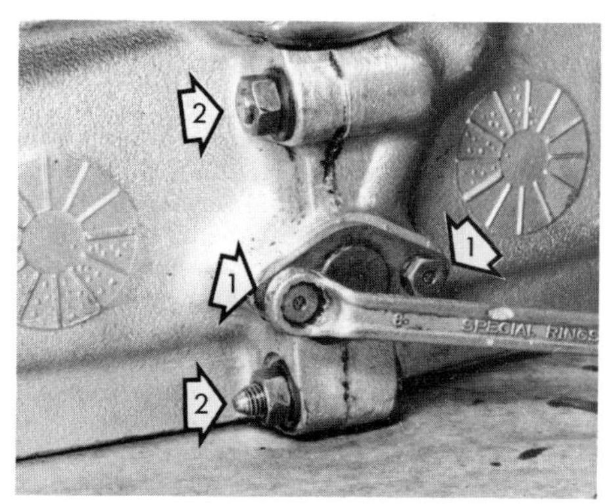

9.15 Unscrew the oil strainer/filter bolts (1) and flange nuts (2)

10 Cylinder heads and barrels – removal (engine in vehicle)

1 The cylinder heads and barrels may be removed from the engine when in the vehicle but the wing panel must first be detached. Refer to Chapter 11 for further details on wing removal for your particular model.
2 Refer to Section 5 and follow the instructions given in paragraphs 2 to 4 and 7 and 8. In paragraph 8, only disconnect those wire connections which are applicable.
3 Disconnect the carburettor throttle control rod and (if fitted) detach the rubber connector from the breather.
4 Although the alternator can be left in position, the drivebelt must be removed. Therefore detach the pulley cover, loosen the mounting bolts and slacken the alternator to disengage the drivebelt.
5 Loosen but do not separate the exhaust and inlet manifold half collar clamps and remove the nuts retaining the manifolds to the cylinder head. When free, raise the manifolds and support them away from the heads by inserting suitable blocks under the housings to wedge them up. Remove the heat exchangers (if fitted).
6 Remove the cylinder cooling cowlings, upper and lower, from each side.
7 The cylinder head is now exposed and ready for removal. Place a suitable drip tray or container under the head to catch the oil spillage as it is removed.
8 Unscrew the rocker cover retaining bolt and detach the cover and gasket. Detach the rocker oil feed pipe from the head.
9 Rotate the crankshaft by means of the starting handle until both valves are in the closed position.
10 The three cylinder head retaining nuts can now be unscrewed, the lower nut first.
11 The cylinder head is now withdrawn together with the pushrods. If required the cam followers (tappets) can be extracted using a piece of wire bent to shape.
12 Repeat the operations on the other cylinder head if desired.
13 If the cylinders are to be removed then they can be simply withdrawn over the head studs. Support the piston as the barrel is withdrawn so that it is not damaged by falling against the studs.
14 Do not mix up the cylinder heads and barrels from the two sides, they are not interchangeable. The heads are marked D – right-hand and G – left-hand.

11 Cylinder heads – dismantling

1 From the pushrod guide tubes, detach the rubber gaskets, cups, springs and thrust washers.
2 To dismantle the rocker gear, unscrew the special spindle retaining bolts using an adjustable spanner. Extract the spindle shaft and withdraw the thrust washers, flexible washers, rocker arms and spacer.
3 To remove the valves a conventional valve spring compressor will be required. Compress each valve spring in turn using the compressor until the two halves of the collets can be extracted from the stem groove. Then release the pressure of the compressor and remove the valve springs, retainer cups, seals and centering collars.
4 If the valve spring is reluctant to be compressed, do not continue to screw down the compressor as damage may be caused. Remove the compressor and strike the stem of the valve with a plastic-faced hammer to free the components, then try again.
5 Withdraw the valves and keep them with their associated components in a compartmented box or something similar so that they can be refitted in the same guide.

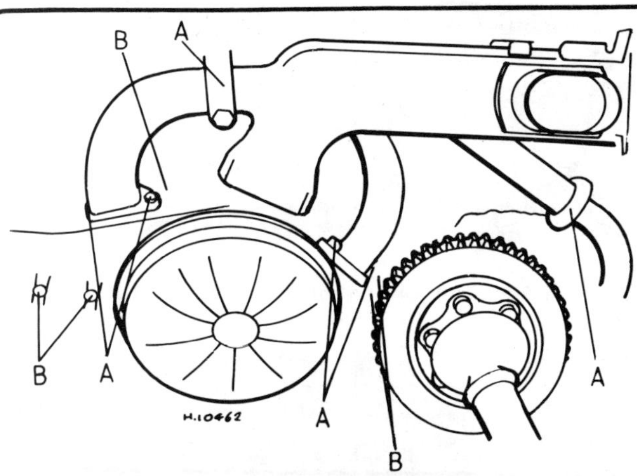

Fig. 1.8 Manifold attachment points and clamps (A) and cooling cowl screws (B) (Sec 10)

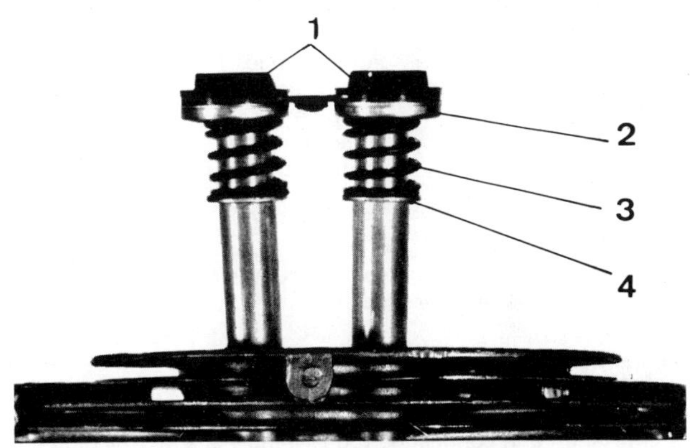

Fig. 1.9 The pushrod guides (Sec 11)

1 Seals
2 Seal cups
3 Springs
4 Washer

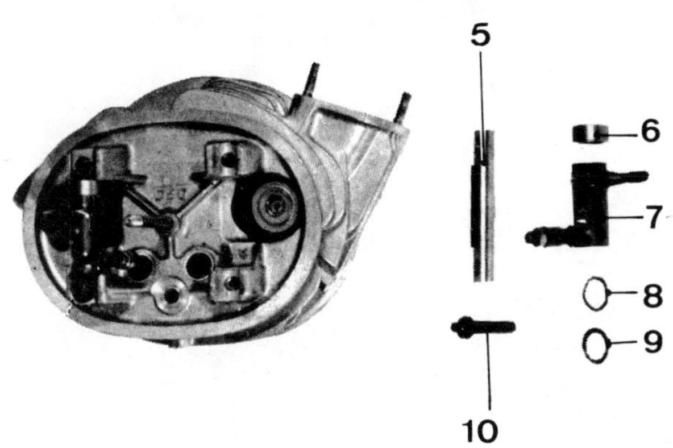

Fig. 1.10 Rocker assembly components (Sec 11)

5 Rocker shaft
6 Spacer
7 Rocker arm
8 Flexible washer
9 Thrust washer
10 Special bolt

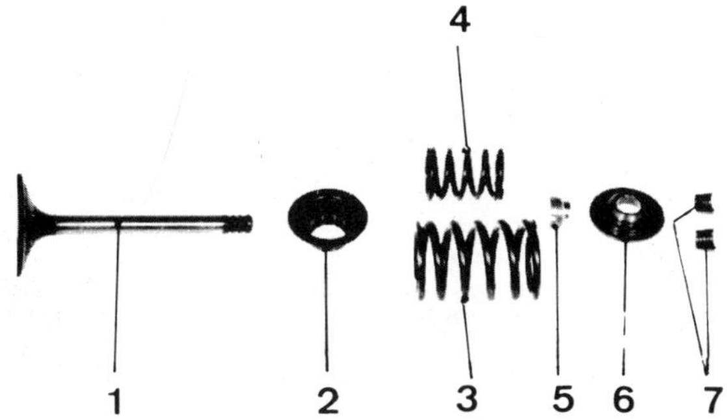

Fig. 1.11 Valve components (Sec 11)

1 Valve
2 Spring retainer
3 Outer spring
4 Inner spring
5 Seal
6 Spring retainer
7 Collets

12 Camshaft – dismantling

1 From the rear end of the camshaft, withdraw the oil pump assembly comprising the pump body and the inner and outer rotors.
2 From the front of the camshaft extract the circlip and withdraw the ignition automatic advance weights assembly. Take care not to distort the springs and note the flat washer fitted between the advance unit and the circlip.

13 Engine – examination and renovation (general)

1 With the engine fully dismantled, the various components can be cleaned and inspected for wear or damage.
2 If the engine is known to have covered a considerable mileage then consideration should be given to renewing the complete unit.
3 The oil cooler can be cleaned externally by brushing with petrol or cellulose thinners, then flushed through with some more of the same solvent and blown through with compressed air.
4 If the crankshaft bearings are known to have run, or there is a history of overheating, the oil cooler and filter must be renewed.
5 On models produced from November 1970, the lubrication pipe plug (Fig. 1.12) must be removed and the oilway cleaned out.
6 Whilst the engine is removed, make an inspection of the mountings. If the rubbers are worn or perished they must be renewed.

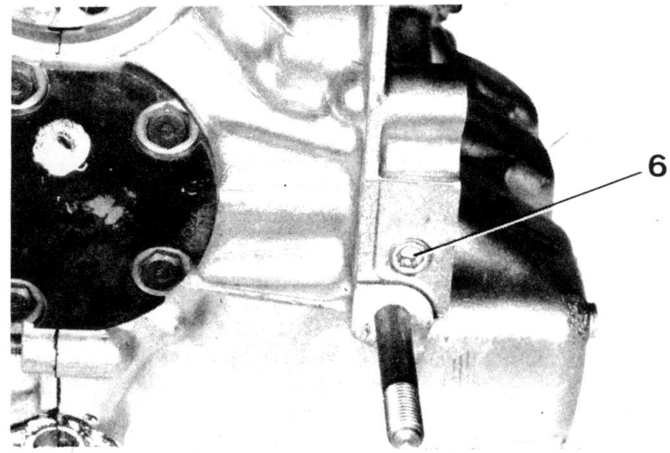

Fig. 1.12 Lubrication pipe plug (6) on engines produced from November 1970 (Sec 13)

14 Crankcase housings – inspection

1 Make a careful examination of the housings for signs of damage and general wear. Inspect the tapped holes and if the threads are damaged in any of them get your Citroën dealer or automotive engineer to fit a thread insert.
2 Check the condition of the core plugs (Fig. 1.13). If any signs of leakage are present clean with a suitable solvent and smear a sealant such as Metalit around the plug concerned.
3 Check that the housing contact faces are perfectly clean and free from damage and score marks. Also check the centering dowels in the journals (photo).
4 Check that the oilways are clean and refit the lubrication pipe plug (if applicable).
5 On engines fitted with a ball type pressure relief valve, inspect the valve seating for signs of wear or damage.

Fig. 1.13 The housing core plugs (2) (Sec 14)

15 Crankshaft and connecting rods – general

1 The crankshaft and connecting rod assembly is a factory built unit and cannot be dismantled by the owner. If the big-end or main bearings are known to have failed or have any diametrical play, then it is necessary to renew the crankshaft/connecting rod assembly; a factory exchange scheme is in operation. The rear main bearing is renewable, but the front bearing is not. If one is worn it is fair to assume the other is too.
2 Small-end bushes can be renewed, but this task must be entrusted to your Citroën dealer or automotive engineer.
3 The crankshaft rear pilot bearing and oil seal can be extracted for renewal. The bearing will be either a needle roller type or a bush. If renewing the latter, immerse the new bush in engine oil for 30 minutes prior to installation. Use a suitable soft drift or tube to drive the new bush into position. If fitting a new needle bearing, smear it with some silicone grease prior to assembly.
4 The oil seal fitted in the rear differs according to the type of bearing used. The seal fitted to the crankshaft with a pilot bush is 4 mm thick, but if a needle bearing is fitted then the seal is 3 mm thick. The seal is always fitted with the maker's name and reference number facing away from the engine.

14.3 Check the centering dowels

16 Cylinders and pistons – cleaning and renovation

1 It is important that any dirt and old oil be cleaned out of the cylinder cooling fins.
2 The ridge at the top of the cylinder bore will give you an approximate idea of the wear in the bores. If the ridge is deep and/or there are score marks down the cylinders then they will almost certainly be in need of replacement. A shallow ridge can be removed

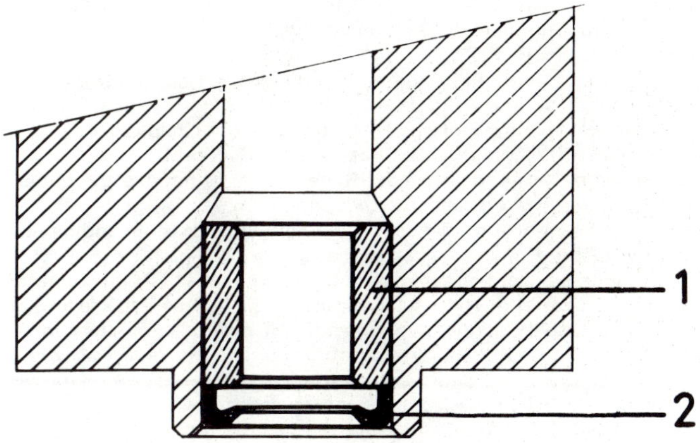

Fig. 1.14 Pilot bearing bush (1) and seal (2) (Sec 15)

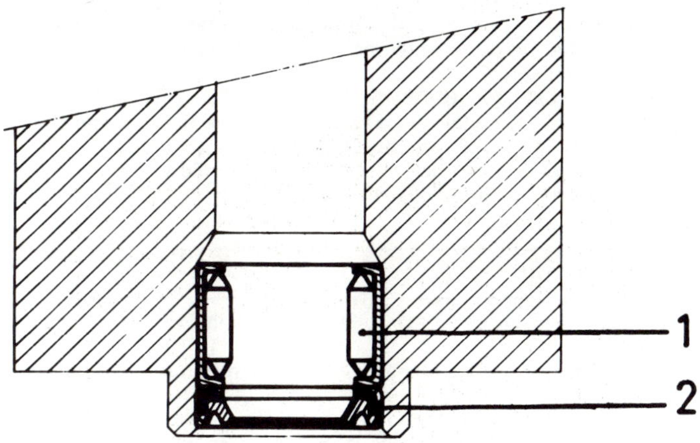

Fig. 1.15 Pilot roller bearing (1) and seal (2) (Sec 15)

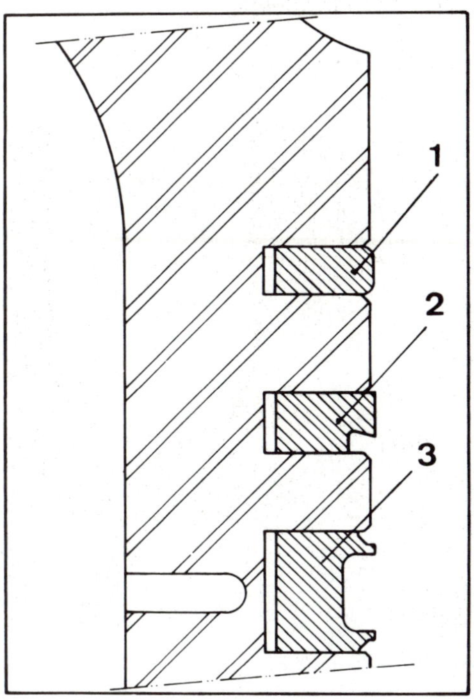

Fig. 1.16 Section showing details of piston rings (Sec 16)

1 Top compression ring
2 Second compression ring
3 Oil control ring

using a de-ridging tool or by carefully rubbing around (not up and down) the top of the bore with some medium emery cloth. No reboring is possible as oversize pistons are not supplied.

3 Clean and inspect the pistons and rings. If the top compression ring is a sloppy fit in its groove then the rings at least are in need of renewal. To remove the rings use a twisting action and carefully slide them upwards over the piston lands. Take care not to cut your fingers, the rings may be sharp. To assist removal insert two or three old feeler blades between the ring and the piston to prevent the rings entering the grooves as they are removed. Never remove or fit piston rings over the bottom of the piston.

4 Clean the grooves and rings free from carbon, taking care not to scratch the aluminium surfaces of the pistons.

5 If new rings are to be fitted, then order the top compression ring to be stepped to prevent it impinging on the wear ridge formed at the top of the cylinder bore.

6 Before fitting the rings to the pistons, push each ring in turn down to its lower limit or normal travel in its respective cylinder bore (use an inverted piston to do this to keep the ring square in the bore) and measure the ring end gap. The gaps are listed in the Specifications.

7 Test the side clearance of the compression rings; they must not bind in the piston grooves.

8 Where necessary a piston ring which is slightly tight in its groove may be rubbed down holding it perfectly squarely on an oilstone or a sheet of fine emery cloth laid on a piece of plate glass. Excessive tightness can only be rectified by having the grooves machined out.

9 It is important that when the rings are fitted to the piston prior to assembly that the ring gaps be spaced at 120° intervals.

10 It is also important to fit the rings the correct way round, the originals being marked 'Haut' 'H' or 'Top'; this marking must face upwards towards the piston crown.

11 If fitting new piston rings in old bores, deglaze the bores with coarse emery paper, being sure to remove all traces of abrasive afterwards.

12 Since June 1972 some 602cc engines have been fitted with 'U-flex' oil control rings. When decompressed the diameter of the 'U-flex' ring is greater than the cylinder bore.

17 Flywheel starter ring gear – removal and refitting

1 Remove the flywheel starter ring by driving it off with a hammer.

2 Clean the contact areas of the ring and the flywheel and ensure the surface is smooth and even.

3 Heat the ring with a blow torch, moving it round the ring all the time to ensure even expansion. Heat the ring to between 200 and 250°C (straw yellow colour) and fit the ring to the flywheel with the teeth lead-in (chamfer) towards the gearbox.

4 Check that the run-out on the starter ring does not exceed 0.3 mm (0.012 in).

18 Cylinder heads – cleaning and renovation

1 After the cylinder heads have been dismantled they should be thoroughly cleaned to remove all carbon deposits in the combustion chambers. Avoid damaging the valve seats when removing the carbon. Check that the oil holes under the valve caps on the exhaust side are clear.

2 Check whether the heads have been blowing. Burning or hammering of the spigot faces must be removed by lapping to an old cylinder barrel or by machining. Do not remove more metal than is necessary or the compression ratio of that cylinder will be altered.

3 Slight pitting of the valves and seats can usually be rectified by lapping with carborundum paste. If the seats are badly pitted or burned they will require grinding. Valve seat angles are shown in Fig. 1.17, but unless you have the necessary equipment (and are skilled in its use) this is a job for an automotive engineering works.

4 The chamfer of the valve heads is given in the Specifications in case the valves need to be ground on a machine. Make a slight chamfer at 'a' (Fig. 1.17) on the valve head to smooth the edge.

5 When lapping-in slightly pitted valves and valve seats with carborundum paste proceed as follows. Apply a little coarse grinding paste to the valve seat and using a suction valve grinding tool, lap the valve into its seat with a semi-rotary movement, lifting the valve from time to time. A light spring under the valve head will assist in this

operation. When a dull matt even surface finish appears on both the valve and the valve seat, clean off the coarse paste and repeat the operation with a fine grinding paste until a continuous ring of light grey matt finish appears on both valve and valve seat. Carefully clean off all traces of grinding paste. Blow through the gas passages with compressed air.

6 Inspect the valve springs for distortion or damage. If in doubt, have your Citroën dealer check the spring loads and lengths, or compare them with new ones. Renew the springs if necessary.

7 Inpect the rocker shaft, rockers and associated components for signs of wear or damage. The thrust washer will probably be worn and should therefore be renewed as a matter of course as should the flexible washer. Earlier engines were fitted with a spring (instead of the flexible washer) and this will almost certainly be in need of replacement.

8 Check the rocker arm on the shaft for excessive play and where necessary renew the rocker arm and/or shaft as applicable.

9 Check the rocker arms for wear at the face which bears on the valve stem and for wear of the adjustment ball end screws. If the wear faces are obviously worn then the rocker arm must be renewed. Slight wear on the valve stem mating wear face can be cleaned down on a grindstone, but take care not to distort the angle of the wear face.

10 Check the pushrods for wear and distortion. Roll them on a straight surface to check for distortion and renew any defective rods.

11 Inspect the pushrod guide assemblies. Always renew the cups and seals. Note that two types of tube joints have been fitted. On models produced from December 1972, there is no centering well in the crankcase for the tube joints. Renewal of the pushrod tubes is a job for your dealer.

12 The valve stem oil seals must be renewed (see Section 27).

19 Crankshaft oil seals – renewal

1 Whenever the engine is fully dismantled, the front and rear crankshaft oil seals should always be renewed. New seals must be fitted only after the crankcase halves have been assembled.

2 The renewal of the rear seal can only be achieved after the engine has been removed from the vehicle and the clutch and flywheel removed. The front seal can be renewed with the engine in the vehicle as described below.

3 Disconnect the battery and detach the wiring from the front grille panel.

4 Remove the front grille panel as described in Chapter 11.

5 Remove the cooling fan as described in Section 8.

6 Depending on model, it may be necessary to remove the generator, oil cooler and air collector seal panel.

7 The crankshaft front oil seal should now be accessible and can be extracted using a puller similar to that shown in Fig. 1.19.

8 To use this puller you will need to drill two holes of 2mm diameter through the seal at diametrically opposite points. Insert the extractor studs into the holes (screw them in) and then lever or screw the central bolt against the end of the crankshaft to remove the seal. *Take great care not to mark or damage the crankshaft in any way during removal,* particularly the oil thrower scrolls and taper face.

9 Clean out the seal housing and then smear a high melting point grease over the new seal outer and inner surfaces to ease assembly.

10 Fit the seal with the manufacturer's name or marking to the front and carefully drive it into position using a tube drift of dimensions 45 mm outside diameter x 31 mm inside diameter x 100 mm long.

11 When fitted the seal should be approximaterely 0.5 mm from the front face of the crankcase.

12 Refit the seal panel (if fitted) and oil cooler or generator.

13 Start and run the engine at a fast idle for a few minutes and check for signs of leakage from the seal.

14 If in order, refit the fan and front grille, adjust the generator drivebelt and top up the oil level to complete.

20 Oil pump – inspection

1 It is obviously essential that the oil pump be in good condition and this can easily be checked.

2 Thoroughly clean the respective components in petrol, wipe dry and reassemble.

3 Check the endfloat of the inner rotor using a feeler gauge inserted between the rotor top edge and a straight-edge placed across the

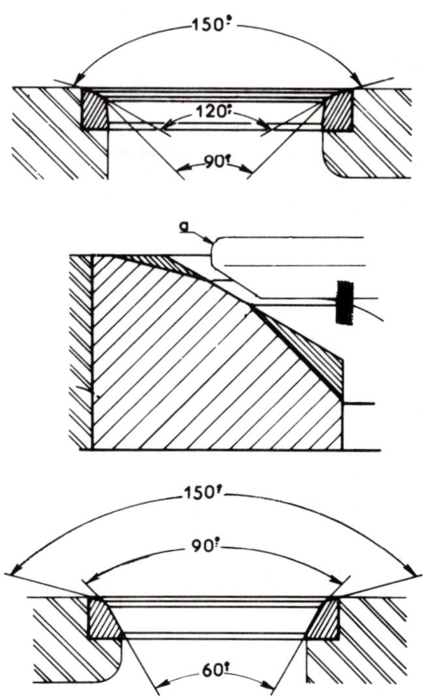

Fig. 1.17 Valve seat angles. For (a) see text (Sec 18)

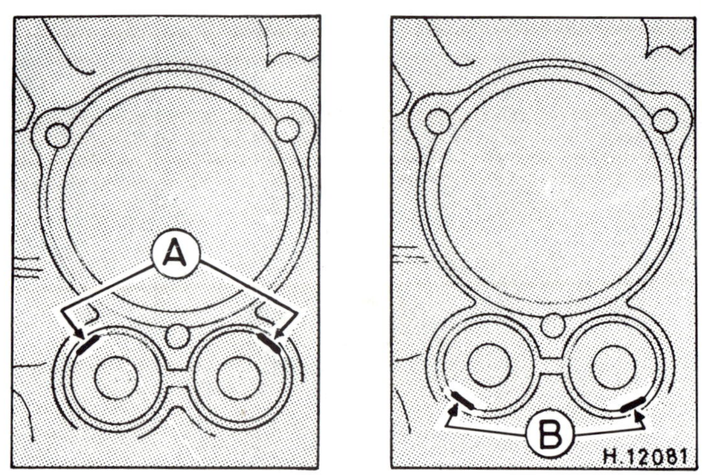

Fig. 1.18 Tube joint positions in crankcase on post-1972 engines (Sec 18)

a 602 cc engines – flats upwards
b 435 cc engines – flats downwards

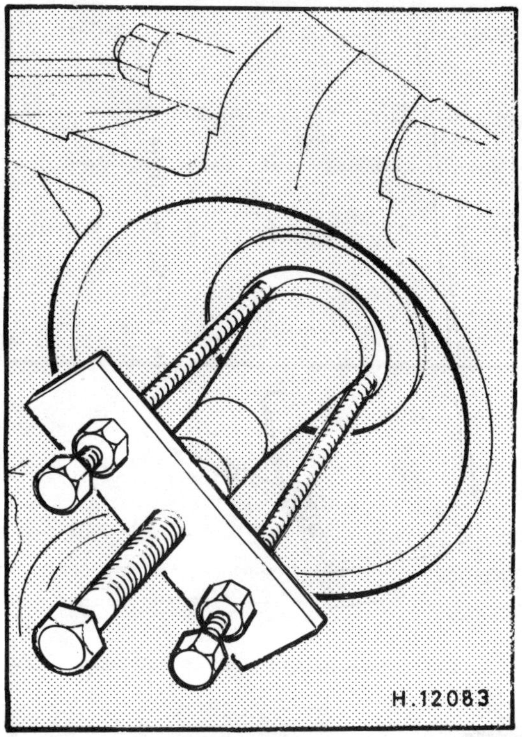

Fig. 1.19 Extracting the crankshaft front oil seal using the special Citroën tool (Sec 19)

pump face. The endfloat must not exceed that given in the Specifications.

4 If the pump body or rotors are obviously worn, scratched or damaged then the pump unit must be renewed complete. It is not possible to repair the pump.

21 Camshaft – examination and renovation

1 Carefully examine the camshaft bearings. If they are worn, damaged or scored then renewal is necessary.

2 The camshaft lobes must also be inspected for signs of damage or excessive wear characteristics. Slight scoring of the lobes can be erased by gently rubbing down with fine emery cloth, but take great care to keep the cam profiles smooth.

3 Examine the camshaft (and crankshaft) drivegears and if the teeth are badly worn or chipped then they must be renewed as a pair. Check the anti-backlash springs for breakage or loss of tension.

4 If possible check the camshaft run-out between fixed centres. It must run perfectly true or the distributor points gap will vary. Renew it if necessary.

22 Tappets (cam followers) – examination and renovation

The faces of the tappets which bear on the camshaft should show no signs of pitting, scoring or other forms of wear. They should also not be a loose fit in their housing. Wear is only normally encountered at very high mileages or in cases of neglected engine lubrication. Renew if necessary.

23 Engine lubrication system – general description

Engine lubricant is distributed in the following manner. Oil from the sump is drawn through a gauze filter into the oil pump on the rear end of the camshaft. From the pump the oil passes through the filter (if fitted) to the main big-end bearings; it also passes along the camshaft to the oil cooler and the cylinder heads. Oil returns to the sump via the pressure release valve. Later models incorporate a low pressure warning switch and a bypass valve, the latter in case the filter becomes clogged.

The sealed breather system maintains a vacuum in the crankcase whilst the engine is running. Thus if an oil leak develops it is most likely to occur when the engine has stopped.

If an oil filter is fitted it is usually of the external cartridge type, although for a short period an internally mounted filter was used (Fig. 1.24). The latest type of filter also incorporates a bypass valve.

24 Engine oil and oil filter – draining, removal and refitting

1 The engine oil must be changed at the specified intervals, or more frequently if operating under unfavourable conditions (mainly short journeys, or very hot or dusty climates). It is best to change the oil immediately after a run, when any impurities are still in suspension in the old oil.

2 The car should be on level ground. Position a container of sufficient capacity underneath the drain plug, wipe the sump clean around the plug and remove the plug. (The drain plug is located immediately adjacent to the half housing joint near the centre of the sump). Allow the oil to drain for at least ten minutes. Clean the drain plug magnet.

3 Access to the oil filter cartridge on early models is made easier by removing the engine/transmission undershield, which is secured to the chassis members on each side by bolts and washers. This is not necessary if Citroën filter wrench 1683-T is available.

4 If available use a strap wrench to unscrew the filter cartridge

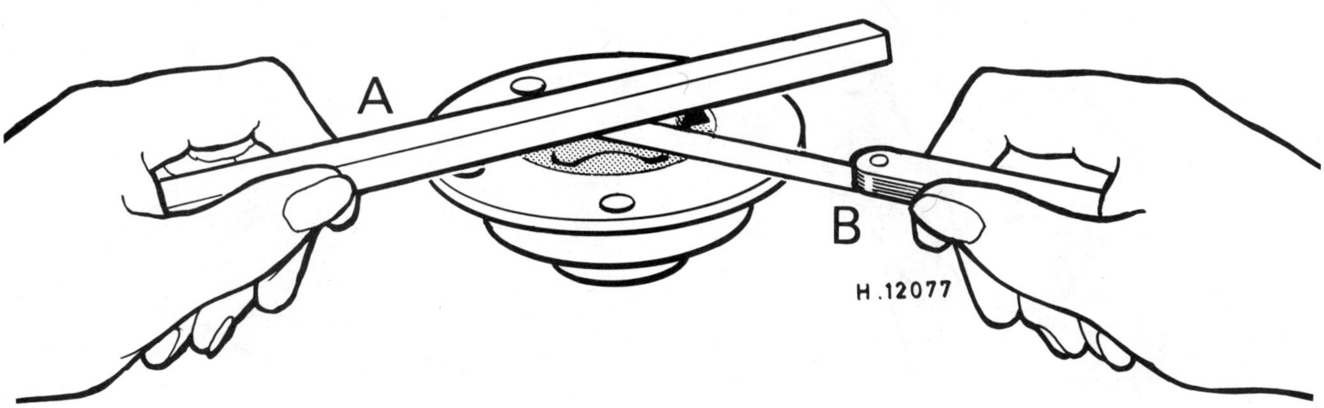

Fig. 1.20 Checking the oil pump endfloat with a straight-edge (A) and feeler gauge (B) (Sec 20)

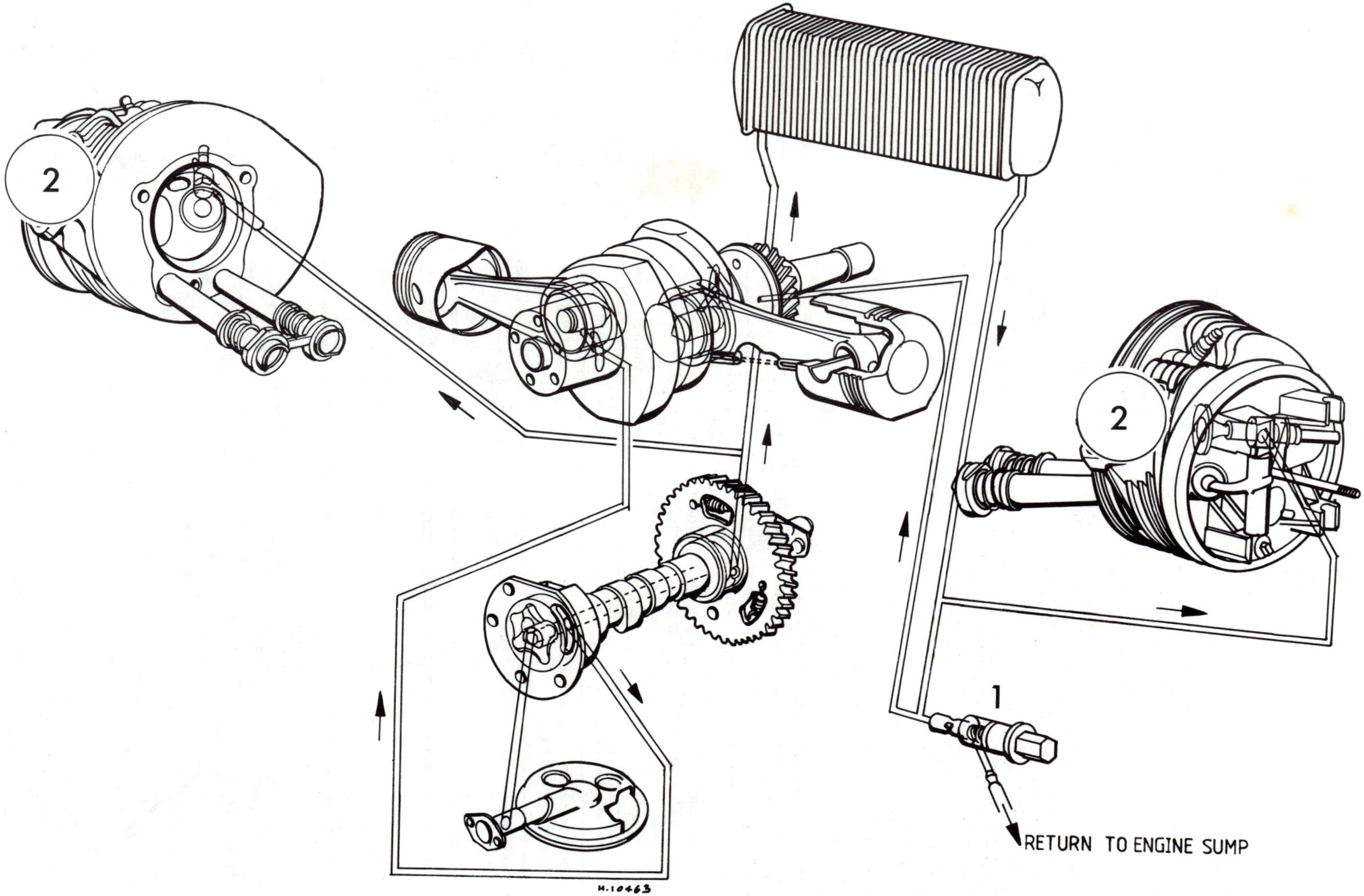

Fig. 1.21 Engine lubrication system – early type (Sec 23)

1 *Relief valve*　　2 *Cylinder heads*

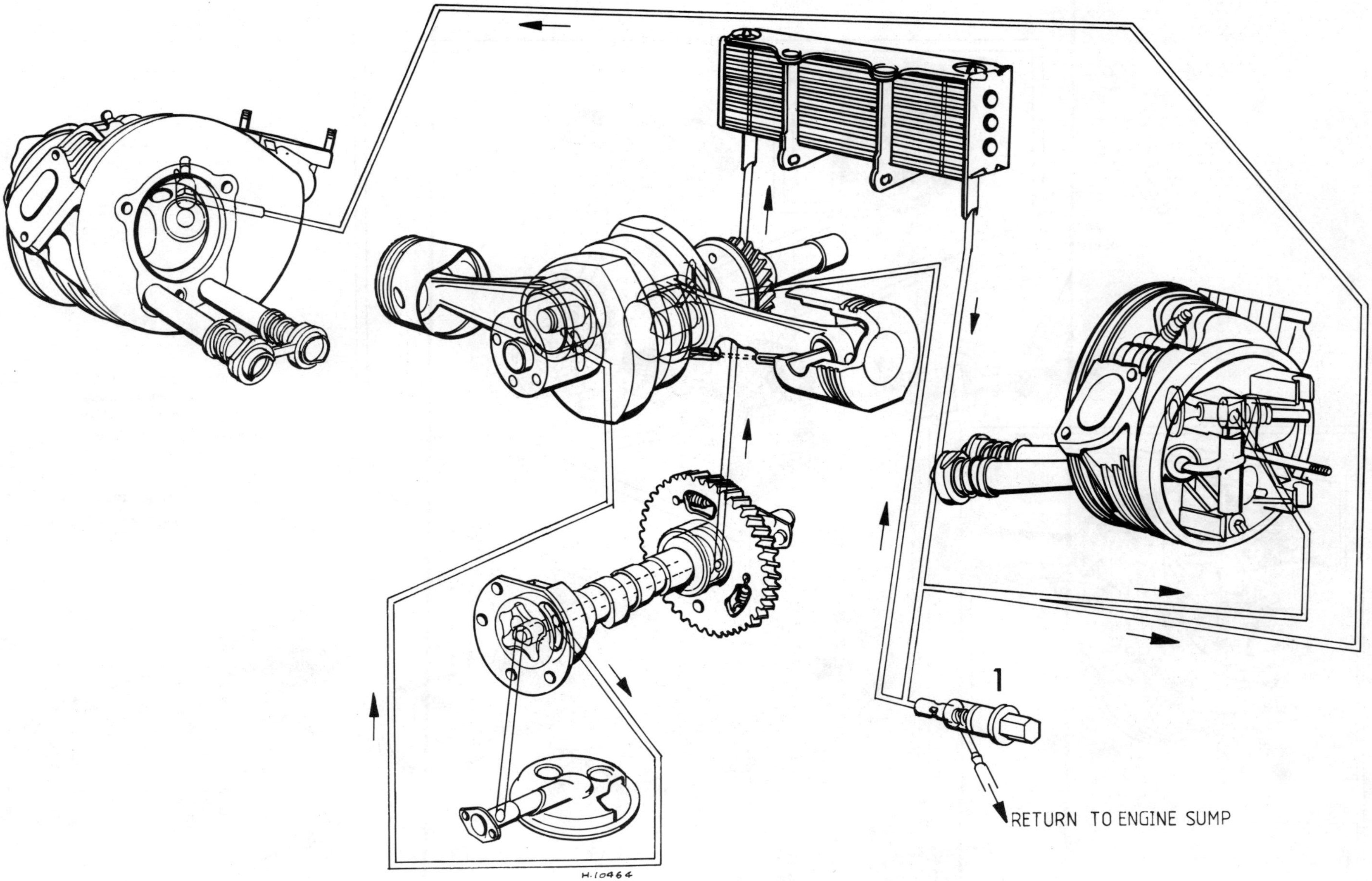

Fig. 1.22 Engine lubrication system – A79/1. M28 and M28/1 engines up to November 1970 (Sec 23)

1 *Relief valve*

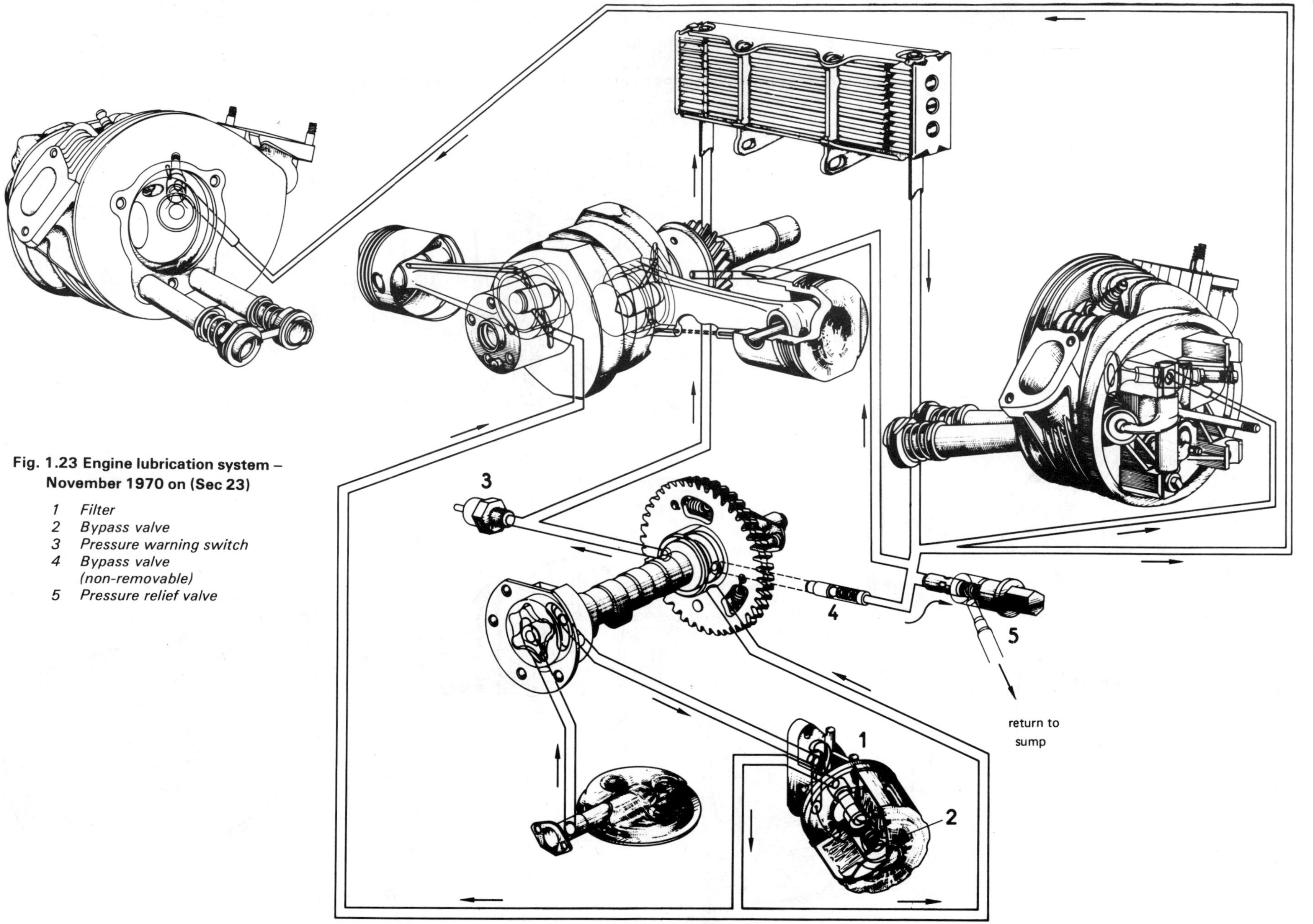

Fig. 1.23 Engine lubrication system – November 1970 on (Sec 23)

1 *Filter*
2 *Bypass valve*
3 *Pressure warning switch*
4 *Bypass valve (non-removable)*
5 *Pressure relief valve*

should it prove too tight to unscrew by hand. Alternatively drive a long punch or screwdriver through the filter casing to use as a lever when unscrewing. Allow for a certain amount of oil spillage from the filter.
5 Always avoid spillage of oil around the engine whenever possible. If spilt oil is not wiped clean, it can assist in clogging up the oil cooler fins and will collect dirt around the other parts of the engine. This in turn will cause the engine to overheat and shorten its working life.
6 Refit and tighten the sump drain plug (do not overtighten it) making sure that the washer is in good condition.
7 Wipe the filter joint face clean, lubricate the new cartridge seal with engine oil and hand tighten the cartridge according to the instructions on the casing. Do not overtighten it, but ensure that it is secure and that the seal is seated correctly.
8 Top up the engine oil level with the recommended grade of lubricant to just above the 'Max' mark, then run the engine up to its normal operating temperature and check around the filter housing for signs of leakage. If in order switch off the engine and refit the undershield (if removed).
9 Recheck the engine oil level before the next run.

25 Engine oil cooler – removal, cleaning and refitting

1 It is of utmost importance that the engine oil cooler be kept clean and in good working condition. Should the cooler unit become blocked then it must be cleaned without delay or the engine will overheat and serious damage may result. Cleaning can be carried out *in situ* after removing the front grille and the fan.
2 To remove the cooler unit, first remove the front grille panel (see Chapter 11), and the fan as described in Section 8.
3 The oil cooler unit is retained to the front of the crankcase by bolts and also by the inlet and outlet pipe unions. When removing the cooler note the distance pieces.
4 Clean out the cooler fins by washing in petrol or a grease solvent and hosing through. Blow through the fins and inspect for damage.
5 If the cooler unit is in order refit in the reverse order. Renew it if defective.

26 Engine reassembly – general

1 To ensure maximum life with minimum trouble from a rebuilt engine, not only must everything be correctly assembled, but also must be spotlessly clean. All oilways must be clear, locking washers and spring washers must be fitted where indicated. Oil all bearings and other working surfaces thoroughly with engine oil during assembly.
2 Before assembly, renew any bolts, studs or screws with damaged threads. The use of new spring washers is advisable.
3 Apart from having a supply of normal tools, a supply of clean rags and an oil can should be available.
4 Before starting work, clear the work area of any unwanted parts and arrange all the components nearby, prepared for reassembly (photo).

27 Cylinder heads – reassembly

1 Refitting of the valves is a reversal of the removal procedure. Always fit new valve seals on reassembly and ensure that the collets are correctly seated in the valve stem groove before fully releasing the valve spring compressor.
2 As each valve is assembled, lubricate the stem with engine oil (photo).
3 When the valve is in position fit the lower centering collar, oil seal, valve springs and upper spring retainer cup (photos). The oil seals can be pushed fully onto the valve guides using a suitable piece of tubing. Use the sleeves provided with new seals to stop the valve stem grooves damaging the seals.
4 Compress the springs and retainer just sufficiently to enable the collets to be inserted in the valve stem groove, then release the compressor. To assist in retaining the collets when assembling, smear the valve stem around the collet area with grease which will hold the collets in position until the compressor is released (photo).
5 When assembled lightly tap the end of each valve stem to check that the collets are fully located and to seat the valve.

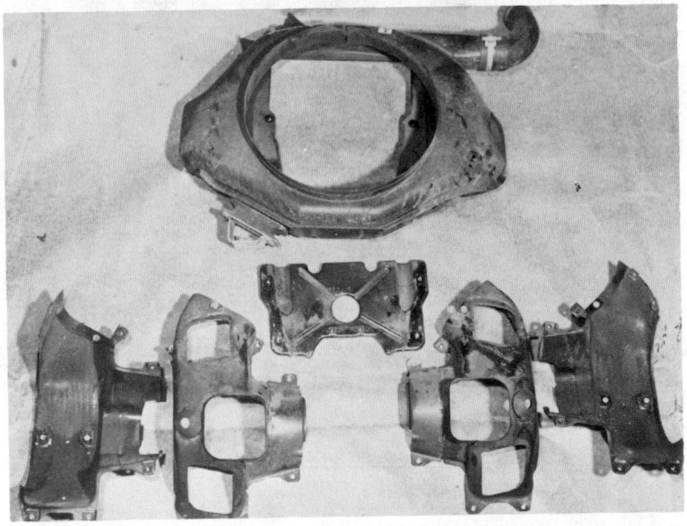

26.4 The engine and fan cowlings cleaned and ready for reassembly

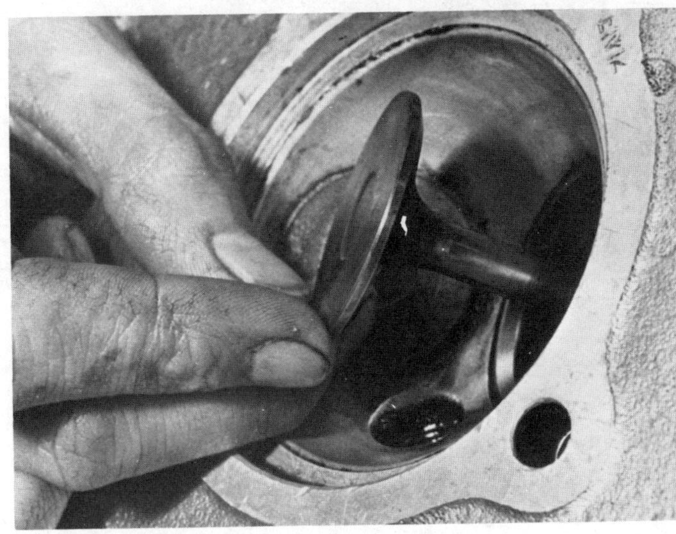

27.2 Lubricate and insert the valve

27.3a Locate the centering collar ...

27.3b ... the valve springs and ...

27.3c ... the spring retainer

27.4 Using a spring compressor to insert the collets

27.8a Fit the washer, spring and cup

27.8b The double joint seals

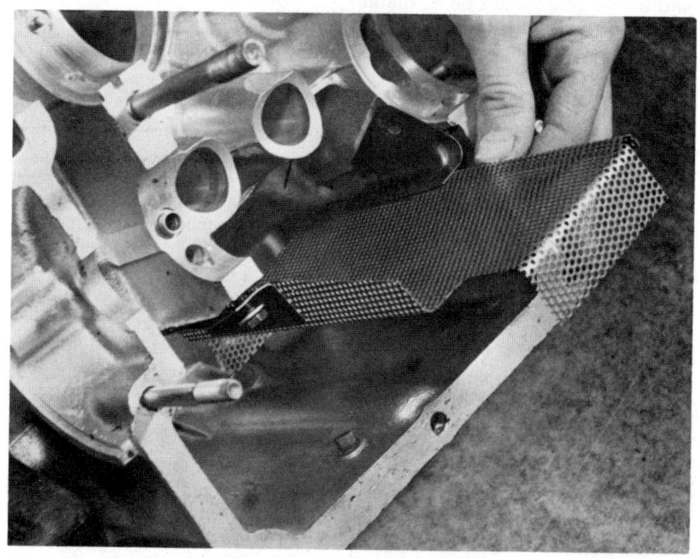
28.1 Locate the emulsion screen

6 The rocker arms and shafts can now be reassembled. Lubricate each rocker shaft with oil and then assemble on it the thrust washer, flexible washer, the rocker arm and spacer collar.
7 Fit the rocker assembly into position in the head and locate the retaining bolt.
8 To assemble the pushrod tube units first locate the thrust washer, then the spring, followed by the cups and double joint. The procedure is the same for each side (photos).

28 Crankshaft/camshaft and half housings – assembly

1 Install the anti-emulsion screen (if fitted) and retain with bolts and washers (photo).
2 Lubricate the crankshaft journals with clean engine oil. Check that the bearing centering dowels are correctly positioned and locate the crankshaft with connecting rod assemblies (photo) into position in the right-hand crankcase.
3 Locate the bearing over the peg as the crankshaft is lowered into position and ensure that the groove in the bearing bushes is level with the left-hand joint face of the half housing.
4 Lubricate the camshaft bearings and carefully place the camshaft into position in the half housings, engaging the drivegears so that the timing marks are in alignment (photo). Check that the camshaft front bearing is fully engaged with the dowel in the housing.

28.2 The crankshaft and connecting rods with main bearings fitted ready for installation

28.4a Align the timing gear marks when ...

28.4b ... fitting the camshaft

28.5 Locate the oil pump body on the rear of the camshaft

28.6 Refit the sump oil strainer with a new O-ring fitted

28.12 Insert the tappets (cam followers)

28.13a Locate the oil pump inner rotor, ...

28.13b ... then the outer rotor, ...

28.13c ... and refit the cover with a new O-ring

28.15 Tightening the main bearing nuts to the specified torque

Fig. 1.24 Internal oil filter (December 1969 to November 1970) (Sec 28)

3 Retaining screw
4 Flange bolt
5 O-ring
6 Filter

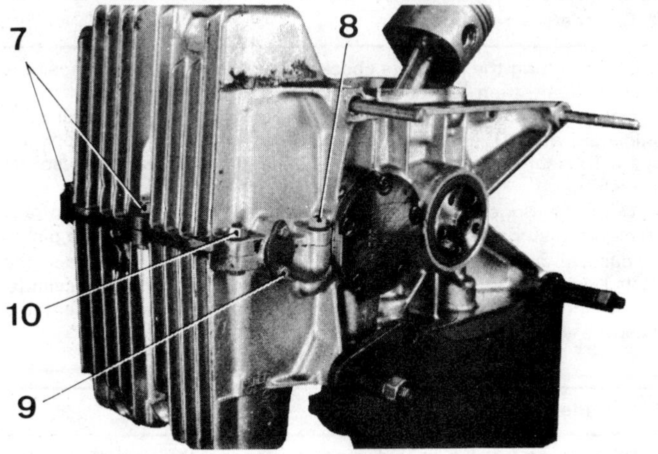

Fig. 1.25 Crankcase retaining bolts. For 7, 8 and 10 see text (Sec 28)

9 *Oil strainer cover flange bolt*

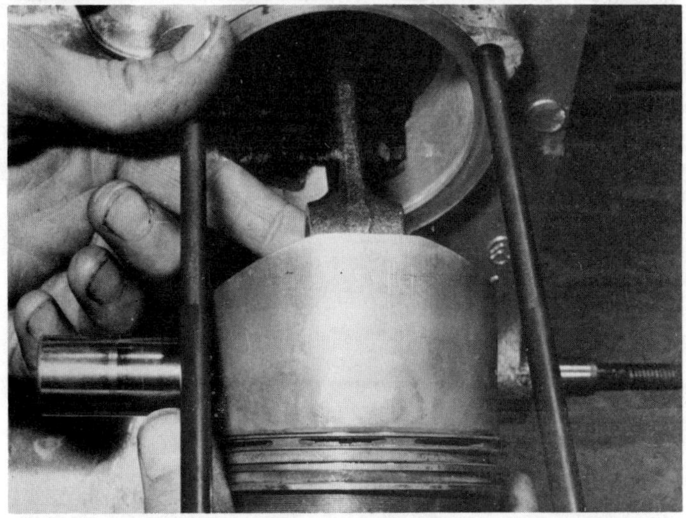

29.3 Locate the piston over the connecting rod

30.3 Fitting the cylinder over the piston and rings (note ring compressor)

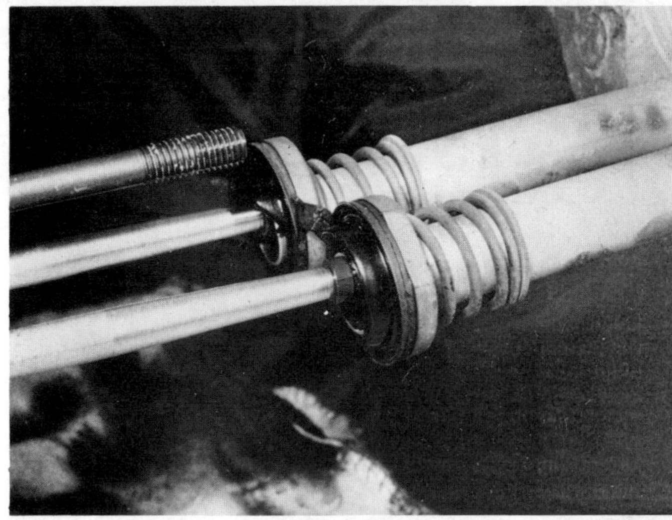

31.2 Insert the pushrods into the guides

5 Locate the oil pump body onto the rear end of the camshaft (photo) and ensure that it is well lubricated. The pump body must be correctly positioned with the oil delivery hole in alignment with that in the crankcase half housing. The bolt holes must also be aligned. Fit a new gasket between the pump body and crankcase. Do not use any form of sealant, fit the gasket dry.

6 The sump oil strainer can now be inserted into position in the casing. Make sure that it has a new O-ring seal (where fitted) up against the end flange (photo). When fitted into position the oil intake hole in the oil strainer must face downwards. Retain in position with a flange bolt and washer. If no O-ring seal is fitted, smear the flange with sealant. Do not fit a seal where there is no provision for one.

7 On vehicles manufactured between December 1969 and November 1970 an internal oil filter is fitted (Fig. 1.24). Fit a new O-ring flange joint seal and locate the filter as shown. Secure in position with a flange bolt on the outside and with the securing screw on the inside of the housing. The threads of the inside screw must be smeared with thread locking compound. When in position there must be a slight clearance between the centre web in the crankcase base and the bottom of the filter. If not, carefully tilt the filter accordingly.

8 The left-hand crankshaft housing can now be located onto the right-hand housing. Evenly smear the two housing mating faces with a suitable sealant on the outer edges.

9 Fit the two housings together after checking that no sealant has entered between the housings and bearings. Locate the housing nuts and flat washers but do not fully tighten just yet. Check that the outer machined flange surfaces around the crankshaft and oil pump housing are flush to within 0.05 mm (0.002 in).

10 Insert the five flange retaining bolts and nuts (with flat washers) and tighten to secure the half housings. Note that the bolt (10 in Fig. 1.25) fitted to the bottom rear corner of the housings (beneath the strainer/filter flange) has a small ground section to facilitate accurate centering of the housings. Referring to Fig. 1.25, tighten bolts 7 and 10 to the specified torque. Then tighten nut 8 to the same pressure. Finally tighten the oil filter/strainer flange bolts to the specified torque.

11 Lubricate the interior and exterior of both oil seals with high melting-point grease. The manufacturer's marking must face outwards. Carefully centralise and press in the seals; they must be flush with or within 0.5 mm (0.020 in) of, the housing outer faces.

12 Lubricate and insert the cam followers (tappets) into their respective bores (photo).

13 Lubricate and assemble the oil pump components commencing with the rotors (inner and outer). Before refitting the cover insert a new O-ring into its groove and smear the joint face of the cover with sealant around the outer edges. Do not apply too much sealant as it must not be allowed to enter the pump assembly when the cover is tightened down (photos).

14 Tighten the pump cover screws to the specified torque.

15 Tighten the crankshaft main bearing stud nuts to the specified torque (photo).

29 Pistons to connecting rods – reassembly

1 Assembly of the pistons to the connecting rods requires a certain amount of care. If refitting the original pistons, be sure to assemble them to their original connecting rods. New pistons will be supplied with new cylinders and gudgeon pins and can therefore be fitted on either side. Where 'U-Flex' scraper rings are being fitted see special note at the end of this Section.
2 To ease the fitting of the gudgeon pin, pre-heat the pistons in warm oil before assembly.
3 With the piston warmed, locate over the connecting rod (photo) with the arrow mark on the piston crown facing the front and insert the gudgeon pin which should be a sliding fit requiring only thumb pressure to install on later models. Early models will require the use of a suitable pressure tool.
4 Using suitable pliers insert the circlips each side to retain the gudgeon pin. Check that the piston can swivel freely on the gudgeon pin without any tight spots.

Special note – 'U-flex' rings

5 Where 'U-Flex' scraper rings have been fitted, the pistons are fitted into the lower section of the cylinders first (with the gudgeon pin hole left exposed beyond the case of the cylinder). The pistons and cylinders are then assembled to their respective connecting rods, the gudgeon pins and circlips fitted and the cylinders pushed fully home.

31.3 Fitting a cylinder head

30 Cylinders – refitting

1 Before fitting the cylinders check that the bores and seal faces are perfectly clean, then lubricate the bores with clean engine oil.
2 Check that the piston rings are correctly located with their gaps equidistant at 120° intervals to each other. Lubricate the pistons and rings with clean engine oil, then locate the piston ring compressor on the piston.
3 With the rings compressed and the piston supported centrally between the studs, locate the cylinder and carefully fit over the piston and push downwards (photo). When the cylinder has enveloped the piston rings, the ring compressor can be removed and the cylinder pushed home and into position against the crankcase. Repeat the procedure with the opposing cylinder assembly.

31 Cylinder heads – refitting

1 Prior to fitting the cylinder heads, loosen the rocker adjuster screws.
2 Lubricate the ends of the pushrods and insert them into their guide tubes (photo) with the coppered ball ends upwards (towards the rocker arms).
3 Each cylinder head can now be fitted into position over the studs and onto its respective cylinder (photo). As each head is fitted, locate the shoulders of the rubber seals (on the guide tube ends) into position in the crankcase.
4 Fit the head retaining nuts and washers. The copper washers are fitted at the top and the steel washer on the lower stud. Progressively tighten the nuts to the initial torque wrench setting specified. Do not fully tighten at this stage.

32 Engine – final assembly

1 If not already installed, fit the new crankshaft pilot bearing and seal as described in Section 15.
2 Locate the flywheel onto the crankshaft flange and progressively tighten the new retaining bolts to the specified torque wrench setting (photo). Refer to Chapter 4 and refit the clutch unit.
3 Referring to Chapter 3 refit the ignition box on the front of the engine, adjust the contact breaker points gap and check the static ignition timing. Renew the points if there is any doubt about their condition.
4 The cylinder head lubrication tubes are now fitted but first check that they are clear, blow through them with an air line if available. Two types have been used. On earlier models with the first type of oil

31.4 Initial tightening of cylinder head bolts

32.2 Tighten the flywheel bolts

32.3 Refit the ignition box

32.5a The oil cooler and protector plate in position

32.5b Oil cooler-to-crankcase securing bolt (arrowed)

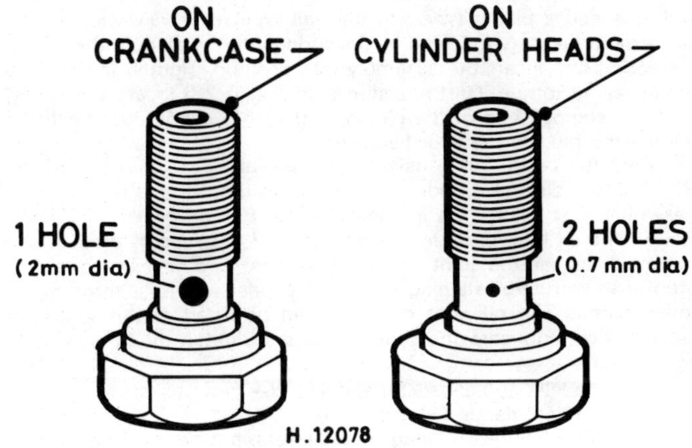

Fig. 1.26 Lubrication tube retaining bolts (Sec 32)

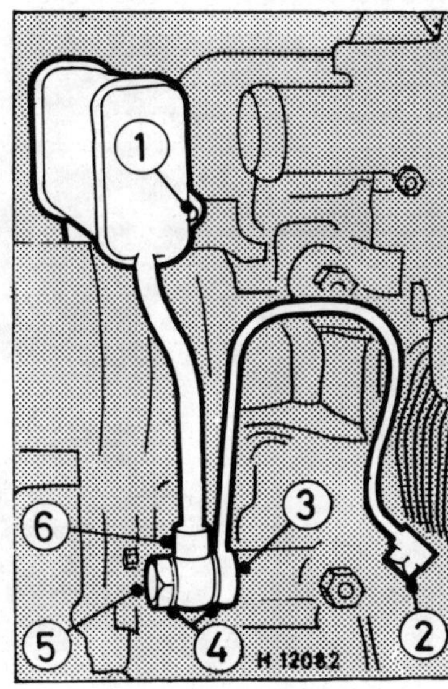

Fig. 1.27 Oil cooler and lubrication tube to crankcase connection (Sec 32)

1 *Retaining screw*
2 *Calibrated union screw*
3 *Oil pipe to cylinder heads*
4 *Washers*
5 *Retaining screw*
6 *Cooler pipe union*

cooler, the tubes are assembled with a double gasket fitted to the cylinder head joint. Fit the protective sleeve onto the tube and tighten the lug screws retaining the tubes. On the second type oil cooler it is important that the union screws are fitted correctly. The crankcase screw has one lubrication hole 2mm in diameter, whilst the screw fitted to the cylinder head has two lubrication holes 0.7mm in diameter (Fig. 1.26). A double copper washer is used on each pipe union. Do not forget the rubber tube and pipe clip.

5 Refit the engine oil cooler unit. On the earlier type cooler, assemble it into position on the front of the engine with its joints and retaining screws which are installed together with the cylinder head oil feed tubes as shown in Fig. 1.27. On engines fitted with the second type oil cooler unit first fit the protector plate into position on the front face of the engine, then with a protector sleeve fitted to the inlet and outlet tubes of the cooler (2mm from end of tube), locate the tube unions and hand tighten the retaining nuts. Check that the tubes are centralised in the joints before tightening, or cross-threading may occur. Before fully tightening these nuts to the specified torque, insert the cooler distance pieces and locate the cooler at the top of the crankcase with the securing bolt (plain washer under head) and nut (with shakeproof washer) (photo).

6 Refit the oil relief valve assembly. Two types have been fitted, a ball type and a piston type. On the ball type relief valve, locate the adjustment washers followed by the spring into the plug, fit the ball to the spring and insert the assembly into position. Tighten the plug to the specified torque. On the piston type (Fig. 1.28) locate the spring over the stepped end of the piston, and with a copper washer fitted tighten the plug to the specified torque.
7 Refit the petrol pump using new gaskets.
8 Reassemble the cylinder cooling plates (photo) and the fan cowl assembly. Also locate the ignition box low tension cable.
9 Fit the oil filter cartridge if applicable. If the support bracket was removed, smear the joint face with sealant and relocate onto the crankcase with two retaining screws. A copper washer is fitted to the lower screw. The oil filter cartridge can be fitted at this stage for convenience. Lubricate the sealing ring and tighten the filter. Do not overtighten.
10 Refit the inlet and exhaust manifolds. Use new gaskets and ensure that the manifold flange faces are clean.
11 Refit the carburettor using new gaskets, but do not fully tighten the bolts yet.
12 Refit the breather and oil filler unit (photo).
13 Locate the ignition box cover (if fitted) and bolt into position (photo).
14 Refit the fan and starter dog onto the front end of the crankshaft (photo), tightening the pulley nut to the specified torque.
15 Refit the alternator/dynamo and engage the drivebelt (photo). Adjust the drivebelt tension as described in Chapter 10. Refit the generator pulley cover (photo).
16 The cylinder head can now be finally tightened to the torque wrench setting specified. Tighten in this order: upper front nut, upper rear nut and then the lower nut. The final tightening of the cylinder heads must only be done after the manifolds have been fitted.
17 The valve clearances can now be adjusted as described in Section 33 and the rocker covers refitted (photo). When fitting the rocker covers check that the joint faces are clean and not distorted. Stick the cover rubber gaskets into position using a suitable adhesive.

Do not forget to insert a new rubber washer between the cover and retaining bolt washer and tighten the nuts to the specified torque. If the cover is not located correctly an oil leak, possibly serious, may develop so take care. Later engines do not have the washer fitted, the nut fitting direct into a recess. If there is an 'O' stamped on the cover, this must be at the top.

18 The engine should now be ready for refitting into the vehicle. If the transmission was removed also then this can be refitted as described in Chapter 5. Make a final check to ensure that all fittings and components are secure and correctly located before lifting into position.

32.8 Refit the cylinder cooling plates

32.12 Refit the oil filler unit

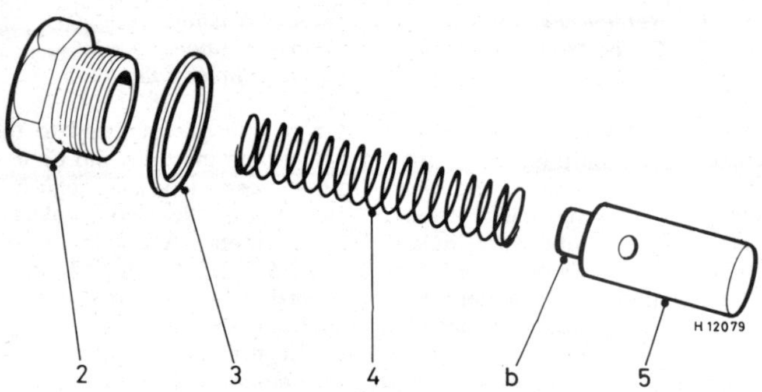

Fig. 1.28 Piston type oil pressure relief valve (Sec 32)

2 Plug
3 Washer
4 Spring
b Step
5 Piston

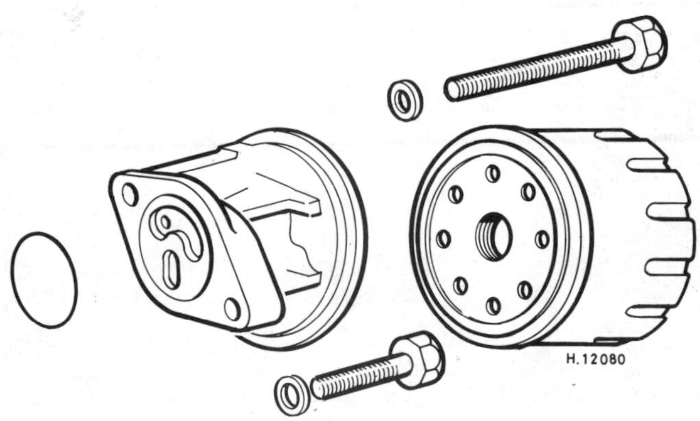

Fig. 1.29 External oil filter assembly components (Sec 32)

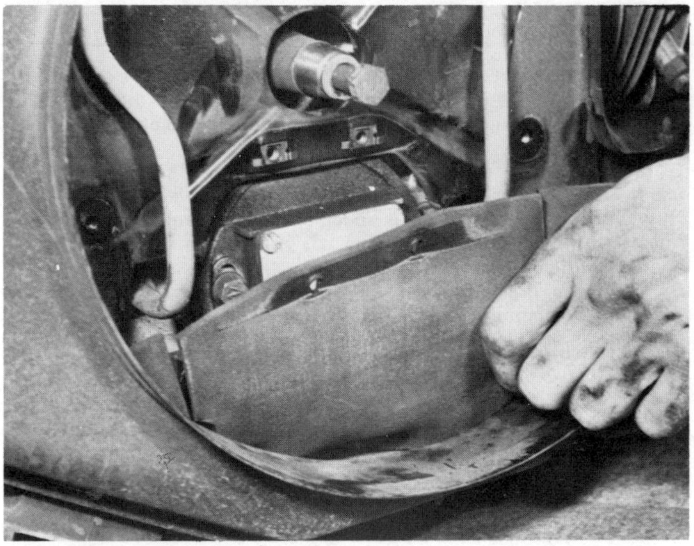

32.13a Locate the ignition box cover (if fitted) ...

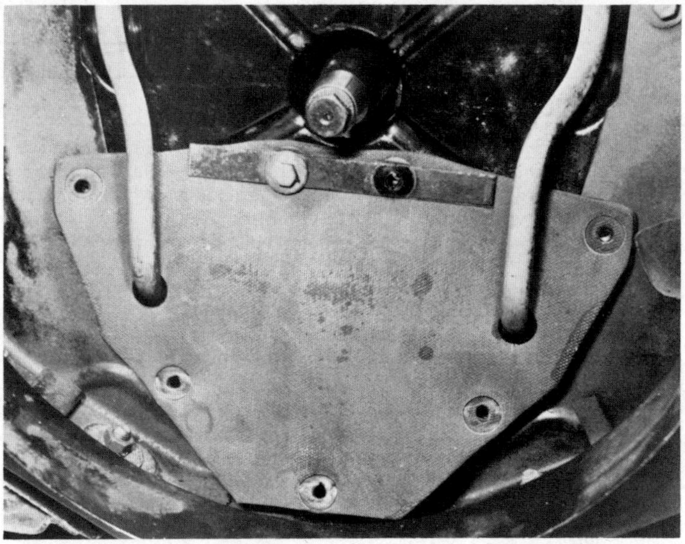

32.13b ... and bolt in position

32.14 Fit the fan and starter dog

32.15a Engaging the generator drivebelt

32.15b Refit the pulley cover

32.17 With the valve clearances set, refit the rocker covers

33 Valve to rocker arm clearance – adjustment

1 The procedure for adjusting the rocker arm to valve clearances is the same whether the engine is in or out of the vehicle. The rocker covers must be removed. If a seal is broken or defective when removed it must be renewed before the cover is refitted.
2 The clearances should be checked and adjustment made when the engine is cold.
3 On 2CV models this task is made easier if the front wings are removeed (see Chapter 11).
4 To check the valve clearances you will need a set of feeler gauges, the blades of which will fit between the valve stem and rocker arm to ascertain the clearance when the valve in question is in the fully closed position.
5 Rotate the engine so that one valve is fully open (spring under compression) and adjust the corresponding valve on the opposite cylinder. Repeat for the remaining three valves. The correct valve to rocker clearance is given in the Specifications.
6 To adjust the rocker clearances you will need a 10mm ring spanner to loosen the locknut and a screwdriver with which to rotate the rocker screw to give the correct clearance (photo). With the engine installed you will need a cranked or very short screwdriver to make this adjustment in Dyane and Ami models.

33.6 Method of adjusting the valve clearances

7 With a feeler gauge of the correct thickness inserted between the valve and the rocker arm, slacken the locknut and turn the rocker adjuster screw to enable the feeler blade to be a firm sliding fit. Holding the screw in this position, retighten the locknut.
8 On very worn engines a slightly smaller clearance can be made to help counteract uneven wear, but this cannot be regarded as good practice. If the clearance is too small the valves may burn.
9 Turn the engine over a couple of times and recheck the clearance. If satisfactory repeat the procedure on the next valve until all four have been adjusted.
10 Wipe clean around the mating surfaces of the rocker covers and refit them together with the gaskets (see Section 32, paragraph 17). Run the engine for a couple of minutes, then stop it and check for oil leaks.

34 Engine and gearbox – refitting

1 Arrange the lifting sling in a similar manner to when the power unit was removed. The engine and gearbox assembly can then be raised and carefully lowered into position through the front of the vehicle. Take care not to foul on the surrounding components.
2 On drum brake models the handbrake cables must be refitted to the crossmember ducts.
3 Engage the rear location studs in the support slots of the mounting. Don't forget to relocate the washers under the bracket.
4 On drum brake models locate the handbrake cables into the lever barrels as the unit is lowered.
5 With the engine mounting re-engaged, insert the retaining bolts using new tab washers and fully lower and remove the lifting sling. Now tighten the bolts to the specified torque wrench settings and make secure by bending over the tab washer ears against the bolt heads. Refit the sealing plugs.
6 On drum brake models refit the following brake components, referring to Chapter 6 for details:

(a) Handbrake cable adjuster nuts (do not tighten yet)
(b) Flexible hose to bracket on gearbox
(c) Rigid brake pipe to flexible hose (use a new seal)

7 On disc brake models refit the following brake components, referring to Chapter 6 for details:

(a) Feed pipe to left-hand brake caliper (use new seal and ensure correct location in support bracket)
(b) Master cylinder hydraulic pipe (use a new seal)
(c) Handbrake cable and return lever connections (use new split pins and a new shakeproof washer)
(d) Handbrake cable stops

8 On all models, bleed the brake hydraulic system on completion (Chapter 6).
9 The driveshafts can now be relocated and the bolts fitted on each side. Tighten the bolts, which have spring washers under the heads, to the specified torque.
10 Refit the speedometer cable into the gearbox and tighten the securing bolt.
11 Reconnect the clutch cable to the pedal lever within the vehicle and adjust the operating clearance (Chapter 4).
12 Smear some exhaust sealant around the exhaust pipe-to-expansion box connections and loosely fit the half clamps. On disc brake models, locate the protector shield under the half collar retaining bolts.
13 Refit the heater ducts and heat exchangers. Tighten the exhaust pipe half clamps and secure the heater ducts.
14 Reconnect the gearlever rod to the selector, and the battery earth cable to the special bolt head on the gearbox top cover.
15 Reconnect the petrol pipe to the pump.
16 Reattach the accelerator and choke cables (see Chapter 2 for details).
17 Refit the front body panel and bumper. On 2CV models refit the headlight bracket assembly, the front wings and the side panels. Check that all panels are correctly aligned.
18 Reconnect the electrical leads to the lights, coil, horn, starter and alternator. Do not forget the earth connections (where applicable). Secure the leads in their clips.
19 Reattach the headlight control cables.
20 Reattach the heater control cables.
21 Reconnect the bonnet release cable and check for satisfactory operation.
22 Check that the engine and gearbox drain plugs are tight, then refill the units with oil (if not already done). Remember that as the engine is presumably being refilled from dry, and with a new oil filter, more oil will be required than at a routine oil change. See Specifications for details.
23 Refit the air cleaner unit.
24 Before connecting the battery terminals, make a final check to ensure that all fittings are securely connected. Reconnect the battery and refit the spare wheel carrier.
25 Before restarting the engine refer to Section 36.

35 Engine only – refitting

1 The engine refitting procedure is roughly a reversal of removal, but note the following.
2 When the engine is being lifted into position, ensure that the clutch disc is centralised to allow engagement with the gearbox input shaft. Do not allow the weight of the engine to be taken by the input shaft during installation.
3 When the engine and gearbox are bolted together the engine mounting bolts can be refitted and tightened to the specified torque. Use new tab washers and bend the ears flush to the bolt heads when tightened to secure.

4 On disc brake models the cooling ducts must be reattached.
5 The remaining refitting procedures are given in Section 34. Follow the instructions given for your particular model, ignoring those operations concerning the gearbox and driveshaft installation.
5 Before restarting the engine refer to Section 36.

36 Engine – initial start-up after major overhaul

1 Before starting up make a visual inspection around and under the engine and transmission to ensure that no rags or tools have been left lying around. Check the oil and fuel levels. Make sure that the throttle return spring is operating correctly.
2 Set the choke and start the engine. It may take a while for the pump to supply fuel to the carburettor.
3 When the engine has started, run it at a fast idle and check for any signs of fuel or oil leaks. Check that the oil pressure light (if fitted) is extinguished.
4 When the engine has warmed up, adjust the idle speed (see Chapter 2).
5 Check the oil level after the engine has been stopped for a few minutes.
6 Before taking to the road, refit the bonnet (if removed) and spare wheel and check the operation of brakes, lights and controls.
7 If new piston rings, pistons and barrels or crankshaft have been fitted, the engine should be treated as though it were new and progressively run-in for the first 500 miles or so. Change the engine oil and filter after the first 500 miles, and loosen and retighten the cylinder head nuts as described in Section 32, paragraph 16. Check the valve clearances and reset if necessary as described in Section 33.

37 Fault diagnosis – engine

Symptom	Reason(s)
Engine will not turn over when starter switch is operated	Flat battery Bad battery connections Bad connections at starter motor and/or solenoid switch Starter motor jammed Defective solenoid Starter motor defective
Engine turns over but fails to start	No spark at plug No fuel reaching the engine Too much fuel reaching the engine (flooding)
Engine starts but runs unevenly and misfires	Ignition and/or fuel system faults Incorrect valve clearances Burnt out valves Worn piston rings and cylinders
Lack of power	Ignition and/or fuel system faults Incorrect valve clearances Burnt out valves Worn piston rings and/or cylinders
Excessive oil consumption	Oil leaks from pipe unions and gaskets of lubrication system Oil leaks from crankshaft oil seals Worn valve guides and/or defective valve stem seals Worn piston rings and cylinders (indicated by excessive blue smoke from exhaust)
Excessive mechanical noise from engine	Wrong valve clearances Worn crankshaft bearings Broken piston ring
Unusual vibrations	Misfiring Loose mounting bolts Defective mountings

Note: When investigating starting and uneven running faults do not be tempted into snap diagnosis. Start from the beginning and follow it through. It will take less time in the long run. Poor performance from an engine in terms of power and economy is not normally diagnosed quickly. In any event the ignition and fuel system must be checked first before assuming any further investigation needs to be made

Chapter 2 Fuel and exhaust systems

For modifications, and information applicable to later models, see Supplement at end of manual

Contents

Specifications

Carburettor – general

Make (all models) ..... Solex

Application:	Carburettor type	Identification No
A53 (2CV)	28 IBC	$32^1/30^1$
	28 CBI	$32^1/30^1$
A79/0 engine (Dyane 4)	32 PICS/PCIS	38/39
A79/1 (2CV4, Dyane 4)	34 PICS/PCIS 4 or 5	101/102
	34 PICS/PCIS 6*	121/122
M4 (Dyane 6, Ami 6)	40 PICS/PCIS 3	$44^3/45^3$
	30 PICS	–
M28/1 (2CV6, Dyane 6)	34 PICS/PCIS 4 or 5	103/104
	34 PICS/PCIS 6*	123/124
M28 (Dyane 6, Ami 6 & 8)	26/35 CSIC/SCIC	$110^2/111^2$
	26/35 CSIC/SCIC*	$113^1/114^1$
	26/35 CSIC/SCIC*	127/128

**Emission control device fitted*

Carburettor specifications

28 IBC and CBI:		
Venturi bore	22 mm	
Main jet	125	
Air corrosion jet	EI	
Choke jet	80	
Idling jet	42.5	
Needle valve seat	1.2	
32 PICS/PCIS:		
Venturi bore	28 mm	
Main jet	150	
Air correction jet	215	
Idling jet	55	
Pump injector	40	
Needle valve seat	1.3	
Float weight	5.7 g	
34 PICS/PCIS 4 and 5:	**101/102**	**103/104**
Venturi bore	28 mm	28 mm
Main jet	155	160
Air correction jet	AB	AB
Idling jet	40	42.5
Bypass jet	55	55
Pump injector	35	40
Needle valve seat	1.3	1.3
Float weight	5.7 g	5.7 g
34 PICS/PCIS 6:	**121/122**	**123/124**
Venturi bore	28 mm	28 mm
Main jet	155	165
Air correction jet	AB	AC
Idling jet	40	42.5
Bypass jet	50	52.5
Pump injector	35	40
Needle valve seat	1.3	1.3
Float weight	5.7 g	5.7 g

Carburettor specifications (continued)

30 PICS:	
Venturi bore	26 mm
Main jet	140
Air correction jet	AB
Idling jet	47.5
Needle valve seat	1.3
Float weight	5.7 g
40 PICS/PCIS 3:	
Venturi bore	32 mm
Main jet	170
Air correction jet	AC
Idling jet	50
Pump injector	40
Needle valve seat	1.3
Float weight	5.7 g

26/35 CSIC/SCIC:	110/111/113/114	127/128
Primary venturi bore	21 mm	21 mm
Secondary venturi bore	24 mm	24 mm
Primary main jet	125	125
Secondary main jet	75	82.5
Primary air correction jet	1F1	1F1
Secondary air correction jet	2AA	2AA
Pump injector	40	40
Idling jet	50	40
Needle valve seat	1.7	1.7

Idle speed settings

Up to September 1972:	
Models with single choke carburettor	800 to 850 rpm
Models with twin choke carburettor	750 to 800 rpm
Models with centrifugal clutch	Clutch drag speed minus 50 rpm
From September 1972:	
Dyane 4, 2CV4, 2CV6	800 to 850 rpm
Dyane 6, Ami 6, Ami 8	750 to 800 rpm

Fuel pump

Make	Guiot or SEV-Marchal
Type	Mechanical, driven by pushrod from camshaft

Fuel tank capacity

2CV (425 and 435 cc) and Dyane 4	20 litres (4.4 gal)
Ami 6, Dyane 6 and 2CV (602 cc)	25 litres (5.5 gal)
Ami 8	30 litres (6.6 gal)

Fuel octane rating

M28 engine	97 to 99 octane (UK 4-star)
All other engines	91 to 93 octane (UK 2-star)

1 General description

The fuel system comprises a fuel tank located at the rear of the vehicle, a fuel pump mounted on and worked by the engine, a Solex single or double barrel carburettor (according to model) and an air filter. Throttle linkage is by cable or by rod.

The fuel tank capacity varies according to model, but all have a filter unit on the base of the fuel supply pipe in the tank and this is located together with the sender unit to the petrol gauge.

The fuel pump, mounted on the front left-hand side of the engine crankcase, draws the fuel from the tank and relays it to the carburettor. The level of petrol in the carburettor is governed by a float-operated needle valve. Petrol flows past the needle until the float rises sufficiently to close the valve. The fuel pump will then 'freewheel' under the back pressure until the petrol level in the float chamber drops, allowing the float to drop and thus reopen the needle valve. This permits a further controlled flow of fuel into the carburettor.

The fuel/air mixture is drawn into the combustion chambers on the induction stroke of each piston in the conventional manner.

The exhaust system comprises a transverse expansion box into which each downpipe is connected. Interconnecting pipes from the expansion box and silencer convey the exhaust gases to the rear of the car.

2 Air cleaner element and unit – removal and refitting

Air cleaner element

1 The air cleaner unit fitted to your vehicle depends on the type and on the date of manufacture. Two types have been fitted, these being of Miofiltre or Lautrette manufacture.

2 The element in all types can be removed by unscrewing the thumb screw retaining the element cover, or by unscrewing the cover itself as in the latest type shown (photos).

3 When the element is extracted from the housing, it can be washed in petrol, dried and then soaked in clean engine oil. Allow the element to drain off and clean around the inside of the filter housing.

4 Refit the element and locate the cover, ensuring that it is correctly seated.

Air filter unit

5 Remove the spare wheel from its carrier.

6 Disconnect the flexible hose from the silencer to the carburettor.

7 Detach the flexible hose from the fan cowl to the filter housing (M28 engines only) (photo).

8 Detach the hose to the oil filler tube.

9 Noting the adjustment position registered, remove the accelerator

2.2a The earlier type of air filter

2.2b The latest air filter unit with element attached to cover

2.7 Disconnect the hose attachments

2.10 Removing the air cleaner unit

return spring tensioner from the lug on the front panel.
10 The cleaner unit mounting bracket retaining nuts can now be removed and the cleaner unit withdrawn (photo). Note that on some models it will be necessary to detach the left-hand spark plug lead and to disengage it from the location guide on the air cleaner body if the cleaner unit is to be completely lifted clear.
11 Refitting of the cleaner unit is a direct reversal of the removal procedure. Check that all connections are secure and renew any damaged or perished hoses or distorted clips.

3 Fuel pump – removal and refitting

1 The fuel pump is located on the left-hand side of the crankcase directly beneath the air cleaner unit.
2 Remove the air cleaner unit as described in Section 2.
3 Loosen the outlet pipe hose clip from the pump to the carburettor at the pump end and detach the pipe.
4 To disconnect the inlet pipe from the fuel tank at the pump is not quite so easy. It is better to disconnect the pipe from its joint adjacent to the left-hand side member (working under the wing panel). Block the pipe on separation to prevent fuel leakage and the ingress of dirt (photo).

3.4 Block the pipe with a suitable bolt as shown

3.5a Removing the fuel pump – note spacer

3.5b Withdraw the operating rod if necessary

5 Unscrew and remove the retaining bolts and withdraw the pump (photo). If required the operating rod can be extracted from the crankcase (photo).
6 Refitting of the fuel pump is a direct reversal of the removal procedure. Be sure to use new gaskets and check that the jointing faces are clean. On restarting make a check of the fuel pump connections to ensure that there are no leaks.

4 Fuel pump (Guiot type) – servicing

1 Remove the pump from the crankcase as described in Section 3 and clean off the exterior surfaces.
2 Unscrew and remove the upper housing retaining screws and separate the upper and lower housings. Note their relative positions.
3 Unscrew and remove the diaphragm retaining nut and washer. Withdraw the three diaphragms, the thrust cup, return spring and cup.
4 Remove the pushrod.
5 Withdraw the two washers and special split washer.
6 The respective components can now be washed in petrol and cleaned ready for inspection. Do not attempt to remove the suction delivery valves from the upper housing. If they are known to be defective then the upper housing must be renewed.
7 Inspect all components for signs of wear or damage and renew as necessary. The most likely items to be in need of replacement will be the diaphragms.

8 Reassembly is a direct reversal of the removal procedure. When assembling the upper and lower housings ensure that the iniet pipe is aligned with the control lever. Do not smear the diaphragms with any form of sealant – they must be assembled dry.

5 Fuel pump (SEV-Marchal) – servicing

1 Remove the fuel pump from the crankcase as described in Section 2 and clean off the exterior surfaces.
2 Unscrew and remove the retaining screws from the upper and lower half housings. Note the relative positions of the housings and carefully separate them.
3 Unscrew and remove the bracket-to-operating lever screw and remove the bracket and operating lever from the lower housing.
4 Carefully remove the diaphragm with pushrod and spring from the lower housing.
5 Mark the relative position of the upper housing to the cover, then remove the retaining screws and detach the cover and seal gasket.
6 The respective components can now be washed in clean petrol and cleaned ready for inspection. Do not attempt to remove the suction delivery valves from the upper housing. If they are known to be defective, renew the upper housing.
7 Inspect all components for signs of wear or damage and renew as necessary. The most likely item requiring replacement will be the diaphragm.

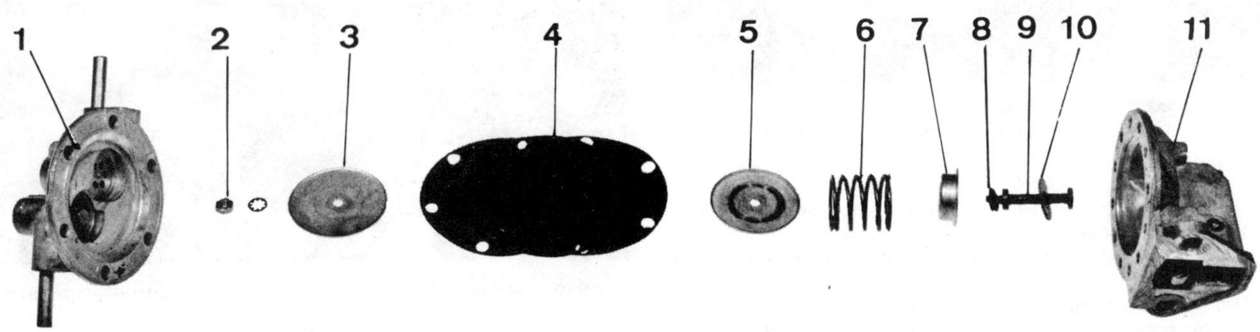

Fig. 2.1 The Guiot fuel pump (Sec 4)

1 Upper housing
2 Diaphragm nut
3 Washer
4 Diaphragms (3 off)
5 Thrust cup
6 Return spring
7 Cup
8 Washers
9 Pushrod
10 Special washer
11 Lower housing

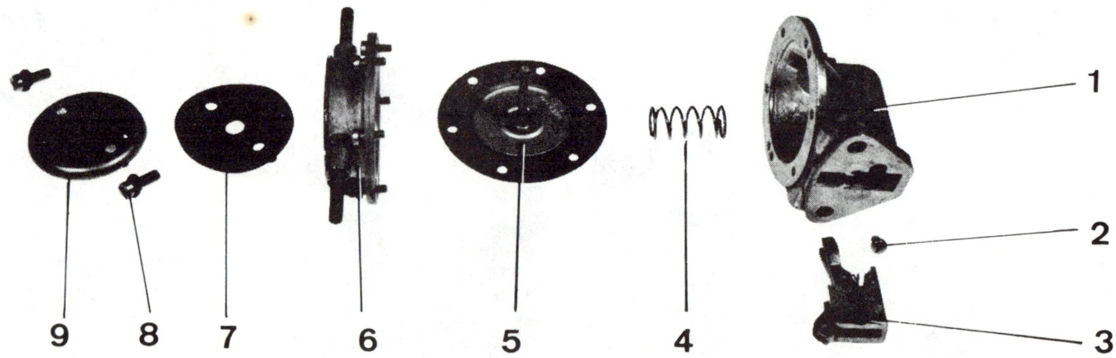

Fig 2.2 The SEV-Marchal fuel pump (Sec 5)

1 Lower housing
2 Screw
3 Operating lever and support
4 Return spring
5 Diaphragm and pushrod
6 Upper housing
7 Gasket
8 Cover retaining screw
9 Cover

8 Reassemble in the reverse sequence to dismantling. Remember to correctly align the upper housing and cover, the inlet pipe to be in line with the operating lever. Do not smear the diaphragm with any form of sealant – it must be fitted dry.

6 Choke cable – removal and refitting

1 Unscrew the inner cable clamp bolt from the carburettor connection and release the cable.
2 Unscrew the outer cable clamp screw and release the outer cable from the carburettor (photo).

6.2 Choke cable clamp bolts (arrowed)

3 On models where the choke control knob is located in the facia panel, unscrew and remove the panel retaining screws and remove the panel sufficiently to gain access to the choke cable connection on the inside.
4 Unscrew the outer cable locknut from the control and then pull the inner and outer cables through the bulkhead aperture and the facia connection to remove.
5 Refit in the reverse order, placing the locknuts onto the cable as it is passed between the facia and bulkhead apertures. Relocate the inner and outer cables at the carburettor and check that the knob is in the off position before tightening the outer cable retaining screw. Then adjust and tighten the inner cable to allow 3 to 5 mm free play at the control knob.

7 Throttle (accelerator) control cable – removal, refitting and adjustment

1 Not all the models covered in this manual have a throttle cable. Some models have a rod linkage, the disconnection of which from the carburettor is described in Section 13.
2 Remove the spare wheel.
3 Extract the retaining clip from the clevis pin at the carburettor throttle lever, and withdraw the clevis pin to detach the cable tension limiter.
4 Withdraw the outer cable from the support bracket slot.
5 Detach the cable from the demister shutter cable and then from the rubber guide at the bulkhead.
6 Working within the vehicle, slide the front seat back to give more room and then detach the stop clip from the outer cable stop on the bulkhead panel.
7 Detach the cable from the throttle pedal and free the cable.
8 Refit in the reverse order, locating the rubber grommet onto the cable and threading the cable through the spare wheel support hole. Refit the grommet.
9 Fit the cable through the scuttle panel. Fit the stop clip to the outer cable and reconnect the inner cable to the pedal.

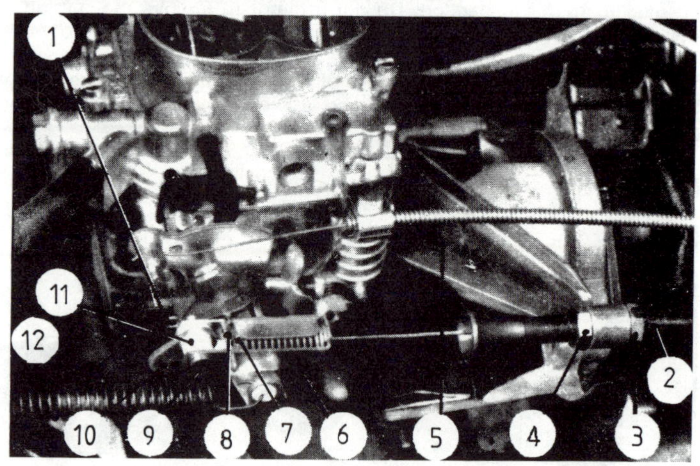

Fig. 2.3 Throttle cable connection to the carburettor (Sec 7)

1 Pin clip
2 Adjusting sleeve
3 Adjusting nut
4 Locknut
5 Bracket
6 Tension limiter
7 Cable stop
8 Pin
9 Clevis pin
10 Lever
11 Plastic bush
12 Return spring

10 At the carburettor end, relocate the adjusting sleeve over the outer cable, then connect the tension limiter unit to the operating lever and secure with clevis pin and clip.

Adjustment

11 To adjust the accelerator cable, slacken off the locknut at the cable location bracket, then with the accelerator pedal fully depressed put a 4 mm thick packing piece between the throttle pedal and the carpet. Adjust the nut to give a maximum operating clearance of 1.5 mm between the cable stop and the pin of the tension limiter unit. Remove the pedal packing and check that the throttle control on the carburettor returns fully to give the correct idle speed. Retighten the locknut.
12 Where a centrifugal clutch is fitted, check the throttle closing dashpot adjustment as described in Section 11.

8 Carburettors – general

All models are fitted with a Solex carburettor and this can be of either single or twin choke design according to model and type.

Carburettors fitted to those vehicles equipped with a centrifugal clutch differ slightly in that they incorporate a decelerating delay device, in which a dashpot is interconnected to the throttle flap and delays the engine speed drop when the throttle is released. This ensures the correct disengagement of the centrifugal clutch which would otherwise be actuated prematurely. An adjustment to the time delay, which is crucial to the satisfactory operation of the centrifugal clutch, can be made as described in Section 11.

The identification number is marked on the outer casing of each carburettor. A note should be made of this to ensure that correct adjustment procedures are followed and also to obtain the correct replacement parts should they be required to effect a repair.

9 Carburettor adjustments – general

1 Although various models of Solex carburettor have been fitted over the years, the adjustment procedures are basically the same. Detail differences are given below.
2 In 1972, the Solex range was modified to meet the European anti-pollution requirements and the throttle stop screw was pre-adjusted at the factory. It is therefore not necessary to touch the throttle stop screw on models produced from September of 1972 in order to adjust the carburettor performance. Any interference with this screw will only add to the adjustment problems and cause additional emissions of carbon monoxide (CO) from the exhaust.
3 On vehicles produced between September 1972 and September 1975 the only adjustments that can be made are via the air regulator screw (for idle speed) and/or the mixture control screw (for idle mixture strength).
4 From September 1975 all adjustments, with the exception of the idle speed, have been preset at the factory and must not be interfered with.
5 Before any adjustments are made to the carburettor the following items must be known to be in good condition and correctly adjusted where applicable:

(a) *Ignition system – the timing must be accurate and the spark plugs in good condition (Chapter 3)*
(b) *Valve/rocker clearances (Chapter 1)*
(c) *Carburettor and air cleaner must be clean and in generally good order*

6 On all engines, run the engine up to its normal operating temperature being making any adjustments.

10 Solex carburettors: idle speed adjustments

Pre-September 1972 models (conventional clutch)

1 With the engine at its normal operating temperature, check that the choke control is fully off and then using a suitable screwdriver, adjust the throttle stop screw (Fig. 2.6) to enable the engine to idle at approximately 800 rpm.
2 Now tighten the mixture adjuster screw until the engine just starts to falter, then back off the screw by $\frac{1}{3}$rd of a turn. The throttle stop screw can now be readjusted to obtain the specified idle speed. For a really accurate adjustment of the idle speed a tachometer will be required which can be connected up temporarily.

Fig. 2.4 Solex single choke carburettor. Arrow shows sealed volume control screw found on later models (Sec 9)

Fig. 2.5 Solex dual choke carburettor. Arrow shows sealed volume control screw found on later models (Sec 9)

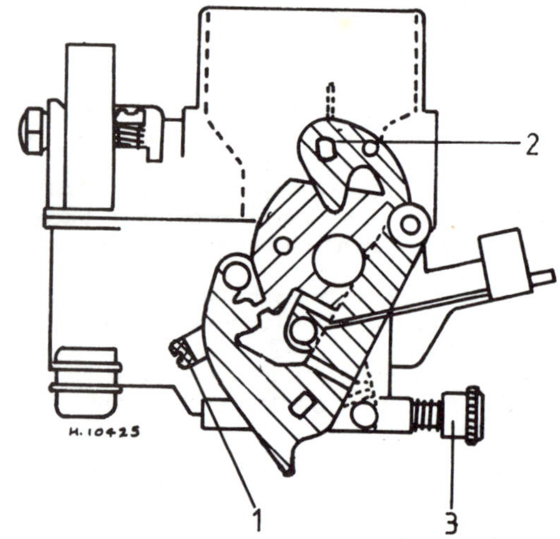

Fig. 2.6 Solex carburettor adjustment points (pre-September 1972 models) (Sec 10)

1 *Throttle stop screw*
2 *Choke lever*
3 *Mixture screw*

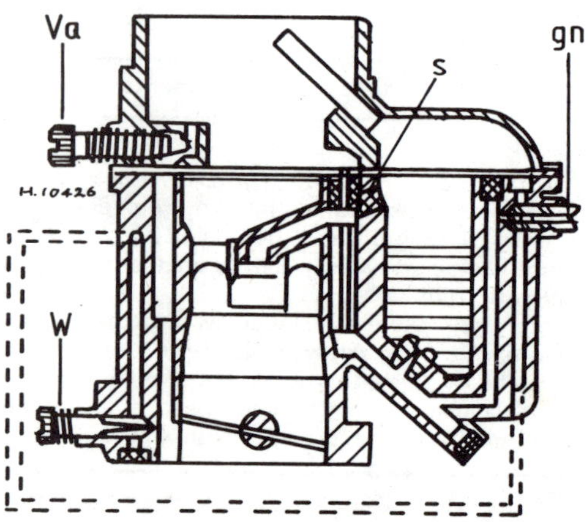

Fig. 2.7 Section of Solex 34 PICS/PCIS carburettor fitted from Sept 1972 to Sept 1975 (Sec 10)

Va *Idle air regulator screw*
W *Idle mixture control*
Gg *Main jet*
gn *Idle jet*
s *Mixture tube*

September 1972 to September 1975 models (conventional clutch)

3 With the engine at its normal operating temperature adjust the air regulator screw (Fig. 2.7) to give the specified idle speed. Turn the mixture screw in or out to achieve the fastest possible idle speed without faltering, then screw it in so that the idle speed falls very slightly (10 to 20 rpm).

4 Readjust the air regulator screw if necessary to bring the idle speed back within limits, then readjust the mixture screw.

5 If a carbon monoxide (CO) analyser is available, measure the exhaust gas CO content. It should be between 0.8% and 1.6% on 602 cc engines and 1.8 and 2.5% on 435cc engines.

Models after September 1975 (conventional clutch)

6 The only adjustment possible on these carburettors is at the throttle stop screw which is not locked. With the engine at normal operating temperature and the choke off, turn the screw in or out to achieve the specified idle speed. If the mixture must be altered for any reason, such as following a major overhaul, remove the tamperproof cap and adjust the mixture screw, using a CO analyser to obtain the correct setting. The CO content should be as for the September 1972 to September 1975 models.

Models with centrifugal clutch

7 Adjust as given above according to model year, but increase the idle speed to the point where the centrifugal clutch just starts to engage, then reduce by 50 rpm.

11 Throttle closing dashpot (centrifugal clutch models) – adjustment

1 The carburettors fitted to vehicles with a centrifugal clutch employ a dashpot control system to prevent the engine speed from dropping too quickly.

2 The progressive drop in engine speed is essential to allow for correct clutch disengagement. If the clutch is allowed to disengage too quickly, caused by a sudden drop in engine speed, there will be no engine braking in the gears. This could prove dangerous under certain driving conditions and must therefore be rectified if faulty.

3 Referring to Fig. 2.9 or 2.10, operate the dashpot lever and check that it is not binding. Open up the accelerator to its maximum position and then release it. When the throttle lever comes into contact with the dashpot, there should then be a delay of 1 to 2 seconds before the end of the throttle stop screw comes into contact with the choke control arm.

4 Should adjustment be necessary, relocate the throttle return spring to the next notch on the adjuster lug. Increasing the spring tension decreases the engine deceleration time. Decreasing the spring tension lengthens the deceleration time.

5 On some models the adjuster spring is located by a tab on the rod as shown in Fig. 2.11. Move the tab up or down the rod to alter the spring tension.

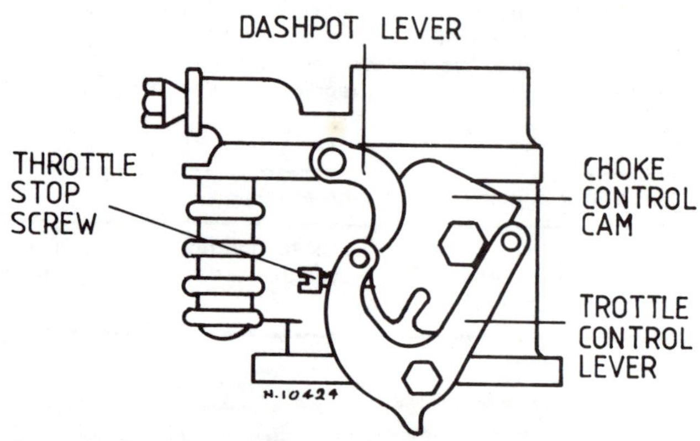

Fig. 2.8 Dashpot closing adjustment (models with centrifugal clutch) (Sec 11)

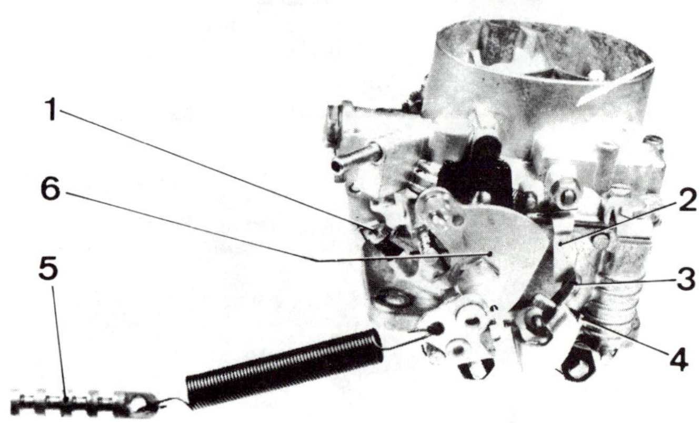

Fig. 2.9 Solex 26/35 carburettor with throttle closing dashpot (centrifugal clutch models) (Sec 11)

1 *Mixture screw*
2 *Dashpot lever*
3 *Control lever*
4 *Butterfly stop screw*
5 *Throttle closure adjuster*
6 *Choke control cam*

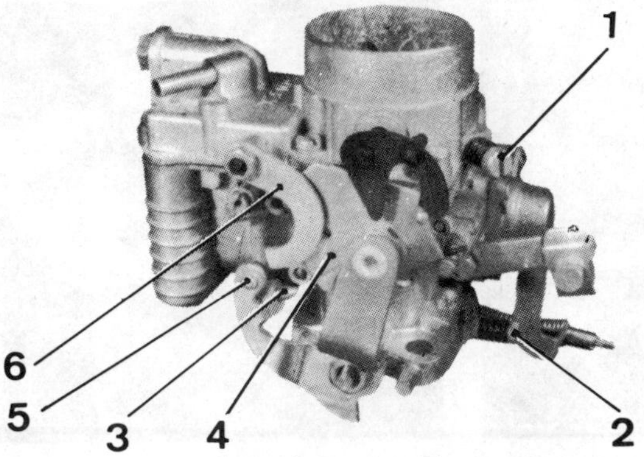

Fig. 2.10 Solex 34 series carburettor with throttle closing dashpot (centrifugal clutch models) (Sec 11)

1 *Air control screw*
2 *Mixture screw*
3 *Butterfly stop screw – do not adjust the setting*
4 *Choke cam*
5 *Butterfly control lever*
6 *Dashpot lever*

Fig. 2.11 The return spring (7) and adjuster/retainer tab (8) fitted to some models (Sec 11)

12 Float level – adjustment

1 If the carburettor float level is incorrect this will induce poor starting and fuel consumption, and erratic performance.
2 The float level on all carburettor models is adjustable by simply bending the float lug upwards or downwards to lower or raise the fuel level in the float chamber.

Solex 34 PICS and 34 PCIS carburettors

3 Unscrew the air filter-to-carburettor pipe connections and detach the pipe from the carburettor.
4 Loosen off, but do not remove, the six screws retaining the carburettor top cover. When all the screws are slackened off, retighten two of them – any two diagonally opposed to each other – and then start and run the engine for about a minute.
5 Switch off the engine and then remove the top cover, taking care not to break or damage the gasket.
6 Position the cover on a clean rag on top of the engine, leaving the fuel feed pipe connected. Use a piece of wire and hook the float from its chamber, taking care not to lose the pivot pin.
7 Using a depth gauge, measure the distance from the top edge of the float chamber to the fuel level. When correct this distance should be 25 mm (63/64 in) which includes the gasket thickness.
8 If the float level is incorrect, adjustment can be made by bending the lug on the top face of the float by the amount required to raise or lower the fuel level. Bend the lug upwards to lower the level or downwards to raise the level.
9 Reinsert the float and refit the top cover. Use a new gasket if the old one was damaged.
10 With the cover refitted, run the engine for a suitable warm-up period. If it still seems unsatisfactory, recheck the float level as described above. It may be necessary to make a slight adjustment to the idle speed.

Solex 26/35 CSIC and SCIC carburettors

11 Disconnect the rubber tube from the air cleaner at the carburettor by loosening the retaining clamp.
12 Detach the fuel feed pipe at the carburettor.
13 Remove the six screws retaining the carburettor top cover.
14 Lift and invert the top cover to check the float levels, which should be 18 ± 1mm (0.72 ± 0.04 in), measured between each float centre line and the cover joint face including the gasket. Each float level must be equal to within 1 mm (0.04 in).
15 The floats can be individually adjusted by carefully bending the lug that contacts the end of the needle valve stem. Check after bending that the floats do not rub on the sides of the float chamber.
16 Refit the cover and make secure with the retaining screws. Renew the gasket if the old one was damaged during removal
17 Reconnect the fuel pipe and air cleaner tube.
18 On restarting the engine check for any signs of leakage around the carburettor top cover and also from the fuel line connection. Warm the engine up and if necessary readjust the idle speed.

Fig. 2.12 Checking float level on Solex 26/35 carburettor. Dimension h must be as specified (Sec 12)

13 Carburettor – removal and refitting

1 Remove the air cleaner unit as previously detailed.
2 Unscrew the fuel inlet pipe retaining clip at the carburettor and detach the pipe. To prevent fuel leakage and the ingress of dirt, plug the end of the pipe with a suitable size bolt and temporarily retighten the clip.
3 Loosen the choke cable retaining bolt, and extract the cable. Unscrew the outer cable retaining bolt and detach the cable from the carburettor.
4 Disconnect the accelerator control from the carburettor. Where an accelerator cable is fitted, first disconnect the spring tensioner from its location on the front cross panel (noting its position) and then extract the retaining clip from the cable clevis pin. Remove the clevis pin that retains the tension limiter to the control lever on the carburettor and detach the cable. On those models fitted with an accelerator control rod instead of a cable, pivot forwards the retaining clip and disengage the rod from the throttle arm on the carburettor (photos).
5 Unscrew and remove the carburettor-to-manifold retaining nuts and carefully lift the carburettor clear (photo). The distance piece can also be removed. Try not to damage the gaskets as they may serve as useful patterns should replacements not be readily available.
6 Carburettor refitting is a direct reversal of the removal process. Always fit new gaskets whenever possible. Reconnect the choke and accelerator linkages and also the throttle return spring, locating it in its original notch position on the front panel lug.
7 Refit the air cleaner and run the engine up to its normal operating temperature, then adjust the carburettor if necessary.
8 Check that there are no fuel leaks from the reconnected fuel line.

13.4a Accelerator rod and retaining clip

13.4b Pivot the clip to withdraw the rod from the lever

13.5 Carefully lift the carburettor clear of the manifold and spacer

14 Solex single choke carburettors – dismantling, inspection and reassembly

1 With the carburettor removed from the vehicle, wash the exterior surfaces clean and blow dry with an air line or tyre pump. Remove it to a clean work area for dismantling and inspection.
2 Commence dismantling by unscrewing the carburettor top cover screws and removing the cover, taking care not to break or damage the sealing gasket. Although this gasket should be renewed on assembly it may be useful for short-term use or as a pattern should a replacement not be readily available.
3 From the top cover remove the filter plug and filter.
4 Unscrew the float needle retaining nut and remove the needle. Note the copper washer under the nut.
5 From the main body lift out the float from the float chamber. Take care not to lose its pivot pin.
6 On centrifugal clutch models, remove the throttle closure lever, piston, spring and centering washer.
7 Unscrew and remove the main jet and slow running jet, noting their respective positions.
8 Remove the non-return valve and nozzle.
9 Unscrew and remove the accelerator pump cover and carefully remove the diaphragm and spring. The nut regulating the fuel delivery must not be removed.
10 Wash all parts clean in petrol and blow dry with an air line or foot pump, then lay out the respective components in order for inspection.
11 Inspect the accelerator pump diaphragm; if defective in any way it must be renewed. If the jets are blocked, wash and blow through them to clear. Do not use a piece of wire to clean them as this will damage the finely machined surface in the bore.
12 Renew any defective or suspect components and also check that the float is not punctured.
13 Always renew gaskets and washers whenever the carburettor is dismantled.
14 Reassemble in the reverse order to dismantling. Do not over-tighten the various components and take care not to cross-thread the jets when inserting them into position.
15 Prior to refitting the top cover check the float level and readjust if necessary. This procedure is described in Section 12.
16 When the carburettor is refitted to the engine, adjust the idling speed (Section 10) and (if fitted) the throttle closing dashpot (Section 11).

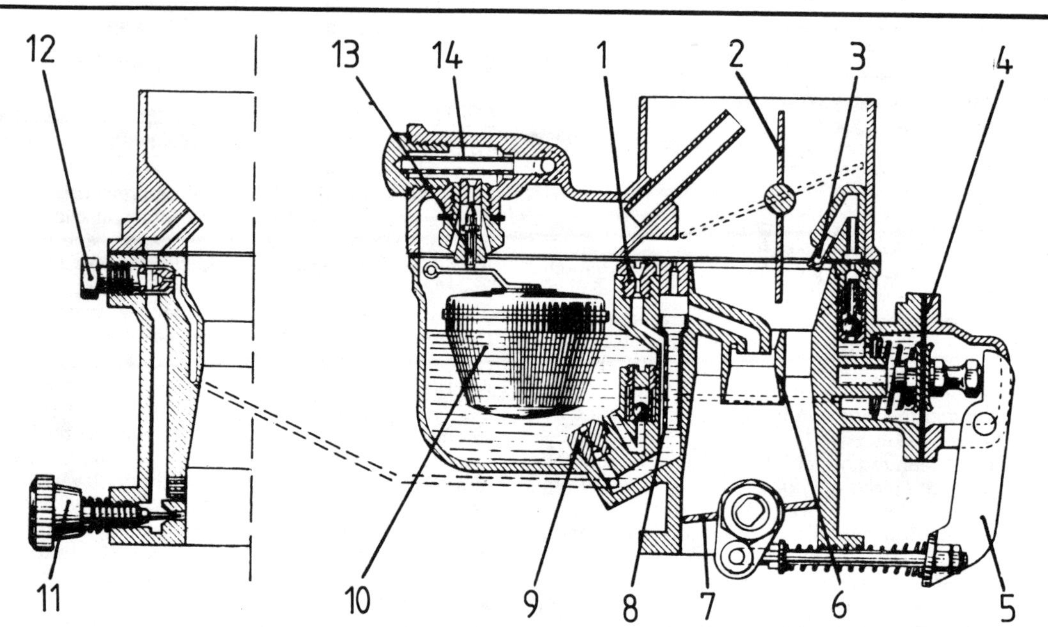

Fig. 2.13 Sections of Solex 32 series single choke carburettor. Series 40 is virtually identical (Sec 14)

1 Air correction jet
2 Strangler flap
3 Pump injector
4 Pump diaphragm
5 Pump operating lever
6 Choke
7 Throttle butterfly
8 Mixing tube
9 Main jet
10 Float
11 Idle mixture control screw
12 Idle jet
13 Needle valve
14 Filter

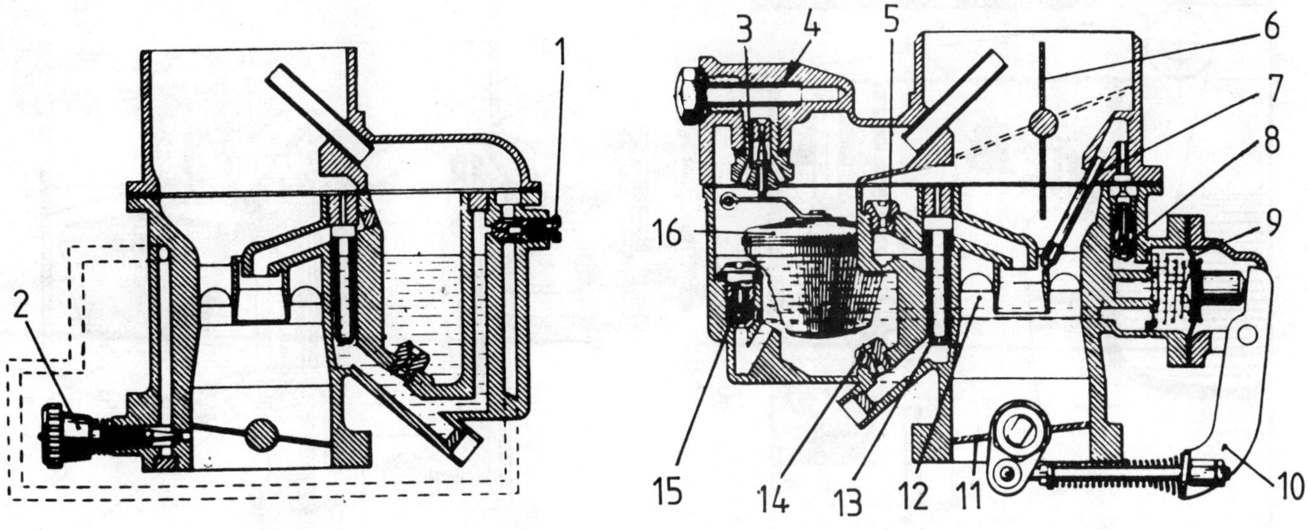

Fig. 2.14 Sections through the Solex 34 PICS/PCIS 4 series carburettor (Sec 14)

1 *Idle mixture*
2 *Idle jet*
3 *Needle valve*
4 *Filter*
5 *Air correction jet*
6 *Strangler flap*
7 *Pump injector*
8 *Ball seat*
9 *Pump diaphragm*
10 *Pump control lever*
11 *Throttle butterfly*
12 *Choke*
13 *Mixer tube*
14 *Main jet*
15 *Ball seat*
16 *Float*

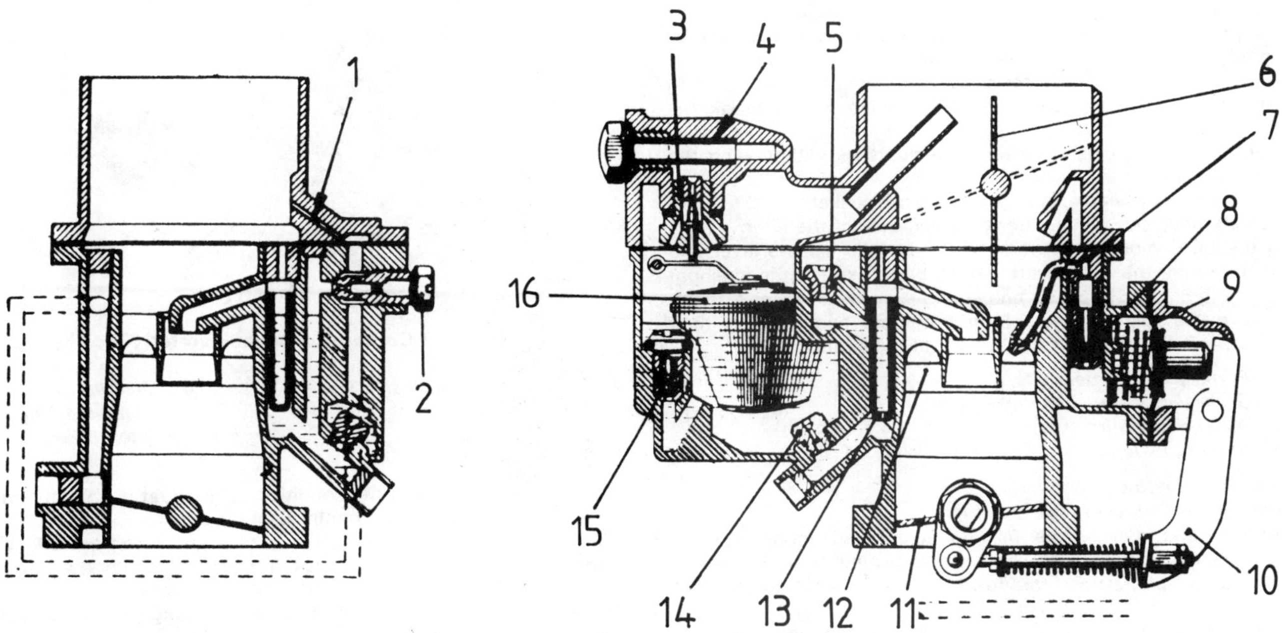

Fig. 2.15 Sections through the Solex 34 PICS/PCIS 5 series carburettor (Sec 14)

1 *Calibrated orifice*
2 *Bypass jet*
3 *Needle valve*
4 *Filter*
5 *Air correction jet*
6 *Strangler flap*
7 *Pump injector*
8 *Ball seat*
9 *Pump diaphragm*
10 *Pump control lever*
11 *Throttle butterfly*
12 *Choke*
13 *Mixer tube*
14 *Main jet*
15 *Ball seat*
16 *Float*

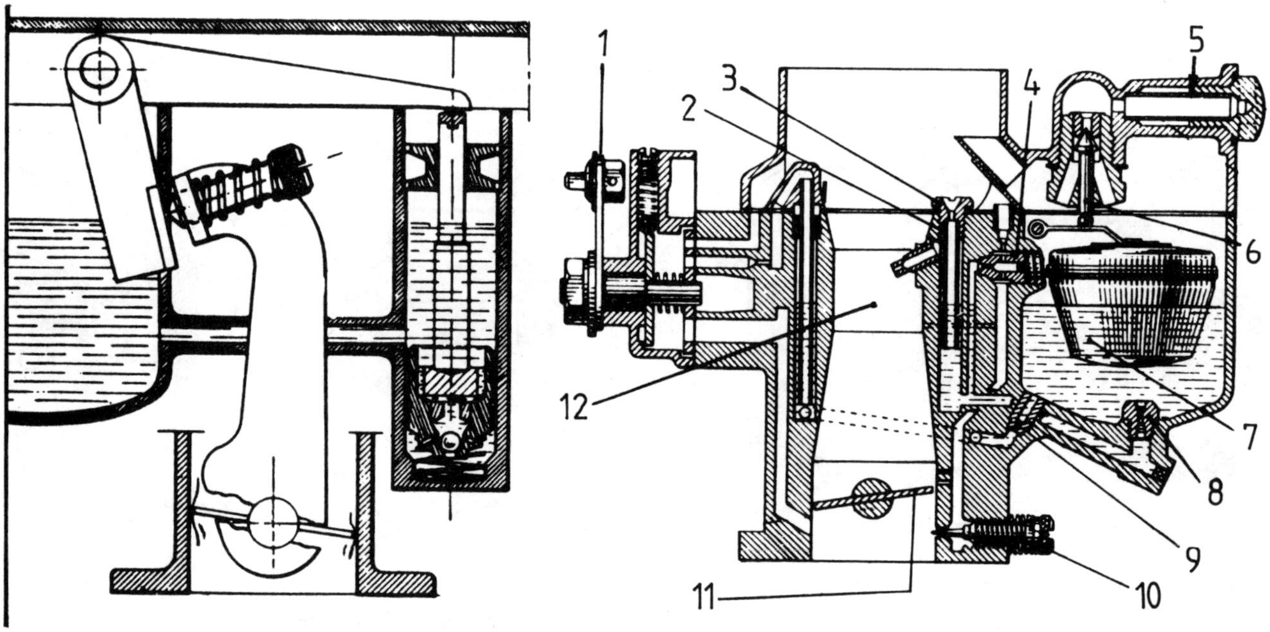

Fig. 2.16 Sections through the Solex 28 CBI/IBC series carburettor (Sec 14)

1 *Choke lever*
2 *Mixer tube*
3 *Air correction jet*
4 *Idle jet*
5 *Filter jet*
6 *Needle valve*
7 *Float*
8 *Main jet*
9 *Choke jet*
10 *Idle mixture control*
11 *Throttle butterfly*
12 *Choke*

15 Solex 26/35 SCIC and CSIC carburettors – dismantling, inspection and reassembly

1 With the carburettor removed from the vehicle, clean off the outer surfaces prior to placing it on clean work area where it can be dismantled and the components laid out in order for inspection.
2 Unscrew and remove the six screws retaining the top cover in position. Remove the top cover carefully, trying not to break the gasket.
3 Invert the top cover and remove the floats by withdrawing the retaining pin.
4 Extract the float needle, spring and copper gasket.
5 Unscrew and remove the filter plug and extract the filter.
6 On the SCIC model only, remove the throttle closure lever and stop lever. From the main carburettor body extract the dashpot pushrod, centering bush, piston and spring.
7 Remove the following jets from the main body, noting their respective positions so that they do not get mixed up:

(a) Primary choke main jet
(b) Secondary choke main jet
(c) Air correction jet
(d) Slow running jet

8 Remove the pump injector.
9 Remove the emulsion tube and support.
10 Unscrew and remove the mixture screw and spring. Do not attempt to remove or reset the primary and secondary choke throttle stop screws on carburettors fitted from September 1972 to 1975, as the screws are preset at the factory.
11 To dismantle the accelerator pump, remove the cover retaining screws and withdraw the cover from the pump with diaphragm and spring.
12 Wash the various components with clean petrol and blow dry with an air line or tyre pump if available. Do not clean out the jets using a piece of wire or any other similar item which could damage the precision finish of the bores.
13 Renew any damaged or suspect components, but do not discard the old parts until the new ones are obtained, fitted and found to be satisfactory. Always renew the gaskets and washers whenever the carburettor is dismantled.

Fig. 2.17 Carburettor cover inverted (Sec 15)

3 *Throttle closure lever*
7 *Gasket*
8 *Float*
9 *Float pivot pins*
10 *Needle*
11 *Needle spring*
12 *Stop lever*

14 In particular inspect the condition of the float needle, the mixture screw and the accelerator pump diaphragm.
15 Do not attempt to remove the throttle and choke butterfly valves. If they are obviously worn or slack in the spindles then the carburettor must be renewed as a unit. Check that the floats are not punctured.
16 Reassembly is a reversal of the dismantling procedure, but take care not to overtighten the jets or cross-thread when fitting them – silly mistakes can prove expensive!
17 Make sure that the jets are correctly fitted to their respective chokes.
18 Before refitting the top cover, check the float levels as described in Section 12. Adjust if necessary and check that the needle valve is not sticking or binding.
19 When the carburettor is reassembled to the engine, reconnect the choke and throttle cables and make any adjustment necessary to the idle settings (Section 10) and (if fitted) the throttle closing dashpot (Section 11).

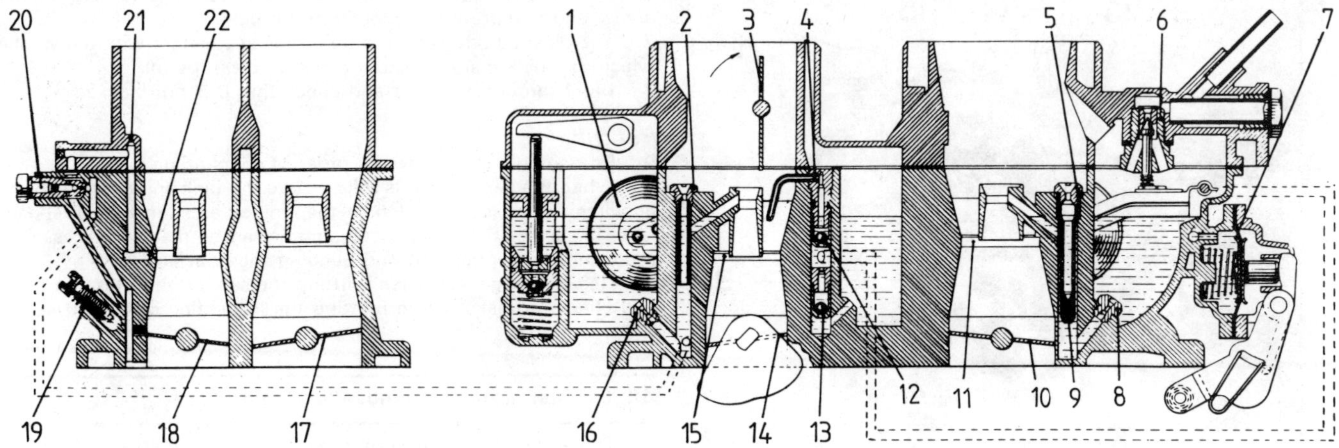

Fig. 2.18 Sections through the Solex 26/35 CSIC/SCIC carburettor fitted up to September 1972 (Sec 15)

1 Float
2 Air correction jet
3 Strangler flap
4 Pump injector
5 Air correction jet
6 Needle valve
7 Pump diaphragm
8 Main jet
9 Mixer tube
10 Throttle butterfly
11 Choke
12 Ball seat
13 Ball seat
14 Throttle butterfly
15 Choke
16 Main jet
17 Throttle butterfly
18 Throttle butterfly
19 Idle mixture control
20 Idle jet
21 Calibrated orifice
22 Calibrated orifice

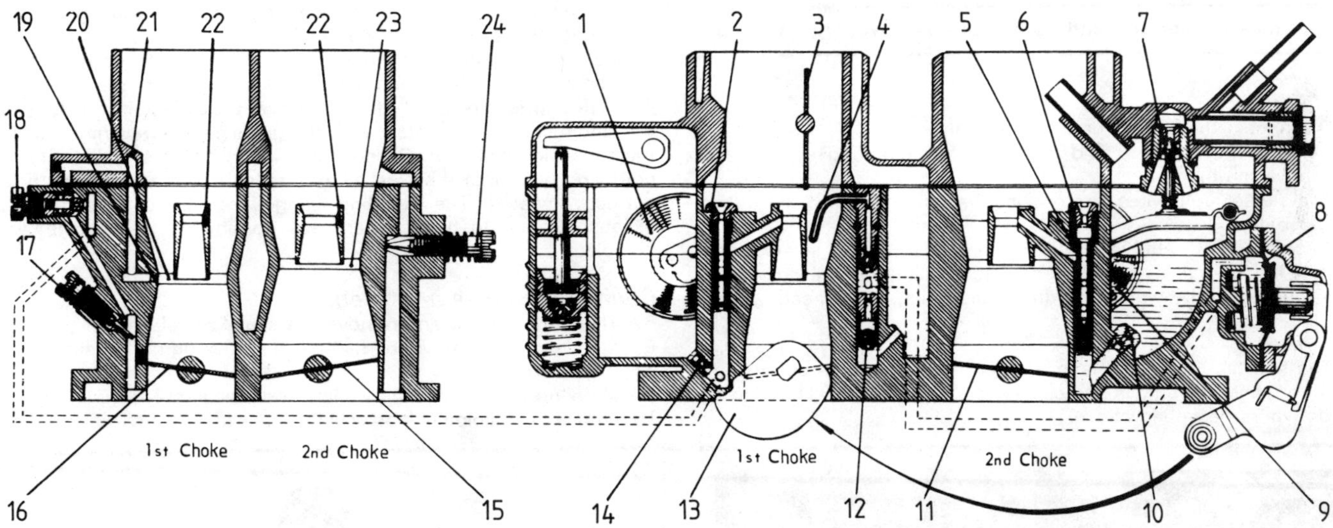

Fig. 2.19 Sections through the Solex 26/35 CSIC/SCIC carburettor fitted from September 1972 (Sec 15)

1 Float
2 Air correction jet
3 Strangler
4 Pump injector
5 Mixer tube
6 Air correction jet
7 Needle valve
8 Pump unit diaphragm
9 Float
10 Main jet
11 Throttle butterfly
12 Ball seat
13 Pump cam
14 Main jet
15 Throttle butterfly
16 Throttle butterfly
17 Idle mixture control
18 Idle jet
19 Calibrated orifice
20 Choke
21 Calibrated orifice
22 Diffusers
23 Choke
24 Secondary air screw

16 Fuel tank – removal and refitting

1 The fuel tank is located at the rear of the car and is removed from underneath the vehicle.
2 Disconnect the battery earth lead connection.
3 Unscrew the drain plug (if fitted) and empty any fuel left in the tank into a suitable container (not plastic). Fit a cover over the container and remove it to a safe place.
4 Raise and securely support the vehicle at the rear to gain access to the tank.
5 Remove the rear seat.
6 Unclip the inspection cover (if fitted) from the floor above the fuel tank, then detach the fuel gauge sender unit wires and the pick-up tube hose. Later models do not have an inspection cover, so the hose and wires must be removed as the tank is lowered.
7 Working underneath the car, support the tank and unscrew the four retaining bolts, one each side and two at the front.
8 Carefully lower the tank and detach the filler pipe.
9 If the fuel tank is damaged or faulty do not attempt to repair it – renew it or have it repaired by a specialist.
10 Refit in the reverse order to removal. On completion refill the tank and check for leaks, especially around the hose connections.

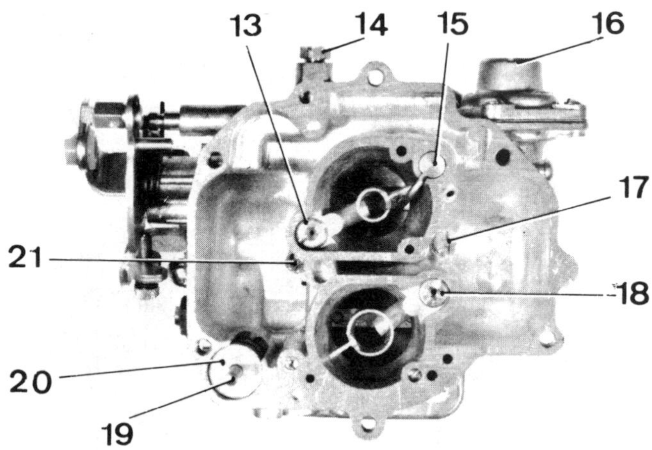

Fig. 2.20 Solex 26/35 carburettor main body with cover removed (Sec 15)

13 Emulsion tube carrier
14 Slow running jet
15 Pump injector
16 Accelerator pump cover
17 Secondary main jet
18 Air correction jet
19 Pushrod
20 Dashpot bush
21 Primary main jet

17 Fuel tank sender unit and tank filter – removal and refitting

Sender unit

1 Disconnect the battery earth connection.
2 Remove the rear seat and unclip the inspection cover from the floor above the fuel tank.
3 The sender unit wires can now be disconnected, also the outlet tube hose.
4 Unscrew and remove the sender unit retaining screws and carefully lift the unit clear. It will have to be tilted during removal to allow the float to be extracted without distorting its connecting rod.

Fuel filter

5 The fuel tank filter unit is located on the base of the outlet tube within the tank. To remove and clean it the sender unit will have to be withdrawn as described above.
6 To dismantle the filter (Fig. 2.22), remove the lower cup retaining screw and withdraw the filter from the pipe.
7 The plastic body can then be removed together with the washers which can be separated and washed in clean petrol.
8 Blow through the pipe and check that it is not blocked.

Refitting

9 Reassemble in the reverse order of dismantling.
10 When the sender unit is refitted into the tank and the fuel line and all wires reconnected, switch on the ignition and check the fuel gauge level for accuracy. A slight adjustment can be made if necessary by removing the sender unit and bending the float arm.
11 Use a new gasket when refitting the sender unit. Run the engine and check for leaks before refitting the inspection cover and seat.

18 Exhaust system – removal and refitting

1 The exhaust system comprises twin downpipes, one from each cylinder, which are attached via coupling flanges to a transverse expansion box. The expansion box is located between the two undershields and just to the rear of the gearbox. A separate pipe conveys the exhaust gases from the expansion box to the silencer and tailpipe, which are mounted flexibly on the left-hand underside of the vehicle.

Expansion box

2 To remove the expansion box, raise the bonnet, remove the spare wheel and detach the downpipe clamps on each side at their connecting flanges to the expansion box.
3 Detach the coupling collars retaining the heat exchangers to the inlet tube of the expansion box and then unscrew and remove the expansion box-to-gearbox mounting bolts (photo). Raise the front of the car and lower the expansion box to remove from the vehicle.
4 Refitting is a reversal of the removal procedure, but ensure that the clutch cable is in contact with the guide clip to prevent it touching the expansion chamber. Do not fully tighten the respective retaining bolts and nuts until they are all assembled and the expansion box is correctly located. The coupling flanges can be smeared with an exhaust sealant to help prevent any possibility of a leakage when complete.

Connecting pipes and silencer

5 Raise the bonnet and remove the spare wheel.
6 Unscrew and remove the half collars retaining the exhaust pipe to expansion box (photo).
7 Working underneath the vehicle, loosen the silencer/pipe clamps. To remove the tailpipe unit as well (which is usually advisable), remove

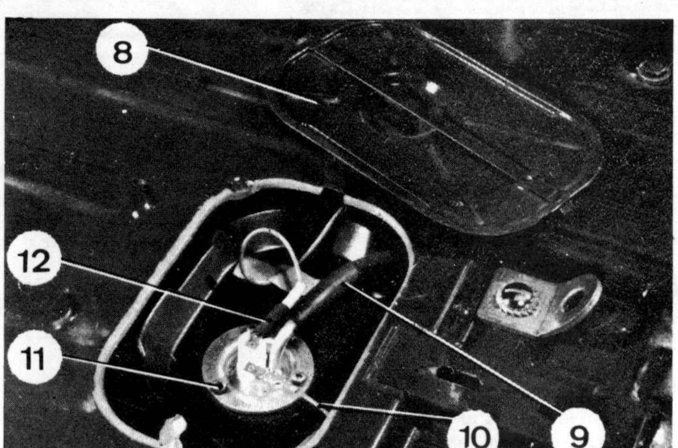

Fig. 2.21 Fuel gauge sender unit and fuel outlet pipe connection to tank (Sec 17)

8 Cover
9 Outlet pipe
10 Earth wire
11 Retaining screw
12 Wire connector

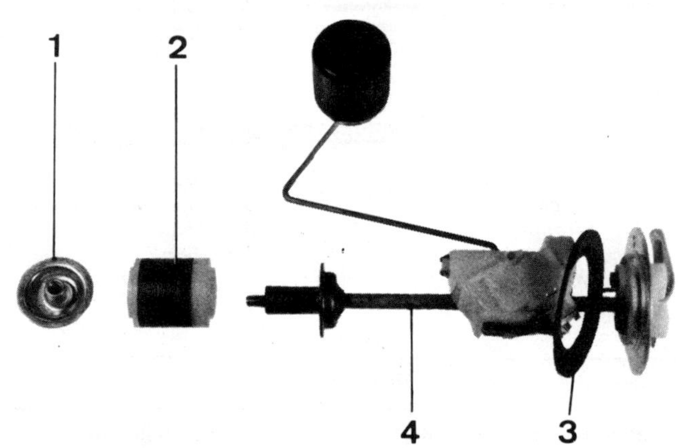

Fig. 2.22 Fuel gauge sender and filter unit (Sec 17)

1 Lower cup
2 Filter unit
3 Sealing ring
4 Outlet pipe

18.3 The expansion box disconnected from the mountings each side of the transmission

18.6 Typical exhaust downpipe flange connection

18.7 The silencer pipe mounting bracket and hanger strap

the retaining bolts from the rear bumper clamp bracket and the silencer hangers (photo).
8 Once the pipe and silencer assemblies are removed from the vehicle they can be separated and renewed as required.
9 Refitting is a reversal of the removal process, but relocate the complete pipe/silencer assembly before retightening any of the retainer fastenings. Smear pipe joints with some exhaust sealant to help prevent any leakages, and finally tighten all clamps and fastenings after the engine has been brought to operating temperature.

19 Fault diagnosis – fuel and exhaust system

Unsatisfactory engine performance and excessive fuel consumption are not necessarily the fault of the fuel system or carburettor. In fact they more commonly occur as a result of ignition faults. Before working on the fuel system it is necessary to check the ignition system. Even though a fault may lie in the fuel system it will be difficult to trace unless the ignition is correct. The table below, therefore, assumes that the ignition system is in order.

Symptom	Reason(s)
Smells of petrol when engine is stopped	Leaking fuel lines or unions Leaking fuel tank
Smell of petrol when engine is idling	Leaking fuel line between pump and carburettor Overflow of fuel from float chamber due to wrong level setting ineffective needle valve or punctured float
Excessive fuel consumption for reasons not covered by leaks or faults in other systems	Float level incorrect or float punctured Choke control not set correctly Worn needle valve Sticking needle valve
Difficult starting, uneven running, lack of power, cutting out	One or more jets blocked or restricted Float chamber fuel level too low or needle valve sticking Fuel pump not delivering sufficient fuel

Chapter 3 Ignition system

Contents

Specifications

System type	Contact breaker and coil. No distributor, cam driven directly from camshaft, centrifugal advance only
Spark plugs	
Make and type	Champion L85 (except Dyane 6 and Ami 8) or L87Y, AC42F, Marchal 35 or 34S, NGK B6HS, or equivalent
Electrode gap	0.65 to 0.75 mm (0.026 to 0.030 in)
Coil	
Make and type:	
6 volt	Ducellier 2768
12 volt	Ducellier 2769
Adjustment data	
Contact breaker gap	0.35 to 0.45 mm (0.014 to 0.018 in)
Dwell angle (percentage):	
Up to February 1970	142° to 146° (78% to 81%)
February 1970 on	106° to 112° (58% to 62%)
Static ignition timing:	
M28 and M28/1 engines	8° BTDC
All other models	12° BTDC
Dynamic ignition timing:	
All models	12 to 17° BTDC at 1000 rpm 18 to 25° BTDC at 2000 rpm 32 to 42° BTDC at 3000 rpm

1 General description

In order that the engine can run correctly it is necessary for an electrical spark to ignite the fuel/air mixture in the combustion chamber at exactly the right moment in relation to engine speed and load. The ignition system is based on feeding low tension voltage from the battery to the coil where it is converted to high tension voltage. The high tension voltage is powerful enough to jump the spark plug gap in the cylinders many times a second under high compression, providing that the system is in good condition and that all adjustments are correct.

The ignition system is divided into two circuits, low tension and high tension.

The low tension circuit (sometimes known as the primary) consists of the battery, lead to the control box, lead to the ignition system, lead from the ignition switch to the low tension or primary coil windings (+ terminal), and the lead from the low tension coil windings (– terminal) to the contact breaker points and condenser attached to the points box.

The high tension (HT or secondary) circuit consists of the coil secondary windings and the HT leads, one from each end of the secondary winding, to the plugs. There is no distributor as found on conventional multi-cylinder engines; instead each plug sparks both on the compression and on the exhaust stroke, and additionally one plug operates in reverse polarity, wear occurring at the side instead of at the centre electrode. For these reasons it is important to renew the plugs at the specified intervals.

The points box (sometimes erroneously referred to as the distributor) is mounted on the front of the crankcase, the points cam being retained on the end of the camshaft by a circlip. Access to the points is only possible after removing the front grille panel and fan. This is not such a problem as may at first appear because the points operate in a more favourable environment than that found in a conventional distributor. They should only be disturbed if the ignition timing or dwell angle need adjusting.

There is no vacuum-operated advance/retard mechanism used on these engines, ignition advance being undertaken entirely by centrifugal weights and springs.

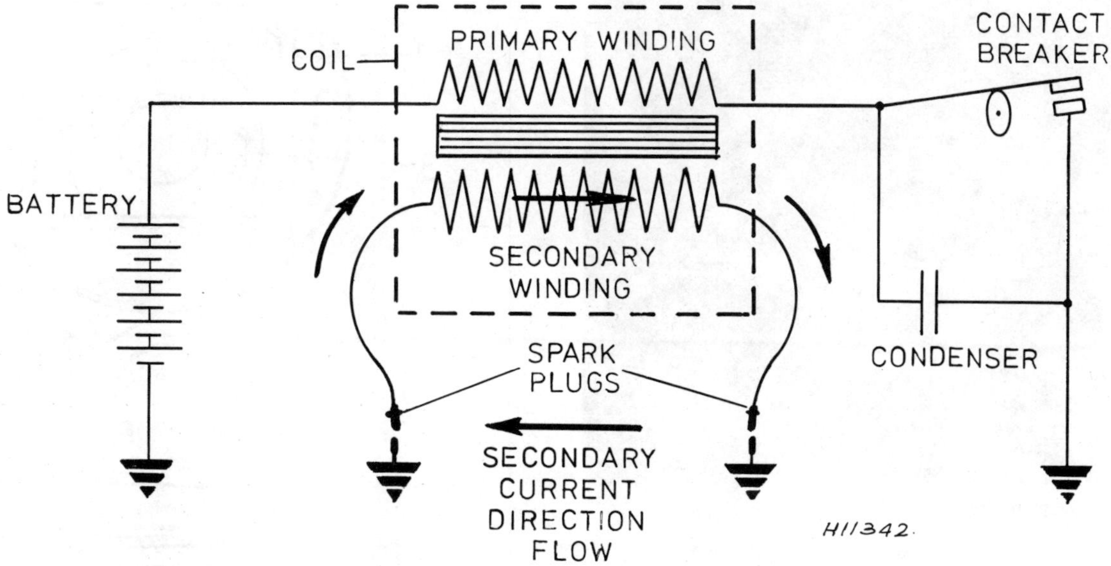

Fig. 3.1 Circuit diagram of ignition system (Sec 1)

2 Spark plugs and high tension (HT) leads

1 The correct functioning of the spark plugs is vital for the correct running and efficiency of the engine. The plugs fitted as standard are listed on the Specifications page.
2 At intervals of 3000 miles (4800 km) the plugs should be removed, examined, cleaned and if worn excessively, renewed. The condition of the spark plug will also tell much about the overall condition of the engine. If the plugs are interchanged between the cylinders the effects of reverse polarity can be minimised.
3 If the insulator nose of the spark plug is clean and white, with no deposits, this is indicative of a weak mixture, or too hot a plug. (A hot plug transfers heat away from the electrode slowly – a cold plug transfers it away quickly).
4 If the top and insulator nose is covered with hard black-looking deposits, then this is indicative that the mixture is too rich. Should the plug be black and oily, then it is likely that the engine is fairly worn, as well as the mixture being too rich.
5 If the insulator nose is covered with light tan to greyish brown deposits, then the mixture is correct and it is likely that the engine is in good condition.
6 If there are any traces of long brown tapering stains on the outside of the white portion of the plug, then the plug will have to be renewed. as this shows that there is a faulty joint between the plug body and the insulator, and compression is being allowed to leak away.
7 Plugs should be cleaned by a sand blasting machine, which will free them from carbon more thoroughly than cleaning by hand. The machine will also test the condition of the plugs under compression. Any plug that fails to spark at the recommended pressure should be renewed.
8 The spark plug gap is of considerable importance, as, if it is too large or too small the size of the spark and its efficiency will be seriously impaired. The spark plug gap should be set to the specified gap for the best results. File the central electrode flat with a points file before setting the gap.
9 To set it, measure the gap with a feeler gauge, and then bend the outer plug electrode until the correct gap is achieved. The centre electrode should never be bent as this may crack the insulation and cause plug failure, if nothing worse.
10 When refitting the plugs, fit them in the opposite cylinders to equalise wear. Use new plug washers if the old ones are in poor condition. Do not overtighten; one quarter of a turn more than hand tight is enough.
11 The HT leads require no attention other than being kept clean and dry. Renew them if they are cracked.

3 Dwell angle – checking and adjustment

1 Dwell angle is the angle through which the contact breaker cam rotates whilst the points are closed. It is directly proportional to the contact breaker points gap. Since access to the points is relatively difficult, the dwell angle is measured to ascertain that the gap is correct.
2 Dwell angle is measured by connecting a dwell meter in accordance with its maker's instructions – usually between the coil LT lead and earth – and taking a reading with the engine idling, then at higher rpm. If the angle is within the specified limits, no further action is necessary. If the angle is not within the specified limits, or varies by more than 6° when the engine speed is altered, the contact breaker points require attention (Section 4).
3 Reducing the points gap increases the dwell angle, and vice versa.
4 If a dwell meter is not available, a Citroën dealer may measure the angle for a small charge. Alternatively some system may be devised for accurately measuring angular rotation of the engine and a test lamp connected as for the static timing check (Section 8). It is possible to count the number of flywheel gear teeth which pass in the periods when the test lamp is lit and when it is not, and thus compute the dwell angle. For anybody with sufficient patience, the number of teeth which should pass whilst the lamp is illuminated is 84 to 87 for early models (up to Feb 1970) and 63 to 67 for later models. Obviously this method cannot measure changes in the dwell angle occurring with variations in engine speed.

4 Contact breaker points – adjustment

1 Remove the front grille panel as described in Chapter 11.
2 Loosen the generator mounting bolts and pivot it towards the engine to slacken the tension on the drivebelt.
3 The fan must now be removed. To unscrew the retaining bolt of the starter dog and fan you will need a long 14 mm box spanner. To prevent the engine turning over when loosening the bolt, jam a screwdriver blade between the flywheel starter ring teeth and the starter mounting.
4 On removal of the retaining bolt it may be found that the fan/starter dog unit is reluctant to be withdrawn due to being jammed on the taper of the crankshaft. This being the case refer to Section 8 of Chapter 1, where further special instructions on the fan removal are given. As the fan is withdrawn disengage the alternator drivebelt.
5 Unscrew and remove the seven bolts and washers securing the

4.6 Remove the cover and seal

4.8 Check the points gap with feeler gauges

4.11 Points adjustment/retaining screw (1) and adjustment lug (2)

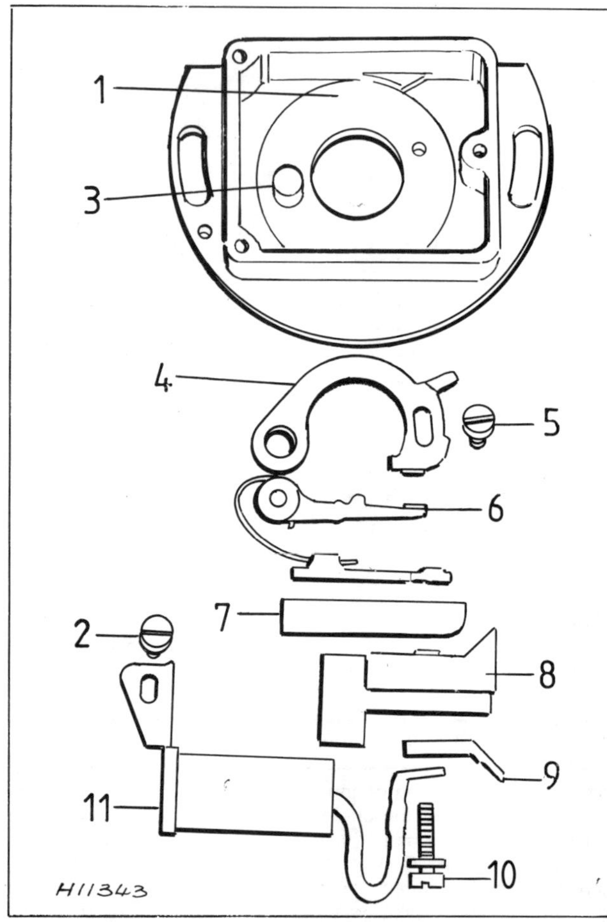

Fig. 3.2 The contact breaker points box assembly (Sec 4)

1 Contact box
2 Condenser retaining screw
3 Contact pivot post
4 Fixed contact
5 Retaining screw
6 Moving contact
7 Insulator
8 Support
9 Terminal
10 Screw and shakeproof washer
11 Condenser

rubber shield (if fitted) in position over the front of the points box. Earlier models did not have this fitting.

6 Clean the area around the points box and then unscrew and remove the three box cover retaining screws, the cover and the rubber seal (photo).

7 The points are now fully accessible for inspection, adjustment and if necessary replacement.

8 To check the points gap they should be fully open on the heel on the cam. Insert a clean feeler blade of the specified thickness between the point faces (photo). Take care not to contaminate the point faces with oil. The blade of the feeler gauge should be a firm sliding fit at this gap, not a loose or tight fit. Check the gap with the points open on both cam lobes. If the gap measurement differs on each lobe by 0.05 mm (0.002 in) or more, then this is indicative of a worn cam which should be renewed.

9 If on inspection the contact points are badly worn or pitted they should be renewed.

10 If adjustment to the points gap is necessary then the ignition timing must be reset (Sections 8 and 9).

11 To adjust the points gap, loosen the contact retaining screw and move the fixed point as necessary (photo). Retighten the retaining screw and recheck the clearance.

12 Set the timing as described in Section 8 or 9.

13 Refit the points cover and (if fitted) the rubber shield. Refit the fan and generator drivebelt and tighten the retaining bolt to the specified torque. Refit the grille panel to complete.

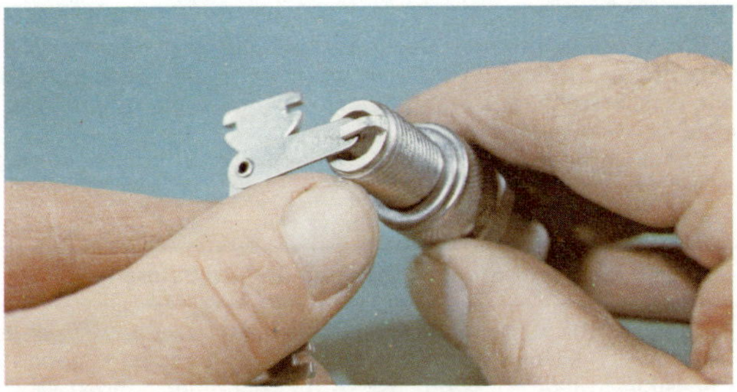

Measuring plug gap. A feeler gauge of the correct size (see ignition system specifications) should have a slight 'drag' when slid between the electrodes. Adjust gap if necessary

Adjusting plug gap. The plug gap is adjusted by bending the earth electrode inwards, or outwards, as necessary until the correct clearance is obtained. Note the use of the correct tool

Normal. Grey-brown deposits, lightly coated core nose. Gap increasing by around 0.001 in (0.025 mm) per 1000 miles (1600 km). Plugs ideally suited to engine, and engine in good condition

Carbon fouling. Dry, black, sooty deposits. Will cause weak spark and eventually misfire. Fault: over-rich fuel mixture. Check: carburettor mixture settings, float level and jet sizes; choke operation and cleanliness of air filter. Plugs can be re-used after cleaning

Oil fouling. Wet, oily deposits. Will cause weak spark and eventually misfire. Fault: worn bores/piston rings or valve guides; sometimes occurs (temporarily) during running-in period. Plugs can be re-used after thorough cleaning

Overheating. Electrodes have glazed appearance, core nose very white – few deposits. Fault: plug overheating. Check: plug value, ignition timing, fuel octane rating (too low) and fuel mixture (too weak). Discard plugs and cure fault immediately

Electrode damage. Electrodes burned away; core nose has burned, glazed appearance. Fault: pre-ignition. Check: as for 'Overheating' but may be more severe. Discard plugs and remedy fault before piston or valve damage occurs

Split core nose (may appear initially as a crack). Damage is self-evident, but cracks will only show after cleaning. Fault: pre-ignition or wrong gap-setting technique. Check: ignition timing, cooling system, fuel octane rating (too low) and fuel mixture (too weak). Discard plugs, rectify fault immediately

5 Contact breaker points – removal and refitting

1 Referring to the previous Section, follow the instruction given in paragraphs 1 to 6 inclusive.
2 Unscrew and remove the two bolts retaining the contact box to the crankcase. Withdraw the box and detach the wire spade connector (photo).
3 The points can now be removed. Unscrew the fixed contact retaining screw.
4 Unscrew and remove the capacitor/insulator retaining screw and then extract the contact arm and spring, followed by the fixed contact.
5 Clean out the points box before commencing reassembly. Lightly smear the points pivot post with grease. In view of its low cost, it is not a bad idea to renew the condenser at the same time as the points.
6 Refitting of the points and condenser is a direct reversal of the removal procedure. Lightly lubricate the cam lobes and check that the spring and moving contact arm are securely fitted to each other.
7 Adjust the points gap (Section 4) and check the dwell angle (Section 3) and the timing (Section 8 or 9) before refitting the fan and front grille.

6 Condenser (capacitor) – description, removal and refitting

1 The condenser is fitted in parallel with the contact breaker points. Its main function is to prevent excessive sparking between the point faces which would otherwise occur every time the LT circuit was interrupted.
2 If the condenser fails in the short-circuit mode, the points will no longer be able to interrupt the ignition circuit and total failure of the ignition system will occur. If the condenser fails in the open-circuit mode, or becomes disconnected, there will be excessive arcing across the points and difficult starting and rough running will result.
3 It is not possible to test the condenser without special equipment and the surest test is by substitution of a new unit. In view of its low cost and inaccessibility, it is well worth renewing the condenser every time new contact breaker points are fitted.
4 To remove the condenser, proceed as described in Section 4, paragraphs 1 to 6, then undo the securing screws and remove the points box and condenser.
5 Refitting is the reverse of the removal procedure.

7 Ignition cam and centrifugal weights – removal and refitting

1 Refer to Section 5 and remove the ignition points box from the front of the crankcase.
2 Extract and remove the protector plate (photo).
3 Remove the circlip from the groove in the end of the camshaft and then withdraw the thrust washer, the cam and the advance/retard control weights, noting their locations.
4 Refitting is a reversal of the removal procedure. Ensure that all components are clean and serviceable prior to assembly. Lightly lubricate the cam and advance/retard spindles with engine oil before assembling. Check that the circlip is fully located in its groove. Refit the protector plate, contact box and points.
5 Adjust the points gap (Section 4) and check the cam play. If the points gap is checked on the two lobes and a difference in measurement is shown then either the cam or camshaft is defective and should be renewed.
6 Check and adjust the timing (Section 8 or 9) before refitting the fan and front grille.

8 Static ignition timing – checking and adjustment

1 To check the static ignition timing it will be necessary to obtain or make a tool similar to that shown in Fig. 3.4. If access is good it may be possible to use a straight rod (6 mm diameter approx) as shown (photo). The Dyane will need a longer rod than that shown.
2 Insert the rod through the hole in the left-hand top half of the crankcase so that it bears on the front of the flywheel. Slowly rotate the flywheel whilst applying pressure to the rod; when the rod enters the hole in the flywheel face, the engine is at the correct static firing point.

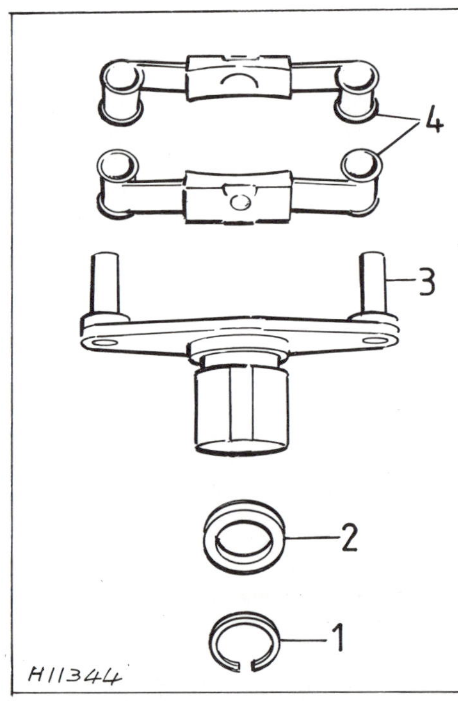

Fig. 3.3 The points cam and centrifugal weights (Sec 7)

1 Circlip
2 Thrust washer
3 Centrifugal weight pivots and cam
4 Advance weights

5.2 Remove box retaining/timing adjustment bolts (1) and detach the spade connector (2)

7.2 Remove the protector plate

8.1 Insert rod through access hole to check timing

3 Paint alignment marks on one flywheel tooth and the starter motor housing for future reference, then remove the rod.

4 Connect a 12V test lamp between the coil terminal which feeds the contact breaker (slide back the blue sleeve) and earth. Turn on the ignition. Remove the plug caps so that the engine cannot fire. If the test lamp is correctly connected, it will light when the points are open and extinguish when they are closed.

5 *Check that the timing rod is removed,* then rotate the flywheel. As the timing marks made in paragraph 3 come into alignment, the lamp should just come on – ie the points must just be separating. If not, remove the fan and grille (if not already done), slacken the points box retaining bolts and move the box in the required direction. Tighten the bolts and recheck the timing.

6 Due to backlash, a variation in the specified timing may be evident when adjusting the ignition timing. If timing is being done statically, then, if the crankshaft is rotated one revolution after setting, the timing marks could appear to be one tooth different between the piston firing points.

7 When checking dynamically, the tolerance given for the BTDC figures in the Specifications allows for this. If the difference between the two cylinder firing points is greater than one tooth (3°) suspect a worn cam.

8 When refitting the fan, position the timing mark on the flywheel vertically (12 or 6 o'clock) and the slots in the starter dog horizontally. Lightly grease the tapers of the fan and crankshaft.

9 Dynamic ignition timing – checking and adjustment

1 If a stroboscopic timing light is available, the ignition timing can be checked dynamically, ie with the engine running.

2 If not already done, make timing marks on the flywheel and starter motor housing as described in Section 8, paragraphs 1 to 3.

3 Connect the timing light to one of the HT leads in accordance with the maker's instructions.

4 Check that the timing rod is removed, then start the engine and shine the timing lamp on the timing marks. The marks should appear in alignment and stationary.

5 If the marks are not in alignment, remove the fan and grille (if not already done), slacken the points box adjustment bolts and rotate the box as necessary to bring the marks into alignment. The engine will idle for 10 minutes or so without the fan or alternator, so it is possible to make the adjustment without refitting the fan every time to check.

6 When the marks appear to be satisfactorily aligned, increase the engine speed and check that the marks appear to drift away from each other as the centrifugal advance mechanism comes into operation. It may be that the cam, camshaft or centrifugal weights are worn, in which case there will be some flutter or spread.

7 Disconnect the timing light and (if removed) refit the fan and grille.

10 Fault diagnosis – ignition system

1 Ignition faults can usually be divided into two groups: faults causing total ignition failure, resulting in refusal to start or failure to restart, and faults causing misfiring. The latter may be intermittent or regular, and this may give a clue as to the origin of the fault.

2 A fault which may give rise to no more than a misfire on a four-cylinder car will have a much more noticeable effect on a two-cylinder engine. It is seldom, therefore than an ignition fault will remain undetected for long.

3 In cases of poor starting or indifferent running, always check the spark plugs first. If in doubt as to their condition, substitute new ones if possible.

Engine fails to start

4 If the engine fails to start and the car was running normally when it was last used, first check there is fuel in the fuel tank. If the engine turns over normally on the starter motor and the battery is evidently well charged, then the fault may be in either the high or low tension

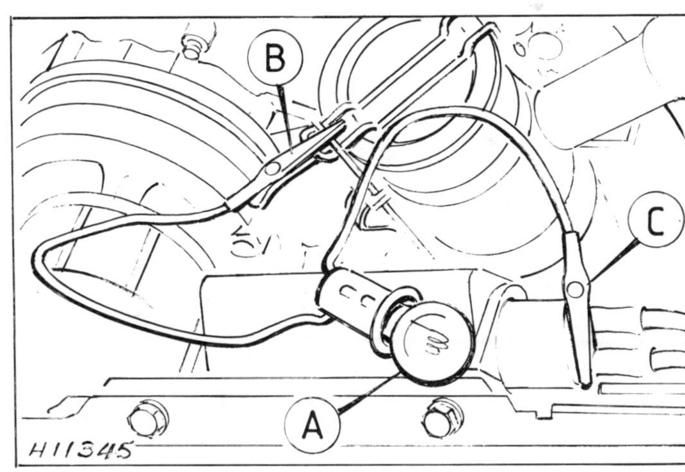

Fig. 3.5 Typical timing test light connections, bulb (A) interconnected between earth (B) and coil feed wire connection (C) (Sec 8)

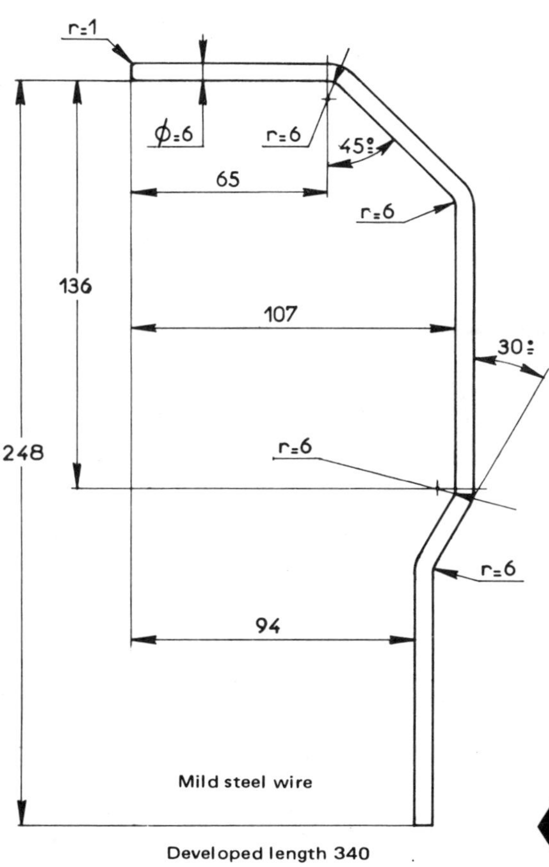

Fig. 3.4 Special timing adjustment tool (Citroën number MR 630-51/15) (Sec 8)

circuits. First check the HT circuit. Note: if the battery is known to be fully charged, the ignition light comes on, and the starter motor fails to turn the engine, check the tightness of the leads on the battery terminals and also the security of the earth lead to its connection to the body. It is quite common for the leads to have worked loose, even if they look and feel secure. If one of the battery terminal posts gets very hot when trying to work the starter motor this is a sure indication of a faulty connection to that terminal.

5 Check that HT current is reaching the plugs. Remove a plug cap and unscrew it to expose the end of the HT lead, or insert a nail or piece of wire so that the live metal can be held about $\frac{3}{16}$ in (5 mm) away from the block. Hold the lead with rubber or an insulated tool to avoid electric shocks. Spin the engine on the starter (ignition on). Sparking from the lead to the block should be fairly strong with a regular blue spark. If it is, check the plugs; if they are in order, the fault must lie elsewhere.

6 If there is only a weak spark, this may be due to a discharged battery. In that case it should be possible to start the engine by using the starting handle. Keep your hand open when pressing down on the starting handle to avoid dislocating the wrist or thumb if the engine kicks back.

7 If there is no spark at either plug lead, check with a 12V test lamp that current is reaching the coil LT connections. With the ignition on, there should be a continuous reading at the wire from the battery and (as the engine is rotated) an intermittent reading at the contact breaker terminal as the points open and close.

8 No reading at the coil battery terminal suggests a break in the wire from the ignition switch or a defective switch; it may be possible to run a wire from the battery + terminal directly to the coil as a 'get-you-home' measure.

9 A reading at the coil battery terminal but none at the contact breaker terminal may be due to a defect in the coil (open circuit primary), short circuit condenser or defective points. It could also be due to the wire from the coil to the points box being earthed somewhere along its length. Disconnect the wire and check again; if the lamp now lights the fault is probably not in the coil.

10 A reading at the coil battery terminal combined with a continuous reading at the contact breaker terminal when the engine is turned over may be due to a broken wire from the coil to the points box or contamination or physical damage at the point faces. In any event it suggests that the next move should be to examine the points.

11 Even if the LT system appears to be in order, it is possible for coil or condenser faults to exist which will prevent the engine running. Test by substitution if possible, but do not substitute more than one thing at a time or you will not know what was causing the fault.

Engine misfires

12 As mentioned above, 'misfiring' on a two-cylinder engine will probably involve the loss of half the available power and so will not go unnoticed for long.

13 If the misfire is regular, it is almost certainly in the HT circuit. Removing the plug cap from the surviving 'good' cylinder will cause the engine to stop; removing the cap from the defective side will make no difference. The plug and the HT lead are the only items to investigate, since there is no distributor to consider.

14 An irregular misfire is usually caused by a loose connection, although it can be due to a faulty condenser or coil. Check that all connections are clean and tight and that the points are in good condition and correctly gapped; renew the condenser as a matter of course if your investigations proceed so far as to make it accessible.

Chapter 4 Clutch

For modifications, and information applicable to later models, see Supplement at end of manual

Contents

Specifications

General

Clutch type	Single dry plate, cable-operated. Centrifugal clutch ('Trafficlutch') also fitted on some models
Driven plate diameter	158.75 mm (6.25 in)
Makers' identification:	
Early models (generally pre-68)	Ferodo PKH3 or PKH4
Later models (generally post-68)	Ferodo PKHB4 or PKHB5
Thrust bearing type:	
PKH3 or PKH4	Graphite
PKHB4 or PKHB5	Ball race

Adjustment data

Clutch pedal height:	
Chassis-mounted pedal	Same as brake pedal
Pendant pedal:	
Ami 8 after Nov 1971	135 ± 2.5 mm (5.3 ± 0.1 in)
All other models	130 ± 5.0 mm (5.1 ± 0.2 in)
Pedal free play:	
Graphite thrust bearing	10 to 15 mm (0.39 to 0.59 in)
Ball race thrust bearing	20 to 25 mm (0.78 to 0.98 in)
Operating lever clearance:	
Graphite thrust bearing	0.5 to 1.0 mm (0.019 to 0.039 in)
Ball race thrust bearing	1.0 to 1.5 mm (0.039 to 0.059 in)

Torque wrench settings

	lbf ft	kgf m
Pressure plate-to-flywheel (or drum) bolts	7.2 to 9.5	1.0 to 1.3
Centrifugal ring-to-flywheel bolts	6.5 to 10.0	0.9 to 1.4
Clutch drum nut	22 to 29	3.0 to 4.0

1 General description

The standard clutch fitted to all models is a single dry plate type and is cable operated.

When the clutch pedal is operated, the connecting cable actuates the clutch lever in the bellhousing which in turn slides the thrust bearing assembly along the input shaft and into contact with the clutch toggle. This action compresses the clutch springs and releases the pressure plate from the clutch disc (driven plate). The clutch disc is located on the splines of the gearbox input shaft and when the pressure from the clutch plate is released the drive between the engine and gearbox is disengaged, the disc friction surfaces no longer being in contact with the pressure plate on one side and the flywheel on the other.

Some models are fitted with a centrifugal clutch ('Trafficlutch') as an optional extra. This device is designed to allow automatic clutch disengagement when the engine speed drops below approximately 1000 rpm, allowing the vehicle to stop without the driver using the clutch pedal and preventing the possibility of stalling. When the engine speed rises again the clutch automatically takes up the drive. The car can move off in 1st or 2nd gear without use of the clutch pedal.

Where a centrifugal clutch is fitted, the carburettor has a throttle closing dashpot fitted which delays the drop in engine speed when the throttle pedal is suddenly released. If the throttle closing is too abrupt, it is possible for the clutch to disengage whilst the vehicle is travelling at speed. Should this occur, reengage the clutch by 'blipping' the throttle slightly.

Wear of the clutch disc (or stretch of the cable) can be taken up by adjusting the cable as described below.

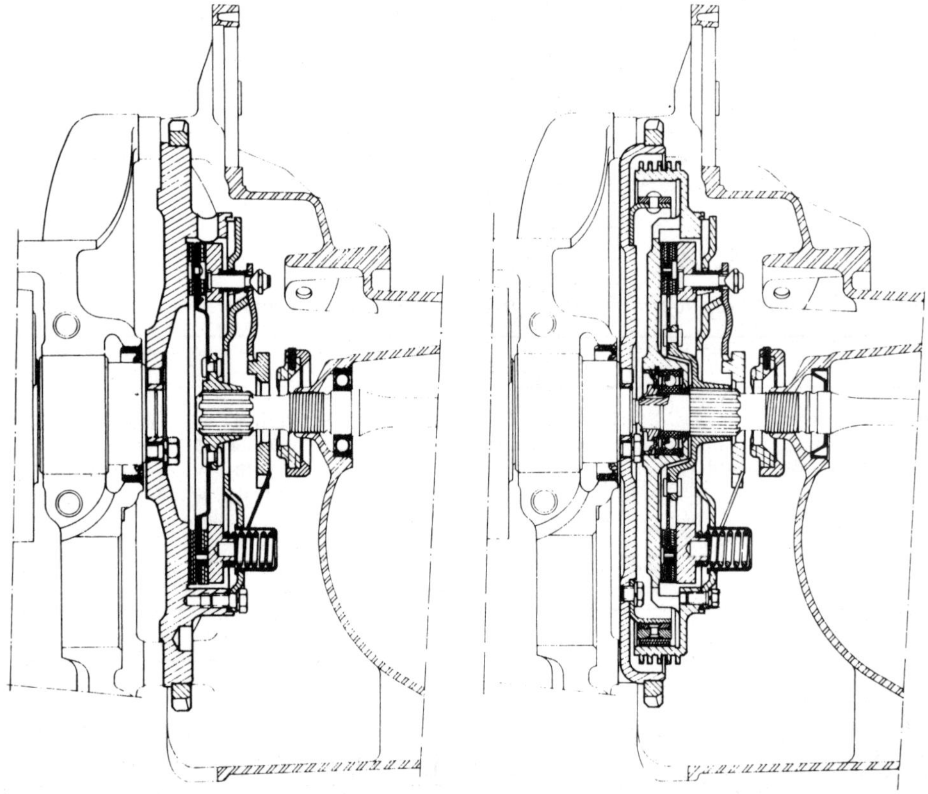

Fig. 4.1 Sectional views of the earlier type standard clutch (left) and centrifugal clutch (right) (Sec 1)

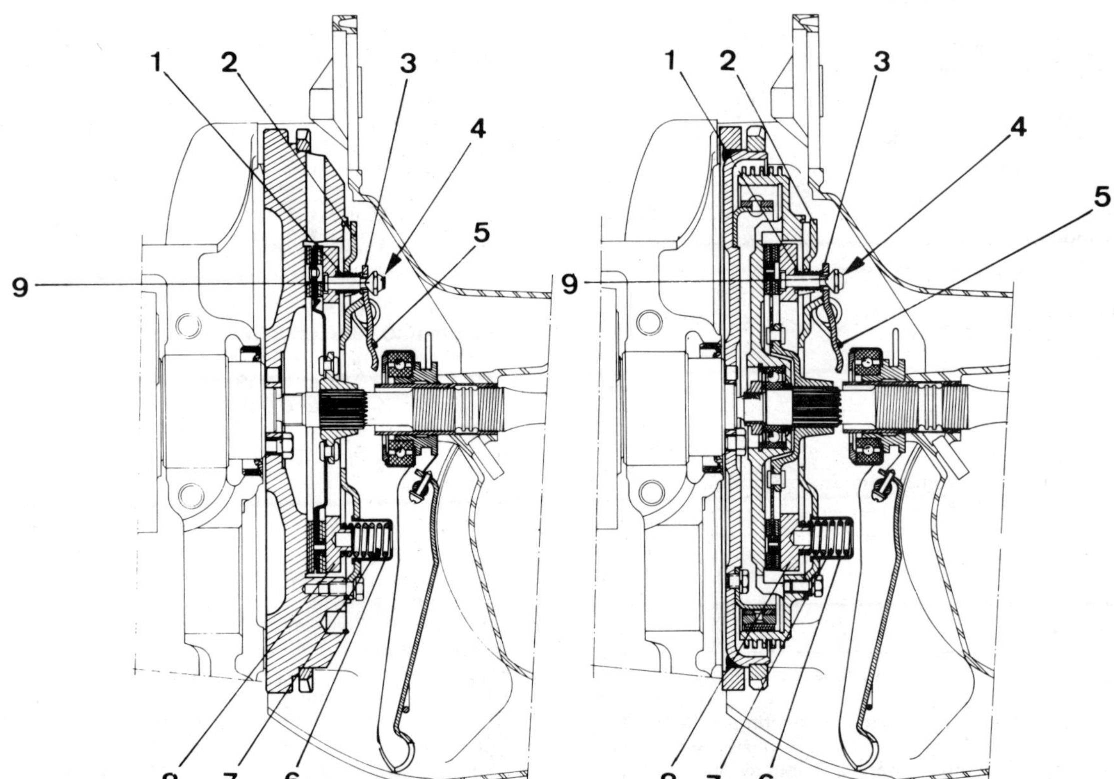

Fig. 4.2 Sectional views of the later type standard clutch (left) and centrifugal clutch (right) (Sec 1)

1 Coil spring
2 Toggle plate
3 Toggle
4 Preset adjuster screw (do not alter)
5 Thrust spring
6 Cup
7 Pressure spring
8 Pressure plate
9 Adjuster screw locknut

1.1 Standard clutch unit and flywheel

6.4 Disconnect the cable from the clutch operating lever

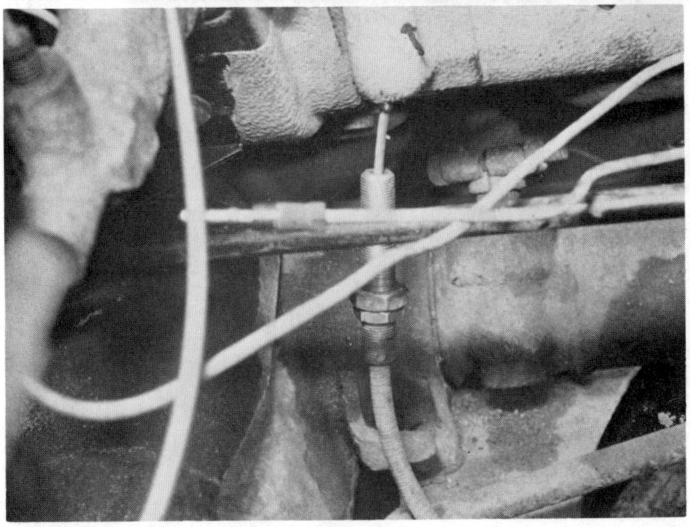

6.7 Reinserting the cable up through the bulkhead. Note the adjuster sleeve and nuts

2 Clutch – maintenance

1 Routine maintenance consists only of checking, and if necessary adjusting, the clutch pedal free play.

2 Where a centrifugal clutch is fitted, particular attention should also be paid regarding the engine idle speed and the throttle closing dashpot adjustment (see Chapter 2).

3 Apart from the above items, an occasional check should be made on the condition of the operating cable and linkages, which should be lubricated periodically.

3 Clutch adjustment – chassis mounted pedal

1 Measure the clutch pedal freeplay; if it exceeds the specified figure it must be adjusted.

2 First check the clutch pedal height, which must be the same as the brake pedal. If not, adjust by relocating the split pin into another hole in the pedal shaft to give the correct setting.

3 To adjust the operating clearance, loosen the locknut at the threaded end of the cable and then turn the adjuster nut to give a clearance of 0.5 to 1.0 mm (0.019 to 0.039 in) between the nut and lever. When making this check/adjustment the cable must be kept taut by pulling at the threaded end and applying a light pressure on the clutch lever so that the thrust bearing contacts the operating lever ring. When set correctly the pedal free play should be as given in the Specifications. Tighten the locknut to secure.

4 Clutch adjustment – pendant pedal

1 Pendant pedal models have the operating pedal mounted from the bulkhead as shown in Fig. 4.3 and not from the chassis as with earlier models.

2 First check that the pedal height is correct by measuring between the floor pan and the bottom edge of the pedal. The correct height is given in the Specifications.

3 To adjust the pedal height, bend the stop to suit.

4 Adjustment of the clutch operating clearance is carried out at the pedal end. Slacken the locknut and turn the adjuster nut as necessary to achieve the specified pedal free play; this should correspond to a clearance of 1.0 to 1.5 mm at the operating lever.

5 Tighten the locknut when the clearance is correct.

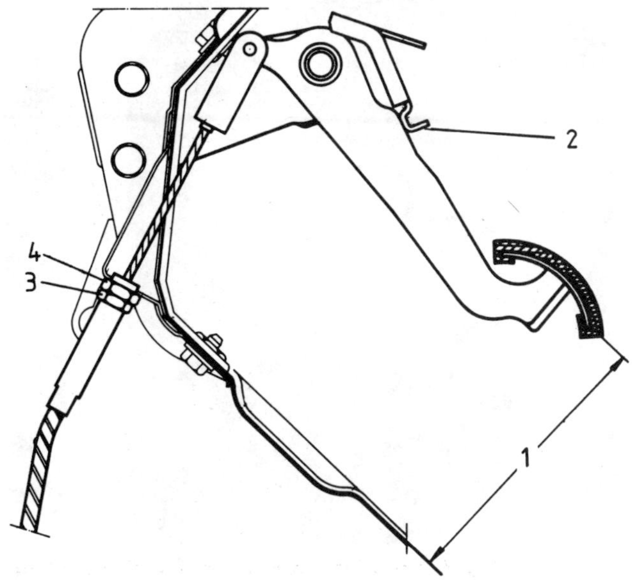

Fig. 4.3 Clutch adjustment – pendant pedal (Sec 4)

1 Pedal height
2 Stop lever
3 Locknut
4 Adjustment nut

5 Clutch cable renewal – chassis mounted pedal

1 Unscrew the cable locknut and adjuster nut, then detach the inner cable at the pedal end.
2 Disconnect the cable at the bottom end at the gearbox and bellcrank and withdraw the cable.
3 Lubricate the inner cable prior to refitting.
4 Refit in the reverse order, ensuring that the cable has no sharp bends in it and that it does not interfere with adjacent components and fittings.
5 Adjust the pedal operating clearance as given in Section 3.

6 Clutch cable renewal – pendant pedal

1 Raise and support the front end of the vehicle so that there is sufficient room to work underneath in safety.
2 Referring to Fig. 4.3, unscrew the cable locking and adjuster nuts on the sleeve.
3 Disconnect the inner cable from the pedal clevis.
4 Working underneath the vehicle, disconnect the inner cable from the operating fork (photo) and pull the cable clear, disconnecting the outer cable from the bottom of the clutch housing.
5 Before fitting the new cable, lubricate it and ensure that it is clean.
6 Refitting is a reversal of the removal procedure, but check that the cable is clear of the exhaust system. Lightly grease the end of the cable before locating it into the operating lever.
7 Pass the top end of the cable up through the bulkhead (photo) and reconnect it to the clutch pedal.
8 Readjust the clutch operating clearance as described in Section 4 and lower the vehicle.

7 Clutch unit – removal

1 To remove and inspect the clutch unit it will be necessary to remove the engine from the car. This is described in Chapter 1.

Standard clutch

2 Mark the relative positions of the clutch pressure plate unit and the flywheel, then unscrew the retaining bolts in a progressive manner. On removal of the bolts, withdraw the pressure plate assembly and clutch disc from the flywheel (photo).

Centrifugal clutch drum removal

3 Bend back or drill or chisel away the metal peened over to retain the central locknut in position, then unscrew the locknut (*left-hand thread*). To prevent the flywheel from rotating, engage a gear and chock a front wheel on one side. Unscrew the nut.
4 Withdraw the clutch drum unit, taking care not to use too much pressure from the rear of the drum.
5 Unscrew the clutch assembly bolts in a progressive sequence and then remove the clutch plate assembly, the clutch disc and the adjuster distance piece.
6 Extract the circlip from the groove in the central aperture and press or drift out the bearing.

8 Clutch unit – inspection and renovation

1 It is not recommended that the clutch units be dismantled any further since this requires the use of special tools, and apart from this, if the assembly or part of it is generally worn, it is normal practice to renew the complete unit.
2 Clean the various components but do not get any oil or grease onto the linings – they may be reusable.

Fig. 4.4 Centrifugal clutch drum securing details (Sec 7)

1 Clutch drum
2 Securing nut (left-hand thread)
a Peened metal

7.2 Removing the pressure plate and disc assemblies from the flywheel

Fig. 4.5 If wear face (b) is refaced, thrust surface (c) must be machined by an equal amount (Sec 8)

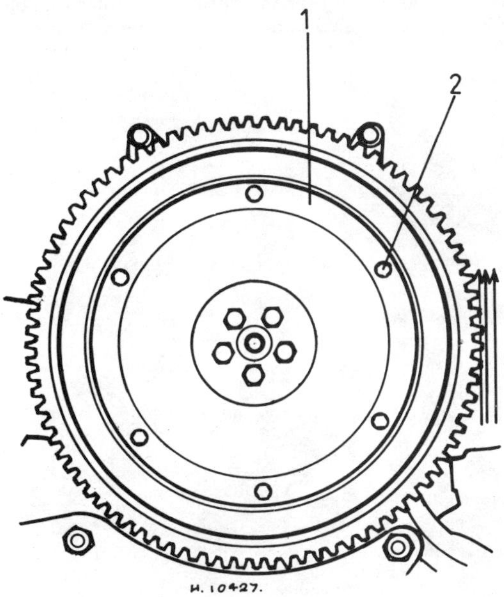

Fig. 4.6 Centrifugal clutch ring (1) and one of the securing bolts (2) (Sec 8)

3 Examine the various components starting with the clutch disc. If this is badly worn or contaminated with oil then it must be renewed. The source of the oil leakage, probably the rear main bearing seal on the crankshaft or possible the gearbox input shaft seal, must be traced and repaired.
4 Check that there are no loose or broken damper springs or rivets on the disc and that the hub splines are in good condition.
5 Examine the flywheel friction face and the corresponding face on the pressure plate. If the clutch disc was worn down to the rivets then it is possible that the wear faces have been scored. A deeply scored flywheel will have to be refaced and this is a job for a competent auto machinist.
6 If the pressure plate assembly is scored or has broken springs then it must be renewed as an assembly.
7 On centrifugal clutch models the procedure is the same as for the standard clutch, but note that if the clutch drum (flywheel) wear face is being refaced, it will be necessary to machine a corresponding amount from the bearing surface of the toggle carrier plate as shown in Fig. 4.5.
8 If on inspection the inner contact surface of the drum is scored or worn then it will be necessary to renew the drum unit as this surface must not be reground. The corresponding linings on the weight ring cannot be renewed if they too are worn or oil soaked, but the assembly must be renewed. Unscrew the five retaining bolts to remove the ring unit from the flywheel.
9 Whilst the clutch is dismantled also make an inspection of the spigot bearing, release bearing and fork assembly. Renew any defective parts. It is sound policy to renew the release bearing as a matter of course whenever the driven plate is renewed, to avoid dismantling again at a relatively early date.

9 Clutch unit – refitting

Standard clutch

1 Locate the clutch disc as shown (photo) with offset boss to the gearbox.
2 If the original clutch cover assembly is being refitted, line up the marks made at removal, position the clutch disc and fit the cover assembly to the flywheel. Fit the washers and retaining bolts, screw them in evenly just enough to grip the driven plate but not enough to prevent it being moved.
3 Before tightening the retaining bolts it is necessary to line up the centre of the clutch disc with the centre bush of the crankshaft. This is easily done if you have an old central shaft or a mandrel with the same spigot diameter as the central shaft. It can also be lined up by eye, but this is not so reliable. If the clutch disc is not centred correctly, it will be impossible to fit the engine to the gearbox and the central shaft may get damaged while attempting to do so.
4 With the clutch disc correctly positioned, proceed to tighten the retaining bolts in a progressive and even manner to the specified torque. Remove the centralising tool.

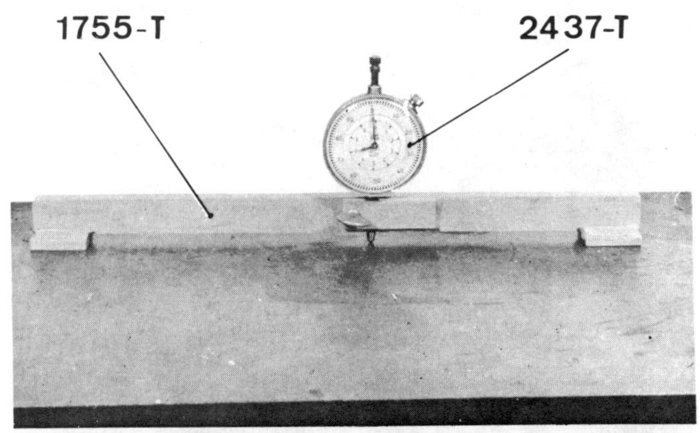

Fig. 4.7 Zero the dial gauge (2437-T) with the straight-edge (1755-T) on a flat surface (Sec 9)

9.1 Locate the disc with the offset hub away from the flywheel

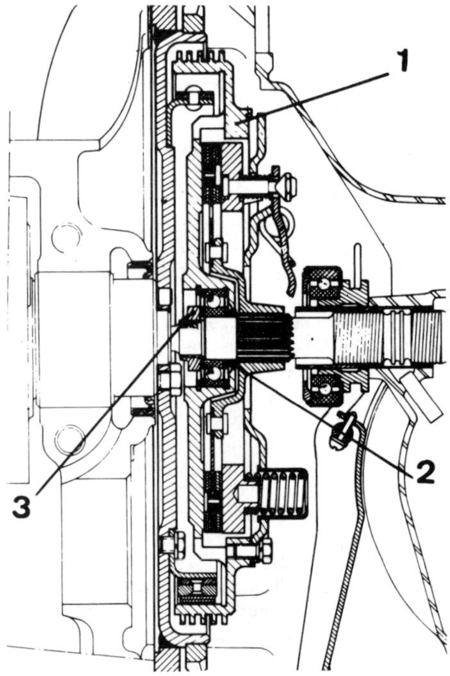

Fig. 4.8 Detail of centrifugal clutch assembly (Sec 9)

1 Clutch drum
2 Distance piece
3 Retaining nut

Fig. 4.9 Checking the clutch drum position with the dial gauge, straight-edge and standard gauge bush (3101-T). For 'a' see text (Sec 9)

Centrifugal clutch

5 If the clutch drum bearing has been removed, take care when inserting the replacement and always use a new circlip to retain it in position.

6 If a new centrifugal ring unit is being fitted, locate and tighten the retaining bolts.

7 If the clutch drum has been renewed then the drum position must be checked and if necessary adjusted. This operation should also be undertaken if the gearcase or mainshaft has been renewed. To check the adjustment you will need special Citroën tools, namely a straight-edge and dial gauge as shown in Fig. 4.7 and a standard gauge bush.

8 Set the dial gauge on the straight-edge face plate and zero the dial with the large pointer, noting the position of the small pointer.

9 Locate the distance piece onto the drive shaft, taking a note of the distance piece thickness. Fit the clutch drum without the disc or mechanism and locate and tighten the central retaining nut (*left-hand thread*).

10 Locate the straight-edge as shown in Fig. 4.9 across the clutch housing thrust bosses and calculate the distance (a) between the distance bush rim edge and the zero reading set on the dial gauge. This should be between 5.12 mm (0.201 in) and 5.42 mm (0.213 in). If the reading taken is outside these tolerances then adjust by fitting a distance piece of the required thickness. Various thicknesses are available.

11 Having checked the drum position remove the retaining nut, the drum and the distance piece.

12 Assemble the clutch disc and pressure plate assembly as for the standard clutch and centralise the disc.

13 Tighten the retaining nut (*left-hand thread*) to the specified torque and peen over the locking metal to secure in position.

14 With the clutch fully assembled and the engine refitted into the vehicle, reconnect the operating cable and adjust the clutch operating clearance as described previously.

10 Clutch release bearing and operating mechanism – removal and refitting

1 To gain access for the inspection and removal of the clutch release bearing and operating fork mechanism you will need to remove the engine from the vehicle as described in Chapter 1. The release mechanism is then accessible (photo).

2 To remove the bearing (or thrust ring on earlier models), remove the retaining clip and then withdraw the bearing and support (photos).

10.1 General view of the clutch release bearing and mechanism

10.2 (a) Remove the clip and ...

10.2 (b) ... withdraw the bearing

10.2 (c) Close-up of the release bearing (1). Note retaining clip (2), bush (3), spring (4), shaft securing screw (5) and operating lever (6)

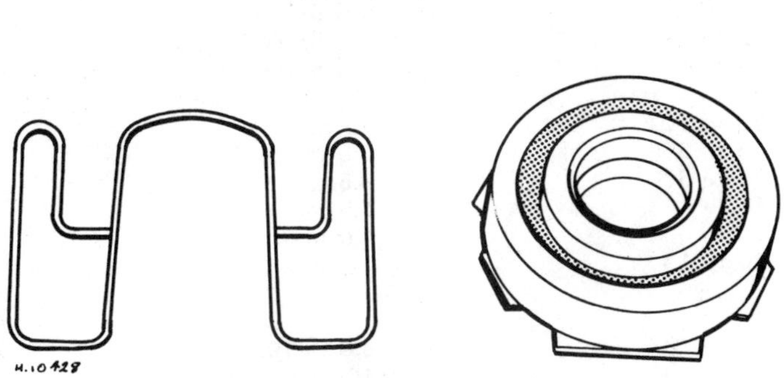

Fig. 4.10 Release bearing and clip fitted to later models (Sec 10)

3 To remove the clutch fork, unscrew and remove the shaft retaining screw. Extract the plug from the hole in the side of the housing and withdraw the shaft, disengaging the respective coil springs, washers and the operating fork. As they are removed note how they are fitted to avoid confusion on reassembly.

4 A self-centering clutch thrust bearing was fitted from September 1973 and this can be used on earlier models provided that a new type securing clip is also fitted.

5 To reassemble, lubricate the shaft and insert it into position, locating the spring and operating fork lever. Insert and tighten the shaft retaining screw. Lubricate the support lightly with oil, fit the bearing and slide it into position. Ensure that the retaining clip is correctly located to complete.

11 Fault diagnosis – clutch

1 Clutch faults can normally be divided into three categories: judder, spin and slip. A squealing noise when the pedal is depressed usually denotes a worn release bearing. There are also some faults peculiar to the centrifugal clutch.

Judder when taking up drive

2 This can be due to loose or worn engine or gearbox mountings. badly worn or contaminated clutch disc friction surfaces, or (rarely) worn splines on the clutch disc or gearbox input shaft. Rectify any source of oil contamination before fitting a new clutch plate.

Clutch spin

3 Clutch spin is evident as difficulty in engaging or disengaging gear. It may be due to excessive free movement at the pedal, in which case adjusting the cable should cure it.

4 Clutch spin may also be caused by the clutch disc sticking to the pressure plate – usually after the vehicle has been standing idle for some time. It may be possible to free the clutch by engaging top gear, depressing the pedal and starting the engine; when the engine is running, slip the clutch until normal disengagement is possible.

5 Clutch spin may also be caused by a damaged or misaligned pressure plate assembly. Renewal of the pressure plate is the only remedy.

Clutch slip

6 Clutch slip is evident when an increase in engine speed is not accompanied by a corresponding increase in road speed. It may be due to wear, maladjustment, or contamination of the linings.

7 If the slip is due to maladjustment – insufficient free play in the cable – adjustment will cure it.

8 If the slip is due to wear it will at first be evident only when the car is heavily loaded or on steep hills; as the linings wear further, slip will become apparent even under light acceleration on the flat. Remedial action should be taken before the linings wear down to the rivets, otherwise the flywheel and/or pressure plate will be scored.

9 Clutch slip can also be caused by oil contamination. It may be possible to achieve temporary relief by squirting a volatile solvent into the clutch housing, but this must be regarded strictly as an emergency measure. Attend to the source of contamination and renew the plate as soon as possible.

Centrifugal clutch faults

10 The centrifugal clutch drum may sometimes emit a squealing noise when engaging or disengaging. This is due to resonance of the drum and is not harmful.

11 Assuming that the clutch components are in good condition, failure to disengage at idle or premature disengagement when the throttle is released will probably be due to carburettor maladjustment. Check the idle speed and the operation of the throttle closing dashpot as described in Chapter 2.

Chapter 5 Transmission

For modifications and information applicable to later models, see Supplement at end of manual

Contents

Specifications

Gearbox

Number of gears	4 forward, 1 reverse
Synchromesh	2nd, 3rd and 4th

Gear ratios (:1):	1st	2nd	3rd	4th	Rev	Final drive
2CV (up to 1970)	7.410	3.572	2.133	1.473	7.980	3.625
2CV van (up to 1968)	7.410	3.572	2.133	1.473	7.980	3.875
Dyane (1967 to 1968)	7.822	3.595	2.133	1.555	8.423	3.625
2CV van (1968 to 1972)	7.822	3.595	2.133	1.555	8.423	3.875
Dyane 6 (1968) and Ami 6 (1968 to 1969)	5.602	2.860	1.923	1.315	5.602	3.625
Dyane 6 (1970 on) and Ami 8 (1969 on)	5.748	2.934	1.923	1.350	5.748	3.875
Dyane 4 (1968 on), 2CV4 (1970 on) and 2CV van (1972 on)	6.961	3.553	2.133	1.473	6.961	4.125
Dyane 6 (1968 to 1970) and 2CV6 (1970 on)	5.202	2.656	1.785	1.315	5.202	4.125

Gear adjustments:	
Endfloat – 2nd gear idler	0.05 to 0.35 mm (0.002 to 0.014 in)
Endfloat – laygear (see text):	
Plain thrust washer, 18 mm wide front bearing	0.05 to 0.35 mm (0.002 to 0.013 in)
Plain thrust washer, 16 mm wide front bearing	0.45 to 1.00 mm (0.018 to 0.039 in)
Roller thrust race	0.10 to 0.20 mm (0.004 to 0.008 in)

Differential

Crownwheel and pinion backlash:	
Models with gear lever on rear upper cover	0.13 to 0.23 mm (0.005 to 0.009 in)
Models with gear lever on upper cover	0.14 to 0.18 mm (0.005 to 0.007 in)

Lubrication

Lubricant type	EP80 gear oil
Lubricant capacity	0.9 litre (1.6 pints)

Torque wrench settings

	lbf ft	kgf m
Mainshaft nut	50 to 65	7.0 to 9.0
Pinion shaft nut (LH thread)	50 to 61	7.0 to 8.5
Driveshaft flange bearing bolt	18	2.5
Driveshaft bearing nut	86 to 101	12 to 14
Drain plug	25 to 32	3.5 to 4.5
Clutch casing – bearing bolt	25 to 32	3.5 to 4.5
Clutch casing bolt (7 mm diameter)	10 to 14	1.5 to 2.0
Level plug	7 to 10	1.0 to 1.5
Upper cover bolts (7 mm diameter)	10 to 14	1.5 to 2.0
Differential shaft ball bearing ring nut:		
2CV from Feb 1970, Dyane from October 1968, 2CV from Jan 1972, 3CV van from May 1968	43 to 72	6.0 to 10.0
Above models previous to dates shown	72 to 101	10.0 to 14.0
All other models	72 to 86	10.0 to 12.0
Differential crownwheel bolt	50 to 57	7.0 to 8.0
Input shaft flange plate bolt	18	2.5
Input shaft bearing nut	86 to 101	12 to 14
Pinion shaft rear bearing flange bolts	18	2.5
Gearbox rear cover bolts	10 to 14	1.5 to 2.0
Hub to gearbox/clutch housing nuts	28 to 30	3.8 to 4.2
Differential hub bearing bush nut (drum brakes)	43 to 54	6.0 to 7.5
Hub retaining bush nut (disc brakes)	43 to 50	6.0 to 7.0
Bush nut on differential shaft (disc brakes)	100 to 114	14.0 to 16.0

1 General description

The transmission system on all models is basically the same, a four forward and one reverse speed gearbox having synchromesh on 2nd, 3rd and 4th gears. (A synchro hub is fitted to bottom gear but does not operate as no spring ring is fitted). The detachable clutch housing and the front section of the gearbox house the differential unit, which transfers the power to the driveshafts of the front wheels.

Drive from the clutch is transferred via the input shaft which passes through the differential housing section and into the gearbox. Power is then transferred to the mainshaft, either direct or by means of the intermediate gear cluster (laygear) and the mainshaft gears, and thence via the constant mesh pinion at the tail of the mainshaft and the reduction gear on the pinion shaft to the pinion shaft. When 4th (top) gear is engaged, the mainshaft is not actually part of the power train, but it still turns because of the continuous engagement of the reduction gear and the constant mesh pinion. The speedometer drive is taken from the rear of the mainshaft. The laygear runs on the pinion shaft; the shaft incorporates the final drive bevel pinion at its front end. Fig. 5.2 explains this more succinctly.

It is important when topping up the gearbox oil that the car be stood on level ground. Always allow excess oil to drip out before refitting the filler/level plug, otherwise the synchromesh may be rendered inoperative. Although Citroën specify an oil of viscosity 80 or 85, some owners find that EP90 oil results in quieter running. Very old and noisy gearboxes may benefit from the use of a multigrade gear oil (85W/140) if available.

Some small changes have taken place in the transmission over the years, so always quote the car model and year when ordering spare parts.

2 Gearbox – removal and refitting

1 The gearbox can only be removed as a complete unit together with the engine, or the engine can be removed first and then the gearbox. These operations are given in Chapter 1, Sections 5 and 6.
2 The refitting procedures are given in Chapter 1, Section 34.
3 When separating and assembling the engine and gearbox units, do not allow the weight of the engine to be taken fully by the gearbox input shaft.

3 Gearbox overhaul – special notes

1 If the gearbox has been removed due to an internal malfunction, the following special points should be noted before any attempt is made to dismantle it.
2 If the gearbox is dismantled and then reassembled using the same components (which is unlikely if a fault exists!) then the dismantling and reassembly procedures can be undertaken without the use of special tools (apart from the selector fork adjustments).
3 The intermediate gear cluster shaft also incorporates the differential bevel pinion. Therefore, whenever this part of the gearbox is renewed, the crownwheel must also be renewed since they are a matching pair and identically marked. In addition, during reassembly the pinion must be set accurately in relation to the crownwheel to provide the correct backlash and meshing of the respective gears. To do this accurately requires the use of special tools and knowledge and is not a job for the average DIY mechanic.
4 If therefore you find problems with the intermediate gear/pinion shaft, have the new components installed by a transmission specialist

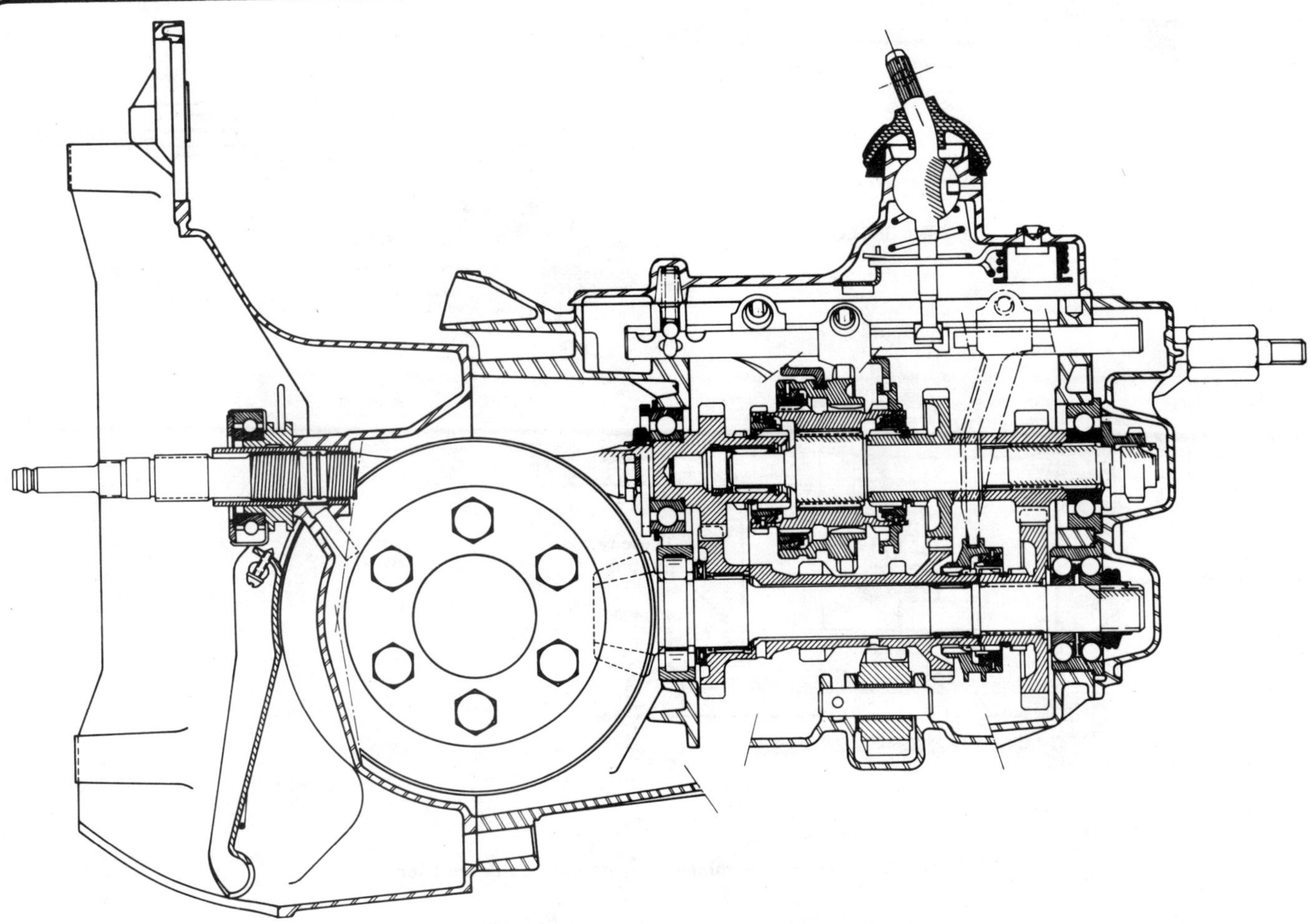

Fig. 5.1 Sectional view of the later type gearbox (Sec 1)

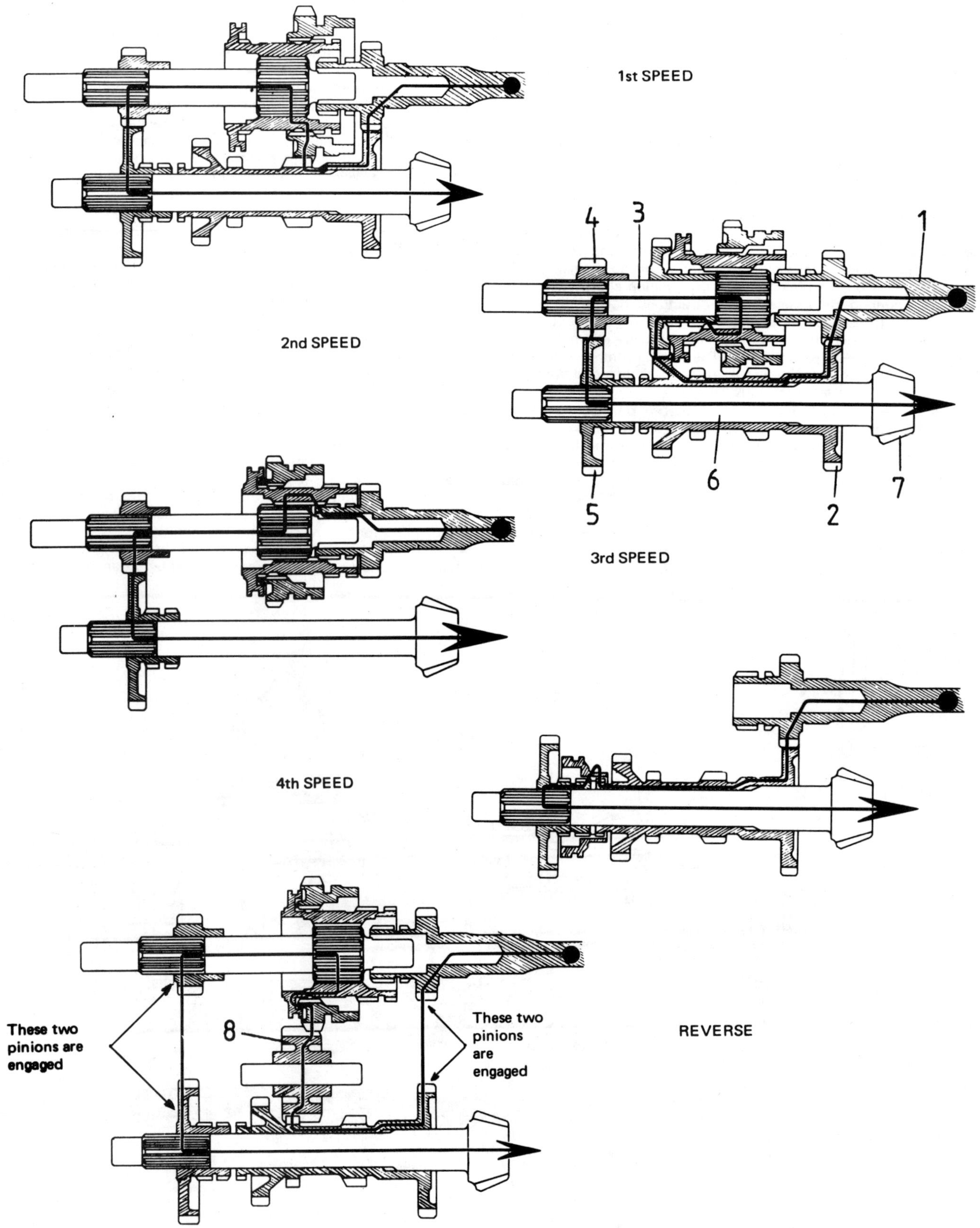

Fig. 5.2 Power transmission in the various gears (Sec 1)

1	*Input shaft*	3	*Mainshaft*	5	*Reduction gear*	7	*Final drive pinion*
2	*Laygear*	4	*Constant mesh pinion*	6	*Pinion shaft*	8	*Reversing pinion*

who is equipped to perform this task.
5 In view of the above, this Chapter describes the reassembly of the pinion/intermediate gearshaft assembly assuming that the original components are being used.
6 When dismantling the gearbox the differential unit will have to be removed. Although this is easily achieved, the refitting process can be more involved depending on the extent of work undertaken. If when the gearbox is assembled the original clutch housing, crownwheel and pinion and differential unit roller bearings are being re-used, then the assembly is a reversal of the removal sequence. If however any of those items mentioned are renewed, then the crownwheel and pinion adjustment will have to be reset, and as mentioned previously this entails the use of special tools and should therefore be entrusted to a transmission specialist.
7 Prior to dismantling the gearbox, assess whether it is worthwhile from the cost angle. Check also the availability of parts. If the gearbox is known to have covered a considerable mileage and is generally worn, then the cost of the replacement parts, not to mention the extra time involved, could be more expensive than simply fitting an exchange unit.
8 If in spite of the above you have decided to dismantle the gearbox, first clean the outer casing and attachments in preparation. As the parts are dismantled lay them out in order ready for cleaning and inspection.
9 Read through the respective operations first to ensure that you can complete the procedures given, particularly the assembly of the various components.

4 Gearbox – dismantling

1 Drain the oil from the gearbox. (The drain plug is located on the right-hand side of the casing towards the rear). Place the gearbox on a clean work surface and have available some wooden blocks and wedges to secure it whilst dismantling. Remove the clutch release bearing and lever (Chapter 4).
2 Refer to Section 12 and remove the differential driveshaft/hub units. *Mark the number and location of the adjustment shims* between the differential bearings and the hubs to ensure correct meshing of the crownwheel and pinion on reassembly. Remember that if any of the differential bearings, gears or housings are to be renewed, the old shims will not necessarily be correct and the assembly will have to be set up by a Citroën dealer.
3 The gearbox top cover(s) can now be removed. Two types have been fitted. On the first type (Fig. 5.3), unscrew the retaining nuts or bolts and remove also the fork control turret and the selector fork tip. On the second type (Fig. 5.4), remove the top cover setscrews. Lift the cover clear, noting that the 2nd/3rd selector shaft detent ball spring is located under the later type cover (photo). Retrieve the ball and spring. Note also that early type covers have a gasket, later ones do not.
4 Unbolt and remove the rear cover. On removal of the cover note the adjustment shims on the mainshaft bearing; unless the mainshaft and/or rear cover are renewed, these shims must be refitted in the same position on reassembly.

Selector forks and shafts

5 The selector shafts are drawn out to the rear. First mark the selector fork positions on their respective shafts to give a guide for correct positioning on reassembly.
6 Unscrew and remove the clamp bolts and withdraw the shafts (photos). Pull each shaft rearwards and rotate it half a turn to allow it to be removed. Keep a finger over the interlock holes to prevent the balls being ejected. Remove the balls and the springs.
7 Remove the selector forks (except 4th gear selector fork), noting how they are located, and fit them back onto their respective shafts to avoid confusion. The 4th gear selector fork cannot be removed until the mainshaft has been removed.

Clutch bellhousing and differential unit

8 Refer to Chapter 4 and remove the clutch release bearing and mechanism.
9 Using a box or socket spanner, unscrew and remove the bellhousing retaining screws and nuts from the front end face.
10 Separate the bellhousing from the gearbox, supporting the differential so that it does not fall out. Note that the differential taper bearing cups are not interchangeable between left and right and must therefore be marked accordingly.

4.3 Remove the top cover. Note detent spring protruding from case

4.6a Unscrew and remove the selector/rod clamp bolts

4.6b Withdraw the shafts rearwards. Note finger preventing ejection of detent ball

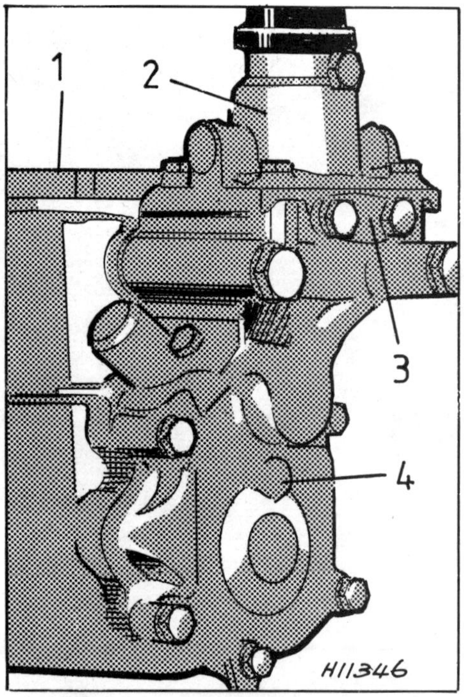

Fig. 5.3 Earlier type top cover (1) and gearchange lever turret at rear (2). Note also selector fork tip (3) and rear cover (4) (Sec 4)

Fig. 5.4 Later type top cover (1), with central gearchange, and rear cover (2) (Sec 4)

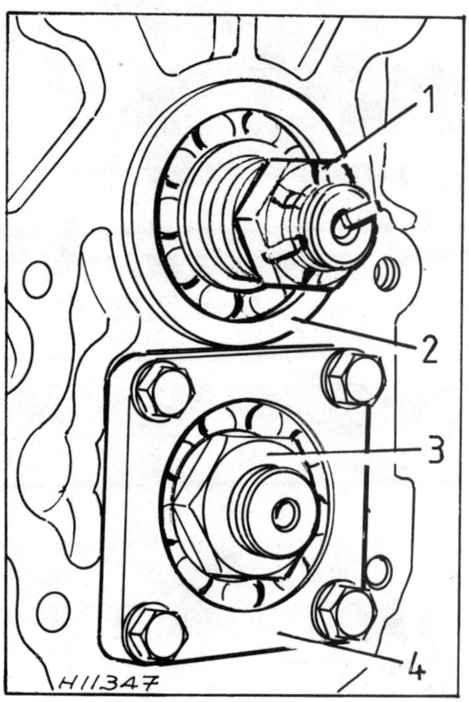

Fig. 5.5 Early type gearbox with rear cover removed (Sec 4)

1. *Speedometer drivegear retaining nut*
2. *Mainshaft rear bearing*
3. *Pinion shaft nut*
4. *Rear bearing retaining flange*

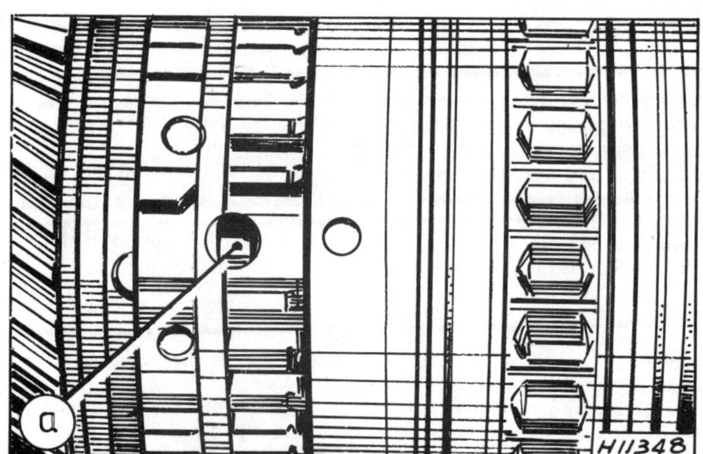

Fig. 5.6 Insert wire through hole (a) (Sec 4)

4.13 Remove the rear bearing

4.17 Extracting the pinion shaft – note the half roller bearings and shims (arrowed)

4.19a Remove the circlip from the input shaft outer race

4.19b Removing the input shaft and bearing rearwards from inside the gearbox

4.22 Reverse gear pinion showing the roll pin in position

Mainshaft and gears

11 Engage two gears to lock the shaft.

12 Relieve the peened-over metal securing the speedometer drive pinion nut and the pinion shaft securing nut. Unscrew the speedometer drive nut and remove the drive pinion. (Early models may have the nut secured by a split pin. Extract the split pin and remove the nut). Remove also the distance piece and flexible washer (if fitted).

13 The rear bearing can now be removed, either by careful levering under the flange, or by judicious tapping on the constant mesh pinion with a soft-headed hammer. In any event take care not to damage the bearing, the pinion or the gearcase (photo).

14 Unscrew and remove the pinion shaft nut *(left-hand thread)* and on earlier models remove the endplate and distance pieces. (It is necessary to do this now whilst the two shafts are still locked up).

15 Withdraw the constant mesh pinion and spacer from the rear of the mainshaft.

16 Engage 4th gear and withdraw the mainshaft and gear assemblies from inside the gearbox. Have ready a piece of stiff wire, slightly curved, to insert into the hole in the 2nd/3rd gear unit (a in Fig. 5.6). This is necessary to retain the needle bearing cage in position. Remove the 4th gear selector fork.

Pinion shaft

17 Drive the rear end of the intermediate shaft towards the front with a copper mallet. Withdraw the pinion and shaft from the front, leaving

the laygear in the gearbox. Note the shims and keep them with the pinion (photo).

Input shaft

18 Unscrew the retaining bolts and remove the flange plate from the front of the bearing.

19 If the input shaft gears are of lesser diameter than the bearing housing, the shaft assembly can be withdrawn forwards. Otherwise, remove the circlip from the bearing outer race and drive the bearing and shaft through from the front. Use a tube drift to locate on the bearing outer race, or gently tap the nose of the shaft with a soft-faced hammer (photo).

Laygear

20 With all the above components removed, the laygear can be lifted out of the gearcase.

21 The pinion shaft rear bearing can be extracted if wished with a suitable tube drift.

Reverse gear pinion

22 Extract the roll pin which locates the reverse gear shaft (photo). Use a pair of pliers and pass a 4 mm split pin through the roll pin to improve leverage.

23 Push the shaft through and remove the gear. If it is to be re-used reposition it onto the shaft facing in the same direction as when it was fitted.

5 Gear assemblies – dismantling

1 With the gearbox dismantled, the sub-assemblies and their various components can be further dismantled and inspected for wear and damage as required.

2 As they are dismantled lay the components out in order of appearance and facing the way in which they were fitted. This will help to avoid any confusion during assembly (photo).

Mainshaft

3 Withdraw the following components from the mainshaft:

(a) *The 1st/reverse gear sliding pinion*
(b) *2nd/3rd gear sliding pinion*
(c) *2nd gear idler pinion and synchro unit*

Input shaft

4 Bend the locktab straight away from the nut and support the shaft in a soft-jawed vice. Unscrew the nut *(left-hand thread)* and remove it.

5 The bearing can now be withdrawn from the shaft. Support the bearing and press or drive it free, using a suitable tube drift which will locate on the bearing outer race.

6 Extract the circlip from the needle bearing aperture. The circlip can be pressed away from its groove by inserting a 2 mm pin through the adjacent hole from the outside. Hook the circlip and pull it free.

7 Withdraw the needle bearing and (where fitted) the distance piece.

Pinion shaft and laygear

8 Remove the thrust washer from the shaft and extract the circlip retaining the bearing in position.

9 If the front bearing is to be removed, use a suitable tube and drift or press the bearing down the shaft to free it.

10 Remove the synchro ring from the reduction gear. The synchro rings must always be renewed when the gearbox is reassembled.

11 Remove the gear cluster bushes from the aperture at each end.

12 On later models the intermediate gear cluster runs on needle roller bearings at each end. Instead of, or in addition to, a single thrust washer at the front, there is a radial needle bearing thrust race with two thrust washers (one each side), as shown in the photo.

Speedometer driven gear

13 This can be removed from the rear end cover by unscrewing the retaining bolt and withdrawing the driven gear unit.

5.2 Lay the gear assemblies out for inspection (mainshaft and input shaft shown)

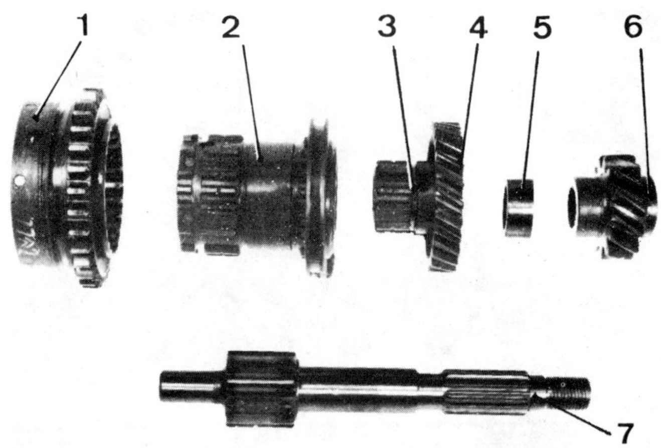

Fig. 5.7 The mainshaft components (Sec 5)

1 *1st/reverse gear*
2 *2nd/3rd gear sliding pinion*
3 *Synchro ring*
4 *2nd gear pinion*
5 *Spacer*
6 *Constant mesh pinion*
7 *Mainshaft*

5.12 The intermediate gear cluster (laygear) and pinion shaft assembly

6 Gearbox components – inspection and renewal

1 Wash and clean all parts in petrol ready for inspection.
2 Inspect each part in turn, looking for defects and/or obvious signs of wear.
3 Check the respective bearings and bushes for signs of wear, binding and coarseness. Renew any defective bearings.
4 Inspect the gear teeth and look for chips or signs of damage. When one gear is renewed then its opposite number should likewise be renewed so that they can bed in together. Meshing a new gear with a worn one is not good practice and can promote gear whine.
5 The crownwheel and pinion are a carefully matched pair and therefore if either is damaged or badly worn then they must both be replaced by a new matching pair (see also Section 3).
6 Make a careful inspection of the gearcase for any signs of hairline cracks or damage. Check the mating flange surfaces which must be free of score marks and any other defects likely to cause distortion and leakage when assembled.
7 Check the selector mechanism and renew any defective or worn parts.
8 Before reassembling the gearbox, check and adjust the mainshaft and pinion shaft endfloats as described in the following Section.

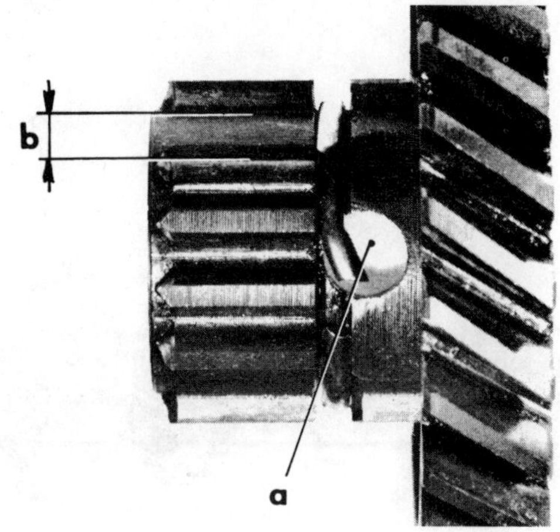

Fig. 5.8 Synchro ring tag must locate in cutaway (a). Wide splines (b) must align with other gears – see text (Sec 7)

7 Mainshaft, pinion shaft and laygear – reassembly and endfloat adjustment

1 Check that all parts are perfectly clean prior to reassembling and checking the respective endfloats.

Mainshaft

2 Fit a new synchromesh ring to the 2nd gear idle pinion, taking care not to distort the ring when fitting. Arrange it so that the location tag is positioned in the circular cutaway.
3 Slide the 2nd gear idle pinion onto the mainshaft together with the distance piece and constant mesh pinion. Now check that the 2nd gear rotates freely and has the specified endfloat. If endfloat adjustment is needed, change the distance piece for one of the required thickness to take up the play.
4 Align the wider splines of the 2nd gear idler pinion with the corresponding splines on the mainshaft.
5 Fit the 2nd/3rd gear sliding pinion, together with the collar, against 2nd gear idler. Position so that the wide splines on the synchromesh cones are aligned with the wide splines of the shaft (Fig. 5.10).
6 Locate the sliding gear with the dogs of the 2nd gear idle pinion.
7 Now assemble the 1st/reverse gear sliding pinion with the teeth rearwards. Align the dogs in the wider splines, then push the sliding gear unit fully into position. Check that the cones rotate freely and that the sliding pinion doesn't stick.

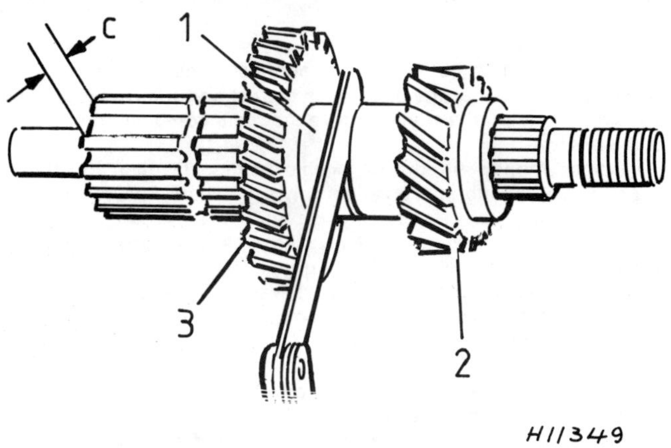

Fig. 5.9 Check endfloat with feeler gauges (Sec 7)

1 Spacer
2 Constant mesh pinion
3 2nd gear pinion
C Align wide splines with those shown in Fig. 5.8

Pinion shaft and laygear

8 As mentioned during the dismantling procedure, there are two types of laygear cluster thrust washer and bearing layouts. The assembly of the bush and fixed thrust washer type is described below; the needle bearing type is described from paragraph 16.
9 Press the front bearing carefully onto the pinion shaft, ensuring that it is fully located. Note that there are two widths of bearing used, 16 and 18 mm wide. If for any reason you have renewed the bearing and it is of a different thickness to the original one fitted then you must also change the thrust washer and front gear cluster bush accordingly.
10 Fit the circlip, taking care not to score the bearing face of the front bush.
11 Smear the thrust washer with grease and locate on the shaft with the flat faces in alignment. If the washer has a chamfered edge this must face towards the bearing.
12 Smear the laygear end bushes with grease and insert them into position. Then slide the laygear into position on the pinion shaft.
13 Assemble a new synchromesh segment to the reduction gear. Locate the reduction gear onto the shaft with the gear offset to the rear.
14 Check that the reduction gear can rotate freely on the shaft whilst it is against the shaft shoulder. The endfloat can be checked at this stage and must be as given in the Specifications. An alternate width

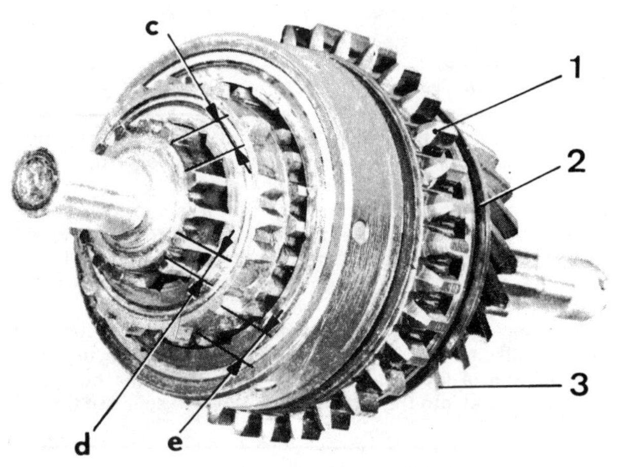

Fig. 5.10 Align the wide splines (c, d and e) as shown (Sec 7)

1 1st/reverse sliding pinion
2 Collar
3 2nd gear pinion

Fig. 5.11 Check the reduction gear/laygear endfloat with feeler gauges (Sec 7)

1 Final drive pinion
2 Laygear
3 Reduction gear

of thrust washer must be fitted if the endfloat does not comply.

15 Having ensured that the endfloat is correct and that the reduction gear moves freely on the shaft, remove the reduction gear and laygear from the shaft.

16 On those models fitted with needle bearing laygear and thrust race, press the bearing into position down the shaft. Ensure that it is fully located and rotates freely.

17 Thrust washers are now selected to give the correct endfloat between the laygear and the reduction gear.

18 Slide a thrust washer of any thickness down the pinion shaft, followed by a thrust washer 2 mm thick (the same thickness as the needle bearing thrust race). Slide the laygear into position down the shafts.

19 Locate the synchromesh ring on the reduction gear and place the gear onto the pinion shaft against the shoulder. Now select a thrust washer which will slide into the gap between the laygear and the reduction gear and allow an endfloat clearance within the specified limits. Obviously a selection of washers will be handy to make this adjustment, but failing this, calculate the thickness required and obtain the required washer.

20 When the washer thickness is selected, remove the reduction gear and laygear from the pinion shaft and also the 2 mm thick washer.

21 Now slide the needle thrust bearing into position against the front thrust washer and then fit the selected rear thrust washer. Smear them with grease to keep them in position against the front ball bearing of the pinion shaft.

8 Input shaft – reassembly

1 Smear the inside of the needle bearing aperture in the rear end of the shaft with some grease and insert the needle roller bearing unit (also greased). Fit the distance piece (where fitted).

2 Insert the retaining circlip and check that it is correctly located.

3 To fit the ball bearing, locate it on the front of the shaft with the circlip groove in its outer race offset to the front. Use a suitable tube and drift or press the bearing into position in the shaft. Check that the bearing is fully located and rotates freely when in position.

4 Fit the retaining nut *(left-hand thread)* and washer. Tighten the nut to the specified torque. Bend over the lockwasher to secure the nut in position. Where a lockwasher is not used, stake the nut using a punch or small chisel into the indent of the exposed spline of the shaft.

9 Gearbox – reassembly

Reverse gear pinion

1 If it was removed, refit the reverse gear pinion into position in the base of the gearbox. Slide it between the lugs with the chamfered

9.4 Locate the laygear in the bottom of the gearbox

9.5a Insert the input shaft

9.5b Refit the circlip to the bearing outer race groove. Pinion shaft should not have been fitted yet!

Fig. 5.12 The input shaft (Sec 8)

10 Retaining nut (LH thread)
11 Synchro ring
12 Bearing
a Locknut flange staking groove

9.7 Insert the pinion shaft

Fig. 5.13 Driving the input shaft home using a tubular drift (A) (Sec 9)

9.11a Insert the mainshaft assembly and ...

edge of the gears to the front and slide the shaft into position, aligning the roll pin hole.

2 Locate and drive the roll pin (use a new one) into position, and check that the gear is free to rotate.

Laygear

3 Check that the bushes or needle bearings are in position in each end of the laygear and suitably lubricated.

4 Engage the reduction gear and sliding pinion onto the rear end of the laygear and place in position in the bottom of the gearbox (photo).

Input shaft

5 The input shaft can now be refitted. Where the driving gear is larger than the bearing, the assembly must be inserted from within the gearbox (photo). If the gear outside diameter is smaller than that of the bearing the assembly can be fitted from the front. Whichever way it is inserted, ensure that the bearing is correctly aligned before driving the assembly into position using a suitable tube drift. When the bearing is in position, fit the new circlip into the groove in the bearing outer race (photo).

Pinion shaft

6 Slide the needle roller bearing and/or thrust washers as applicable into position in the shaft at the pinion end. Grease them well to enable them to be retained in position on the shaft against the ball bearing retaining circlip.

7 The pinion shaft can now be inserted into position. Pass it carefully through the laygear and align the splines to correspond with those of

9.11b ... install the 4th gear selector fork

9.13a Slide on the distance collar and ...

the reduction gear at the rear end. Slide the shaft fully home so that the bearing is in position in the housing (photo).

8 Fit the distance washer onto the rear of the pinion shaft and then the bearing. Support the pinion at the front end and carefully drive the rear bearing into position with its flange flush to the housing.

9 Fit the retaining nut *(left-hand thread)* but do not tighten at this stage.

10 On those models with a retaining flange for the pinion shaft rear bearing, relocate and secure the flange (and shims as applicable), tightening the bolts to the specified torque.

Mainshaft

11 Insert the assembled mainshaft gear cluster and mainshaft into position in the gearbox (photo), and locate the 4th gear selector fork into the groove of the reduction gear sliding hub on the pinion shaft (photo).

12 Check that the mainshaft nose is correctly located in the needle bearings in the input shaft.

13 Slide the distance collar and constant mesh pinion onto the rear end of the mainshaft (photos).

14 Relocate and secure with bolts and spring washers the input shaft bearing flange retainer (photo). Tighten the flange bolts to the specified torque.

15 Locate the mainshaft rear bearing (photo), and carefully drive it

9.13b ... the constant mesh pinion

9.14 The input shaft bearing flange retainer

9.15 Fit the rear mainshaft bearing

9.16 Refit the speedometer drivegear assembly

into position with a tube drift. Check that the mainshaft can rotate freely.

16 Refit the speedometer drivegear, screwing it into position against the bearing (photo). On earlier models this drivegear is fitted together with a distance piece and flexible washer.

17 Engage two gears at once and lock the shafts. Now tighten the pinion shaft rear nut and the mainshaft rear nut to their specified torque (photo). Remember that the pinion shaft nut has a left-hand thread.

18 When the nuts are tightened, peen the outer nut flange into the shaft to lock it in position. On earlier models align the nut (at the specified torque) to the nearest pin hole and insert a new split pin to make it secure.

Selector forks and rods

Early models (rear cover gearchange)

19 Locate the 2nd/3rd and the 1st reverse selector forks into the respective grooves of their sliding pinions (all fixing screw heads must be to the left).

20 Locate the rear interlock springs and balls into position in the gearcase (Fig. 5.14).

21 Insert the 4th gear selector shaft and locking segment. Oil the shaft before fitting, compress the ball and spring from the inside and push the shaft through, rotating it a quarter of a turn to stop it from locking. As it passes through engage it in its selector fork, and when in the neutral position rotate it back to its normal position.

22 Now insert the 1st/reverse gear selector shaft in a similar manner.

23 Finally insert the 2nd/3rd selector shaft, but before sliding the shaft into position in the front housing, locate the locking spring and balls into the front section of the case, positioning them as shown in Fig. 5.15. Rotate this shaft half a turn when fitting and engage with the selector fork; with the lock balls and springs compressed from the front side, push the shaft into position and rotate it back to the neutral position.

Later models (top cover gearchange)

24 Locate the 2nd/3rd and 1st/reverse selector forks into their respective sliding pinions. Position so that the fixing screw heads will face to the left (photo).

25 Referring to Fig. 5.17, insert the lock springs (10 and 6) into the rear casing apertures within the reverse and 4th selector shaft bores.

26 Lubricate the selector shafts and insert the 4th gear shaft into its bore in the casing from the rear (photo). Push the shaft through, engaging with the selector fork, and up to but not yet into the front of the housing.

27 Grease the shaft locator balls (7 and 9) and insert them into the positions shown in Fig. 5.17.

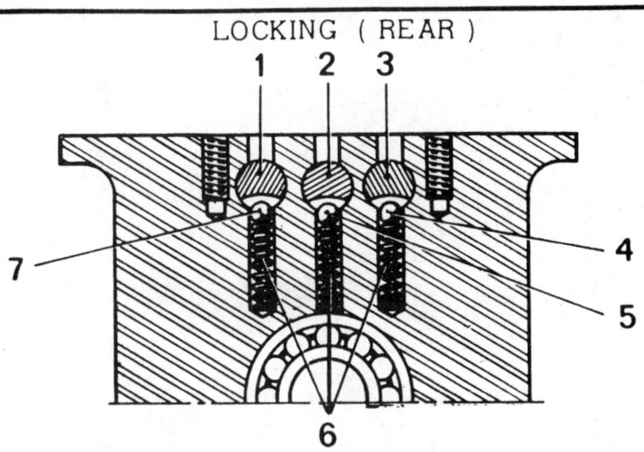

Fig. 5.14 Selector shaft locking spring and ball locations, rear (early models with rear cover gearchange) (Sec 9)

1 *4th gear selector rod*
2 *2nd/3rd selector rod*
3 *1st/reverse selector rod*
4 *1st/reverse ball*
5 *2nd/3rd ball*
6 *Springs*
7 *4th gear ball*

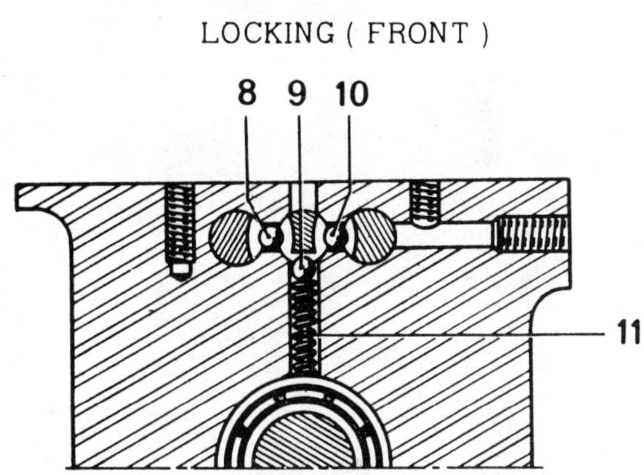

Fig. 5.15 Selector shaft locking spring (11) and ball (8, 9 and 10) locations, front (early models) (Sec 9)

Fig. 5.16 Selector shafts and forks (Sec 10)

3 *1st/reverse selector rod*
4 *2nd/3rd selector rod*
5 *4th gear selector rod*
6 *Clamp bolts*

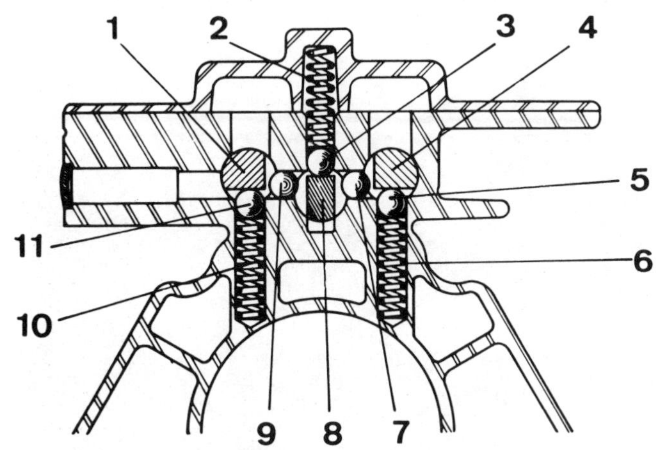

Fig. 5.17 Selector shaft locking springs and balls (later models with top cover gearchange) (Sec 9)

1 *4th gear selector rod*
2 *2nd/3rd spring*
3 *2nd/3rd ball*
4 *1st/reverse selector rod*
5 *1st/reverse ball*
6 *1st/reverse spring*
7 *Interlock ball*
8 *2nd/3rd selector rod*
9 *Interlock ball*
10 *4th gear spring*
11 *4th gear ball*

9.17 Tighten the nuts to the specified torque

9.24 Refit the selector forks

9.26 Insert 4th gear selector shaft

9.28 Insert 2nd/3rd selector shaft

9.34 Refit the rear end cover

9.36 Fit the top cover

28 Insert the 2nd/3rd selector shaft, passing it through to engage in its selector fork as shown (photo).
29 Grease and insert the 2nd/3rd ball (3) into position and locate the shaft in the neutral position.
30 Insert the 1st/reverse gear shaft in a similar fashion.
31 Position the location balls (5 and 11) on top of their springs in the housing and compress each one in turn as the shafts are fully inserted into position.

Peripheral components

32 The rear end cover can now be refitted. Check that the mating surfaces of both the cover and the gearbox are perfectly clean. On early models with the gearchange lever on the rear cover, the mainshaft bearing flange shims must be fitted into position.
33 To check the thickness of shims required, use a depth gauge and measure the amount of bearing projecting from the face of the gearbox. Now measure the depth of the bearing recess in the rear cover and calculate the difference between the two. The difference calculated, plus 0.05 mm, is the shim thickness requirement. When making this check, ensure that the bearing flange is flush against the rear face of the gearbox. The shims can be held in position with grease during assembly.
34 Smear the joint faces of the gearbox and rear cover with a suitable sealant and refit the cover and securing bolts, which must be tightened to the specified torque (photo).
35 Before the top cover is refitted, the selector forks must be checked and adjusted. This is described in Section 10.
36 When fitting the top cover, first check that the mating surfaces are clean and in good condition. Smear the faces with sealant and locate the selector lever in neutral (also the gears). Lower the cover carefully into position, engaging the protruding interlock spring of the 2nd/3rd selector shaft if applicable (photo). Tighten the securing bolts to the specified torque.
37 Turn the gearbox and position it on its rear end. Check that the differential housing is clean, especially the bearing half housings.
38 Refit the differential unit. The carrier bearings must be lubricated before assembling. If the differential position is correct, the crownwheel will be directly in line with the drain plug (photo).
39 Providing that the original clutch housing, crownwheel and pinion, and roller bearing assemblies have not been renewed, the clutch housing can be refitted. If however any of the above mentioned items have been renewed then it will be necessary to have the bearing clearances readjusted – see Section 3.
40 Refit the clutch housing. As the housing retaining nuts are tightened, check that the bearing faces of the shaft hubs are in exact alignment (photo).
41 Locate the adjustment shim washers into the left-hand drive hub

9.38 The crownwheel and differential unit installed

9.40a Locating the clutch housing

9.40b Check that the flange faces are flush

9.41 Refit the correct amount of washers into the left-hand hub

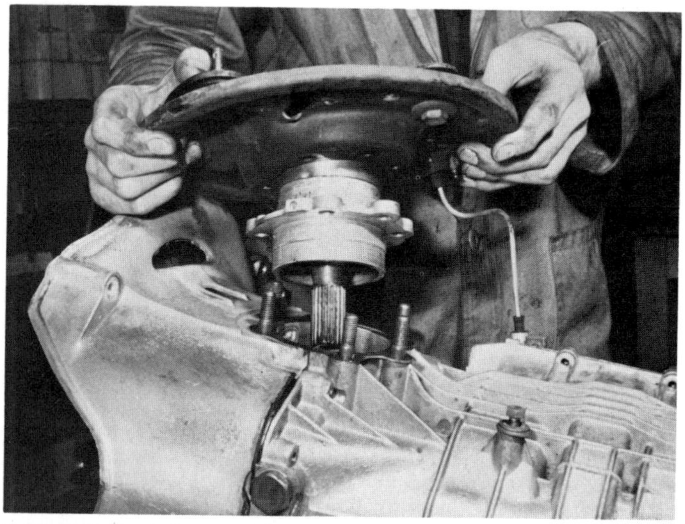

9.42 Refit the hub assembly

housing on top of the taper bearing (photo). Only fit those washers which were originally removed from the left-hand housing as they determine the correct bearing adjustment.

42 Locate the two gaskets over the hub housing studs and then fit the left-hand hub housing into position (photo). Make secure with the nuts and tighten to the specified torque. Repeat the procedure on the right-hand side.

43 Reassemble the clutch release bearing assembly as given in Chapter 4.

44 Reassemble the brake drum or caliper assemblies on each hub as applicable – see Chapter 6. The brake hydraulic fluid pipes can also be relocated on the gearbox.

45 The gearbox should now be ready for reinstallation into the vehicle, but make a final check before fitting.

10 Gearbox selector forks – adjustment

1 The gear selector forks may be adjusted during the process of rebuilding the gearbox, or with the gearbox in position in the vehicle.

2 If the gearbox is in the vehicle, it will be necessary to remove the top cover. To do this the heater duct, heater cables, brake pipes (drum brake models) or handbrake cable (disc brake models) will have to be removed first, and the gearchange linkage disconnected. Slacken the selector fork securing bolts so that the forks can move on the selector shafts.

3 To adjust the 2nd/3rd selector fork locate the fork selector rod in the neutral position. On models with the gear lever located in the upper cover, the 2nd/3rd gear locking ball and spring protrude from the top face. In order that the rod be retained in the correct position, the spring should be compressed during adjustment. To do this fabricate a suitable bar as shown in Fig. 5.18 which can be bolted or clamped in position across the top face of the gearbox to compress the spring.

4 You will now need an adjuster shim 1.8 mm (0.07 in) thick. If available use Citroën special tool number 1786-T. Position the adjuster shim on the synchro segment of the mainshaft as shown in Fig. 5.19.

5 Now move the 2nd/3rd gear selector fork to enable the sliding pinion to make contact with the adjuster shim. Tighten the selector fork clamp bolt in this position so that there is a clearance of 1.8 mm between the input shaft dogs and the sliding pinion. Remove the adjuster shim on completion.

6 Now adjust the 1st/reverse selector fork. Commence by checking that the selector fork rod is in the neutral position, then locate the 1st/reverse gear sliding pinion (Fig. 5.20) at the middle of its movement on the 2nd/3rd sliding pinion. This is correct when the rear of the 1st/reverse pinion unit (a) is flush with the rear of the ground section of 2nd/3rd gear pinion unit (b). When set in this position, tighten the selector fork clamp bolt to secure.

7 To adjust the 4th gear selector fork, check that the fork rod is in the neutral position. You will now require a special adjuster shim, the thickness of which varies according to vehicle type as follows. For AZ models up to February 1970, AZU models up to January 1972, and Dyane (AYA) models from August 1967 to March 1968, use special tool number 1785-T which is 1.50 mm (0.06 in) thick. On all other models use special tool number 3153-T which is 2.70 mm (0.106 in) thick.

8 Slide the selector fork along so that the 4th gear sliding pinion comes into contact with the adjuster shim, see Fig. 5.21. Tighten the selector fork clamp bolt to secure and set the required clearance between the idle reduction gear pinion dogs and the 4th gear sliding pinion.

9 Remove the adjuster shim. Check the operation of the respective selectors and ensure that the gear engagement is satisfactory.

10 Remove the bar retaining the 2nd/3rd selector rod detent ball and spring in position.

11 If the gearbox is still in the car, refit the top cover and the gearchange linkage. Check that all gears can be engaged, then refit the other components which were removed to gain access.

Fig. 5.18 Citroën special tool MR. 630-64/21 for compressing 2nd/3rd locking spring (Sec 10)

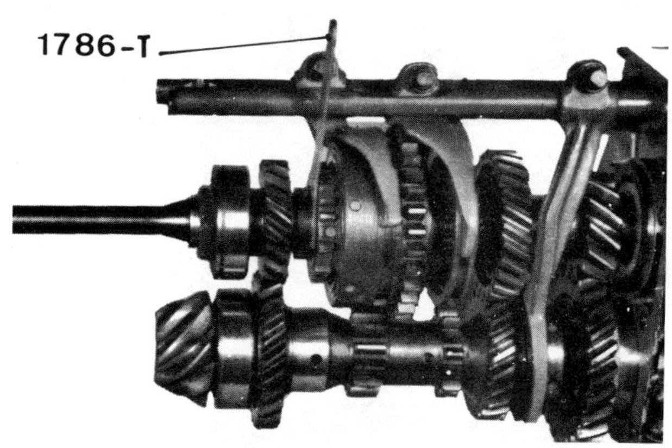

Fig. 5.19 Citroën tool 1786-T in position for adjusting 2nd/3rd selector fork (gearcase removed for clarity) (Sec 10)

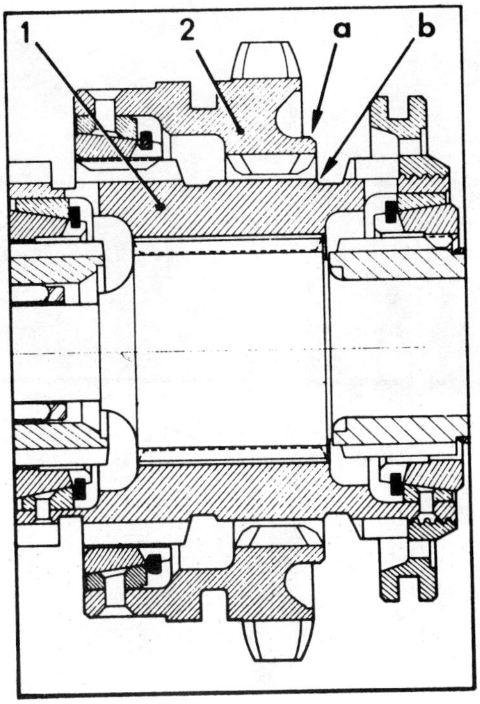

Fig. 5.20 Checking 1st/reverse selector fork – when correctly adjusted, a and b will be flush (Sec 10)

1 2nd/3rd pinion 2 1st/reverse pinion

Fig. 5.21 Citroën special tool 3153-T in position for adjusting 4th gear selector fork (gearcase removed for clarity) (Sec 10)

11 Differential unit – removal and refitting

1 As mentioned in Section 3, differential unit renewal is really a specialised operation, requiring special tools and knowledge to re-adjust the crownwheel and pinion backlash.
2 Dismantling of the differential unit also requires special tools and is generally beyond the scope of the average DIY mechanic.
3 If you wish to remove the differential unit for inspection only, then this can be achieved by removing and dismantling the gearbox as described earlier in this Chapter.

12 Differential driveshaft/hub unit – removal, dismantling, reassembly and refitting

Renewal of the differential oil seals must be carried out immediately if any leakage is observed. Although a drain hole is provided on drum brake hubs (Fig. 5.26), it is not impossible for the friction pads or linings to become contaminated with oil.

Removal

1 Disconnect and remove the driveshaft concerned (Chapter 8).
2 Refer to Chapter 6 and remove the brake drum or disc as applicable. On drum brake models also remove the brake shoes and disconnect the handbrake cable.
3 On drum brake models unscrew and remove the six hub unit retaining nuts (Fig. 5.22) and remove the hub unit, driving free from the rear if necessary using a block of wood and mallet (photo). Extract the shims and keep separate.
4 On disc brake models, use a strap wrench or chain spanner to remove the large special hub retaining nut (Fig. 5.23). This nut is locked in position by peening and this must first be relieved.Do not use any other type of spanner to remove this nut or it will be damaged and need replacing. Withdraw the hub and shaft unit, tapping free to separate from the differential housing using a block of wood and mallet (if necessary). Extract the shim washers from the bearing housing and keep separate.

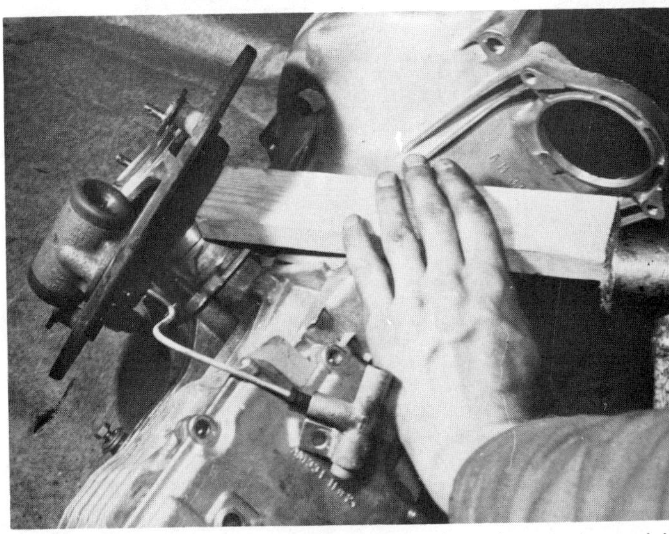

12.3 Method of freeing the hub/backplate unit on drum brake models

Dismantling

5 On drum brake models, secure the shaft flange in a soft-jawed vice and chisel away the locking peen of the differential shaft nut. Use a box spanner to unscrew the nut, then press out the differential shaft to separate from the bearing. Support the unit by resting the backplate over two blocks. Remove the backplate and hold the hub in a soft-jawed vice, then chisel free the bush nut peened locking section and unscrew the nut with a strap wrench or chain spanner. The sealing bearing, spacer and bush can then be removed and inspected or renewed as necessary.
6 On disc brake models relieve the peened section of the bush nut and unscrew the nut. Withdraw the spacer, taking care not to damage it as any scratches will cause oil leaks when assembled. Remove the sealed bearing and bush nut using a suitable puller. Always renew the seal in the differential hub and when removing the old one note which way round it is fitted. If the shim washers are being removed from the housing keep them separate and reinsert the same washers prior to installing the new seal.
7 Inspect all parts for signs of wear or damage. Inspect the spacer

Fig. 5.22 Two of the hub retaining nuts (1) on drum brake models (Sec 12)

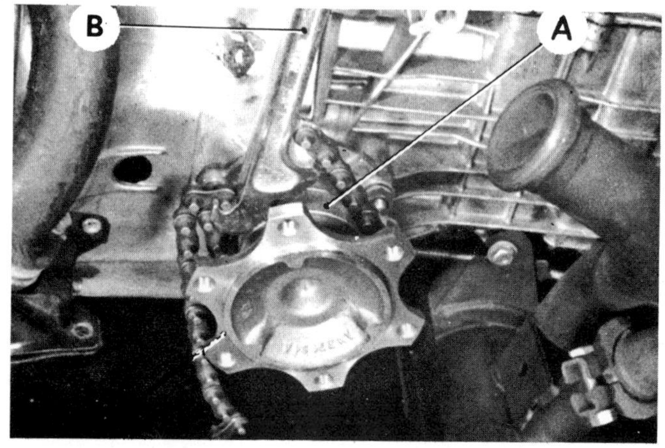

Fig. 5.23 Unscrew the nut (A) with a strap or chain wrench (B) (disc brake models) (Sec 12)

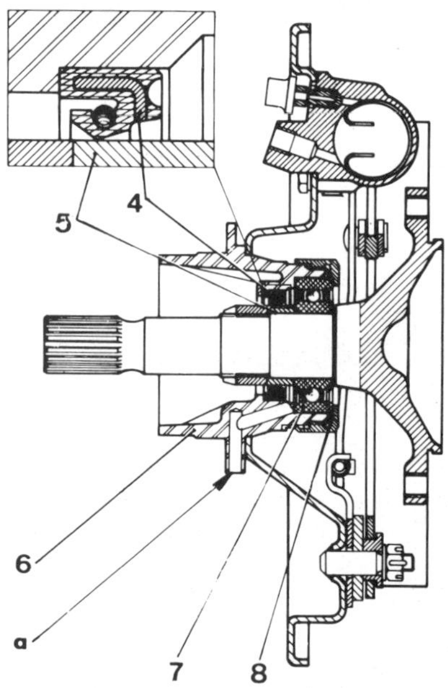

Fig. 5.24 Sectional view of drum brake differential shaft hub (Sec 12)

4 Oil seal
5 Spacer
6 Hub
7 Bearing
8 Bush nut
a Flange oil drain hole

Fig. 5.25 Hub shaft – disc brake models (Sec 12)

1 Nut peened into groove
2 Nut
3 Spacer
4 Bearing
5 Bush nut

Fig. 5.26 Drain hole (arrowed) in flange must face downwards (Sec 12)

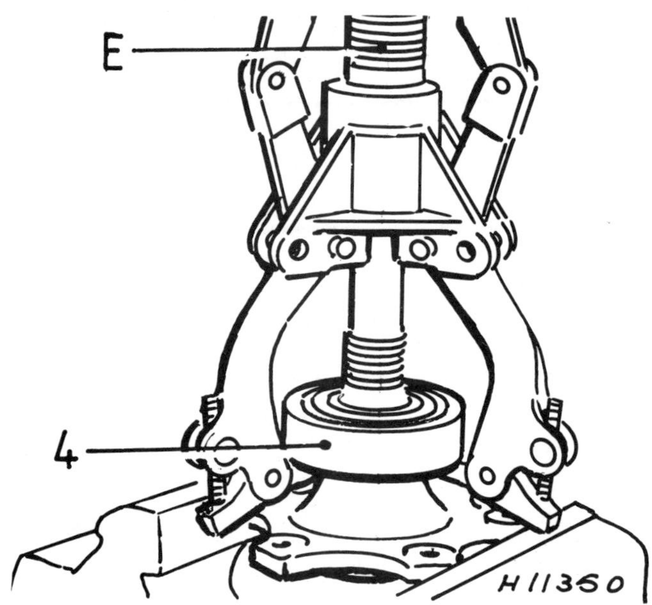

Fig. 5.27 Using an extractor (E) to remove the bearing and bush nut (4). Take care not to damage the shaft (Sec 12)

seal surface for signs of wear or scratching and renew if necessary. Excessive play in the hub bearing warrants renewal also.

Reassembly and refitting

Drum brake models

8 Lubricate the oil seal and spacer and assemble the seal facing the correct way round as removed. Fit the spacer into the seal from the outside. Locate the bearing squarely around the housing edge and press it carefully into position. Screw the bush nut into position and tighten to the specified torque, using a strap wrench or chain spanner and a spring balance. Peen over the nut into the hub splines to secure.
9 Relocate the shaft into the hub and refit the backplate (with the handbrake cable hole to the rear). The shaft must be pressed into the bearing in the hub, so support the hub with a tube of suitable diameter. Relocate the nut and tighten to the specified torque. Peen the nut into a shaft spline, using a punch or small chisel, to secure.
10 Locate a new gasket into position on the hub studs and insert the bearing shims (the exact amount as removed) against the differential bearing. Refit the hub unit with the hole in the flange edge downwards (Fig. 5.26). Fit and tighten the retaining nuts to the specified torque. Always use new shakeproof washers with these nuts.

Disc brake models

11 If removed, insert the differential bearing thrust washers – the exact quantity and thickness removed – then lubricate and fit the new oil seal into the hub.
12 Locate the bearing onto the shaft, then the spacer and bush nut. Tighten to the specified torque and peen over the nut to secure. The nut must be free from any roughness on the lock face.
13 Refit the hub unit into position in the differential housing, tapping it into position using a soft mallet. Retighten the bush nut to the specified torque using a strap wrench and a spring balance. Do not damage the nut when tightening it. Lock in position by peening over into a shaft spline groove.

All models

14 Reassembly for both drum and disc brake models is now a reversal of the removal procedure, but note the following:

(a) Tighten all fastenings to the specified torque
(b) Bleed and adjust the brake system as given in Chapter 6 on completion, including handbrake adjustment

13 Fault diagnosis – transmission

Symptom	Reason(s)
Ineffective synchromesh. Jumps out of one or more gears (on drive or overrun)	Worn synchro units Weak lockball springs, worn selector forks or worn gears
Noisy, rough, whining and vibration	Worn bearings and gears Crownwheel and bevel pinion out of adjustment
Difficulty in engaging gear/s	Worn clutch Worn selectors or out of adjustment Excessive or insufficient oil in gearbox

Note: It is sometimes difficult to decide whether it is worthwhile removing and dismantling the gearbox for a fault which may be nothing more than a minor irritant, considering the amount of work and cost involved. Gearboxes which howl, or where the synchromesh can be 'beaten' by a quick gear change, may continue to perform for a long time in this state. A worn gearbox usually needs a complete rebuild to eliminate noise.

Chapter 6 Braking system

For modifications, and information applicable to later models, see Supplement at end of manual

Contents

Specifications

Braking system – general

System type	Hydraulic to all four wheels. Inboard discs or drums at front (according to model and year), drums at rear
Handbrake	Mechanical to front wheels
Hydraulic fluid type:	
All drum brake models	Castrol Girling Universal Brake and Clutch Fluid or equivalent to SAE J 1703
All disc brake models	Castrol LHM or equivalent

Drum brakes

Wheel cylinder bore:	
Front	28.57 mm (1.125 in)
Rear	16.0, 17.5 or 19.0 mm (0.630, 0.689 or 0.748 in)
Drum diameter:	
Front	200 or 220 mm (7.87 or 8.66 in)
Rear	180 mm (7.09 in)
Drum regrind tolerance	+ 2 mm (0.078 in) maximum
Drum ovality	0.1 mm (0.004 in) maximum
Minimum lining thickness	2 mm (0.078 in)

Disc brakes

Disc diameter	244 mm (9.61 in)
Disc thickness:	
New	7 mm (0.275 in)
Minimum after grinding	4 mm (0.157 in)
Maximum disc run-out	0.2 mm (0.008 in)
Caliper piston diameter	42 mm (1.653 in)
Minimum pad thickness	2 mm (0.078 in)

Master cylinder

Bore:	
Drum brake models	20.6 or 22.0 mm (9.81 or 0.87 in)
Disc brake models	17.5 mm (0.69 in)
Pushrod to piston clearance	0.5 mm (0.02 in) maximum

Torque wrench settings

Torque wrench settings	lbf ft	kgf m
Front brake drum nuts (4 studs)	18	2.5
Front brake drum bolts (6 bolts)	32.5	4.5
Caliper assembly bolts	32.5 to 36	4.5 to 5.0
Brake pipe unions	5.8 to 6.5	0.8 to 0.9
Disc-to-driveshaft retaining bolts	32.5 to 36	4.5 to 5.0
Handbrake centre bolts	29	4.0
Handbrake cable locknut	11	1.5
Master cylinder pushrod nut	7 to 18	1.0 to 2.5
Backplate retaining nuts	28 to 30	3.8 to 4.2
Rear hub bearing locknut	252 to 295	35 to 40
Ring nut-rear hub bearing	252 to 295	35 to 40

1 General description

The braking system employed depends on the model concerned. All earlier models had drum brakes front and rear. Later models have disc brakes at the front and retain drum brakes at the rear.

The front brakes on all models are inboard. Disc brakes have airflow ducting for cooling purposes. The brake drums on the front are finned to assist in this respect.

The brakes are hydraulically operated by a master cylinder which is bolted to the bulkhead directly in front of the brake pedal.

The handbrake operates the front brakes only and is cable operated. On disc brake models the disc calipers incorporate separate pads for the foot and hand brakes. On front drum brake models the handbrake operates the brake shoes in the normal manner via a lever connected between the shoes and the cable.

Two types of hydraulic fluid are used: LHM (Liquide Huile Minerale) in cars having disc brakes, and 'ordinary' brake fluid in cars having all-drum brakes. Refer to Section 2 for further details. The two fluids are **not** compatible: use of the incorrect fluid will rapidly damage the rubber seals in the brake hydraulic system. In an emergency, SAE 20 engine oil may be used in place of LHM, but the system must be flushed with the correct fluid as soon as possible thereafter.

Apart from routine maintenance, many of the tasks on the braking system may appear very daunting, but with the right approach should present no more difficulty than a 'normal' car to a novice mechanic. This is mainly due to the inboard front brakes which are not readily accessible. In addition, the manufacturers specify the use of certain special tools; although these tools make the work easier, we were able to overhaul the brakes using tools readily available to the DIY mechanic, and only needed to fabricate one tool. Before starting work on the braking system, therefore, read through the details of the relevant operation to make sure that the necessary tools and materials are available.

2 Routine maintenance

1 Under normal operating conditions the brakes require very little attention, and should therefore need only to be checked over at the intervals specified in Routine Maintenance at the start of the book.

2 The following items are the most important ones in need of regular checks and (where necessary) further attention:

- (a) *Check the hydraulic fluid level in the master cylinder reservoir, and top up as necessary. Frequent topping-up indicates a leak in the system*
- (b) *Inspect the disc brake pads for wear and renew as necessary (where applicable)*
- (c) *Check and adjust the drum brakes as necessary*
- (d) *Check and adjust the handbrake as necessary*
- (e) *Inspect the various hydraulic brake pipes and connections for signs of deterioration and/or damage. Repair or renew as necessary*

3 On models equipped with drum brakes all round it will be necessary to drain and renew the brake fluid every 18 months. Always use the fluid specified.

4 On later Ami and Dyane models fitted with disc brakes on the front, it is not necessary to drain the fluid periodically, but it is essential that when topping up, the specified LHM fluid be used. This green mineral oil is similar to engine oil and has a higher boiling point than 'normal' (synthetic) hydraulic fluid; in addition it is moisture repellent.

5 Never interchange the fluid types in the two systems as the seals are designed specifically to be used with the prescribed type of fluid. *Seals for systems using synthetic brake fluid are colour-coded red or white; systems using LHM are colour-coded green.*

6 When cleaning brake hydraulic components, use methylated spirit or synthetic brake fluid on front drum brake systems and petrol or LHM on disc brake systems.

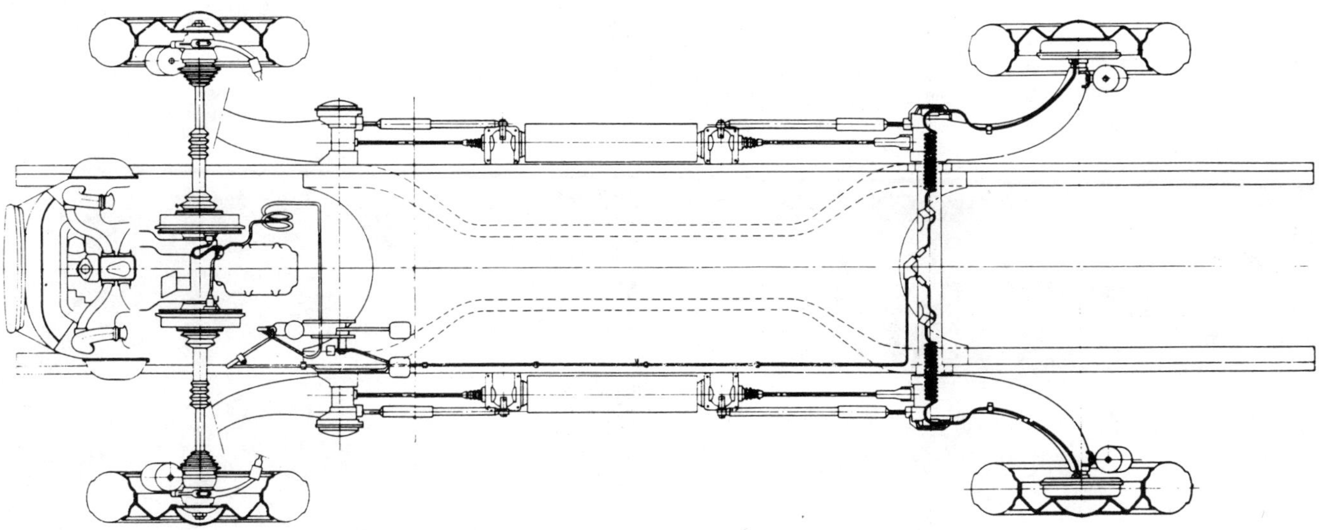

Fig. 6.1 Braking system layout – LHD with drum brakes all round. RHD is similar (Sec 1)

3 Drum brakes – adjustment

Front

1 Park the vehicle on firm level ground and place chocks under the rear wheels. Release the handbrake. There is no need to jack up the front of the car as there is sufficient play in the driveshaft joints to check for freedom of rotation.
2 Working from above and down through the engine compartment, rotate a brake drum and using a 14 mm open-ended spanner, turn the adjuster cam on the brake backplate in the direction of the arrow (Fig. 6.2).
3 When the drum is felt to 'drag', the shoes are in contact with the inside of the drum. The adjuster can then be unscrewed just sufficiently to allow the drum to rotate freely.
4 Retighten the adjuster so that the drum can rotate freely but the brake shoes are just dragging on the inside. *Never complete the adjustment by backing off the adjuster.*
5 If the adjuster is found to be stiff, apply a light coating of penetrating oil to help free it. Do not overlubricate it as the oil may find its way onto the linings.
6 Repeat this operation for the other brake shoe and then on the other front brake. When complete, pump the brake pedal several times and then recheck the rotational freedom of the drums by pushing the car forwards. If binding occurs at any point, readjust and recheck at the position where binding occurs.

Rear brakes

7 Apply the handbrake and chock a rear wheel on one side. Jack up and raise the opposite side at the rear. Make secure with an axle or chassis stand.
8 The adjustment can now be made in a similar fashion to that described for the front brakes. Rotate the wheel and turn the adjuster accordingly, tightening until the shoes are just felt to drag.
9 Repeat the procedure on the opposite rear wheel brake.
10 If the drums contain a lot of brake dust it can sometimes be difficult to judge when the brakes are binding due to the dust on the linings. To remove the dust, tap around the drum with a soft-headed mallet and extract the dust using a vacuum cleaner with the nozzle located between the drum and backplate. *Do not blow the dust out.* Asbestos is extremely harmful when inhaled.

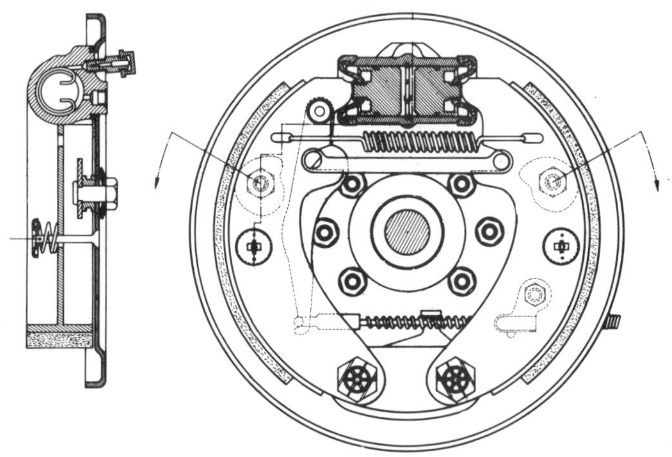

Fig. 6.2 Front drum brake layout. Arrows indicate direction of adjustment to take up wear (Sec 3)

Fig. 6.3 Rear brake adjustment. Arrows indicate direction of adjustment to take up wear (Sec 3)

4.4 One of the handbrake cable adjusters – drum brake models

4.9 The disc brake adjuster for the handbrake. Note adjuster nut and locknut (arrowed)

4 Handbrake – adjustment

1 Before making any adjustments to the handbrake check that the front brakes are correctly adjusted. Where disc brakes are fitted the pads must be above the specified minimum thickness.
2 Raise and securely support the front of the vehicle so that the front wheels are clear of the ground. Chock the rear wheels.

Drum brake models

3 Fully release the handbrake and then pull it on three notches.
4 The handbrake cable tension is now adjusted by means of two wing nuts which are situated at the rear of the gearbox on the chassis crossmember (photo). Increase the tension by screwing up the wing nuts until the brake shoes are felt to bind on the drums when they are tuned.
5 Pull the handbrake lever to the fifth notch and try turning the brake drums. They should be fully locked in position.
6 Now release the handbrake lever and check that the drums are free to rotate without binding. Lower the car to complete.

Disc brake models

7 Adjustment to the handbrake on disc brake models is achieved by moving the eccentrics to the prescribed setting.
8 Disconnect and remove the flexible heater ducts.
9 Loosen the eccentric securing screws, and then loosen the cable lock and adjuster nuts (photo).
10 Set the eccentrics with notches so that the notches are at the top. Eccentrics without notches should be set to give the pads maximum clearance from the disc. Check that the operating levers are making contact with the stop lugs on the caliper housing.
11 Rotate the eccentrics in opposing directions (the left one clockwise, the right one anti-clockwise) until the pads just contact the disc. This contact must occur at the postion of maximum disc run-out – turn the wheel to check.
12 Retighten the eccentric securing screws – ensuring that the eccentrics do not rotate when tightening. This is difficult with some types of eccentric and, in the absence of the Citroën tool 2115-T, something will have to be made up to fit the 24 mm eccentrics.
13 Now check the cable adjustment. Turn the adjuster nuts on the cable end of each caliper so that when the handbrake operating lever is applied, the brakes start to operate on the third notch and are fully applied on the fifth.
14 When adjusted correctly the lengths of the threads beyond the locknuts on the right and left-hand should be the same to within 5 mm (0.196 in). Tighten the locknuts to secure.
15 Operate and release the handbrake cable a few times to check that the handbrake operation is effective.
16 Lower the front of the vehicle when complete.

5 Bleeding the hydraulic system

Note: *Before topping up or bleeding the brake hydraulic system, ensure that you have the correct brake fluid (see Specifications and Section 2).*
1 If any of the hydraulic components in the braking system have been removed or disconnected, or if the fluid level in the master cylinder has been allowed to fall appreciably, it is inevitable that air will have been introduced into the system. The removal of all this air from the hydraulic system is essential if the brakes are to function correctly, and the process of removing it is known as bleeding.
2 There are a number of one-man, do-it-yourself, brake bleeding kits currently available from motor accessory shops. It is recommended that one of these kits should be used wherever possible as they greatly simplify the bleeding operation and also reduce the risk of expelled air or fluid being drawn back into the system.
3 If one of these kits is not available then it will be necessary to gather together a clean jar and a suitable length of clear plastic tubing which is a tight fit over the bleed screw, and also to engage the help of an assistant.
4 Before commencing the bleeding operation, check that all rigid pipes and flexible hoses (if fitted) are in good condition and that all hydraulic unions are tight. Take care not to allow hydraulic fluid to come into contact with the vehicle paintwork, otherwise the finish will be seriously damaged. Wash off any spilled fluid immediately with cold water.
5 If hydraulic fluid has been lost from the master cylinder, due to a leak in the system, ensure that the cause is traced and rectified before proceeding further or a serious malfunction of the braking system may occur.

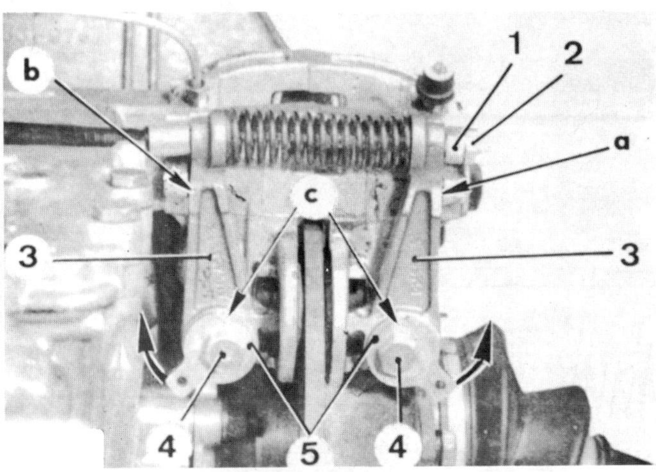

Fig. 6.4 Handbrake adjustment – disc brake models (Sec 4)

1 Cable adjuster nut
2 Cable adjuster locknut
3 Actuating arms
4 Eccentric securing screws
5 Eccentrics
a Stop lug
b Stop lug
c Eccentric notches

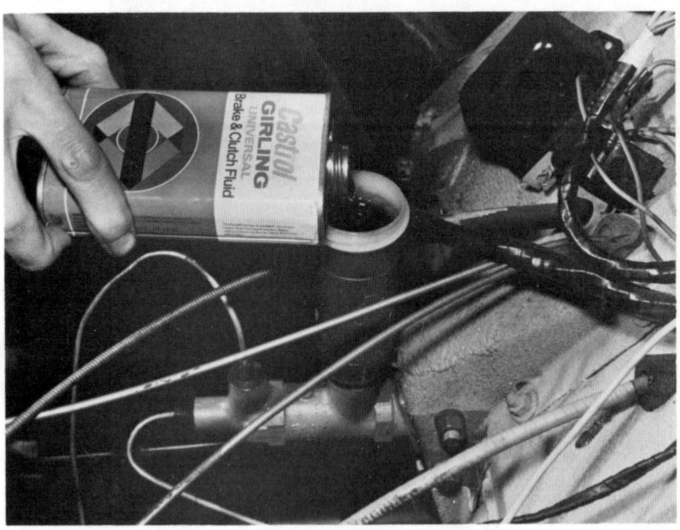

5.7 Topping up the master cylinder (drum brake system – using J 1703 fluid)

6 To bleed the system, clean the area around the bleed screw at the wheel cylinder to be bled. On cars with disc brakes there is only one bleed nipple at the front, on the top of the left-hand caliper. If the hydraulic system has only been partially disconnected and suitable precautions were taken to prevent further loss of fluid, it should only be necessary to bleed that part of the system. However, if the entire system is to be bled, start at the wheel furthest away from the master cylinder.

7 Remove the master cylinder filler cap and top up the reservoir (photo). Periodically check the fluid level during the bleeding operation and top up as necessary.

8 If a one-man brake bleeding kit is being used, connect the outlet tube to the bleed screw and then open the screw half a turn. If possible position the unit so that it can be viewed from the car, then depress the brake pedal to the floor and slowly release it. The one-way valve in the kit will prevent dispelled air from returning to the system at the end of each stroke. Repeat this operation until clean hydraulic fluid, free from air bubbles can be seen coming through the tube. Now tighten the bleed screw and remove the outlet tube.

9 If a one-man brake bleeding kit is not available, connect one end of the plastic tubing to the bleed screw and immerse the other end in the jam jar containing sufficient clean hydraulic fluid to keep the end of the tube submerged. Open the bleed screw half a turn and have your assistant depress the brake pedal to the floor and then slowly release it. Tighten the bleed screw at the end of each downstroke to prevent expelled air and fluid from being drawn back into the system. Repeat this operation until clean hydraulic fluid, free from air bubbles, can be seen coming through the tube. Now tighten the bleed screw and remove the plastic tube (photos).

10 If the entire system is being bled the procedures described above should now be repeated at each wheel, finishing at the wheel nearest to the master cylinder. Do not forget to recheck the fluid level in the master cylinder at regular intervals and top up as necessary.

11 When completed, recheck the fluid level in the master cylinder, top up if necessary and refit the cap. Check the 'feel' of the brake pedal which should be firm and free from any 'sponginess' which would indicate air still present in the system.

12 Discard any expelled hydraulic fluid as it is likely to be contaminated with moisture, air and dirt which makes it unsuitable for further use.

6 Brake hoses and pipes – inspection, removal and refitting

1 Inspect the condition of the flexible hoses (if fitted). If they are swollen, damaged or chafed they must be renewed. Rigid brake pipes must be renewed if corroded.

2 Wipe the top of the brake master cylinder reservoir and unscrew the cap. Place a piece of polythene sheet over the top of the reservoir and refit the cap. This is to stop hydraulic fluid syphoning out during subsequent operations.

3 Always use new flexible hose seals when overhauling a section of the hydraulic system.

5.9a Bleeding the rear brakes

5.9b Bleeding the front brakes

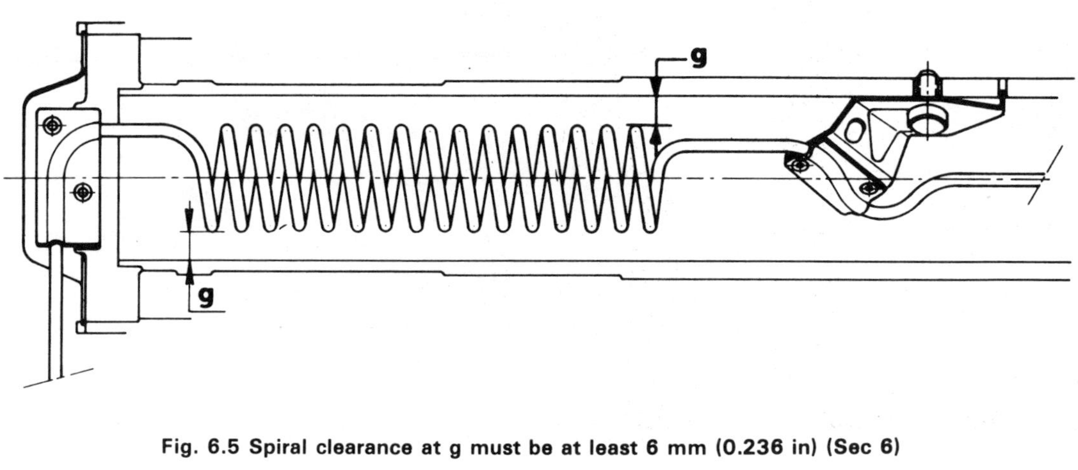

Fig. 6.5 Spiral clearance at g must be at least 6 mm (0.236 in) (Sec 6)

Front brake hose

4 Early models have a flexible type front brake hose (later models use rigid pipes). To remove a hose, wipe the unions and bracket free of dust, and undo the union nut from the metal pipe end.

5 Withdraw the metal clip securing the hose to the bracket on top of the gearbox (where applicable) and detach the hose from the bracket (photo). Unscrew the hose from the wheel cylinder/caliper.

6 Refitting is the reverse of the removal procedure, but ensure that the hose is connected at the wheel cylinder end first. On completion, the front brakes must be bled of air, as described in the previous Section.

Rear brake pipe (spiral tube type through crossmember)

7 To replace the spiral tube from the rear three-way adaptor to the brake drum you will first need to remove the petrol tank (see Chapter 2).

8 Unscrew and loosen the clip retaining the circular cover on the forward end of the rear suspension arm and prise the cover free (photo).

9 Unscrew the pipe union nut to the wheel cylinder (photo) and disconnect the pipe.

10 Unscrew the bolt which secures the 3-way connector to the crossmember (photo).

11 Remove the spiral tube retaining nut in the crossmember, and the bolt from the two-way screwed union.

12 Prise free the rubber bushes from the three-way connector to the crossmember and then unscrew the respective union nuts as applicable. Withdraw the spiral tube and three-way connector as required.

13 Refitting is a reversal of the removal procedure, but note the following points:

- *(a) To prevent the union nut from sliding down the tube when fitting, temporarily retain the nut in position with sticky tape*
- *(b) Do not fully tighten any of the retaining nuts and bolts until the tubes are fully located*
- *(c) Always use a new joint seal of the correct type at the wheel cylinder-to-tube connection*
- *(d) When in position the spirals of the feed tube must have a clearance of 6 mm (0.236 in) between the outside diameter at the spiral and the inside diameter of the crossmember. This is shown in Fig. 6.5 and can be checked using a bolt of suitable diameter and length*
- *(e) Use a new retaining clip to retain the end cover in position*
- *(f) Top up and bleed the brake hydraulic system and check for any signs of leakage around the connections*

Rear brake hoses (flexible type)

14 On models built up until 1972 flexible hoses are fitted. The fitting instructions are as for the front brake hoses. Always use new seals of the correct type and ensure that the pipes have sufficient clearance for the chassis and suspension components.

6.5 The T-piece connector on top of the gearbox

6.8 The rear suspension arm cover and hydraulic pipe

6.9 The pipe to the rear wheel cylinder union (bleed screw arrowed)

6.10 The three-way connector

7 Brake pedal clearance – adjustment

1 The adjustment of the brake pedal should be maintained in accordance with the appropriate diagram according to model and year of production.

2 The pedal height must be measured between the centre of the upper surface of the pedal pad and the metal surface of the floor (carpet removed).

3 If necessary, adjust the pedal height by bending the stop bracket above the pedal arm.

4 The pedal free movement should be adjusted by releasing the locknut and rotating the pushrod.

5 Finally adjust the stoplight switch so that it completes the stoplight circuit immediately the foot pedal is depressed; refer to Section 8.

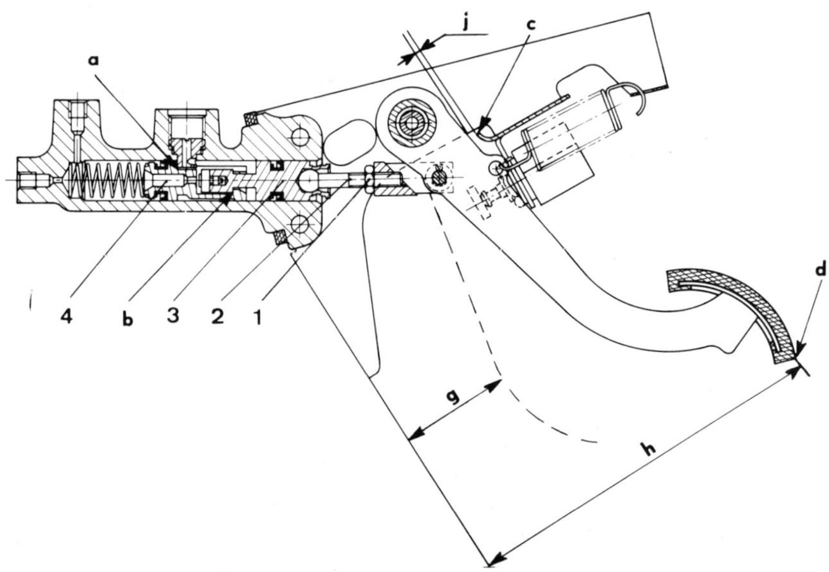

Fig. 6.6 Brake pedal and master cylinder (Sec 7)

1 Locknut
2 Pushrod
3 Piston
4 Piston
a Piston stop
b Piston stop
c Stop bracket
d Pedal pad
g Pedal travel
h Pedal height
j Free movement

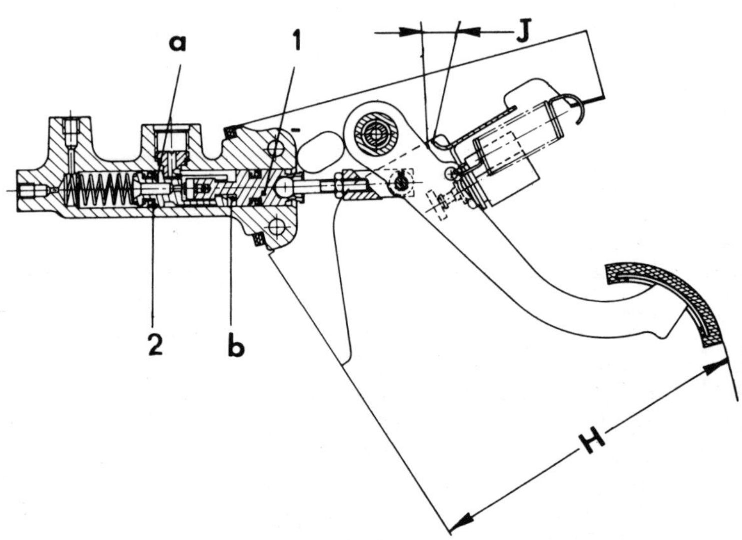

Fig. 6.7 Pedal height setting diagram (Sec 7)
Ami models September 1969 to October 1971

1 Piston seal
2 Piston seal
a Piston stop
b Piston stop
H = 122.5 to 127.5 mm (4.8 to 5.0 in)
J = 2.0 mm (0.08 in)

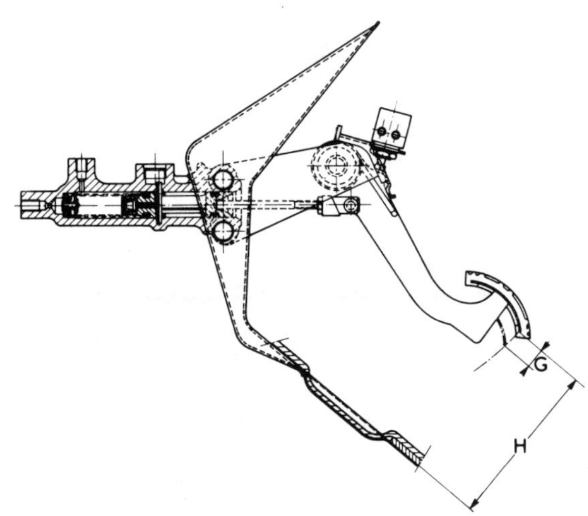

Fig. 6.8 Pedal height setting diagram (Sec 7)

2CV models
Dyane models up to 1976
Ami models up to September 1969
G Free movement = 5.0 mm (0.20 in)
H = 125.0 to 135.0 mm (4.9 to 5.3 in)
Dyane models July 1977 on
G = 5.0 mm (0.20 in)
H = 139.0 to 147.0 mm (5.5 to 5.8 in)

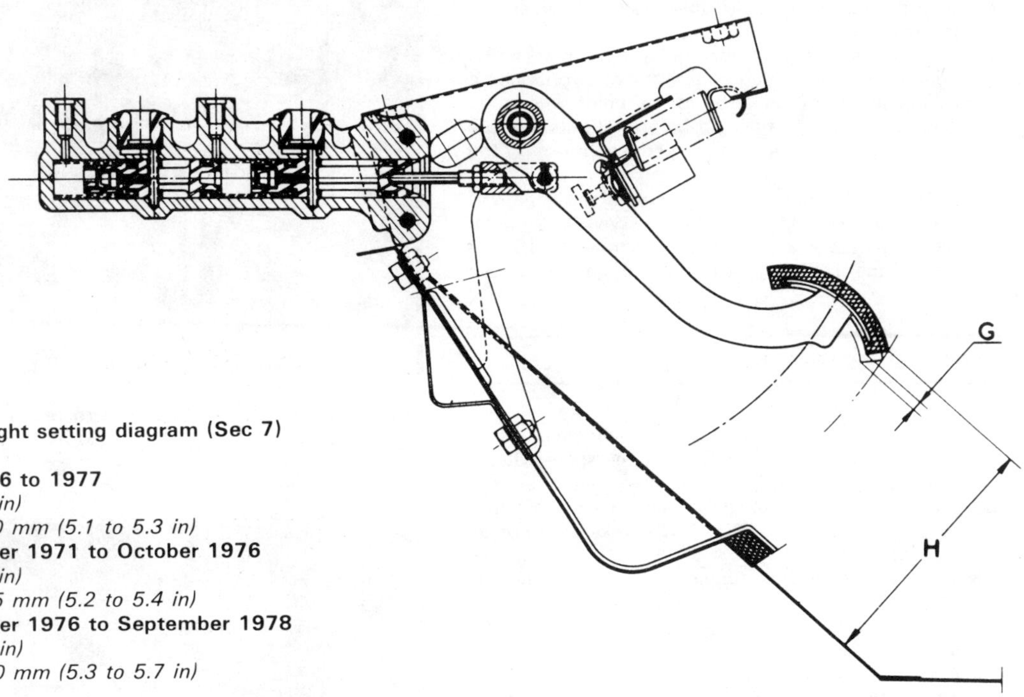

Fig. 6.9 Pedal height setting diagram (Sec 7)

Dyane models 1976 to 1977
G = 5.0 mm (0.20 in)
H = 129.0 to 134.0 mm (5.1 to 5.3 in)
Ami models October 1971 to October 1976
G = 5.0 mm (0.20 in)
H = 132.5 to 137.5 mm (5.2 to 5.4 in)
Ami models October 1976 to September 1978
G = 5.0 mm (0.20 in)
H = 135.0 to 145.0 mm (5.3 to 5.7 in)

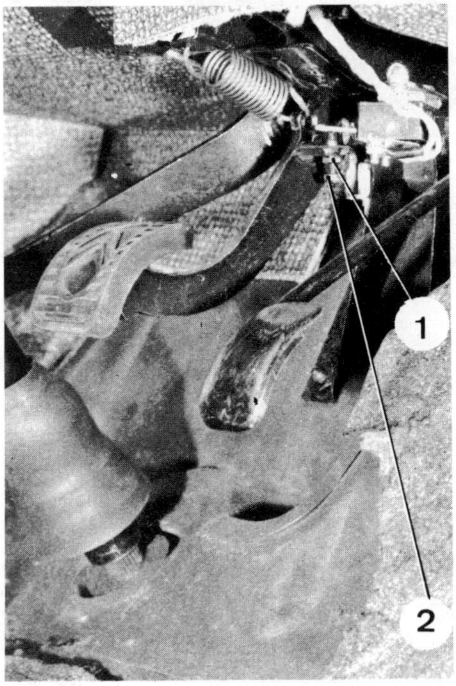

Fig. 6.10 The stoplight switch (Sec 8)

1 *Locknut* 2 *Adjuster screw*

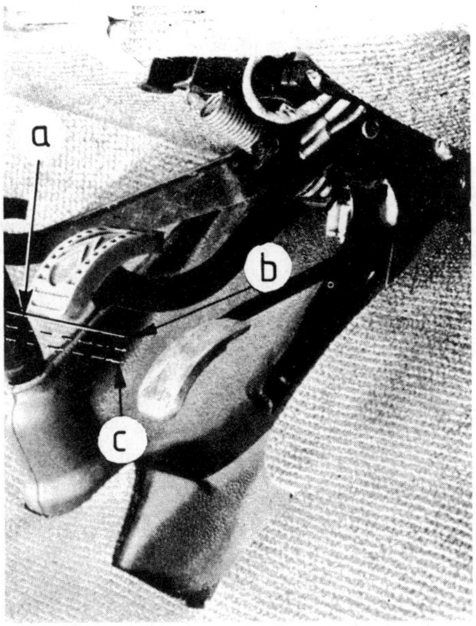

Fig. 6.11 Stoplight switch operation (Sec 8)

a *Resting position – switch off*
b *1.5 mm (0.06 in) – switch off*
c *10 mm (0.4 in) – switch on*

8 Stoplight switch – contact adjustment

1 First check that the pedal height and free play clearances are correct as described previously.
2 *On front drum brake models,* turn the ignition on, loosen the switch locknut and undo the adjuster screw until the stoplights come on. Now screw the adjuster screw inwards to the point where the lights go out, and then a further one full turn before retightening the locknut. Recheck the stoplight operation on the pedal and turn off the ignition.
3 *On front disc brake models,* check that with a pedal movement of 1.5 mm (0.06 in) minimum the stop lights do not come on (ignition on). The lights should illuminate when the pedal has travelled 10 mm (0.4 in). If not, adjust the switch bracket to obtain the above requirements.

9 Disc pads – removal and renewal

Footbrake pads

1 Place chocks under the wheels and release the handbrake.
2 Raise the bonnet and where necessary remove the spare wheel.
3 Loosen the retaining band and remove the flexible heater ducting.
4 Using a pipe grip wrench or similar implement, press the brake pads away from the disc on each side (Fig. 6.12). Take care not to damage the disc wear faces.
5 Use a screwdriver and lever the double pad retaining spring down and away from the pads, which can then be removed for inspection or renewal (photo). On Ami models lever the spring upwards and remove the pads from below.
6 When the pads are removed clean and measure them for wear, and renew if necessary. Always renew pads in complete axle sets, even if only one pad is worn to the limit.
7 Refitting of the pads is a reversal of the removal procedure. Push the pads fully into position and check that the retaining spring is fully located in the notch of the lockplate.
8 On completion apply the brake pedal a number of times to ensure that the pedal travel is normal and the brakes are fully operational. Avoid fierce braking until the new pads have bedded in.

Handbrake pads

9 Fully release the handbrake control lever and place chocks under the rear wheels. Raise the vehicle at the front and support with axle stands.
10 Although the pads on Ami models can be removed and refitted without having to withdraw the caliper, the job will be found easier if the caliper is removed, as described in Section 10. On Dyane models the calipers are reversed and it is therefore possible to extract the pads without removing the unit; proceed as follows:

(a) Loosen the handbrake cable locknuts and adjuster nuts. Unscrew and remove the eccentric retaining bolts together with the eccentrics and sleeves (if loose). When fitted remove the anti-rattle springs

(b) Extract the pads from the caliper, using a piece of wire bent accordingly and inserted between the disc and pad

11 If the caliper unit on Ami models was removed, the pads can now be extracted and the eccentric retaining bolts loosened.
12 Refitting is a reversal of the removal procedure. Insert the new pads into position in the caliper unit and check that the anti-rattle springs (if fitted) are located correctly. A piece of rubber is inserted between the pads to retain them whilst the caliper is out of the vehicle.
13 Refit the brake pads and top up and bleed the hydraulic system (Ami). If the caliper was removed, adjust the eccentrics and the handbrake mechanism, see Section 4, and lower the vehicle. Apply the brakes a few times to centralise the pads.

10 Disc brake caliper unit – removal, overhaul and refitting

Removal

1 Disconnect the battery earth terminal lead.
2 Detach and remove the flexible heater duct for access to the right-hand brake unit.
3 Loosen the starter motor securing bolts and withdraw the motor rearwards. Allow it to rest out of the way with its leads still connected.

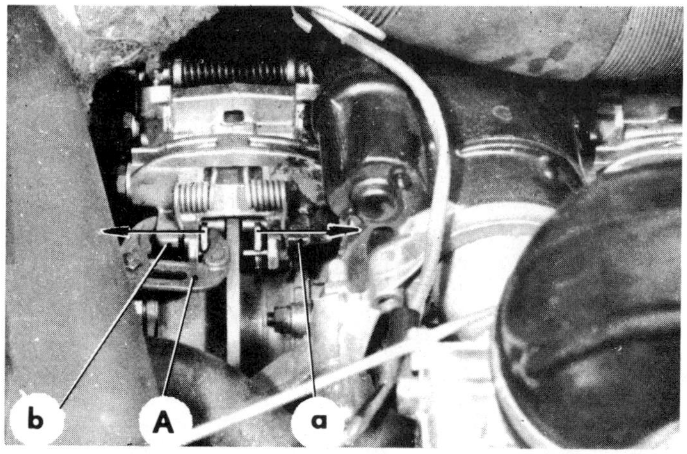

Fig. 6.12 Using pipe grips (A) to press the pads away from the disc. Use bosses (a) and (b) as leverage points (Sec 9)

9.5 Levering the pad retainer to release the pads

Fig. 6.13 The disc caliper unit (Sec 9)

1	*Pads*	*3*	*Eccentric bolts*
2	*Eccentrics*	*A*	*Rubber spacer*

Fig. 6.14 Check the anti-rattle springs (5) (Sec 9)

Fig. 6.15 Caliper securing details (Sec 10)

7 Rear securing nut
8 Handbrake cable locknut
9 Handbrake cable adjuster nut
10 Tube support
11 Rear securing bolt
12 Front securing bolt

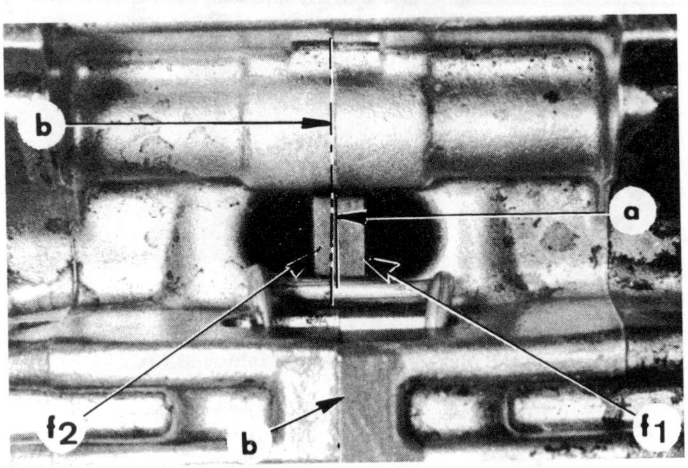

Fig. 6.16 Check the caliper alignment (Sec 10)

a Disc centre-line
b Caliper joint line
f1 Disc edge
f2 Disc edge

4 Extract the footbrake pads from the caliper, see Section 9.
5 Unscrew and detach the respective hydraulic fluid pipes from the unit concerned. Once the pipes are disconnected, plug them to prevent leakage of fluid and the ingress of dirt.
6 Unscrew the unit rear retaining nut and extract the bolt.
7 Loosen and unscrew the forward retaining screw about half a turn and then pivot the caliper unit forwards. Reinsert the rear bolt and locate its nut to clamp the caliper halves together and prevent fluid leakage.
8 Withdraw the front bolt, detach the handbrake cable (from the left side) and lift the caliper unit clear. Take care not to allow the handbrake pads to fall out.

Overhaul

9 To dismantle the caliper unit, remove the rear retaining bolt and separate the two halves of the unit.
10 Apply compressed air to the hydraulic pipe connections and carefully blow the pistons from their bores. Keep them separate.
11 Clean the components in petrol or LHM (**not** normal brake hydraulic fluid, alcohol or methylated spirit).
12 Examine the pistons and bores for scoring, corrosion or any signs of damage and renew any defective components accordingly. New seals must always be fitted on reassembly.
13 Lubricate the new seals and pistons when fitting with some LHM fluid. Do not under any circumstances use any other type of hydrulic fluid or the seals will deteriorate very quickly.
14 Check both the footbrake and handbrake pad thicknesses and renew if necessary.
15 Before refitting the caliper unit, check the disc run-out using a dial gauge if available. If the disc is badly scored, or the run-out exceeds that specified, then the disc must be removed and reground or renewed as applicable.

Refitting

16 When refitting the caliper unit, the two half housings can be clamped together by fitting the rear retaining bolt into position.
17 Check that the mating faces of the caliper and gearbox housing are clean and reposition the caliper unit together with the packing piece originally fitted. If a new caliper unit is fitted then its position must be checked in relation to the disc when the unit is fully assembled.
18 Insert the front retaining bolt to retain the damper in position, tighten the bolt fully and then unscrew it half a turn.
19 Refit the handbrake pads.
20 Remove the rear bolt and nut and pivot the unit downwards to the rear to align the bolt hole. Refit the rear bolt (with plain washer under its head).
21 Check that the packing piece is correctly positioned and then tighten the front and rear caliper retaining bolts and nut to the specified torque.
22 To check that the caliper unit is correctly positioned, scribe a line in the centre of the disc outer edge and see if the caliper half casing joint line is in alignment with it (Fig. 6.16). If the alignment is not within 0.5 mm (0.019 in) then the caliper must be adjusted accordingly by adding or subtracting packing pieces.
23 Refit the footbrake pads (Section 9).
24 Check the adjustment of the handbrake pads and reconnect the handbrake cable, which can then be adjusted (see Section 4).
25 Reconnect the respective hydraulic pipes and use new seals where applicable. Only use seals colour coded green.
26 Top up and bleed the hydraulic system (Section 5).
27 Refit the starter motor and the heater ducting. Reconnect the earth terminal lead to complete.

11 Brake disc – removal and refitting

1 Raise the vehicle at the front and support it with axle stands.
2 Refer to Section 10 and remove the caliper unit.
3 Unscrew and remove the driveshaft flange to disc/transmission drive hub bolts. Separate the driveshaft from the hub and remove the disc.
4 Refitting is a reversal of the removal process. Tighten the retaining bolts to the specified torque, but before refitting the caliper unit, check that the disc run-out is within the limits specified.
5 Check the run-out using a dial gauge or fixed bracket and feeler

gauges mounted from the gearbox. Should the run-out exceed the figure quoted, relocate the disc and check again. There are six possible positions: if they all fail to meet the required tolerance, then the disc must be renewed.

12 Front drum brake shoes – inspection, removal and refitting

1 Due to the relatively poor accessibility of the front drum brakes, it may be worthwhile to remove the wing panels. Depending on your particular model, the extra time taken to achieve this may well be saved later due to ease of access. As a guide the 2CV wing panels can be removed in about 15 minutes, the Dyane wings (complete with wheel arches) in about 20 minutes and the Ami wings in about 30 to 40 minutes. Information on removing the wings is given in Chapter 11.
2 If the drums are being removed for inspection purposes only then it may not be worth removing the wings. However if any dismantling is to be done, their removal will be most beneficial.
3 Remove the spare wheel and disconnect the battery earth lead.
4 Prior to dismantling the driveshaft from the hub/drum unit wipe them clean and also the surrounding components. Cleanliness is essential when working on brake or driveshaft components. Mark the drum/driveshaft hub to ensure original alignment on reassembly
5 Release the handbrake and put chocks under the rear wheels.
6 Back off the brake adjuster cams on the backplates to release the shoes from the drums.
7 On earlier models unscrew and remove the four drum/driveshaft flange retaining nuts. Separate the driveshaft and withdraw the drum.
8 On models fitted with a double crosspin driveshaft CV joint, unscrew and remove the grease nipple from the driveshaft and detach the gaiter retaining rings. Slide the gaiter along the shaft from the transmission followed by the cover. Unscrew and remove the four drum retaining nuts; withdraw the drum and cover.
9 On models fitted with the ball type velocity joints (Rzeppa), unscrew and remove the six driveshaft flange-to-drum retaining bolts. Rotate the driveshaft to gain access to the bolts. Separate the driveshaft by compressing it (photo) and remove the drum.
10 It may be necessary to bend back the engine cooling cowling lug in order to remove the drums. The exhaust clamp should also be loosened and swivelled out of the way.
11 With the drums removed, the brake components can be cleaned and inspected (photo). Be careful not to get any grease or oil onto the brake linings.
12 The brake shoe linings normally wear faster on the leading shoes. Check the lining thicknesses; if any one is below 2 mm, the set of four shoes must be renewed. It may be possible to get the existing shoes relined by a local dealer so, before removing them, mark their relative positions for correct location on reassembly. If relining is not possible, a set of exchange shoes can be obtained from the Citroën dealer.
13 If the linings are found to be in good condition they can be deglazed by rubbing with some emery cloth. Any grease or fluid which may have been embedded in the linings may prove difficult to remove, but a cloth soaked in methylated spirit will erase most of the surface deposits. Badly soaked linings must be renewed.
14 If the wheel cylinder is obviously leaking or looks to be in need of attention, now is the time to do it! Refer to Section 17 for overhaul instructions.
15 Before removing the brake shoes take note of how they are located and the correct location of the return springs.
16 To separate the shoes, rotate the adjuster cam bolts and loosen the handbrake adjuster wing nuts, unscrewing them to the end of the thread.
17 Removal of the brake shoes is much easier if the wheel cylinder is removed. Unscrew and detach the brake pipe at its union from the end of the pipe.
18 Unscrew and remove the two wheel cylinder retaining bolts and withdraw the cylinder. Place an elastic band round the cylinder lengthwise to retain the pistons in position.
19 Adjust the cam bolts to close the shoes.
20 Using a pair of needle nose pliers, engage them in the holes of the shoe retainer washer (photo), then press and turn through 90° to disengage the washer and spring from the pin (photo). Note that the front steady pin must be removed with care or it may fall into the clutch housing. A piece of folded cardboard can be wedged behind the backplate to retain the pin in position. Alternatively an elastic band can be used to retain the pin.
21 Extract the eccentric locknut split pins, unscrew the nuts and remove with the flat washers (photo).
22 Unscrew and remove the eccentrics. They may be corroded in position; if so, a little penetrating oil will help.
23 Pull the shoes off the eccentric bolts. The trailing shoe can then be

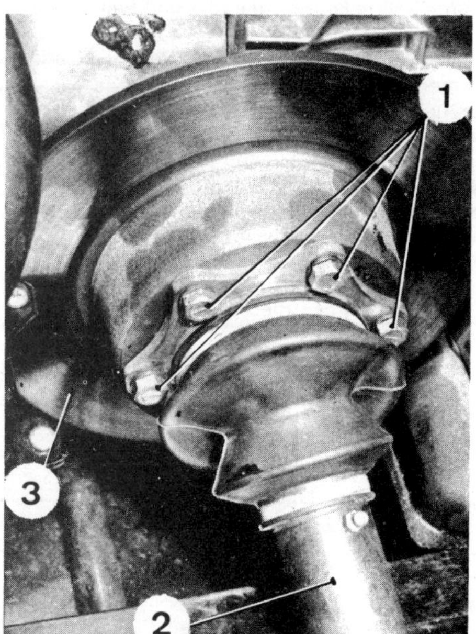

Fig. 6.17 Separate the driveshaft from the hub (Sec 11)

1 *Flange bolts*
2 *Driveshaft*
3 *Brake disc*

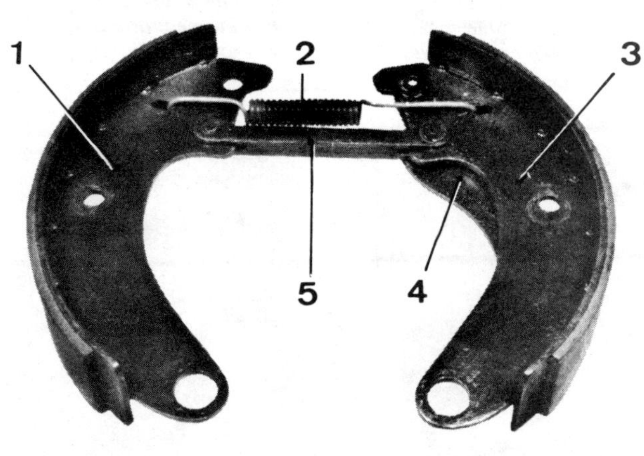

Fig. 6.18 Right-hand front brake shoes removed (Sec 12)

1 *Trailing shoe*
2 *Return spring*
3 *Leading shoe*
4 *Handbrake lever*
5 *Interconnecting lever*

12.9 Detach the driveshaft (engine removed for clarity)

12.11 Clean the shoes and associated brake components for inspection

12.20a Press and twist the washer ...

12.20b ... and release the washer and spring

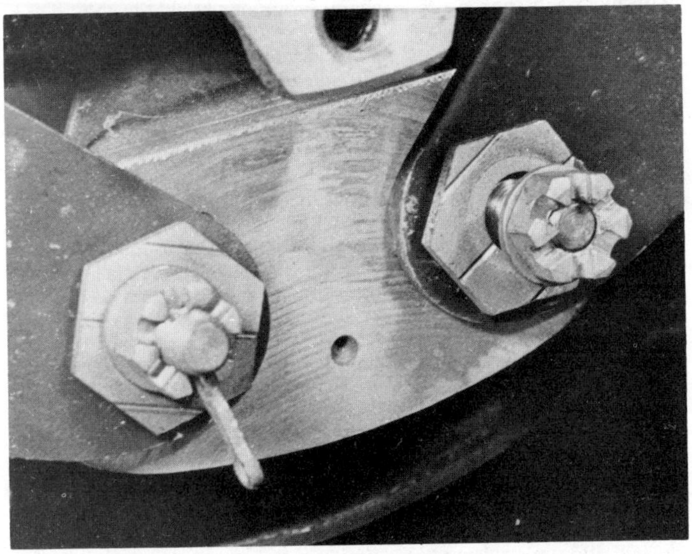

12.21 Remove the split pins, nuts and flat washers

12.28 Locate the handbrake cable

12.29 Fitting the trailing shoe – return spring connected at the top. This is easier if the wheel cylinder is fitted afterwards

12.37 Simple tool fabricated to centralize the brake shoes

12.39 Retain the eccentric in the set position and align the locknut to the nearest split pin hole to secure

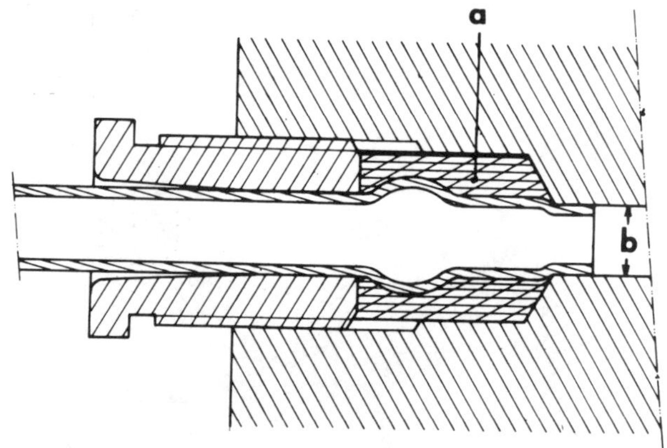

Fig. 6.19 Seal (a) must be fitted so that tip of pipe enters bore (b) (Sec 12)

removed and the return spring can be unhooked from the leading shoe. Pull the leading shoe forward, unhook the handbrake cable and remove the shoe.

24 Before fitting the new shoes, clean the backplate assembly and the brake drum. Clean and check the eccentrics.

25 Check that the respective fittings are secure and in good condition. In particular ensure that the handbrake operating lever assemblies are free to pivot and also check that the eccentrics fit the holes in the new brake shoes. During assembly, do not allow any oil or grease to be smeared onto the new lining surface areas.

26 If the brake drum shoe contact surface area has been badly scored or rusted, the drums can be reground providing the maximum allowable amount is not exceeded. Otherwise, deglaze the brake shoe contact area with emery cloth.

27 As the components are assembled, apply a small amount of PBC or Copaslip to those items with moving contact faces such as the eccentrics, cams and handbrake levers.

28 Commence assembly by engaging the handbrake cable onto the lever of the leading shoe (photo).

29 Attach the return spring to the shoes and relocate the trailing shoe (photo). Make certain that the horizontal handbrake link arm is fully engaged in both shoes.

30 Relocate the eccentrics into position on the bottom pivot pins and locate with the shoes. Fit and provisionally tighten the locknuts (with flat washers).

31 Now turn the cam adjusters to expand the shoes.

32 If removed, the wheel cylinder can now be refitted and secured with bolts and shakeproof washers. Provisionally tighten the bolts at this stage.

33 Insert the shoe steady pins and relocate the springs and slot washers. Rotate the washers through 90° to lock in position.

34 The brake shoes must be centralized to prevent uneven wear and brake squeal.

35 Back off the adjuster cams so that the drum can be located and temporarily secure it in position. On models fitted with ball type constant velocity joints on the driveshafts fit only three of the bolts, with 7 mm spacers (or large nuts) under the heads. The spacers temporarily take the place of the driveshaft flange coupling.

36 Rotate the adjuster cam of the rear brake shoe until it is felt to just make contact with the drum (rotate the drum as the cam adjustment is taken up).

37 With the rear brake shoe set in the required position, carefully remove the brake drum. You will now need to buy, borrow or fabricate a centralizing tool. The official Citroën tool is numbered 3570-T. We manufactured our own and this is shown in the accompanying photo. As can be seen it consists of a piece of flat mild steel, slotted at one end and drilled at the other, and with a crank in the middle sufficient to offset the difference in levels between the axle hub flange and brake shoe outer edge. An old alternator or dynamo adjusting strap suitably modified, will serve admirably. Attached to the hub by as many driveshaft/drum retaining bolts, washers and spacers as necessary, the tool is set at right angles to the brake shoe and has an index screw adjusted within the slot to contact the face of the brake shoe lining.

38 With the index screw touching the outer contact face of the linings, rotate the axle hub and adjust the shoes by means of the cam adjusters on the backplate and the eccentrics at the bottom to enable the index screw to touch the linings through a complete turn.
39 When this has been achieved, retain the eccentrics in position and tighten the locknuts, loosen to the nearest split pin hole and insert new pins to secure (photo).
40 Recheck that the shoes are still centralized and then remove the special tool.
41 Slacken off the adjuster cams, refit the brake drum and connect up the driveshaft.
42 Extract the plug from the brake hose and reconnect it to the cylinder using a new seal of the correct type. With the seal fitted the tube should protrude by 2 mm (0.078 in) and this then enables correct centering when the tube is fitted into the union. Do not overtighten the retaining nut or the seal will distort, causing leakage.
43 Top up the hydraulics and bleed the brakes (Section 5), adjust the footbrakes (Section 3) and handbrake (Section 4).
44 Loosen the wheel cylinder retaining bolts slightly and then operate the footbrake a few times to centralize the wheel cylinder. Retighten the bolts whilst the brake is applied by an assistant.

13 Rear drum brakes – removal, inspection and refitting

1 Before attempting to dismantle the rear brakes, note that the rear hub bearing is incorporated into the brake drum. The removal of the bearing required certain special tools, see Chapter 12 for details: if it is thought that the bearing renewal is necessary, it may be best to entrust the job to your dealer.
2 If it is only wished to gain access to the brakes, a 44 mm ($1\frac{3}{4}$ in AF) socket spanner and a long extension bar will be required for undoing and tightening the hub nut. The nut has to be tightened to a very high torque on reassembly (see Specifications), so a torque wrench of appropriate range will also be needed. The hub grease cups are usually renewed as it is difficult to get them off undamaged.
3 Apply the handbrake, jack up the car on one side at the rear and support securely.
4 Remove the roadwheel.
5 Slacken off the brake adjusters.
6 Lever the hub grease cup from its housing. The easiest way to do this is to pierce the cup with a screwdriver or chisel; obviously a new cup will be needed on reassembly (part No D 42298).
7 The hub nut is now accessible. Relieve the peened section of the nut flange.
8 Fit the 44 mm socket on the hub nut and unscrew it. Considerable pressure will be required: make sure the car is firmly supported, and wedge a wheel chock between the suspension arm and the floor panel to prevent movement (photo).
9 The brake drum can now be removed from the hub, either by judicious levering or by refitting the wheel and pulling on that. Remember that the drum is made of cast iron and will crack or shatter if struck hard.
10 With the drum removed, inspect the brake shoes as described for the front brakes (photo).
11 If the brake shoes are to be removed, prise the U-shaped spring from the holes in the brake shoes (photo). Older cars may have a coil spring instead of a U-spring.
12 Press and twist each shoe steady pin slot washer and withdraw with the coil spring.
13 Bend back the lockwasher tabs and unscrew the lower shoe pivot nuts. Remove the nuts with combination washer/spring clip and then the eccentrics. The shoes can then be removed, but mark them first if they are to be refitted.
14 Whilst the drum is removed, inspect the hub bearing and oil seal (photo). If the bearing is to be renewed, refer to Chapter 9.
15 If the wheel cylinder is to be removed, unscrew and disconnect the hydraulic feed pipe on the inside and plug the pipe. Unscrew and remove the two retaining bolts and withdraw the cylinder.
16 Clean the backplate and adjuster cam assemblies before refitting the brake shoes.
17 If a new oil seal has been inserted into the drum check that the inner lip faces towards the bearing and that the seal face has a clearance of 1.5 mm (0.059 in) from the bearing edge.
18 If new shoes are being fitted, check that the eccentrics fit in them.
19 Refit the brake shoes in the reverse order of removal. If the old

13.8 Use the wheel chock to wedge the suspension arm

13.10 General view of rear brake assembly with drum removed

13.11 Removing the U-spring retainer (later models)

shoes were fitted with a coil type return spring, they can be converted to the later type by drilling out the appropriate holes for the location of the U-spring. You will also need the combination tab washer for the bottom pivot nuts and to secure the spring.

20 Grease the moving parts of the components such as the adjuster cams, pivot bolts and eccentrics, before assembling.

21 When fitted, the shoes must be centralized in a similar manner to that described for the front brakes. However, a different tool must be used to gauge the shoe positions. A stiff piece of wire soldered to the outer edge of the hub nut will do the job. Bend the wire over to meet the outer edge of the brake lining and rotate the nut through a full turn to gauge for centralisation. Adjust the shoes by means of the cam adjusters at the top and the eccentrics at the bottom. Tighten the locknuts of the pivots to secure in position and bend over the ears of the lockwasher. Break free the gauge wire from the nut and file off any protrusion.

22 Lightly lubricate the bearing inner race bore and stub axle before fitting, and ensure that the drum is fitted squarely. Tap the drum carefully into position and refit the large nut. Tighten the nut to the specified torque and peen the flange into the stub axle cutaway to lock in position (photo).

23 Smear a small amount of wheel bearing grease into the new grease cup before fitting. The cup is designed to be fitted together with the bearing locking, but as this requires a special tool it will probably already be in position. Therefore much care must be taken when tapping the cup into position or it will easily distort. Do not tap it in too far or it will interfere with the bearing. It must not be loose when in position.

24 If the wheel cylinder was removed, reconnect the pipe using a new seal of the correct type. Do not overtighten the retaining nut.

25 Adjust the brake shoes. If the wheel cylinder was removed, top up and bleed the hydraulic system as described in Section 5.

26 Slightly loosen the wheel cylinder retaining bolts, operate the brakes a few times, then retighten the bolts whilst the brake is being applied to centralize the cylinder.

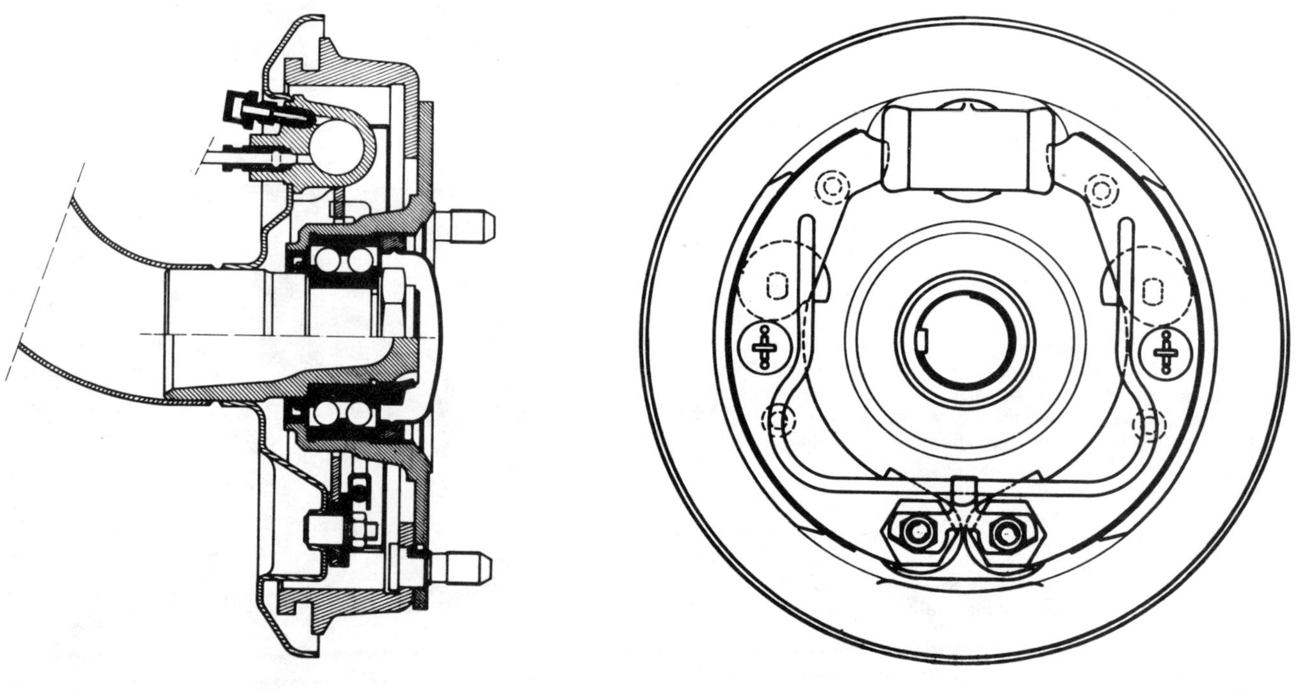

Fig. 6.20 Sectional views of typical rear brake and hub assembly (Sec 13)

13.14 Check the seal and bearing

13.22 Peen over the flange into the groove in the stub axle

14 Master cylinder – removal and refitting

1 Remove the spare wheel.
2 Disconnect the battery earth cable from the terminal. On models with the battery located above the master cylinder, disconnect both cables and remove the battery and tray for better accessibility.
3 Syphon or drain the master cylinder of brake fluid.
4 On front drum brake models, disconnect the pipe from the top of the cylinder unit (to the rear brakes). Unscrew and disconnect the front brake pipe at its connection to the pipe or flexible hose from the master cylinder (at the support bracket on top of the gearbox). Support the bracket nut and unscrew the pipe nut. Disconnect the flexible hose from the bracket by supporting the hose nut (against the bracket) and unscrewing the locknut on the other side of the bracket. Unscrew the flexible pipe from the master cylinder.
5 On front disc brake models (and some drum brake versions) both the front and rear brake pipes can be disconnected at the master cylinder connection (photo).
6 Unscrew and remove the hydraulic fluid reservoir from the top of the cylinder. On some models this is separate from the cylinder, in which case disconnect the feed pipe between the two at the cylinder.
7 Unscrew and remove the bolts securing the master cylinder and pedal assembly to the bulkhead. There are three bolts at the front (underneath the cylinder) and four bolts on the horizontal panel, (to the rear of the reservoir). On most models the cylinder is retained by two transverse through bolts (photo). Unscrew and remove these.
8 Now working inside the car, detach the wire to the stoplight switch.
9 Disconnect the clutch cable from the pedal connection. The master cylinder and pedal can now be withdrawn as an assembly from inside the car (photo).
10 The master cylinder can now be disconnected from the pedal assembly. On front drum brake models there are just two retaining bolts, whilst on front disc brake models the fulcrum pin must also be extracted.
11 On disc brake models, refer to Fig. 6.23 when refitting the master cylinder to the pedal assembly. The yoke (a) must have the longest

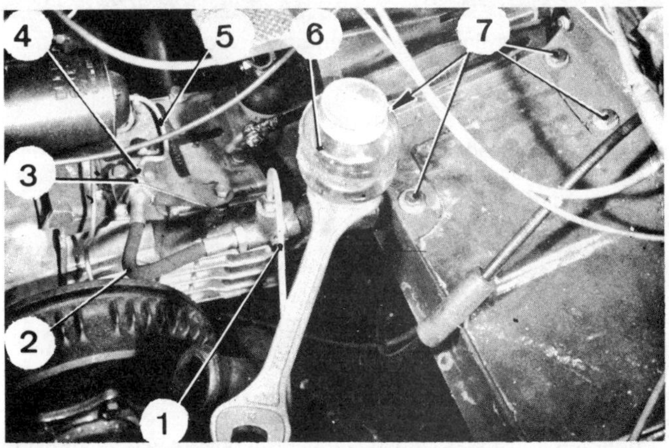

Fig. 6.21 Removing the master cylinder on earlier Ami models. LHD shown, RHD similar (Sec 14)

1 Rear brake pipe
2 Front brake flexible hose
3 Support bracket
4 Union locknut
5 Connecting pipe
6 Reservoir
7 Upper retaining bolts

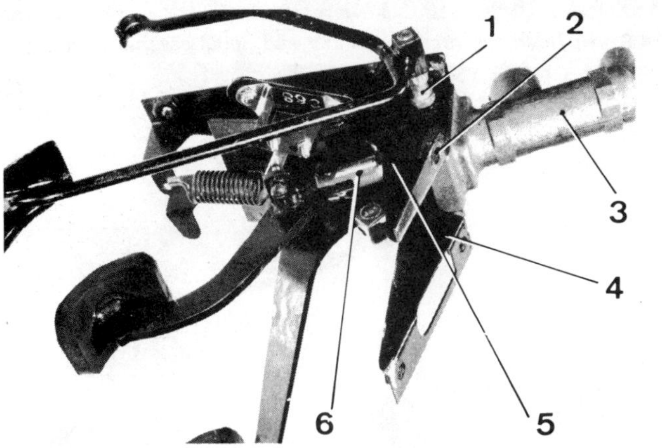

Fig. 6.22 Master cylinder and pedal assembly – drum brake models (Sec 14)

1 Retaining bolt
2 Bolt hole
3 Master cylinder
4 Bracket
5 Pushrod
6 Pushrod clevis

14.5 Disconnect the feed pipes from the master cylinder on the later models

14.7 Remove the two transverse bolts (later models)

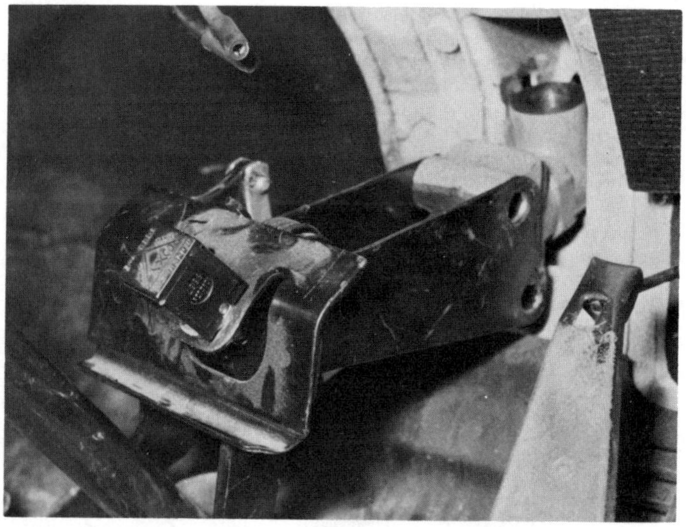

14.9 Withdraw the master cylinder and pedal assembly through the vehicle

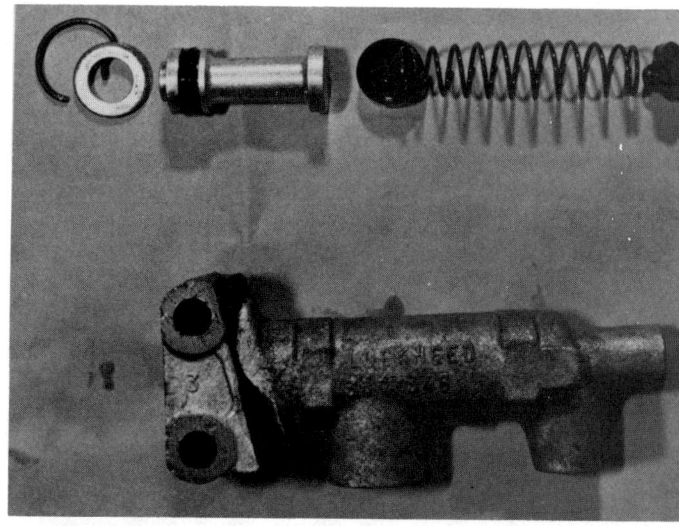

15.3 The master cylinder components removed

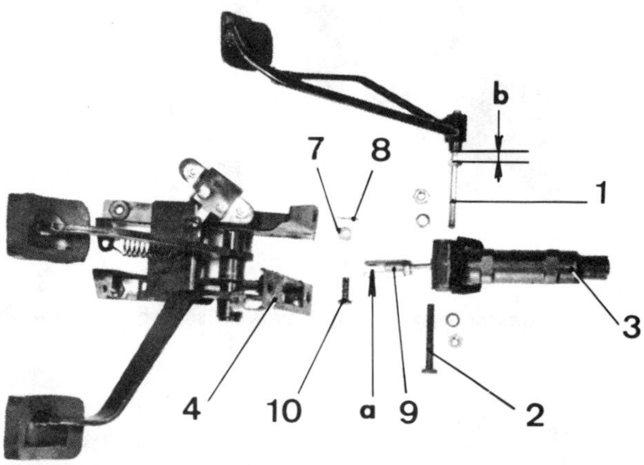

Fig. 6.23 Master cylinder and pedal assembly – disc brake models (Sec 14)

1 Bolt
2 Bolt
3 Master cylinder
4 Bracket
7 Washer
8 Pin
9 Clevis
10 Clevis pin
a Yoke
b = 10 ± 0.25 mm (0.39 ± 0.01 in)

side of its milled section towards the pedal spindle, and dimension b must be as specified.

12 Refitting is the reverse of the removal procedure. Use new seals on reassembly. Bleed the hydraulic system (Section 5) and check the adjustment of the stoplight switch (Section 8).

15 Master cylinder (drum brake models) – dismantling and re-assembly

1 Extract the circlip using a small screwdriver to lever it out, or a pair of needle-nosed pliers.

2 Withdraw the thrust washer, piston (note which way round), cup spring and valve.

3 The respective components can now be cleaned and inspected. Only use the specified brake fluid for your car's system (see Section 2).

4 Inspect the bore of the master cylinder for signs of score marks or corrosion; if present then the cylinder must be renewed. Check that all supply holes are clear.

5 Remove the piston seal and check the piston for signs of wear or damage. Renew if necessary.

6 The seals must automatically be renewed on assembly and if the circlip or spring is distorted then these too must be renewed.

7 As each part is assembled, soak it in clean hydraulic fluid. Refit in the reverse order to removal, starting with the valve spring and cup.

8 Locate the seal into position on the piston and insert the piston into the bore.

9 Refit the thrust washer and compress it down the bore, fitting the circlip to secure. Refit the pushrod and use a new split pin to secure the spindle.

16 Master cylinder (disc brake models) – dismantling and re-assembly

1 In this master cylinder the piston and spring assembly are retained in the cylinder bore by either a screw or a press fit retaining pin visible through and removable via the reservoir aperture. Commence dismantling by removing the screw or pin as applicable. Fit the special tool (Fig. 6.30) to prevent internal parts being lost when the screw or pin is removed.

2 If a pin is fitted you will need to clamp a 3 mm drill in a vice and lower the master cylinder so that the drill locates in the locking pin. Carefully twist the cylinder in a clockwise direction and pull to withdraw the pin.

3 Extract the piston, the valve and spring and the lock coil spring. Remove the cup seals from the piston, taking care not to scratch it.

4 Clean and examine the components as described in Section 15, but using petrol or LHM for cleaning.

5 Reassemble in the reverse order to removal, lubricating each part as it is fitted with clean LHM fluid. Always use new seals.

6 Refit the main spring, the valve and spring and piston. Locate the piston so that the two slots (Fig. 6.28) are vertically positioned in the cylinder.

7 To fit the new locking pin or screw, it is necessary to compress the spring and valve piston assembly in the cylinder. The Citroën special tool for this purpose is shown in Fig. 6.30; a suitably bent piece of stiff wire or thin pipe may serve, but take care not to scratch the cylinder or damage the seals.

8 When the pin or screw hole is in alignment, insert the new pin or screw. The pin split portion should face rearwards. Tap or press the pin home and remove the wire compressing the spring and piston.

9 Check that the pin or screw is correctly located by pushing and pulling on the pushrod.

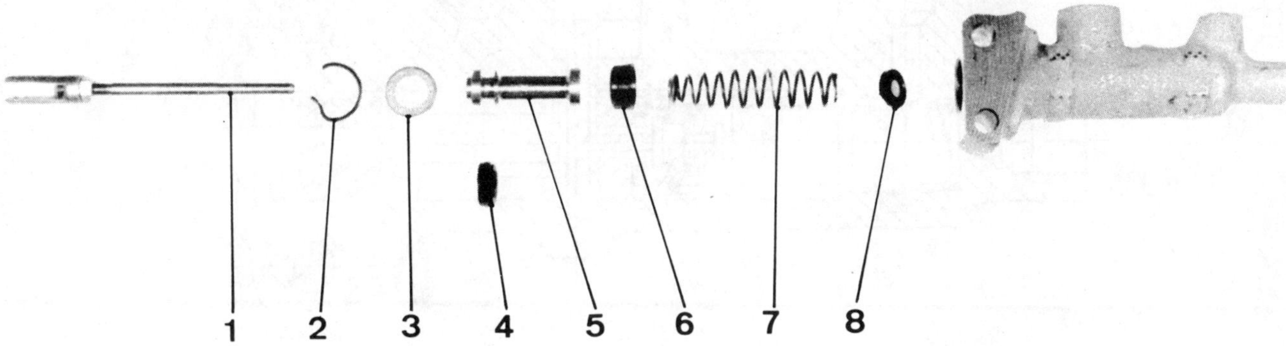

Fig. 6.24 Single piston master cylinder components – four wheel drum brake models (Sec 15)

1 Pushrod
2 Circlip
3 Washer
4 Cup
5 Piston
6 Cup
7 Spring
8 Valve

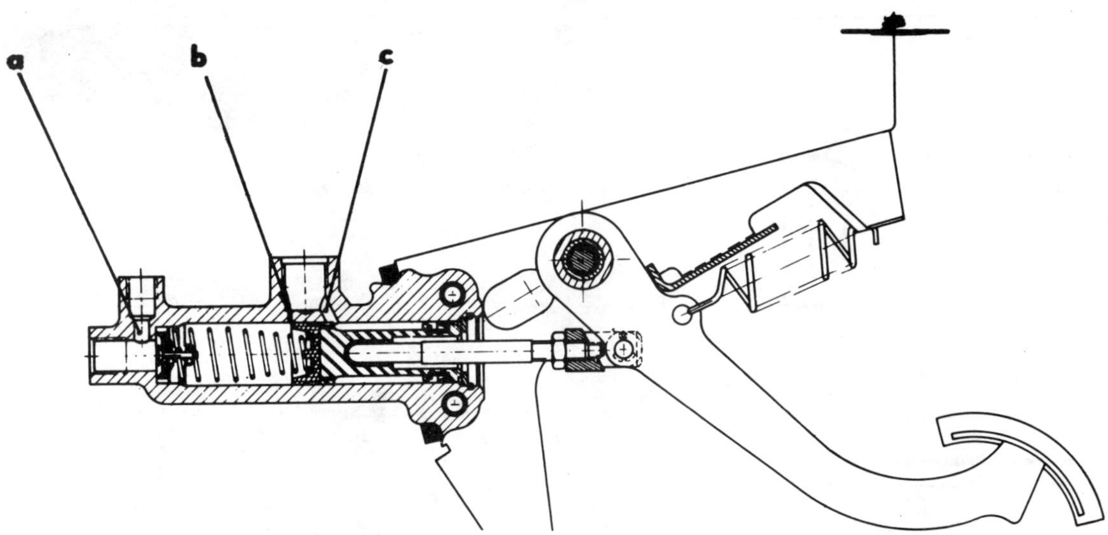

Fig. 6.25 Check that ports a, b and c are clear – four wheel drum brake models (Sec 15)

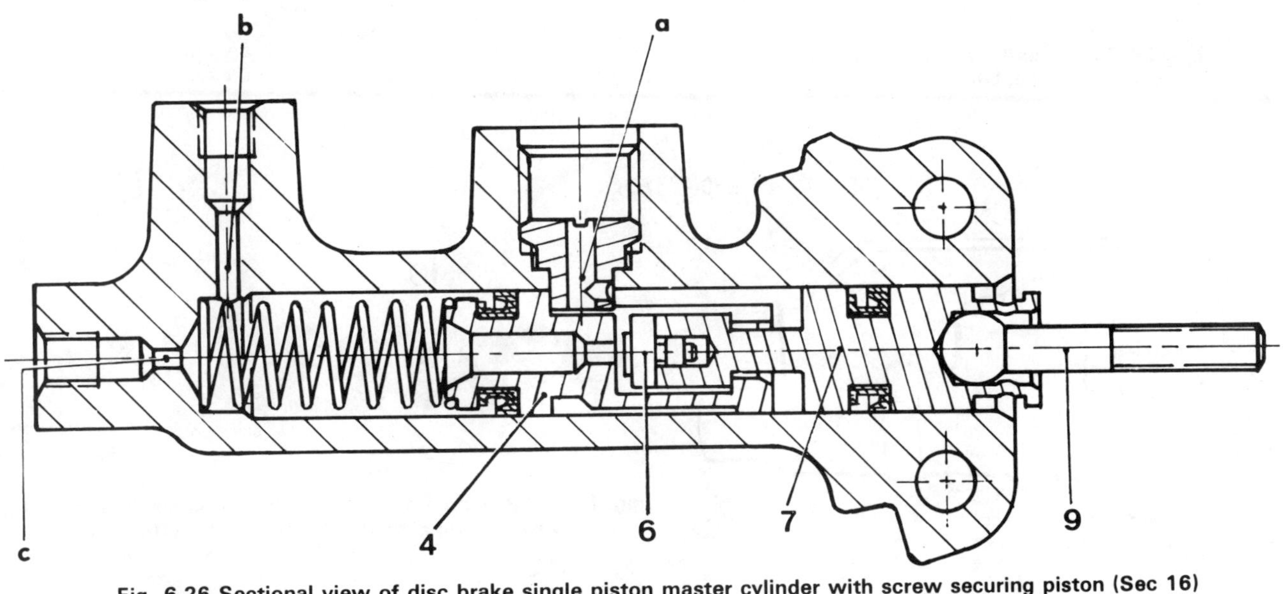

Fig. 6.26 Sectional view of disc brake single piston master cylinder with screw securing piston (Sec 16)

4 Piston front section
6 Valve
7 Piston rear section
9 Pushrod
a Screw
b Outlet port
c Outlet port

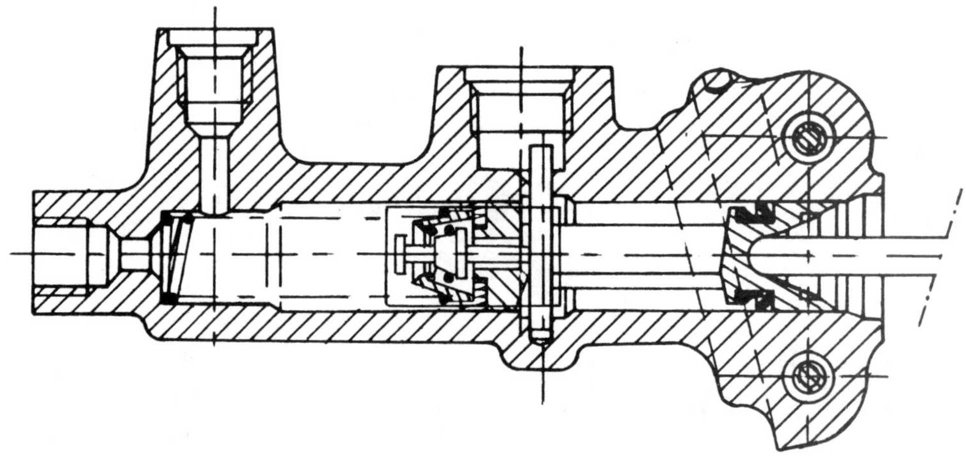

Fig. 6.27 Sectional view of disc brake single piston master cylinder with roll pin securing piston (Sec 16)

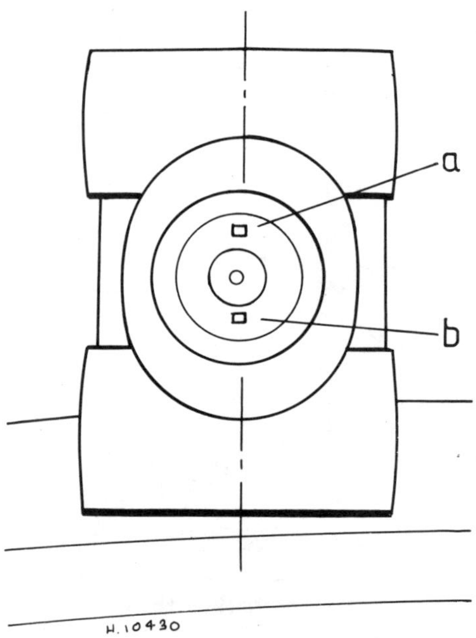

Fig. 6.28 Slots a and b must be vertical (Sec 16)

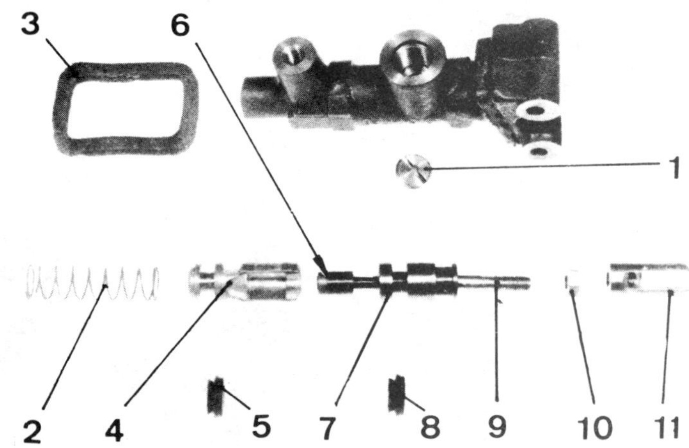

Fig. 6.29 Master cylinder components (Sec 16)

1 Screw
2 Spring
3 Gasket
4 Piston front section
5 Cup
6 Valve
7 Piston rear section
8 Cup
9 Pushrod
10 Locknut
11 Clevis

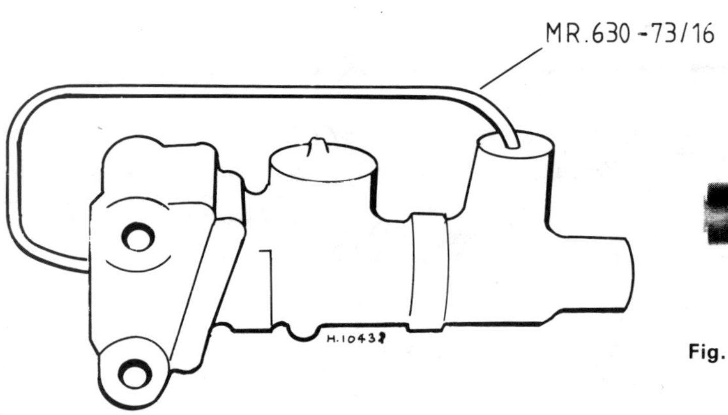

Fig. 6.30 Citroën special tool MR.630-73/16 used to compress the master cylinder components (Sec 16)

Fig. 6.31 Check operation of cylinder unit by pulling on pushrod. Note retaining screw (9) and gasket (10) (Sec 16)

17 Wheel (slave) cylinder – dismantling and overhaul

1 Removal of the wheel cylinders is covered in Sections 12 and 13.
2 Two types of wheel cylinder have been fitted, the main difference being that one has cup seals and the other has O-ring seals. The two types are dealt with separately below.

Wheel cylinder with cups

3 Prise free the dust covers from each end of the cylinder.
4 Extract the pistons, cups and central coil spring.
5 Unscrew and remove the bleed nipple.
6 Discard the dust covers and cups; clean the other components in the correct brake fluid.
7 Inspect the pistons and the cylinder bore for signs of scratches or

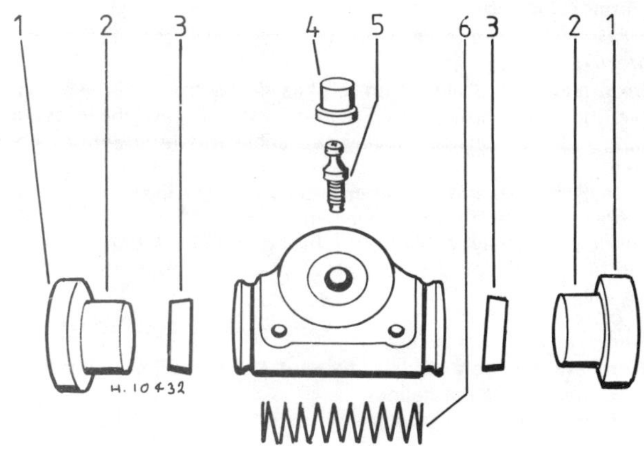

Fig. 6.32 Wheel cylinder components – cup seal type (Sec 17)

1 Dust cover
2 Piston
3 Cup
4 Cap
5 Bleed nipple
6 Spring

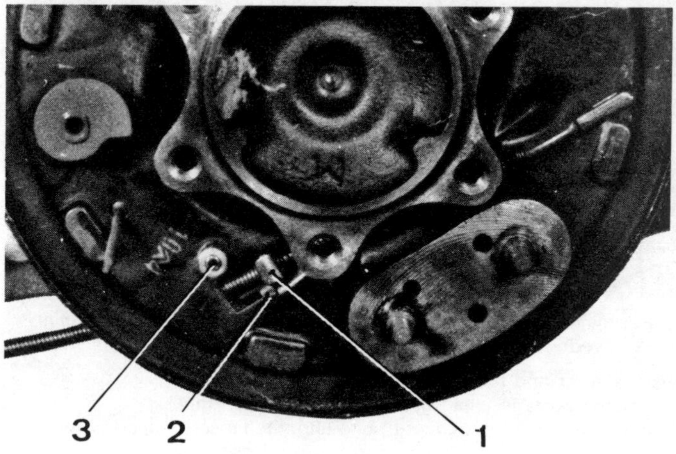

Fig. 6.34 Handbrake cable connection to drum brakes (Sec 18)

1 Clip
2 Stop
3 Retaining nut

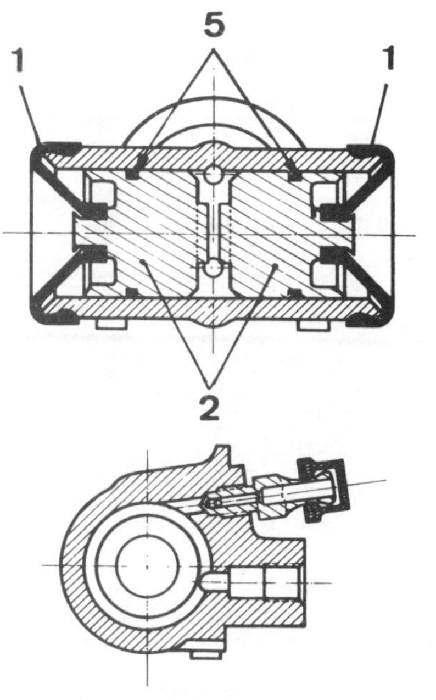

Fig. 6.33 Sectional views of wheel cylinder – O-ring seal type (Sec 17)

1 Dust cover
2 Pistons
5 O-rings

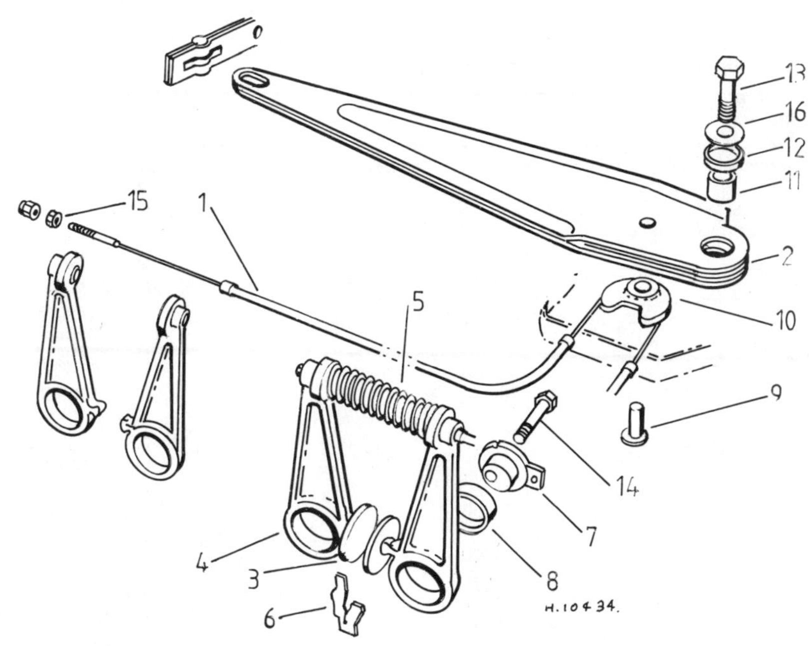

Fig. 6.35 Handbrake linkage details – disc brake models (Sec 18)

1 Cable
2 Lever
3 Pad
4 Caliper lever
5 Spring
6 Anti-rattle spring
7 Eccentric
8 Bush
9 Pin
10 Roller
11 Bush
12 Anti-rattle sleeve
13 Pivot bolt
14 Locking bolt
15 Nut and locknut
16 Washer

18.1 Removing the handbrake outer cable clip nut (the shoes have been removed)

excessive wear and renew if necessary.
8 Coat the parts in clean brake fluid before assembly.
9 Fit a piston and dust cover at one end, then insert a cup followed by the spring. The opposing cup, piston and dust seal can then be assembled onto the other end.
10 Refit the bleed nipple and cap to complete.

Wheel cylinder with O-ring seals

11 Prise the dust covers free from each end of the cylinder.
12 Extract the pistons from each end of the cylinder and note which way round they face. If they are reluctant to exit, remove the bleed nipple and apply some regulated compressed air down the cylinder.
13 Extract the locking circlip (where applicable) and remove the piston O-ring seals.
14 Discard the old seals and end covers as new ones must be fitted on assembly.
15 Clean the parts with clean brake fluid of the correct type. Inspect the pistons and cylinder bore for signs of scoring or wear and renew if necessary.
16 Assemble in the reverse order. Lubricate all parts with clean hydraulic fluid before fitting. Insert the circlip (where applicable) followed by the respective pistons fitted with new seals. Fit the dust covers and bleed nipple to complete.

18 Handbrake cable – renewal

Front drum brake models

1 On models fitted with drum brakes at the front it is necessary to remove the brake drum (see Section 12). Unscrew the outer cable retaining nut (photo) and moving the cable forwards unhook it from the lever.
2 Detach the cable at the other end by unscrewing the adjuster and releasing the cable from the lever arm.
3 Lubricate the new cable before fitting and check that it is securely located on installation. Readjust the brakes to complete.

Disc brake models

4 Remove the spare wheel.
5 Unscrew the cable adjuster locknut and the adjuster nut from the cable connection at the caliper.
6 Withdraw the cable from the actuating levers of the handbrake on the caliper unit.
7 Disconnect the intermediate lever to release the cable at the top end. To remove the intermediate lever, unscrew and remove the pivot bolt and spacer and free the outer cable from the support. Remove the split pin and extract the connecting pin of the intermediate lever and handbrake ratchet control. The intermediate lever and handbrake cable can now be separated as required.
8 Refitting is a reversal of the removal procedure. Lubricate the swivel, the pivot pin and the cable. Tighten the lever pivot bolt to the specified torque. When fitted check that the cables are clear of the exhaust. Readjust the handbrake as described in Section 4.

19 Fault diagnosis – braking system

Symptom	Reason(s)
Pedal travels almost to the floor before brakes operate	Air in hydraulic system Brake fluid level too low Wheel cylinder leaking Master cylinder leaking (bubbles in master cylinder fluid) Brake flexible hose leaking Brake line fractured Brake system unions loose Shoe linings excessively worn Disc pads excessively worn
Brake pedal feels springy	New linings not yet bedded-in Brake drums badly worn or cracked
Brake pedal feels spongy	Air in hydraulic system Wheel cylinder leaking Master cylinder leaking (bubbles in master cylinder reservoir) Brake pipe line or flexible hose leaking Unions in brake system loose
Excessive effort required to brake vehicle	Shoe linings or disc pads badly worn New shoes or pads recently fitted – not yet bedded in Harder linings fitted than standard resulting in increase in pedal pressure Pads or linings and brake drums contaminated with oil, grease or hydraulic fluid Scored drums or discs
Brakes tend to bind, drag or lock-on	Air in hydraulic system Wheel cylinders seized Handbrake cables too tight or binding Weak shoe return springs Incorrectly set foot pedal or pushrod Master cylinder seized Brakes overadjusted Blocked reservoir cap vent hole

Chapter 7 Steering, wheels and tyres

Contents

Specifications

Steering type
Rack-and-pinion

Turning circle (between kerbs)
11.4 m (37.4 ft)

Steering angles

Camber (wheels straight-ahead)	1° (+45′, – 25′)
Castor (non-adjustable)	15°
Toe-out	0 to 3 mm (0 to 0.118 in)
Steering lock	35°

Tyre sizes

2CV and Dyane:	
Standard fitting	125–15X
Alternatives	135–15X, 135–15ZX, 135–15XAS, 135–15XZX, 135– 15X (M+S)
Ami:	
Standard fitting	125–15X (Saloon), 135–15X (Estate),
Alternatives	135–15X, 135–15XZ, 135–15XZX, 135–15X(M+S)

Tyre pressures in lbf/in² (bar)

The following are general recommendations. Consult the operator's handbook supplied with the vehicle for further details

	Front	Rear	Spare*
2CV, Dyane, Ami 6 and 8 Estates	20 (1.4)	26 (1.8)	29 (2.0)
Ami 6 Saloons	22 (1.5)	26 (1.8)	29 (2.0)
Ami 8 Saloons	26 (1.8)	26 (1.8)	29 (2.0)

* *Adjust to correct pressure when in use*

Torque wrench settings

	lbf ft	kgf m
Crossmember bolts	36	5
Pinion retaining nut	101	14
Steering column shaft nut	14	2
Steering pivot/lever bolts	10 to 14	1.5 to 2.0
Steering column-to-pinion clamp bolt	13	1.9
Wheel nuts	29 to 43	4 to 6
Track rod ball-pin 'Nylstop' nuts	29	4
Track rod sleeve clamp bolts	7	1
Anti-roll bar bolts	43	6

1 General description

1 Rack-and-pinion type steering is employed, the rack unit being located within the crossmember which supports the front axle arm. The crossmember is located on the chassis member at each side and is directly in front of the bulkhead and to the rear of the gearbox.
2 The track rod to each steering arm is attached to its respective rack balljoint.
3 As the steering wheel is turned, the column shaft transmits the movement to the pinion which is located by a ball bearing. The pinion in turn operates the rack, from which track rods (photo) transmit the action to the steering arms on the axle on each side, causing the wheels to turn in the desired direction. The steering shaft of the Ami 8 models incorporates upper and lower universal joint units to improve the steering column angle and to collapse safely in a collision.
4 Many of the procedures in this Chapter require the use of special tools. In some instances they can be fabricated, but read through each operation concerned fully before starting work to ensure that you will be able to complete the task at hand.

2 Steering column – removal and refitting

1 Disconnect the battery earth terminal and unlock the anti-theft lock (if fitted).
2 Unscrew the steering shaft-to-flexible joint clamp bolt (Fig. 7.2) and pull the steering wheel upwards to remove.

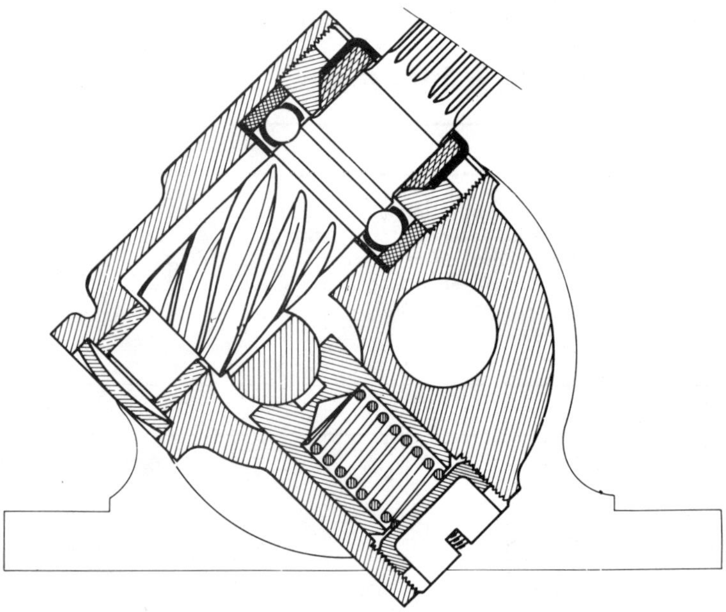

Fig. 7.1 Sectional view of the rack-and-pinion (Sec 1)

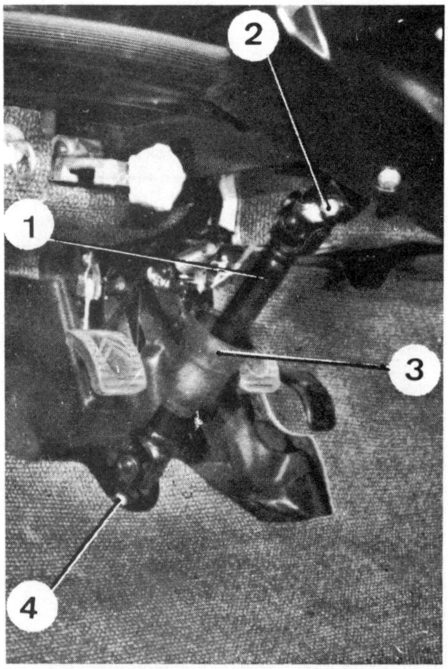

Fig. 7.2 The steering column (Ami shown, others similar) (Sec 2)

1 Steering column
2 Steering wheel shaft clamp bolt
3 Rubber sleeve
4 Lower retaining bolt

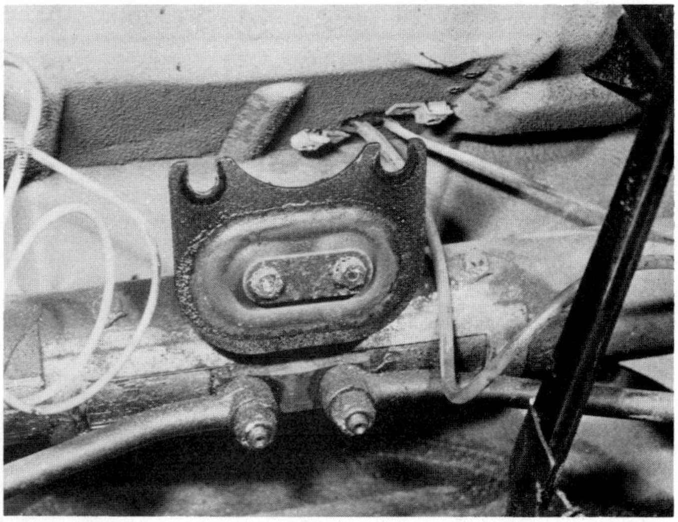

1.3 The track rod connections to the steering rack (engine and gearbox removed)

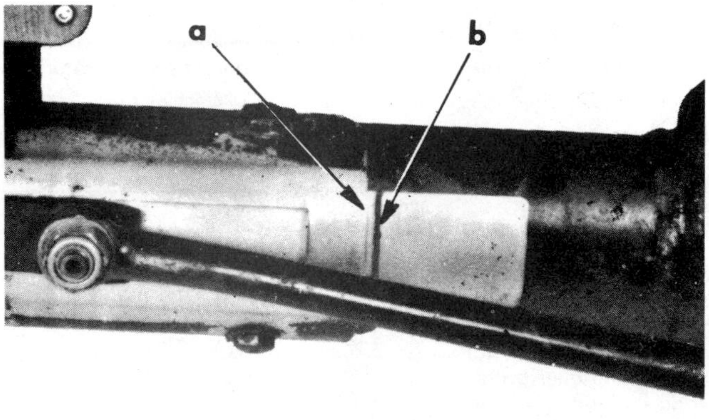

Fig. 7.3 Align the sliding cover reference line (b) with the edge of the slide (a) (Sec 2)

3 Pull back the rubber cover from the lower column joint, unscrew the pinion shaft-to-lower flexible joint clamp bolt and remove the column.
4 The rubber cover can be removed if required, using brake fluid to SAE J 1703 or a non-mineral grease as a lubricant.
5 Refitting is basically a reversal of the removal procedure. Always use new 'Nylstop' nuts on the clamp bolts. Hand tighten these nuts initially until the components are aligned as described below.
6 Rotate the column so that the alignment mark on the sliding cover on the rack housing (crossmember) is in line with the contact guide of the left-hand balljoint (Fig. 7.3).
7 Refit the steering wheel and align the arm at about 30° below the horizontal. Insert the column/shaft clamp bolts and hand tighten the new Nylstop nut.
8 Check that when turned through a complete revolution, the steering wheel does not come into contact with the plastic bush. If it does, lift it until it clears and pinch tighten the clamp bolt.
9 Tighten the clamp bolts and nuts of the column to the specified torque.
10 Slide the rubber protector over the lower flexible joint and operate the anti-theft lock to ensure that it is in order.

3 Steering column tube and anti-theft lock – removal and refitting

Ami models

1 Disconnect the battery earth terminal and remove the spare wheel.
2 Detach the choke cable from the carburettor.
3 Turn the ignition key to the unlocked position and remove the steering wheel by unscrewing the clamp bolt and withdrawing the wheel.
4 Unscrew and remove the bolts securing the upper section of the electrical control housing and detach the upper housing section.
5 Unscrew and remove the lower control housing retaining bolts and remove the housing, but leave the wires connected. Support the housing on the gear lever.
6 Unscrew the anti-theft lock retaining screw, detach the wires and remove the anti-theft unit.
7 The column fixed tube can be removed if required by unscrewing the bracket retaining bolts.
8 Refitting is a direct reversal of the removal procedure. Take care to reconnect the wiring securely and correctly, and if necessary insert a new plastic bush into position at the top of the column (to seal the housing).
9 When complete check that the anti-theft device is fully operational and that all the electric circuits are working.

2CV models

10 Working in the engine compartment, unscrew and remove the steering column-to-rack pinion clamp bolts.
11 Disconnect the battery earth lead.
12 Working inside the car, detach the anti-theft unit wires.
13 Use a short screwdriver and remove the collar retaining screw which protrudes just below the bracket. Withdraw the protection collar.
14 With the anti-theft lock in the unlocked position, unscrew the Allen screws (5mm) and free the lock bush.
15 Extract the securing bolts (special tool 2412-T should be used if available). Withdraw the anti-theft lock and its adjustment shims.
16 If required the steering column and fixed tube, together with the rubber support, can now be removed.
17 Refit in the reverse sequence to removal. Tighten the new anti-theft lock bolts until their heads shear off. Do not overtighten the Allen screw retaining the lock bush.
18 On completion check that the lock operates correctly. Tighten the pinion/column clamp bolt to the specified torque.

Dyane 4 and Dyane 6 models

19 It is not necessary to remove the anti-theft lock if the steering column fixed tube is being withdrawn.
20 Working in the engine compartment, unscrew the pinion-to-column clamp bolt and disconnect the battery.
21 Unscrew and remove the cone nuts retaining the fixed tube mounting plate and anti-theft lock (photo).

Fig. 7.4 Steering column tube and column lock retaining bolts. LHD shown, RHD similar (Sec 3)

7 Tube retaining bolt (upper)
8 Tube retaining bolt (upper)
9 Tube retaining bolt (lower)
10 Lock retaining screw
11 Tube retaining bolt (lower)

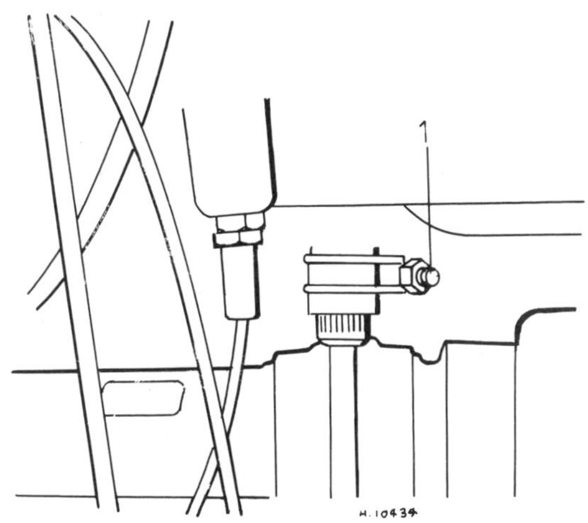

Fig. 7.5 Pinion shaft-to-steering column clamp bolt (1) (Sec 3)

3.21 The steering column lock and tube mounting in the Dyane.

22 Separate the column from the pinion.
23 Detach the wires from the anti-theft lock.
24 Separate the fixed tube and steering column units. The fixed tube can be removed from the column together with the Rilsan bush and rubber bush.
25 To remove the anti-theft lock, drill into the head of the retaining screw using a 3.5 mm diameter drill and then withdraw the screw using a thread extractor. Apply pressure on the ignition key, retain in the locked position and withdraw the lock unit.
26 Refit in the reverse order to removal. Tighten the new lock unit retaining bolt to the break point of its head. Tighten the pinion-to-column clamp bolt to the specified torque. Check the lock operation on completion, also the reconnected electric circuits.

4 Steering wheel – removal and refitting

1 Turn the ignition key to the off position with the column unlocked.
2 Prise back the pad from the centre of the steering wheel spoke and unscrew the wheel-to-column retaining bolts. Remove the wheel, noting its position.
3 On some models it will be necessary to unscrew the upper column clamp bolt and withdraw the steering wheel complete with upper steering shaft section. Note the position of the steering wheel on removal to ensure correct relocation when refitting. Refer to Section 12 if alignment is lost.
4 Refit in the reverse order and tighten the bolts securely.

5 Rack-and-pinion unit – overhaul

1 If the rack-and-pinion unit is to be dismantled for inspection and repair then it must be removed from the vehicle. The unit is housed in the crossmember from which the suspension arms are mounted. Refer to Chapter 8 for the removal procedure.
2 With the crossmember removed, clear a suitable workspace where the various components can be laid out in order as they are removed.
3 Clean the outside of the crossmember and its associated fittings before commencing dismantling. It is most important that no dirt be allowed to enter the rack housing, especially when reassembling.
4 If possible support the unit on the workbench. Commence by disconnecting the track rod ends from the rack ball-pins. You will need to use a ball-pin extractor, or preferably Citroën special tool 3502-T fitted with knurled nut 1965-T. You will have to cut free the rubber anti-rattle plate to facilitate fitting of the extractor.
5 Unscrew and remove the spring guide nut. Withdraw the spring and guide (Fig. 7.13).
6 Remove the slide from its cover and then separate the sliding cover and guide blocks from the ball-pins.
7 Separate the assembly rack and tube from the crossmember.
8 To remove the pinion (if still in position) drill out the locking peg of the special retaining nut using a 4mm (5/32 in) diameter drill and unscrew the nut. If possible special tool 3503-T; if not, fabricate a spanner using a suitable diameter tube and cut away the end section to leave two lugs protruding. Drill a hole through to lever the tube and unscrew the nut. Remove the pinion.
9 Drive out the rack pinion bearing with a shouldered mandrel. The bearing will exit complete with the housing plug. The stepped mandrel should have a small diameter of 13mm (0.511 in) and a large diameter of 17mm (0.669 in).
10 Extract the split pin and remove the ball stop nut (Fig. 7.9).
11 Referring to Fig. 7.10, insert the rack tube with ball-pins and push the seat with the ball-pin to separate the seat from the tube.
12 Separate the rack guide and ball-pins and withdraw the ball-pin, ball seats, spring and spacer, ball seats and spacer in order from the rack tube.
13 The components can now be carefully cleaned and inspected for wear or damage. Any part suspected of being defective must be renewed. In particular check the ball-pins, sliding dust cover, springs and spacers for wear. Check the rack for alignment and inspect the teeth of both the rack and the pinion for wear or damage.
14 Ensure that all components are perfectly clean prior to refitting.
15 Lubricate the ball-pin guide (inside), the fourth ball-pin hole seat and spring, the inner surface of the rack tube and the ball-pins, with general-purpose grease.

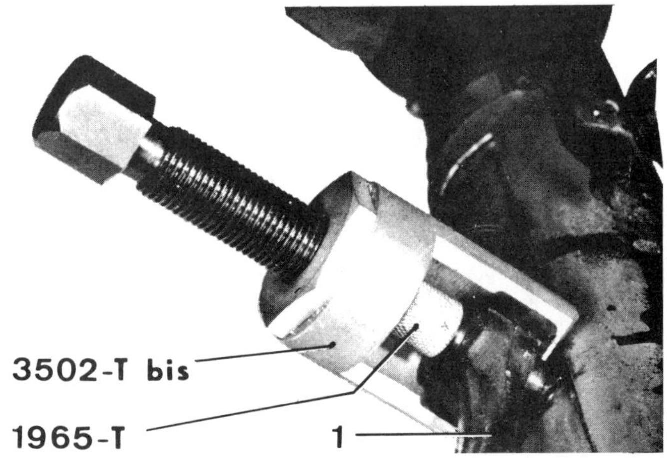

Fig. 7.6 Special Citroën tools 3502-T and 1965-T being used to separate the track rod to ball-pin joint (Sec 5)

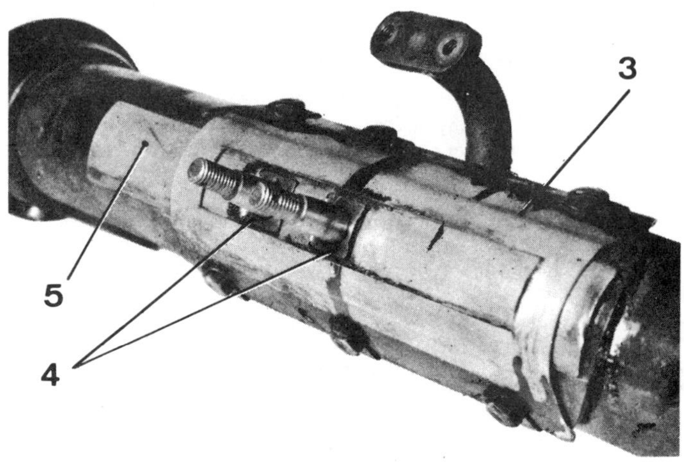

Fig. 7.7 Steering rack sliding joints with track rods removed (Sec 5)

3 *Slide*
4 *Guide blocks*
5 *Sliding cover*

Fig. 7.8 Pinion retaining nut (1) and peened pegs (a) (Sec 5)

Fig. 7.9 The split pin (1) retains the ball stop nut (2) (Sec 5)

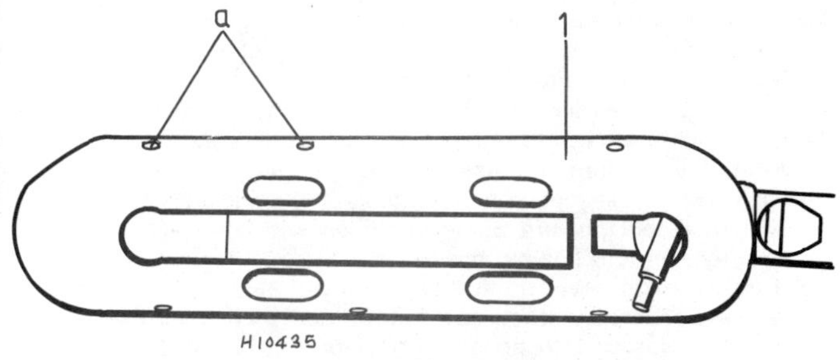

Fig. 7.12 Fitting the rack and ball-pin guide (1). Holes (a) should be at the opposite end to the rack (Sec 5)

Fig. 7.10 Freeing the seat from the rack tube (Sec 5)

3 Ball-pin guide
4 Ball-pin
5 Rack tube

Fig. 7.13 Fit the guide (1), spring (2) and special nut (3) (Sec 5)

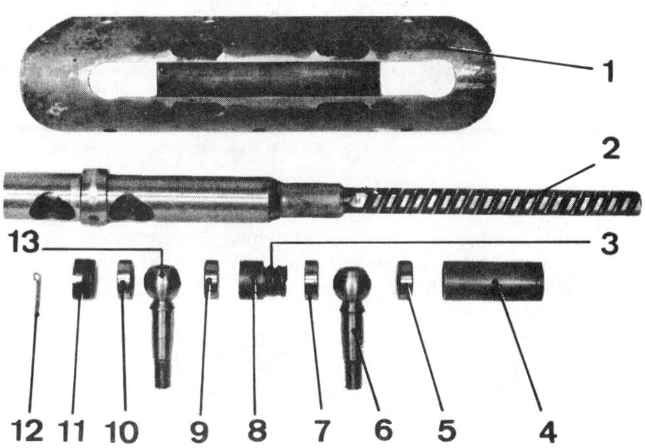

Fig. 7.11 The steering rack components (Sec 5)

1 Ball-pin guide
2 Rack tube
3 Spring
4 Spacer
5 1st seat
6 Ball-pin
7 2nd seat
8 Spacer
9 3rd seat
10 4th seat
11 Thrust nut
12 Split pin
13 Ball-pin

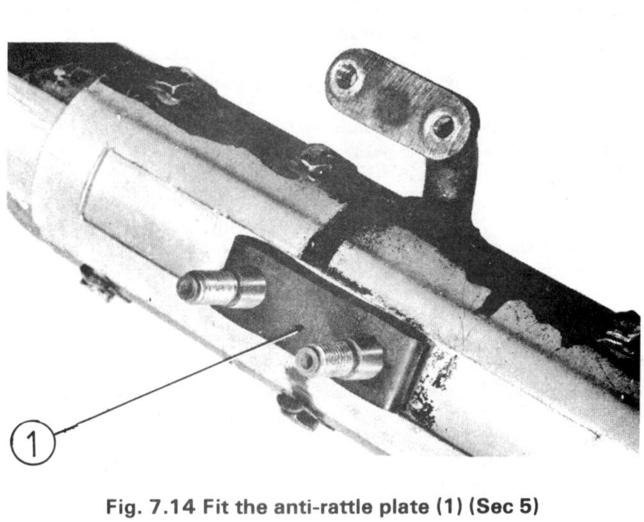

Fig. 7.14 Fit the anti-rattle plate (1) (Sec 5)

16 Insert the following into the rack tube in the order given: the spacer, 1st seat, 2nd seat, spring and spacer, 3rd seat and ball-pin (13 in Fig. 7.11).
17 Now offer the rack tube assembly to the ball-pin guide and ensure that the guide is positioned with the two closer retaining bolt holes ('a' in Fig. 7.12) at the opposite end to the rack.
18 Locate the 2nd ball-pin (6 in Fig. 7.11) and the 4th seat.
19 Screw the thrust nut into position and when tightened, loosen it off by about $\frac{1}{16}$th of a turn and insert a new split pin to secure. Check that the ball-pins can swivel without binding or slackness. Ensure that the ends of the split pin are bent over flush with the rack sleeve, otherwise they may rub against the guide.
20 Locate the pinion bearing into position, carefully tapping it home using the mandrel employed to remove it. Carefully locate and tap the expanding plug washer into position and lubricate the bearing with transmission grease.
21 Before fitting the rack and tube into the crossmember, smear them with grease.
22 Lubricate the pinion teeth and bearing with transmission grease. The pinion rotating part must be smeared with graphite grease. Fit the pinion into the housing and locate the special nut and felt washer. Tighten to the specified torque, but do not lock the nut at this stage.
23 Fit the guide blocks into position on the ball-pin stems, and then locate the sliding cover (which must be smeared with grease). Now position the slide and fit the bolts and new lockwashers. When the bolts are tight, check that the rack can move freely and without binding in the crossmember. Bend over the tabs of the lockwashers to secure the bolts.
24 Lubricate the guide with grease and insert it into position together with the spring and special nut, which must not be fully tightened at this stage. Supporting the crossmember, the rack must now be moved along its complete length of travel by turning the pinion shaft. This should be about $2\frac{1}{2}$ turns.
25 Progressively tighten the special nut to the point where the rack binds (if at all) and then loosen it to adjust its pressure so that the rack can be moved along without any binding. The nut will be retained in the set position by the pressure of the guide spring.
26 Fit the anti-rattle plate over the two balljoint shafts, the tapered sections of which must be wiped clean. Locate the track rods and tighten the 'Nylstop' nuts to the specified torque. To prevent the ball-pins from turning, position an open-ended spanner between the nut and the track rod and tighten the locknut to close up the tapers, then remove the spanner and fully tighten the nut to the specified torque.
27 Before refitting the crossmember assembly, the pinion must be removed and fitted again from inside the car once the assembly is in position. Slide an 8mm thick section of wood down the crossmember to support the rack before the pinion is removed.
28 Unscrew the pinion locking nut and remove it with the felt. Withdraw the pinion and plug the rack housing aperture to prevent the ingress of dirt when fitting the crossmember – this is important.

6 Track rod – removal and refitting

1 Raise the bonnet, disconnect the battery earth cable and remove the spare wheel.
2 Detach the right-hand side heat exchanger.
3 Turn the steering fully left, then cut free the rubber anti-rattle plate and unscrew the track rod retaining nuts. Both nuts must be unscrewed so that a new anti-rattle pad can be refitted on assembly.
4 Raise the front of the vehicle and support it securely.
5 When removing the left-hand track rod, the right-hand rod does not have to be disconnected. However, when removing the right-hand track rod, the left-hand rod must be disconnected from its lever. This is so that the extractor (paragraph 9) can be fitted.
6 Remove the roadwheel(s) on the side(s) being worked on.
7 Detach the track rod from the steering lever by removing the split pin and nut – it may be necessary to clean off some mud first (photo). Extract the ball-pin outer seat and free the dust cover.
8 Locate the hub to align the ball-pin flats in the rod and free the track rod.
9 To separate the rod from the rack ball-pin you will need to use a ball-pin extractor, or preferably Citroën special tool 3502-T with knurled nut 1965-T.
10 Refit in the reverse order to removal. Use new 'Nylstop' nuts to secure the rods to the rack balljoint.
11 Lubricate the ball-pin housings with transmission grease.
12 When the ball-pins are fitted in the rod, tighten the seat retaining nut fully, then back it off $\frac{1}{16}$th of a turn and insert the split pin to secure.
13 Tighten all nuts to their specified torques on completion, check the steering action and lower the vehicle.
14 Check the wheel alignment and check if necessary (Section 7).

6.7 Track rod to steering arm joint may be muddy. Securing nut (arrowed) is just visible

7 Wheel alignment – checking and adjustment

1 The alignment of the front wheels does not normally alter unless the steering linkage or front suspension has been subject to abnormal stress or the track rods have been disturbed or renewed.
2 Specialised equipment is needed to check accurately and if need be adjust the steering and suspension alignment. In addition the wheel bearings and steering and suspension components must be in good order before an accurate check or adjustment can be made.
3 The vehicle height must also be correctly adjusted (Chapter 9) and tyres must have the correct pressures.
4 Basic checks can be made as a temporary measure. Park the car on level ground and ensure that the wheels are in the straight ahead position.
5 Raise and chock the vehicle under the front chassis to give a height of 207mm (8.14 in) between the ground and point 'b' on each side (Fig. 7.15).

Camber angle

6 Use a mark on the steering rack cover to ensure that the wheels are in the straight-ahead position (Fig. 7.3). If this mark is not visible, stretch a piece of string or wire at wheel centre height over the complete length of the vehicle as shown (Fig. 7.16) and check that the front wheels are parallel by measuring the dimensions a1 and a2 which must be equal.
7 You will now require the equivalent of specal tool number 2313-T as used by your Citroën dealer (Fig. 7.18). On this tool a plumb line is suspended from a fixed point level with the top of the wheel rim and a gauge scale is level with the rim at the bottom. If the camber angle is incorrect the problem is probably a defect in the axle arm assembly. No adjustment can be made to correct the camber angle of the wheels.

Front wheel toe-out

8 The front wheels must be set so that they toe out by the amount given in the Specifications. Toe-out means that the wheels are not exactly parallel; the dimension specified is the amount by which the distance between the *outer* edges of the wheel rims at the front of the wheel exceeds the same distance at the back of the wheel.
9 Various tracking gauges are available for the DIY mechanic. Some of these measure the distance between the *inside* edges of the wheels. The specified toe-out thus measured would strictly speaking not be precisely the same, but the difference is unlikely to be significant.

Fig. 7.15 Check vehicle height at point b. h = h (Sec 7)

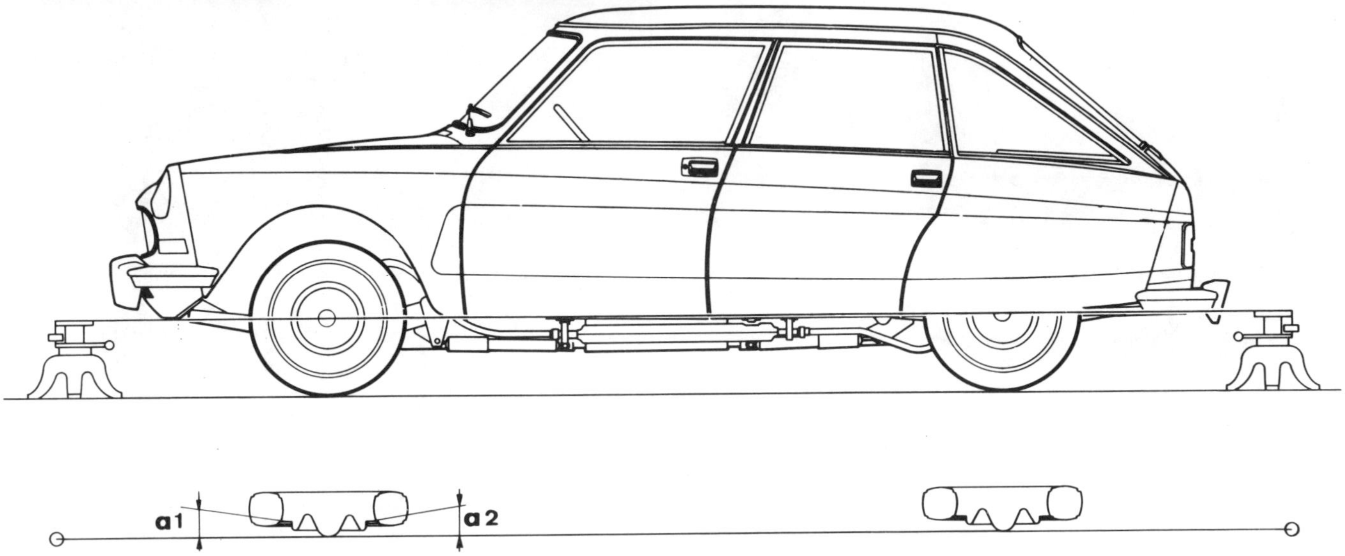

Fig. 7.16 Method of checking the front wheel alignment. a1 and a2 must be equal (Sec 7)

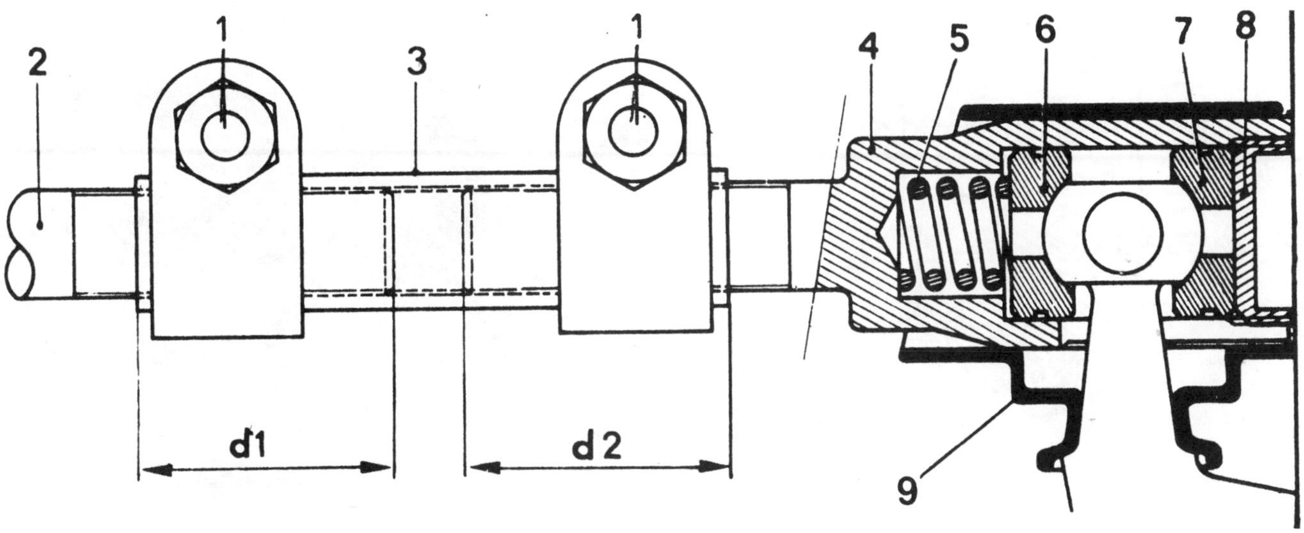

Fig. 7.17 The track rod adjuster sleeve and steering joint (Sec 7)

1 Locknuts
2 Bar
3 Adjuster sleeve
4 Track rod end
5 Spring
6 Ball seat
7 Ball seat
8 Retaining nut
9 Dust cover
d1 = d2 ± 2 mm

Fig. 7.18 Using Citroën tool 2313-T to check the camber angle (Sec 7)

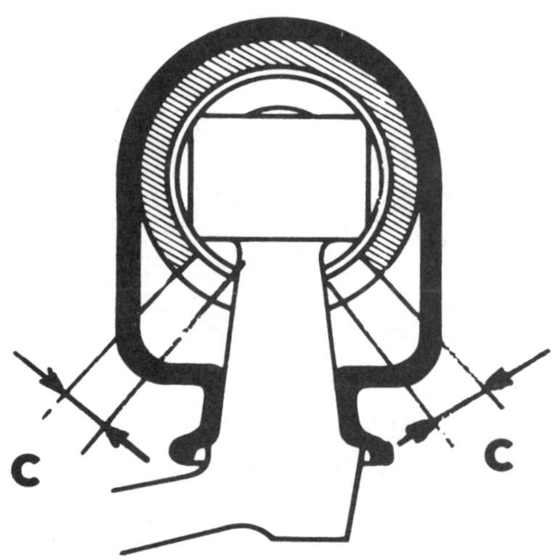

Fig. 7.20 Balljoint movement (c) must be the same on each side (Sec 7)

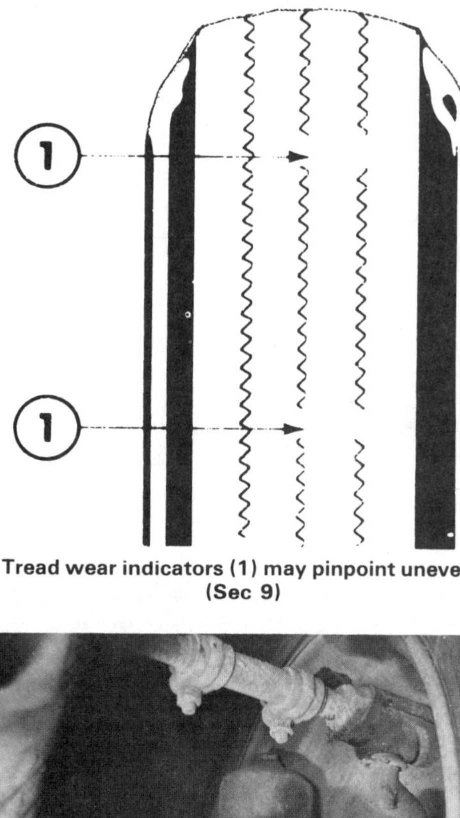

Fig. 7.21 Tread wear indicators (1) may pinpoint uneven tyre wear (Sec 9)

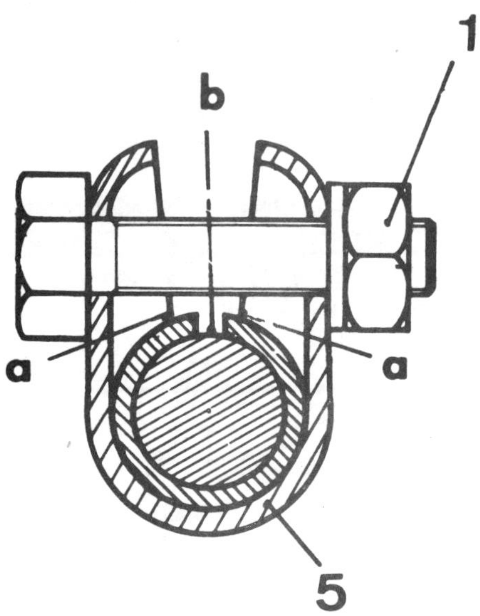

Fig. 7.19 Position sleeve (5) with nut and bolt (1) at the top. Locate slot (b) between gap (a) (Sec 7)

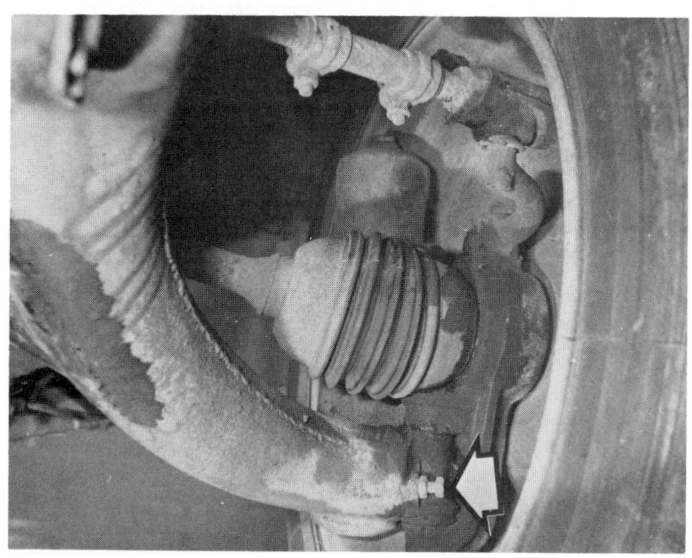

8.4 Steering lock adjuster screw and locknut (arrowed)

10 Measure the distance between the edges of the wheel rims at centre height at the front of the wheels. (The wheels must be in the straight-ahead position – refer to paragraph 6 if necessary). Mark the points between which the measurement is taken with chalk.
11 Roll the car forwards so that the wheels turn through half a revolution, ie the chalk marks are now at the rear of the wheels. Measure the distance again. The distance at the rear should be less than that at the front by the specified amount.
12 If the toe-out is incorrectly set, make an adjustment accordingly by loosening the locknuts of the track rod sleeves (Fig. 7.17) on each side. The sleeves are now rotated as necessary to adjust wheel position. A complete revolution of the sleeve is equal to a 6 to 7mm movement of the wheel. The distance d1 and d2 (Fig. 7.17) must be equal to within 2mm.
13 The sleeve clamps must be positioned vertically with the bolts at the top.
14 The balljoint movement at 'c' (Fig. 7.20) must be equally set and the nuts then retightened to the specified torque.

8 Steering lock – adjustment

1 The vehicle must be parked on a flat level surface, and the body height must be correct.
2 Turn the steering to full lock and check the clearance between the tyre and axle arm in this position, which should be 5mm (0.2 in).
3 Check the clearance between the damper and the arm; this should be 1mm (0.039 in) (vehicles fitted with inertia dampers on the front).
4 To adjust, a locking stop screw is fitted under the arm (photo). Unscrew the locknut and turn the screw as necessary. Retighten the locknut and check the clearances again.
5 Repeat the process on the opposite wheel.

9 Wheels and tyres – general

1 The front tyres will wear faster than those at the back since they are subject to steering stress. If it is wished to equalise wear, front and rear tyres on the same side may be interchanged. It is not good practice to reverse the direction of rotation of a radial tyre, as would happen if the wheels were moved from one side of the car to the other.
2 Wheels may need balancing when they are moved to a different position on the car. When buying new tyres, if two tyres only are being renewed, the new pair should always be fitted to the front wheels, as these are the most important from the safety aspect of steering and braking.
3 Never mix tyres of radial and crossply construction on the same car, as the basic design differences can cause unusual and, in certain conditions, very dangerous handling and braking characteristics. If an emergency should force the use of two different types, make sure the radials are on the rear wheels and drive particularly carefully. If three of the five wheels are fitted with radial tyres, make sure that no more than two radials are in use on the car (and these at the rear). Rationalise the tyres at the earliest possible opportunity.
4 Wheels are not normally subject to servicing problems, but when tyres are renewed or changed the wheels should be balanced to reduce vibration and wear. If a wheel is suspected of damage, caused by hitting the kerb or a pothole which could distort it out of true, change it and have it checked for balance and true running at the earliest opportunity.
5 When fitting the wheels, do not overtighten the nuts. The maximum possible manual torque applied by the manufacturer's wheelbrace is adequate. It also prevents difficulties when the same wheelbrace has to be used for removal of the wheels.

10 Fault diagnosis – steering, wheels and tyres

Symptom	Reason(s)
Excessive free movement in steering wheel	Wear in steering linkage, gear and driveshaft joints
Wander	As above Wheels out of alignment Uneven tyre pressures Worn kingpin bushes
Steering stiff and heavy	Balljoints seized Incorrect wheel alignment Low tyre pressures Kingpins seized
Wheel wobble and vibration	Roadwheels out of balance or damaged Wheel nuts loose Wheels out of alignment Worn wheel bearings Worn balljoints
Uneven tyre wear	Pressures incorrect Camber angle incorrect Toe-out adjustment incorrect

Chapter 8 Front axle and front suspension

For modifications, and information applicable to later models, see Supplement at end of manual

Contents

Specifications

Suspension type
Independent front and rear, interconnected by central cylinder

Shock absorbers

Early models	Inertia dampers, friction or telescopic shock absorbers
Later models	Telescopic shock absorbers only

Vehicle height settings – front

2CV (up to July 1969):	
125-380 X tyres	192.5 to 197.5 mm (7.58 to 7.78 in)
135-380 X tyres	205.5 to 210.5 mm (8.09 to 8.29 in)
2CV4 and 2CV6:	
125-380 X tyres	192.5 to 197.5 mm (7.58 to 7.78 in)
Ami Saloon:	
125-380 X tyres	187.5 to 192.5 mm (7.38 to 7.58 in)
Ami Estate:	
125-380 X tyres	192.5 to 197.5 mm (7.58 to 7.78 in)
Dyane:	
125-380 X tyres	192.5 to 197.5 mm (7.58 to 7.78 in)
2CV van:	
125-380 X tyres	202.5 to 207.5 mm (7.97 to 8.17 in)

Torque wrench settings

	lbf ft	kgf m
Crossmember bolts	36	5.0
Pinion (steering) retainer nuts	101	14.0
Axle arm retaining nut (slotted)	36	5.0
Front hub nut	250 to 290	35 to 40
Hub bush nut	250 to 290	35 to 40
Front shock absorber bracket bolts	29	4.0
Steering column shaft joint nuts	14.5	2.0
Steering pivot (knuckle) lever bolts	10 to 14.5	1.5 to 2.0
Steering column-to-pinion clamp bolt	13	1.9
Inertia damper retaining nuts	43	6.0
Front shock absorber rear end spindle nuts	152	21.5
Connecting lever to pivot bolts	11 to 14.5	1.5 to 2.0
Lower plugs to pivot spindle	43	6.0
Coupling sleeve rod nuts	7	1.0
Wheel nuts	29 to 43	4.0 to 6.0
Steering rod ball-pin 'Nylstop' nuts	29	4.0
Anti-roll bar clamp	43	6.0

1 General description and maintenance

1 Although the front and rear suspension assemblies are independent, on most models they are interconnected by a central suspension cylinder (see Chapter 9).

2 The rear end of the front axle arm pivots on the crossmember unit on each side on taper roller bearings. At the front end the arm curves outwards and forms the axis section of the front axle unit. The axle and hub unit are fitted with taper roller bearings and the hub nut also retains the driveshaft outer section.

3 Some early models were fitted with inertia damper units on the front or front and rear hubs. All models now have telescopic shock absorbers fitted front and rear. These have replaced the friction dampers previously used (refer to Chapter 12).

4 The driveshaft on each side has male and female sliding spline joints to allow for transverse movement of the hub. A constant velocity (CV) type joint provides steering and suspension movements. The driveshaft and steering joints are enclosed in rubber gaiters for protection from dirt.

5 Each axle arm movement is controlled by its connection to the telescopic shock absorbers, which are mounted in line and horizontally on each side, and also by its connection with the tie-rod bars to the central suspension unit. The tie-rods are adjustable to enable the vehicle ground clearance to be corrected when required. Ami models are fitted with a front anti-roll bar.

Maintenance

6 Very little in the way of maintenance is required apart from greasing the sliding joints of the driveshafts (photo) and the kingpins, and occasionally checking/adjusting the chassis ground clearance. Refer to Chapter 9 for details of height adjustment.

7 Lubricate the knife edges and suspension arm brackets and the tie-rod ends (photo). These items are most easily lubricated using a clean paint brush dipped in grease.

8 The inertia dampers can be drained and refilled with the specified oil. The units will have to be removed for draining – see Section 4.

9 Periodic checks must also be made to look for wear or damage in the various joints, pivots and wheel hub bearings.

10 In the unfortunate event of a front end collision, a check must be made on the axle and steering geometry (see Chapter 7). There is no adjustment possible to correct the wheel camber angle and if it is incorrect the axle arm is almost certainly at fault. Have this checked by your Citroën dealer for misalignment and renew if necessary.

2 Anti-roll bar – removal and refitting

1 Raise the car at the front and support with chassis stands. Remove the front wheels and place chocks against the rear wheels.

2 Unscrew and remove the retaining bolts of the bar clamps on the left-hand side. Note the number and orientation of the adjustment and stop shims.

3 Disconnect the retaining bolts and note the shim fittings on the right-hand side.

4 Remove the bar from the left-hand side. Keep the shims separate and in order.

5 To check the anti-roll bar for misalignment, possibly caused through accident damage, place the bar on a perfectly flat surface and referring to Fig. 8.3 ensure that the side marked 'a-b' is kept firmly in contact with the surface area. Now measure any distortion at the opposing side using feeler gauges inserted at point 'c'. A maximum distortion of 3 mm (0.118 in) is allowed, beyond this figure the bar must be renewed. Repeat the procedure on the opposing side reversing the process.

6 To refit the anti-roll bar, locate the retaining clamps if they were removed and relocate the bar. Insert the bar from the left-hand side, curved section facing rearwards.

7 As the bar is fitted, first adjust the left-hand side. Slide a 6 mm (15/64 in) diameter rod between the suspension arm and the bar and insert the retaining bolts with the bar held in this position. The thrust pad round edges must fit towards the clamps. Tighten the bolts to the specified torque.

1.6 The drive shaft sliding joint lubrication nipple

1.7 Lubricating the knife edges

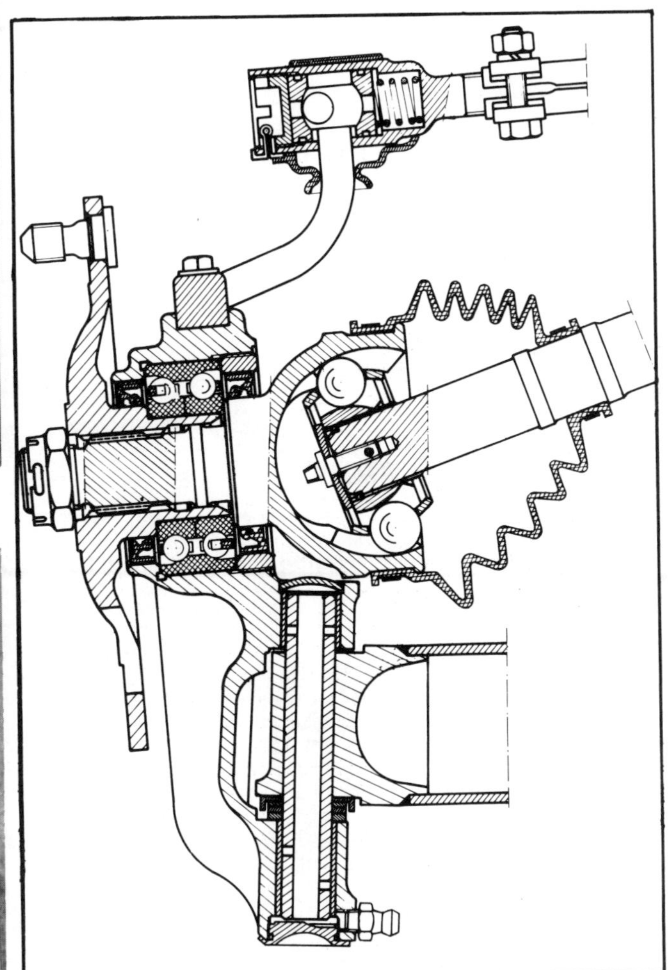

Fig. 8.1 Cross-section of the front hub, driveshaft and steering assembly (Sec 1)

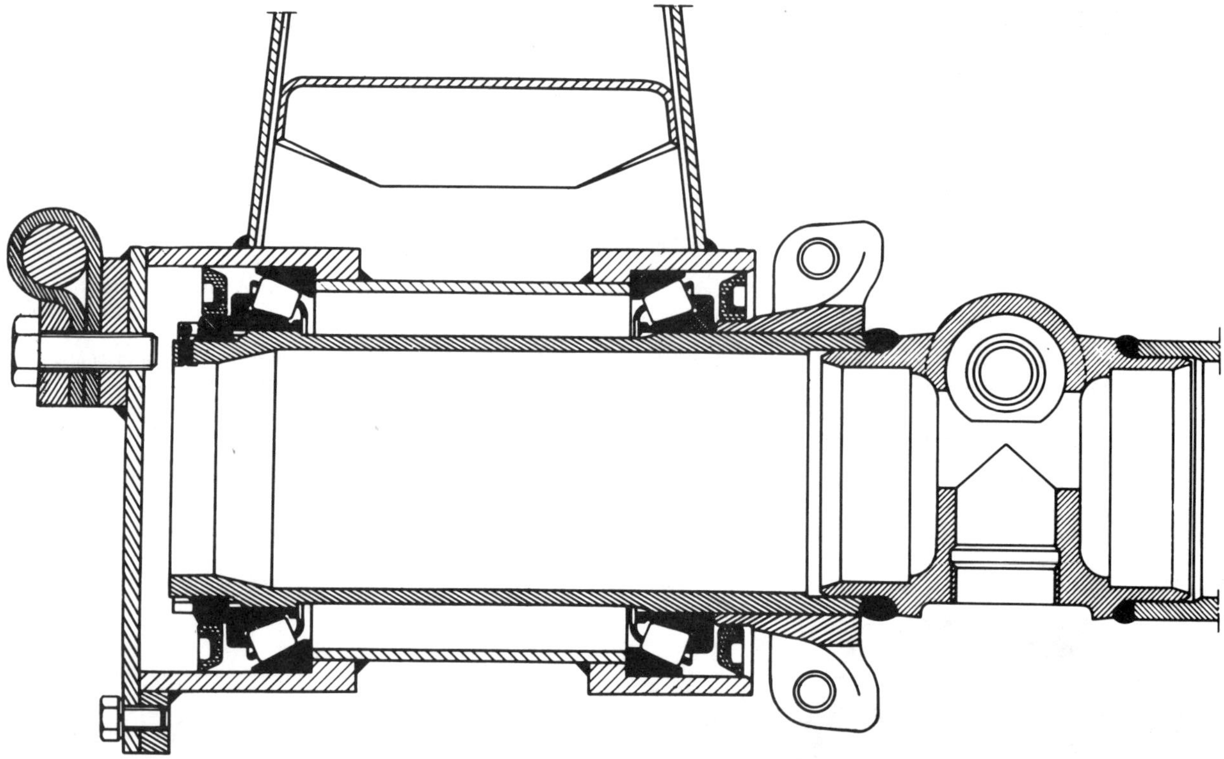

Fig. 8.2 Sectional view of axle arm attachment to crossmember – Ami models (Sec 1)

Fig. 8.3 Checking anti-roll bar alignment. Points a and b must be in contact wiith the flat surface (Sec 2)

A Feeler gauge *c Measure gap here*

8 Now locate the right-hand side of the bar in the same manner as for the left.

9 To adjust the bar endfloat the shim packing thickness required between the damper bracket and the clamps must be calculated, and must give a clearance or interference of 0.5 mm (0.019 in) maximum before fitting the retaining screw. Various shim thicknesses may be needed and these should be obtained from your Citroën dealer or cut out and made to the shape of the originals.

10 When the endfloat adjustment has been completed on one side, repeat the procedure on the other and tighten the bolts to the torque specified.

11 Refit the roadwheels and lower the vehicle to complete.

3 Front shock absorber – removal and refitting

1 If fitted, unscrew and remove the anti-roll bar clamp bolt on the side to be worked on and note the position of shims relative to clamps.

2 Unscrew and remove the shock absorber bracket retaining bolts and separate the bracket.

3 Unscrew and remove the shock absorber rear retaining nut and disconnect the unit with the front bracket.

4 Unscrew the bracket to shock absorber retaining nut to separate them.

5 Refitting is a reversal of the removal procedure, but note the following:

- *(a) Ensure that the shock absorbers are fitted the correct way round with the drain holes facing downwards*
- *(b) The respective washers must be fitted in the correct order as in Fig. 8.5*
- *(c) Tighten the shock absorber spindle at the rear end to the specified torque*
- *(d) Smear 'Masti joint' or equivalent between the faces of the front bracket and crossmember*
- *(e) Reconnect the anti-roll bar (if fitted) as described in Section 2.*

6 If replacement shock absorbers are being fitted to vehicles not equipped with inertia dampers at the front, fit only Lipmesa shock absorber units (coloured black). Models fitted with inertia dampers at the front are equipped with shock absorbers of Boge manufacture (coloured dark blue).

4 Inertia damper unit (front) – removal and refitting

1 Raise the front of the car and support with chassis stands.
2 Remove the roadwheel from the side concerned.
3 The damper unit is retained to the front axle assembly by two nuts. Unscrew the nuts and detach the damper. If one of the retaining screws is tight in its bracket hole, use a soft drift to drive it free.
4 To check the damper unit shake it up and down in the normal upright position (filler plug to top). The damper is serviceable if the inner weight can be felt to be moving, accompanied by a rubbing noise.
5 If the damper is defective it must be renewed.
6 The oil can be replaced by unscrewing the filler plug (retain the copper washer) and inverting the damper. Allow the old oil to drain out. Use a suitable funnel and insert the new lubricant (70 cc of LHM fluid or light oil). Refit the cap and washer.
7 Refitting the damper is a reversal of the removal procedure. Ensure that the filler plug is at the top and tighten the retaining nuts to the specified torque.

Fig. 8.4 Front shock absorber location (Sec 3)

1 Washer
2 Drain holes
3 Rear spindle
4 Rear nut
5 Front nut

3.3 The front shock absorber and tie-rod

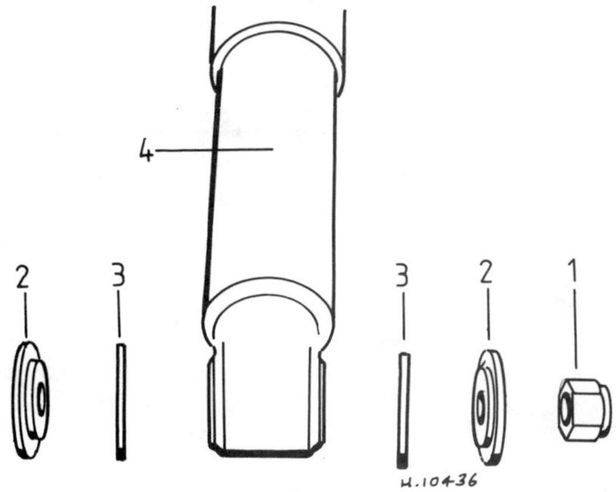

Fig. 8.5 Shock absorber washer locations (Sec 3)

1 Nut
2 Shouldered washer
3 Anti-rattle washer
4 Shock absorber

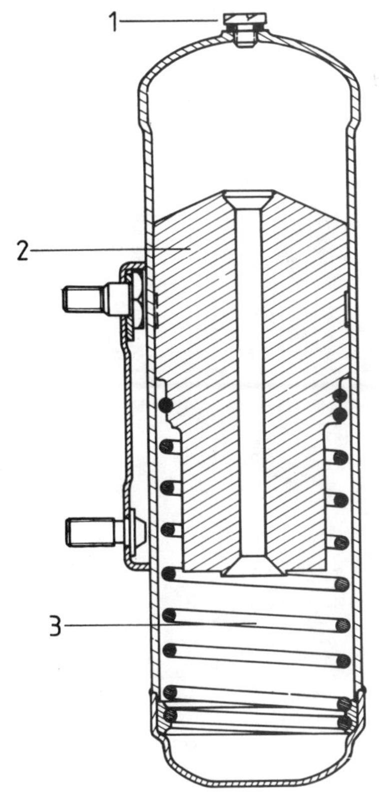

Fig. 8.6 Sectional view of inertia damper unit (Sec 4)

1 Drain/filler plug
2 Weight
3 Spring

5 Driveshafts – removal, inspection and refitting

Outer shaft section (hub end)

1 Raise the vehicle at the front and support with axle/chassis stands. Remove the roadwheel on the side concerned.

2 Extract the split pin from the hub nut and then unscrew and remove the nut. Considerable pressure will be required: to prevent any damage to the steering arm stop, support the axle unit. Lock the hub by passing a 29 mm diameter bar through one of the three holes.

3 Rotate the wheel hub onto full lock and then unscrew the driveshaft protector bellows retaining clip and compress the bellows.

4 Withdraw the driveshaft gearbox outlet on the inside and disengage from the hub on the other end to remove it.

5.7 Unscrew and remove the driveshaft flange bolts

Inner shaft section (gearbox output end) (Ball type CV joints)

5 This can be removed without removing the outer section. Raise and support the front end of the vehicle and remove the roadwheel on the side to be worked on.

6 Unscrew and loosen the rubber protector seal retaining clip on the sliding section.

7 Unscrew and remove the six driveshaft flange retaining bolts to the transmission output hub unit (photo), then compress the inner section and outer shafts together on their splines. Swivel the shaft forwards and separate the two.

Inspection and refitting

8 If on inspection the CV joints are worn, they cannot be repaired and the unit must be renewed. Check the splines for signs of wear and damage and renew if necessary. Remove the old grease with a clean lint-free cloth.

9 The rubber bellow protector seals must be in first class condition. If there are any cracks or defects in them then they must be renewed as defective seals will shorten considerably the life of the joints.

10 Refitting of both inner and outer sections is a reversal of the removal process. Lubricate the constant velocity joint with general purpose grease prior to assembly. Also lubricate the shaft splines. Use new shaft flange-to-transmission output hub bolts and tighten to the specified torque. Retighten the hub nut to the specified torque and insert a new split pin to secure.

6 Front wheel hub and bearing – removal and refitting

1 Raise the vehicle at the front and secure with axle/chassis stands.

2 Blocks up the chassis at the height of the axle crossmember.

3 Remove the roadwheel on the side to be worked on.

4 Remove the driveshaft by extracting the split pin from the hub nut and unscrewing and removing the nut. Separate the stub axle from the hub.

5 Chock the axle arm to support it and drive the hub from the pivot to separate. Use a wooden block or soft drift.

Fig. 8.7 Front wheel hub (Sec 5)

1 Nut
2 Split pin
3 Hub
A Locking bar

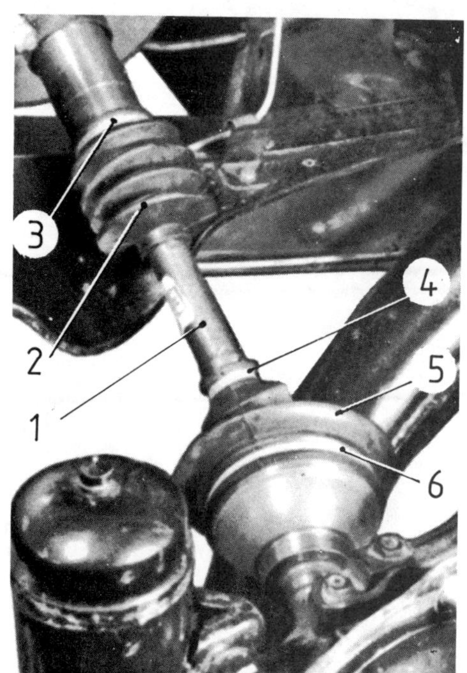

Fig. 8.8 Driveshaft and joint covers (Sec 5)

1 Driveshaft
2 Bellows
3 Clip
4 Clip
5 Bellows
6 Clip

6 If the bearing is to be removed, drill out the centre punch marks securing the bush nut. A 4 mm drill is ideal. Unscrew and remove the bush nut using special tool 3301-T and extension piece and spanner 3304-T. Alternatively a long bar and a strong tube can be used with a suitable socket spanner.
7 Tap the bearing from the pivot bore using a soft drift. To remove the inner bearing race if it is still on the stub axle, use a suitable puller or special tool 1813-T.
8 Prise the oil seals free from the pivot and bush nut
9 Before commencing reassembly, ensure that all components are clean and serviceable.
10 Always fit new oil seals. Position the seal in the bush nut with the lips towards the bearing. The seal must seat so that it is recessed 1.5 mm (0.06 in) from the bearing shoulder (Fig. 8.9).
11 Similarly fit the other seal in the hub bore.
12 Check that the bearing inner races are flush against each other. Pull them together using a suitable bolt and flat washer if necessary. Check the bearings for smooth operation.
13 Lubricate the bearing with general purpose grease and insert it in the pivot bore using a suitable tube 70 mm (2.7 in) diameter, which must bear onto the outer race of the bearing only.
14 Screw the bush nut into position and tighten to the specified torque, then lock it in position by stake punching at diametrically opposed points.
15 Refit the hub using a soft-headed mallet. Drive it home squarely.
16 Remove the chock supporting the axle arm.
17 Refit the driveshaft.
18 Refit the roadwheel to complete and lower the vehicle to the ground.

7 Kingpin (pivot pin) – removal and refitting

1 Refer to Section 5 and remove the driveshaft from the side concerned.
2 Remove the retaining nuts and remove the inertia damper unit if fitted (Section 4).
3 Extract the split pin and unscrew the steering rod to pivot lever joint screw, using a large screwdriver or special tool MR630-16/2 if available.
4 To remove the pivot, unscrew and remove the lower plug (Fig. 8.10).
5 Extract the top plug using a 7 mm (0.275 in) diameter drift 200 mm (7.8 in) long.
6 To remove the pin with the axle arm attached to the vehicle, special tool 1858-T or equivalent will be needed (Fig. 8.11). The arm will require heat from a blowlamp before the pin can be moved. With the arm removed from the vehicle, the pin can be pressed out.
7 Detach the pivot from the friction and thrust washers and also from the dust cover.
8 To dismantle the pivot unit (steering knuckle), remove the hub as described in Section 6 and dismantle it.
9 Unscrew the retaining screws and remove the pivot lever.
10 Clean and check that all parts are fully serviceable before reassembly. In particular check the kingpin and bushes for wear and renew if worn or damaged.
11 Drive or press the old bushes out using a shouldered drift of a suitable diameter.
12 Reassembly is a reversal of the removal process, but you will need

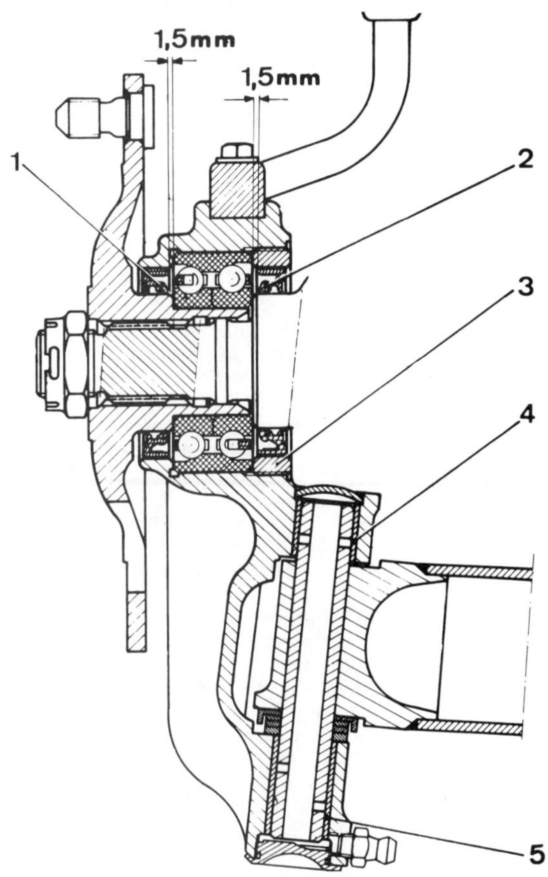

Fig. 8.9 Front wheel bearings and seals (Sec 6)

1 Seal
2 Seal
3 Bush nut
4 Upper kingpin bush
5 Lower kingpin bush

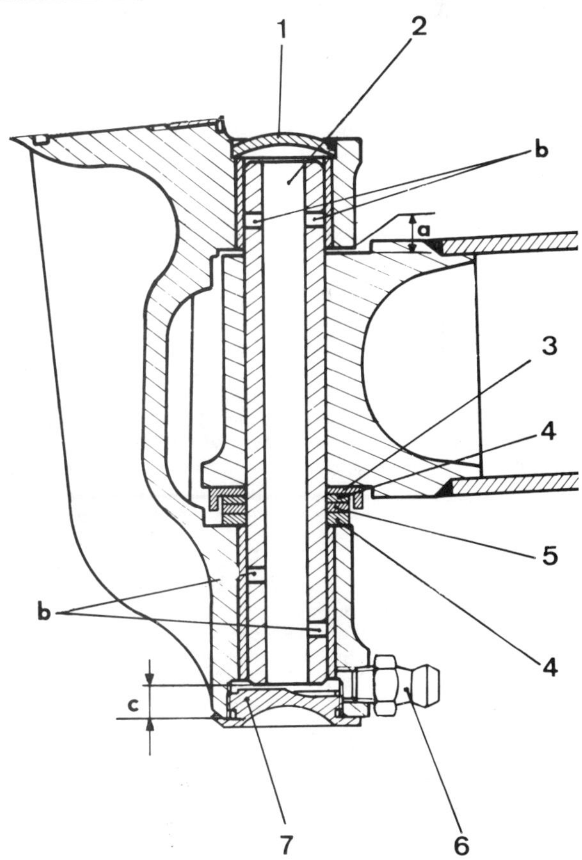

Fig. 8.10 Kingpin (pivot pin) and axle arm assembly (Sec 7)

1 Top plug
2 Kingpin
3 Dust cover
4 Thrust washer
5 Friction washer
6 Grease nipple
7 Bottom plug
a See text
b Lubrication holes
c See text

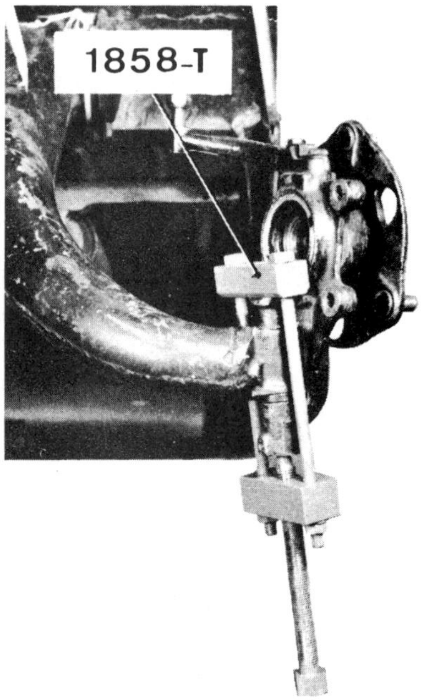

Fig. 8.11 Special tool 1858-T in position to remove the kingpin (Sec 7)

a 'slave' taper pin 16.5 mm (0.6 in) in diameter and 150 mm (5.9 in) long.

13 Fit the new bushes into position in the upper and lower pivot sections and ensure that they are correctly located. Lubricate and check the pin for size. If the pin is too tight then you will need to ream the bushes to suit. Remove the pin.

14 Gather together and lubricate with grease the dust cover, selected thrust washers and the friction washer.

15 Locate the pivot and arm and insert the dust cover, friction and thrust washers. Insert the 'slave' pin to locate them. Measure the clearance at point 'a' (Fig. 8.10) between the pivot and the arm. This clearance should be 0.1 to 0.4 mm (0.0039 to 0.0157 in). To adjust, use an alternative thrust washer to suit.

16 Thoroughly clean and lubricate the new kingpin prior to fitting. Lubricate the bushes with oil. When fitting the pin align the lubrication holes correctly as shown in 'b' (Fig. 8.10). Make sure that the dust cover, thrust washers and the friction washers are fitted *under* the arm.

17 Locate the pin initially using a copper or soft drift, taking great care to align it correctly with the bushes. If misaligned it will damage the bushes during assembly. Complete the insertion using a press or special tool 1858-T. When in position check that the base of the pin protrudes below the pivot inner section by 7.10 to 7.25 mm (0.279 to 0.285 in).

18 Fill the space between the pin and plug at the top and the plug at the bottom with suitable grease. Screw up the lower plug and bend over the collar on the pivot body to secure.

19 Carefully locate the upper plug and tap it into position, taking care not to distort it. Peen over the top ridge of the pivot in a couple of places to secure the plug. Refit the grease nipple.

20 Refit the damper (if applicable).

21 Reconnect the steering rod to the pivot lever, fully tightening the screw then unscrewing it by $\frac{1}{16}$th turn. Insert the split pin to secure.

22 Relocate the driveshaft and tighten the retaining nut to the specified torque. Lock in position using a new split pin.

23 Grease the kingpins and check that there is no severe binding when pivoted.

8 Axle arm and steering rack/crossmember (Ami models) – removal and refitting

1 Disconnect the battery earth lead and remove the spare wheel.

2 Remove the front seat by extracting the pin from the central slide and pushing the seat forwards fully to disengage.

3 Fold back the carpet and remove the rubber plugs from the passenger side floor. Unscrew the gearbox rear support bolt by several turns.

4 Referring to Fig. 8.12, peel back the rubber cover from the universal joints on the steering shaft. Unscrew the upper and lower joint screws to disconnect the steering shaft.

5 Now working within the engine compartment, unscrew the adjuster wing nuts of the handbrake cables (drum brakes only). When loosening the wing nuts, note the number of turns as a rough guide when readjusting the brakes on completion.

6 The gearbox must now be raised. If available use a trolley jack and place a piece of wood between the jack and gearbox to cushion the pressure point. Raise the gearbox just sufficiently to enable the retaining scews to be removed from the rear support.

7 You will now need a block of wood that is 35 mm (1.37 in) thick. This is positioned between the gearbox and the platform crossmember to support the gearbox.

8 Chock the rear wheels and raise the front of the vehicle. Support it securely using axle/chassis stands.

9 Remove the front roadwheels.

10 Unscrew the anti-roll bar retaining clamp bolts on each side and remove the anti-roll bar, taking note of the number and location of the shims. Also note the fitting direction of the bar.

11 Unscrew the securing bolts of the shock absorber brackets and remove them downwards.

12 Detach the exhaust pipe from the joint to the expansion chamber. Use penetrating oil if the joint retaining bolts have rusted badly.

13 Disconnect the driveshafts. Withdraw the split pin, unscrew the hub nut and release the driveshaft from the hub.

14 Extract the split pin retaining the left-hand steering rod joint nut in position. Unscrew the nut using a large screwdriver, or special spanner MR630-16/2 if available. Detach the swivel ball outer seal and free the dust cover from the steering lever.

15 Turn the hub to align the flats of the balljoint to those of the rod and separate the rod.

16 The suspension tie-rods must now be disconnected. To act as a guide when reassembling, mark the relative positions of the tie-rod and the end piece and then unscrew the tie-rod to free the knife edge. Remove the tie-rod rearwards.

17 To remove the left-hand axle arm, withdraw the split pin and unscrew the large slotted nut. If available use special tool 1833-T. Tap the arm underside with a mallet to remove it from the crossmember.

18 Insert a suitable length of wood (8 mm thick) to support the steering rack when removing the pinion.

19 Remove the steering pinion from inside the car. Withdraw the bushes and rubber washer, then drill the securing stake section of the pinion nut using a 4 mm drill. Unscrew the nut (special tool 3503-T) and plug the housing hole. Note that the utmost cleanliness is essential. Plug or seal the pinion housing hole.

20 Detach the crossmember and right arm by removing the four retaining bolts and withdraw the front axle and right-hand steering arm from the right-hand side.

21 Prior to refitting ensure that all parts are perfectly clean and fully serviceable. If a new axle arm and steering unit are being fitted it will be necessary to detach the left-hand axle arm and the rack-and-pinion (unless the engine and gearbox have been removed).

22 Insert the steering unit crossmember and right-hand side axle arm into position from the right-hand side. Locate the unit onto the chassis platform and engage the centering dowels. Fit the retaining bolts with lockwasher and tighten to the specified torque. Bend over the tabs of the lockwashers to secure.

23 Remove the plug from the pinion housing and ensure that no dirt is allowed to enter when fitting the pinion. Lubricate the pinion and its bearing with grease and insert into position in the housing. Refit the felt washer and nut and tighten to the specified torque. Stake punch the nut at two points to make secure. Withdraw the length of wood supporting the rack and insert the rubber bush and washer over the pinion shaft.

24 To fit the left-hand axle arm, lubricate the outer and inner bearings with grease and locate the arm onto the crossmember.

25 Use a suitable tube drift and locate the outer bearing into position. Fit the slotted nut and tighten to the specified torque, aligning the slot to the split pin holes in the housing. Fit a new split pin to secure.

26 Reconnect the left-hand steering rod. Lubricate the swivel housing with general purpose grease. Locate the swivel ball so that flat sections are aligned to suit the steering rod and insert ball into bar.

Fig. 8.12 Disconnect the steering shaft (Sec 8)

1 Column-to-shaft bolt
2 Steering shaft
3 Rubber plugs
4 Protective boot
5 Shaft-to-pinion joint bolt

Fig. 8.13 Suspension tie-rod connection (Sec 8)

1 Pin and clip
2 Tie-rod end
3 Tie-rod

Fig. 8.14 Special tool 1833-T or equivalent is needed to undo the axle arm nut (Sec 8)

4 Nut
5 Arm

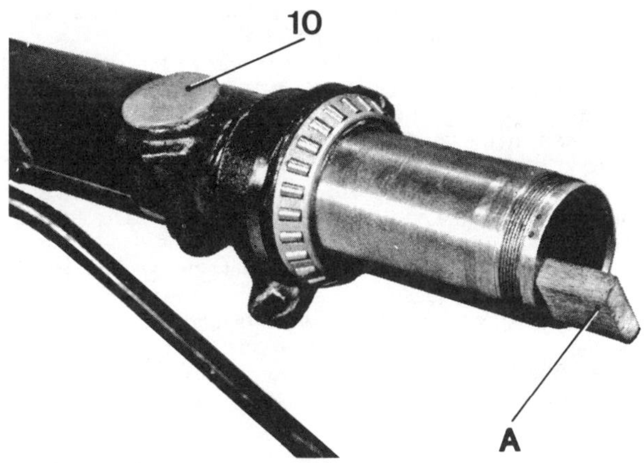

Fig. 8.15 Insert wood (A) to retain rack in position. Note protective plug (10) (Sec 8)

Fig. 8.16 Refitting the pinion (Sec 8)

4 Rubber washer
5 Pinion shaft
6 Bush
7 Pinion nut
a Punch positions

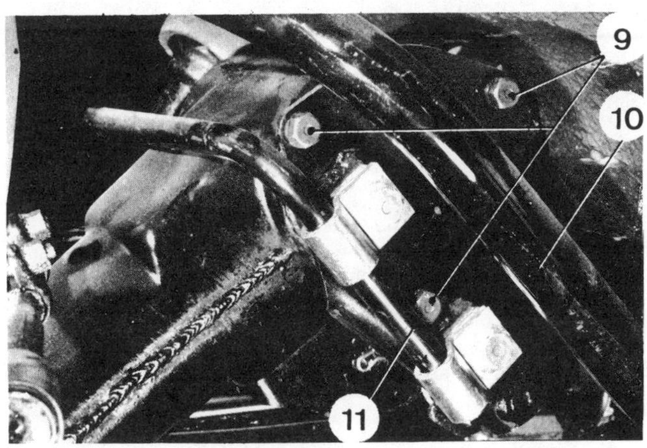

Fig. 8.17 Locating the anti-roll bar (Sec 8)

9 Bracket securing bolts
10 Exhaust pipe
11 Anti-roll bar

27 Fit the dust covers and swivel joint seating. Fit and fully tighten the retaining screw against the ball, then back it off by $\frac{1}{16}$th of a turn and insert a new split pin to secure.
28 To refit the driveshafts, lubricate the splines with grease and relocate the hub. Fit the hub nut and tighten to the specified torque. Insert a new split pin to secure.
29 Reconnect the suspension tie-rods. Lubricate the knife edges with grease and locate the inner spring clip stop.
30 Screw the tie-rod in up to the mark made on removal. Check that the dust cover is located on the suspension cylinder end piece.
31 Reconnect the exhaust pipe to the expansion box joint. Smear the joint with exhaust sealant to ensure a good seal.
32 Reconnect the front shock absorber support brackets. The shock absorber retaining bolts can be loosened to facilitate the bracket location. Retighten the bolts when the brackets are located. Retighten the bolts when the brackets are located. Tighten the bracket bolts to the specified torque.
33 Refit the anti-roll bar using the same number of shims as removed. When located, insert a 6 mm clearance gauge rod between the axle arm and rod (Fig. 8.17). Tighten the bolts on that side and remove the gauge. On the right-hand side repeat the procedure and adjust the endfloat as given in Section 2.
34 Relocate the gearbox with the rear bracket and remove the wooden block.
35 Readjust the handbrake cables.
36 Lower the vehicle from the supports and reconnect the steering with the wheels in the straight-ahead position.
37 Locate the steering shaft to the rack pinion at the bottom and insert the retaining bolt. Do not tighten yet.
38 Check that the steering wheel is in the straight-ahead position and connect the shaft at the top joint. Tighten the securing nuts to the specified torque.
39 Refit the plugs into the floor, refit the carpets and the front seat.
40 The vehicle height must now be checked and if necessary adjusted (see Chapter 9).
41 Check and tighten the anti-roll bar and also the shock absorber bolts to their specified torques.
42 Check and adjust if necessary the wheel alignment.
43 Check that the steering lock is correct (see Chapter 7).
44 Reconnect the battery to complete and check that the various circuits are operational.

9 Axle arm and steering rack/crossmember (all models except Ami) – removal and refitting

1 Disconnect the battery earth terminal and remove the spare wheel.
2 Remove the bonnet, side panels, wheel arches and front wings as described in Chapter 11.
3 Detach the steering column (see Chapter 7).
4 The following operations in the removal procedure closely follow those given for the Ami models. Refer to Section 8 from paragraph 11 on, and disconnect and remove as applicable:

(a) The driveshafts
(b) Right-hand steering rod
(c) Suspension tie-rods
(d) Right-hand axle arm

5 Remove the axle arm and steering rack from the left-hand side.
6 As described for the Ami, check that all components are clean, lubricated where specified and in a serviceable condition as they are refitted.
7 Follow the refitting procedures in Section 8 from paragraph 22, but fit the steering unit and axle arm from the left-hand side. Refit the following:

(a) Right-hand axle arm
(b) Right-hand steering rod
(c) Driveshafts
(d) Suspension tie-rods (see Section 3 for refitting hydraulic shock absorbers)
(e) Relocate the gearbox and adjust the handbrake cables
(f) Reconnect the steering

8 Check the steering for correct operation.

10 Axle arm – removal and refitting

1 Raise the vehicle and support the chassis at axle height.
2 Remove the wheel on the side to be worked on.
3 Refer to Section 2 and remove the anti-roll bar (if fitted) and its support brackets.
4 Unscrew the retaining bolts and remove the shock absorber mounting bracket on the side concerned.
5 If the left-hand arm is being removed, then disconnect the exhaust pipe from the silencer. This does not apply if working on the right-hand side only.
6 Flatten the lockplate tabs and unscrew the bolts which hold the steering drag link to the top of the hub carrier.
7 Remove the driveshaft at the axle end (Section 5).
8 Ensure that the tension in the front suspension is relieved by supporting both sides on jacks or axle stands.
9 Extract the spring clip, drive out the retaining pin, and disconnect the suspension tie-rod. On Dyane models remove the wing valance.
10 To remove the axle arm, extract the split pin and unscrew the slotted retaining nut. Use special spanner number 1833-T if available, or fabricate one from a suitable diameter tube.
11 With the nut removed the arm can be withdrawn. If it is tight tap it off using a soft-headed mallet.
12 To remove the inner taper roller bearing you will need a puller similar to that shown in Fig. 8.18. Alternatively, it may be possible to lever off the bearing using two screwdrivers, if it is not too tight.
13 Disconnect the axle arm from the axle unit.
14 If required, the outer bearing races can be removed from the arm with a suitable drift. If they are to be used again take care not to damage them and mark them on removal for identification.
15 Assemble in the reverse order to removal and note the following:

(a) Do not interchange the bearing cones and cups. When fitting the cups fit them squarely and ensure that they are fully located. Lubricate the races with grease
(b) Always fit a new gasket and seal

16 Fit and tighten the axle arm retaining nut to the specified torque figure and ensure that the arm rotates freely. Align the split pin hole and fit a new split pin to secure, bending over the pin ends into the crossmember bore.
17 When reconnecting the suspension tie-rod, grease the knife edge before refitting. Retighten the tie-rod to the original setting which was marked when dismantling.
18 When connecting up the steering rod refer to Chapter 7 for fitting and adjustment instructions.

Fig. 8.18 Special puller 1829-T being used to remove the inner taper roller bearing cone (1) and seal (2) (Sec 10)

19 Reconnect the driveshaft – see Section 5.
20 Loosen the shock absorber retaining nuts, then refit the supports and retighten the fittings to the specified torque.
21 Relocate the anti-roll bar (if fitted) and adjust it as described in Section 2.
22 Reattach the exhaust pipe, using exhaust sealant to ensure a leakproof joint.
23 Refit the roadwheel and lower the vehicle.
24 Check the vehicle height as described in Chapter 9 and the steering geometry as described in Chapter 7.

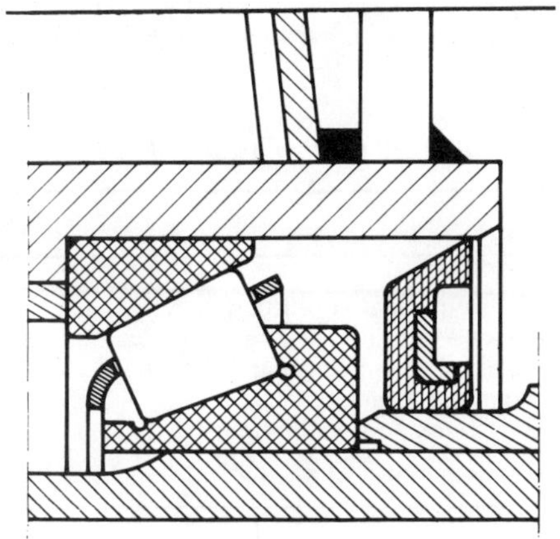

Fig. 8.19 The bearing and seal location (Sec 10)

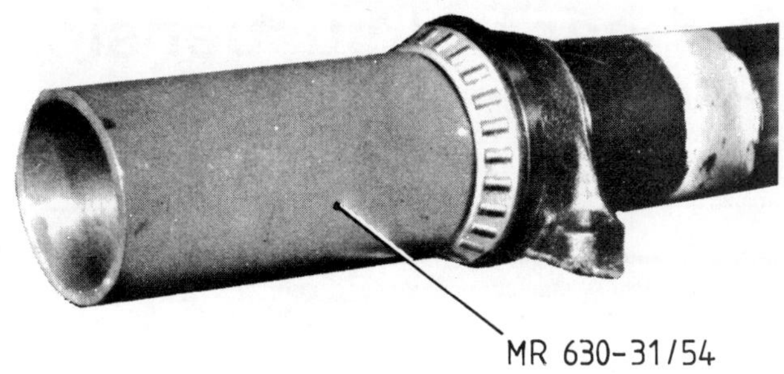

Fig. 8.20 Use the Citroën tubular drift MR630-31/54 or equivalent to fit the bearing cone and seal (Sec 10)

11 Fault diagnosis – front axle and suspension

Before diagnosing faults from the following chart, check that any irregularities are not caused by:

1. *Defective steering*
2. *Incorrect tyre pressures*
3. *Incorrect 'mix' of tyres*
4. *Incorrect wheel alignment*

Symptom	Reason/s
Vibration and rattles	Worn axle arm kingpin and/or bearing Suspension cylinder loose Pipe securing clips and brackets loose Axle unit securing bolts loose Hub bearings worn Driveshaft CV joints worn
Suspension bottoming	Suspension height incorrect Shock absorbers worn or defective Inertia unit/s defective
Suspension stiff, groans and squeaks	Suspension cylinder dry or defective Driveshaft or gaiter fouling wheel arch Driveshaft splined joint dry

Chapter 9 Rear suspension and central suspension units

For modifications and information applicable to later models, see Supplement at end of manual

Contents

Specifications

Type	Independent, trailing arm interconnected to front suspension by central cylinder unit. Double-acting telescopic shock absorbers.

Rear wheel geometry

Toe-in:	
Models up to 1969	0 to 8.0 mm (0 to 0.31 in) (not adjustable)
Models 1969 on	4 mm (0.16 in) toe-out to 4 mm (0.16 in) toe-in (not adjustable)
Camber	0° to 0° 30′ (not adjustable)

Vehicle height settings – rear

2CV (up to July 1969):	
125-380 X tyres	277.5 to 282.5 mm (10.93 to 11.12 in)
135-380 X tyres	288.5 to 293.5 mm (11.36 to 11.56 in)
2CV4 and 2CV6:	
125-380 X tyres	277.5 to 282.5 mm (10.93 to 11.12 in)
Ami saloon:	
125-380 X tyres	277.5 to 282.5 mm (10.93 to 11.12 in)
Ami estate:	
135-380 X tyres	287.5 to 292.5 mm (11.32 to 11.52 in)
Dyane:	
125-380 X tyres	277.5 to 282.5 mm (10.93 to 11.12 in)
2CV van:	
125-380 X tyres	332.5 to 337.5 mm (13.09 to 13.29 in)

Torque wrench settings

	lbf ft	kgf m
Central cylinder rear overrun stop nuts	129 to 158	18 to 22
Central cylinder front end piece nuts	129 to 158	18 to 22
Rear axle arm retaining nut	40	5.5
Inertia damper retaining nuts	43	6
Rear crossmember retaining bolts	29 to 36	4 to 5
Rear damper nuts	68	9.5
Rear brake line clip nuts	7	1
Three-way union bolts	14.5	2
Brake pipe screwed unions	5.8 to 6.5	0.8 to 0.9
Rear hub bush nut	220 to 290	30 to 41
Rear hub bearing nut	220 to 290	30 to 41

1 General description

The rear suspension is interconnected with the front suspension by means of a central suspension cylinder on each side. (Post-1976 Ami 8 models have a fixed central suspension cylinder and thus front and rear suspensions are not interconnected).

Both the front and rear tie-rods are connected to their own coil springs within the cylinder at one end and to the axle arm at the other. The tie-rods are adjustable for length to enable adjustment of the vehicle ground clearance front and rear.

Double-acting telescopic shock absorbers are fitted at the rear and these are mounted horizontally from the chassis at the rear of the central suspension cylinder, and to the axle arm at the other end.

The rear axle arms pivot from a crossmember unit which is located across the chassis near to the forward section of the rear wheel arch. On all post-1972 models the rear brake line has a centrally situated three-way connector and the feed line to each rear brake runs from the connector into the crossmember, where it is coiled to allow for the suspension arm movement and to withstand shock treatment. The brake line then comes out through the crossmember end piece and continues down the axle arm to the brake unit.

Inertia dampers are fitted to the rear hub units on some earlier models.

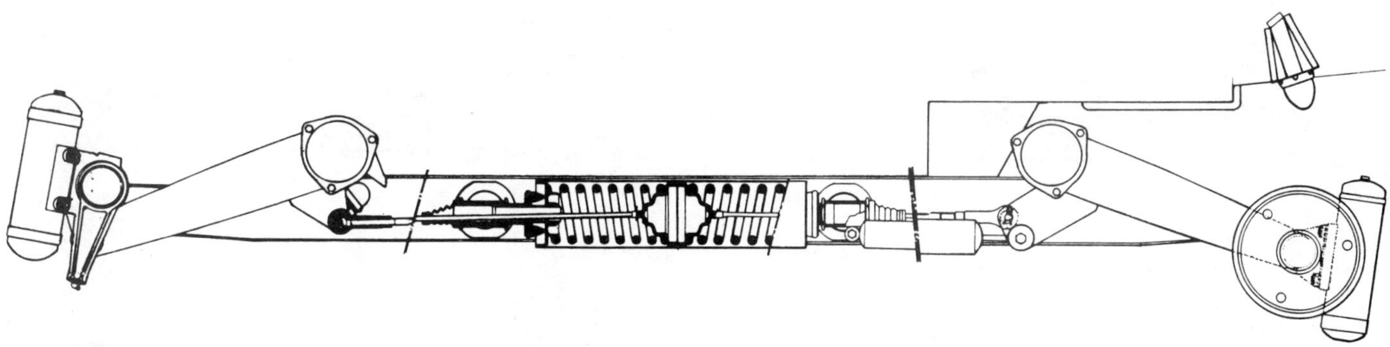

Fig. 9.1 Diagram showing the interconnection of front and rear suspension. (Early model shown – later models similar) (Sec 1)

2 Vehicle height – check and adjustment

1 The vehicle height check should be made occasionally to ensure that it is correct. The correct body height is needed to maintain the required weight distribution and also the correct working angles for the associated suspension components.

Checking

2 Before making a check, ensure that the tyre pressures are correct. The car must stand unladen on level ground and the fuel tank contain about 5 litres (1 gallon) of fuel.
3 You will need a cranked open-ended 9mm spanner and a height measuring gauge of some description.
4 Rock the vehicle up and down a couple of times and allow it to resettle.
5 On all models, check the height by measuring from the ground to the chassis underside between the front and then the rear crossmember mounting bolts (Figs. 9.2 and 9.3).
6 Compare the height measured against that specified for your particular model and adjust if necessary. (Front suspension heights are given in Chapter 8).

Adjustment

7 Raise the car and support it on the side to be adjusted. Place chocks under the other wheels. Slacken the nuts securing the hydraulic shock absorbers (if fitted) to prevent damage to the bushes.
8 To increase the height, screw the tie-rod into the tie-rod end piece, and vice versa to reduce the height. The rod can be turned by the 9mm spanner fitted onto the flat sections of the rod. Initially try turning the rod three complete turns and then lower the car and recheck the height at the point adjusted. Make any further adjustments accordingly until the front and rear heights are correct.
9 Due to the interconnected front and rear suspension system, any adjustments made at one end of the vehicle will alter the height of the other. Therefore, when making adjustments, allow for this factor.
10 Check the front bump stops (see next Section).

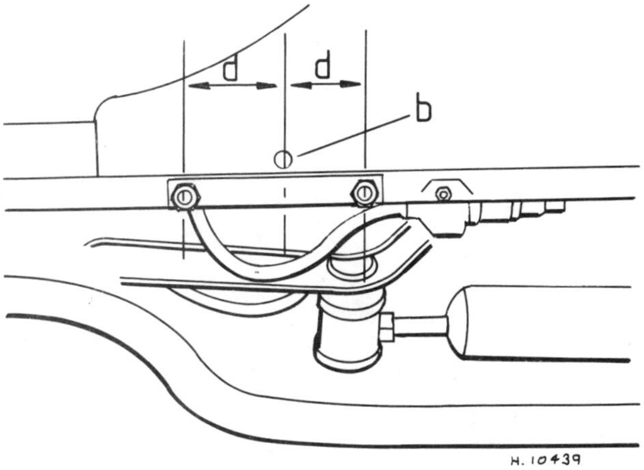

Fig. 9.3 Height measurement point (b) at rear is midway between crossmember bolts (d=d) (Sec 2)

3 Front arm stop – adjustment

1 The front and rear body heights must be correctly set as described in the previous Section.
2 Referring to Fig. 9.4, measure the clearance between the rubber buffer and the arm stop. This should be 3 to 6mm (0.118 to 0.236 in).
3 If adjustment is necessary, insert or extract (as applicable) washers between the buffer and the chassis bracket. Various washer thicknesses are available.

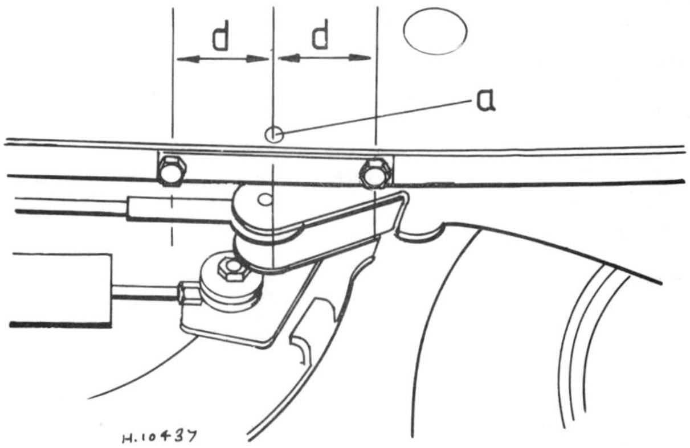

Fig. 9.2 Height measurement point (a) at front is midway between crossmember bolts (d=d) (Sec 2)

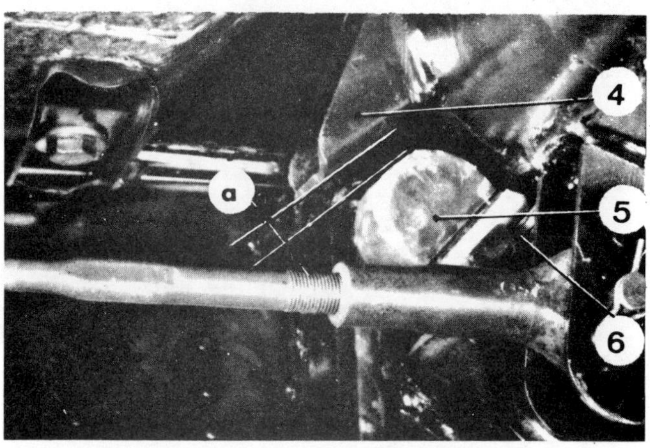

Fig. 9.4 Front arm stop adjustment (Sec 3)

4 Arm stop
5 Buffer
6 Washers
a 3 to 6 mm (0.118 to 0.236 in)

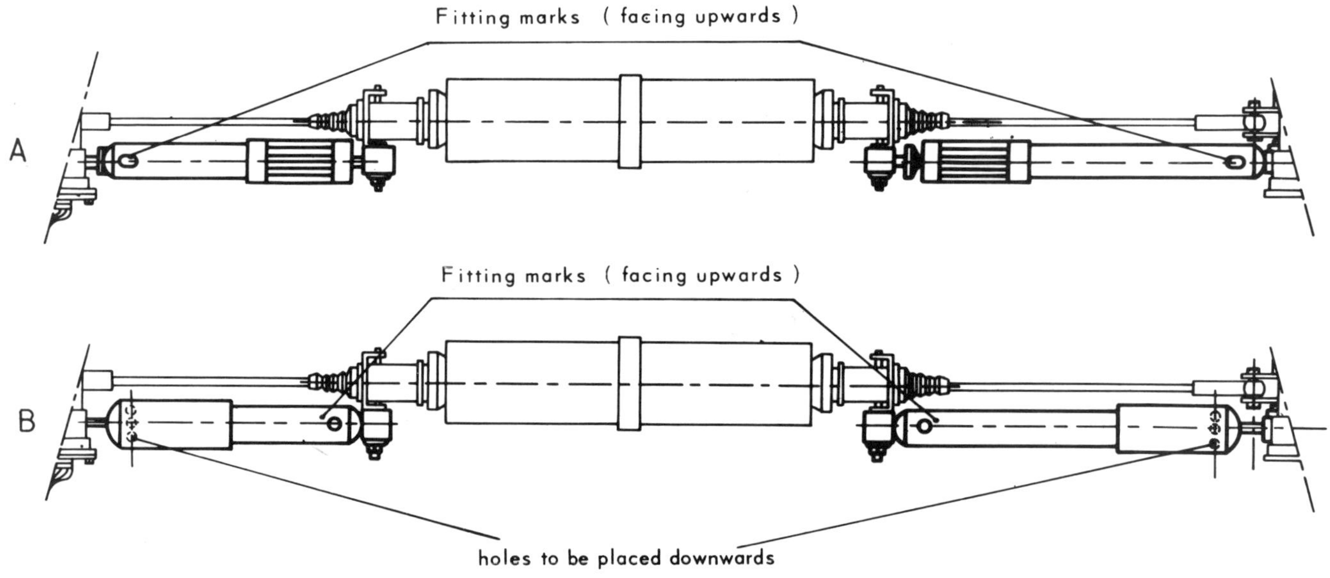

Fig. 9.5 Shock absorber mounting positions (Sec 4)

A Lipmesa type *B Boge type*

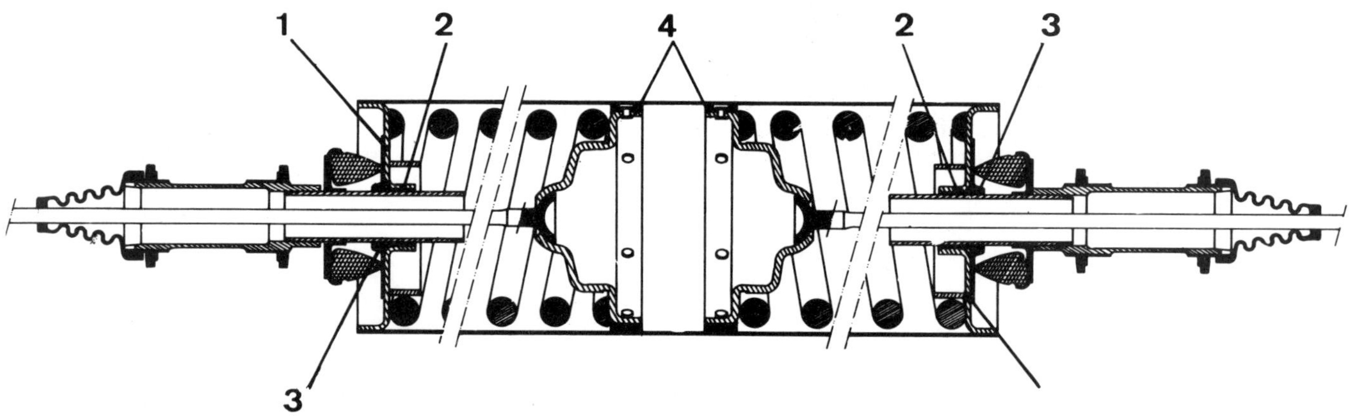

Fig. 9.6 Sectional view of the earlier type central suspension unit (Sec 5)

1 End faces
2 Bushes
3 Washers
4 Compression cups

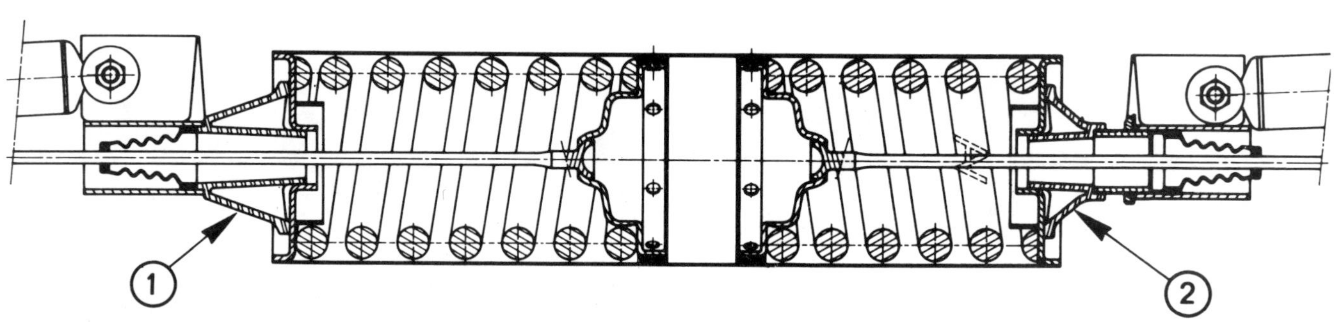

Fig. 9.7 Cutaway view of later type suspension unit (Sec 5)

1 Front buffer *2 Rear buffer*

4 Rear shock absorber – removal and refitting

1 Jack up and support the vehicle on the side concerned, using axle stands to make secure.

2 Note which way round the shock absorber unit is fitted (photo) and then unscrew the retaining bolt nuts at each end. Withdraw the shock absorber unit.

3 If fitting replacement shock absorbers, refer to Section 3 of Chapter 8 concerning Boge and Lipmesa type shock absorbers.

4 Refit in reverse, but only tighten the nuts hand tight initially. Lower the vehicle to enable it to stand normally and then finally tighten the retaining nuts to the specified torque.

5 Central suspension unit – removal and refitting

1 Jack up and support the side of the vehicle on which the central suspension unit is being removed. Support with axle stands to make secure.

2 Remove the front and rear shock absorbers (as applicable). Refer to Chapter 8 for the removal of the front shock absorber.

3 Before disconnecting the tie-rods mark the adjustment point (guide rod to end piece) to act as a guide on reassembly. Extract the spring clip and free the knife edge to lower the end piece. If necessary slacken the rod adjustment to release the tension on the knife edge. Repeat the procedure for both tie-rods.

4 Prise back the rubber seal covers from the adjustable end section of the central cylinder at each end (photo).

5 Detach the respective end sections from the side-member supports. Retain the end section and unscrew the inner adjustment nut. Detach the end pieces and the dust cover.

6 Remove the adjustable end pieces.

7 Detach the rubber support strap (where fitted) using special tool 3457-T or equivalent, then remove the front tie-rod through the slot from the side-member bracket. Remove the central cylinder unit forwards, the rear tie-rod passing through the side-member bracket. Separate the flexible buffers.

8 Although the central suspension units can be rebuilt, specialised equipment is necessary and it is therefore suggested that a defective unit is simply renewed. A cylinder which squeaks may be quietened by injecting some castor oil.

9 To refit the suspension cylinder, commence by locating the rubber buffers into position as shown (Fig. 9.9). Note that the front end of the cylinder, marked AV, must be towards the front of the car.

10 The inner nuts are now placed into position against the buffers and the cylinder unit relocated against the side-member in the reverse order to removal. The rear tie-rod engages in the side-member bracket, followed by the front tie-rod passing through the slot in the front support.

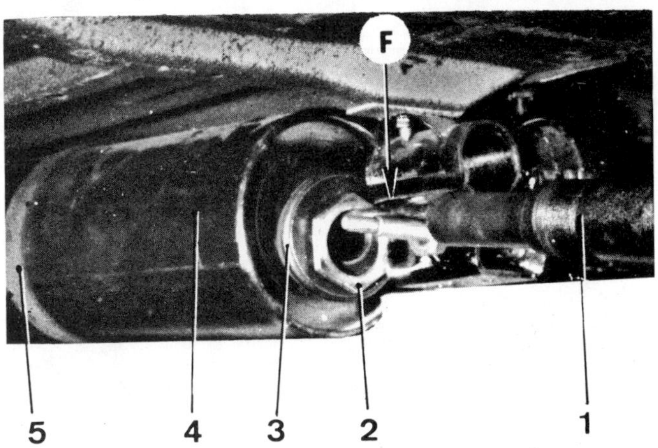

Fig. 9.8 Disconnect the tie-rods (Sec 5)

1 End piece
2 Adjuster nut
3 Flexible buffer
4 Cylinder
5 Rubber support strap
F Tie-rod slot

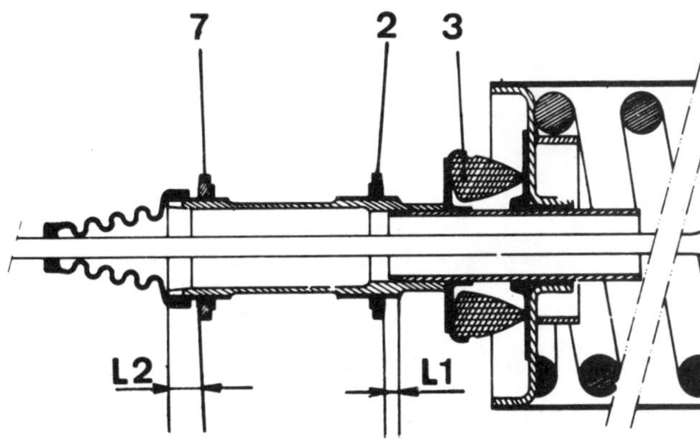

Fig. 9.9 Adjustment of front of central suspension unit (Sec 5)

L1 5 mm (0.196 in)
L2 15 mm (0.590 in)
2 Adjuster nut
3 Buffer
7 Adjuster nut

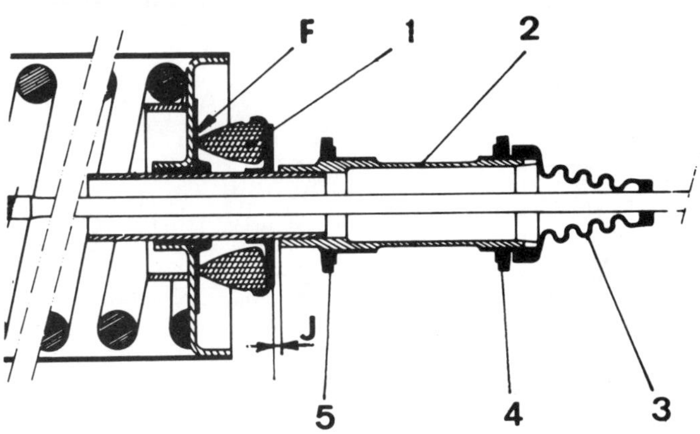

Fig. 9.10 Adjustment of rear overrun stop (Sec 5)

1 Buffer
2 End piece
3 Dust cover
4 Adjuster nut
5 Adjuster nut
F End face
J See text

4.2 The rear shock absorber unit

11 Fit the end piece adjusters in the brackets and then the nuts into position to retain them. Do not tighten at this stage, the end pieces must first be adjusted.
12 To adjust the front end piece, rotate the nuts and adjust the front and piece to give the dimensions shown in Fig. 9.9 at L1 and L2. Once the correct dimensions have been obtained, tighten the locknuts to the specified torque. Retain the end piece in the set position when tightening the nuts.
13 Relocate the dust cover onto the tie-rods and hand tighten the end pieces onto the rods at the marked adjustment position. Locate the knife edges within the end pieces onto the axle arm (having lubricated with grease), and insert the locking clips to retain in position.
14 Lower the vehicle from the supports and adjust the height as described in Section 2.
15 Before refitting the shock absorbers and anti-roll bar, adjust the rear overrun stop. The vehicle must be parked on firm level ground with the front wheels in the straight-ahead position. Release the handbrake but do not position wheel chocks.
16 Referring to Fig. 9.10, position the rear stop against the cylinder end face at F and rotate the adjustment nuts to give the correct clearance at J which must be as follows:

(a) Ami models AM3 and AMB3 – 0 to 1 mm (0 to 0.04 in)
(b) Ami models AMF3, AMC3 and AMU3 – 2 to 3 mm (0.08 to 0.12 in)
(c) All other models – 0 to 2 mm (0 to 0.08 in)

17 With the correct clearance obtained, tighten the locknuts to the specified torque whilst retaining the end piece in the set position.
18 Relocate the rubber cover.
19 Refer to Section 4 and refit the rear shock absorber.
20 Refer to Chapter 8 and refit the front shock absorber.
21 Refer to Chapter 8 and refit the anti-roll bar (if applicable).

6 Inertia damper unit (rear) – removal and refitting

The removal and refitting instructions for the rear inertia unit are the same as those for the front unit (see Chapter 8). Jack up and support the vehicle at the rear instead of the front.

7 Rear axle arm – removal and refitting

1 Loosen the rear roadwheel nuts on the side to be worked on, raise the vehicle at the rear and support it with axle stands. Remove the roadwheel.
2 Refer to Section 4 and remove the rear shock absorber.
3 Refer to Chapter 6 and remove the rear hydraulic brake hose between the wheel cylinder and the three-way (or single) connector as applicable.
4 Disconnect the suspension rear tie-rod from the axle arm. Mark the relative positions of the rod and end piece to act as a guide for vehicle height setting on reassembly. Loosen the rod, extract the clip and remove the knife edge, allowing the arm to hang down.
5 If not already removed, detach the protector cover from the axle arm at the top.
6 Extract the split pin and unscrew the special slotted nut retaining the arm in position. If available use special tool 1833-T. Alternatively, make up a suitable slotted tube spanner. Withdraw the arm, tapping it free from the crossmember with a soft-headed mallet if required.
7 To remove the taper roller bearing cone from the crossmember you will need special puller 1829-T or a similar implement. Take care not to damage the crossmember or bearing during removal. When the bearing is removed, the rubber seal can be withdrawn and renewed.
8 If the axle arm is to be further dismantled, refer to Section 8. If the axle arm is suspected of being out of alignment have it checked by your Citroën dealer. It is not normally possible to straighten or repair the axle arm.
9 To refit the axle arm, commence by fitting a new rubber seal onto the crossmember.
10 Lubricate and locate the taper bearing cone into position on the crossmember shaft using a soft tube drift of a suitable diameter. When in position the flat part of the seal must be in contact with the bearing

5.4 The central suspension unit adjusters and seal

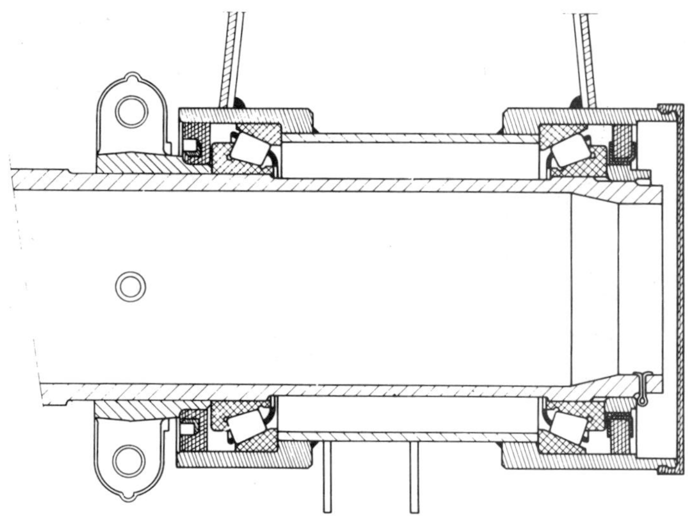

Fig. 9.11 Sectional view of the rear axle arm-to-crossmember fitting, showing the bearing and seal positions (Sec 7)

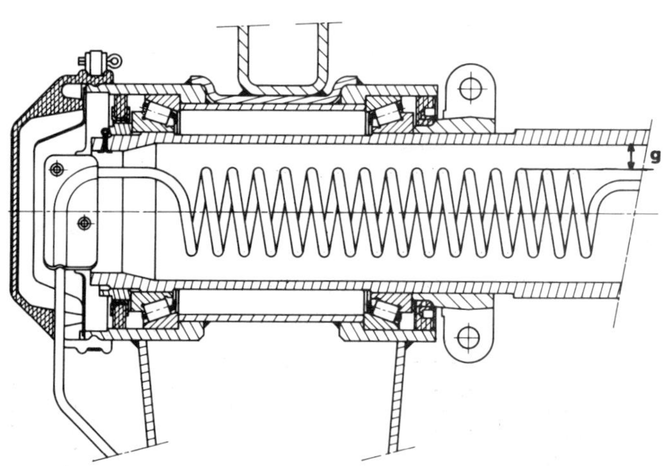

Fig. 9.12 Brake line coil must have sufficient clearance in the crossmember (Sec 7)

g = 6 mm (0.236 in) minimum

cone race. **Note**: *Do not interchange the bearing cups and cones.* Original bearing cones and cups must be kept together. SKF and Timken bearings can be fitted but their cups and cones are not interchangeable due to differing tapers.

11 Smear the bearing cone and rollers with grease and relocate the axle arm with the aid of an assistant, or with a jack placed under the inertia damper unit.

12 Refit and tighten the retaining nut. Tighten to the specified torque and insert a new split pin to secure. Check that the arm pivots freely without binding. When tightening the axle arm nut, do not loosen it to the nearest split pin hole but tighten to the given torque and then tighten further if necessary to the nearest split pin hole position.

13 On vehicles fitted with a flexible external rear brake hose, reconnect it to the wheel cylinder and to the chassis connection, making certain that there is sufficient clearance when secured between the chassis and the axle arm. Always use new seals and tighten union nuts to the torque specified. Refit the axle arm and cover.

14 Reconnect the suspension tie-rods at the rear to the arm, greasing the knife edges and fitting the retaining clip to secure.

15 Refit the shock absorbers (see Section 4) but do not tighten the retaining nuts at this stage.

16 On vehicles equipped with a spiral type brake line between the wheel cylinder and the three-way connector, refer to Chapter 6 and reconnect the brake line as described and allowing sufficient clearance between the inside of the crossmember and the line coil (Fig. 9.12). Be sure to use new seals. Refit the arm cover and tighten the clamp.

17 Top up the hydraulic brake fluid reservoir and bleed the brake system as described in Chapter 6.

18 Lower the vehicle to the ground and tighten the shock absorber retaining nuts to the specified torque.

19 Check the vehicle height and adjust if necessary (Section 2).

8 Rear axle arm – dismantling and reassembly

1 Remove the axle arm from the vehicle as described in Section 7.

2 Remove the rear inertia damper unit (if fitted).

3 Refer to Chapter 6 and remove the brake drum/hub, the brake shoes and the wheel cylinder unit.

4 Use a suitable drift to drive out the axle arm bearing cups. Take care not to damage the housing.

5 Reassembly of the axle arm is the reversal of the removal procedure. The respective bearing cones and cups must be kept together – do not interchange them (see paragraph 10 of Section 7).

6 Take care when fitting the bearing cups. Use a suitable diameter tube drift to press or drive the cups fully into position.

7 Refer to Chapter 6 and refit the brake assemblies and drum/hub unit, renewing any defective or worn components.

9 Rear crossmember – removal and refitting

1 Remove the rear axle arms on each side (see Section 7) and remove the taper bearing cone and seal on each side.

2 On models fitted with front drum brakes, support the fuel tank and remove the two forward retaining screws.

3 On some models it will be necessary to remove the left-hand wing at the rear (see Chapter 11).

4 Unscrew and remove the crossmember retaining bolts on each side. The crossmember can now be removed from the left-hand side, but take care not to damage petrol or brake pipes in the adjacent area.

5 Refitting is a reversal of the removal procedure. Locate the crossmember over the positioning dowels and insert the retaining bolts fitted with new lockwashers. Tighten the bolts to the specified torque and bend over the lockwasher tabs to secure.

6 Refit the rear wing panel.

7 Refit the axle arms and bearings.

8 Relocate the fuel tank bolts (drum brake models).

9 Top up the brake fluid level in the master cylinder and bleed the brakes.

10 Rear wheel alignment check

1 Excessive or uneven tyre wear or vibration can be caused by incorrect wheel alignment, especially if the vehicle has been involved in an accident or the suspension has been subjected to abnormal stress.

2 To check the alignment of each rear wheel, first ensure that the body height is as specified at the front end rear (see Section 2). Also check that the tyre pressures are correct. The vehicle must be parked on level ground and normally laden.

3 You will need the use of a track gauge. The track can then be checked in a similar fashion to that of the front wheels measuring on the outer rim at the centre-line of the hub at the front and rear of the wheels. Rotate the wheels a further half turn and measure again.

4 If the toe-in is not within the specified limits then the axle arm is probably at fault. The track is not adjustable and assumung that the wheel hub bearings and axle arm pivot bearings are in good condition, then the axle arm must be removed and checked by your Citroën dealer.

11 Fault diagnosis – rear suspension and central suspension unit

Symptom	Reason(s)
Vibration and rattles	Loose central suspension unit Knife edges dry Shock absorber mounting bushes worn Inertia damper unit loose/defective
Suspension stiff and squeaks	Suspension cylinder dry Knife edges dry
Suspension 'bottoms'	Rear and/or front suspension heights incorrect Defective suspension unit or shock absorbers
Uneven or abnormal rear tyre wear	Rear axle arm(s) damaged

Chapter 10 Electrical system

For modifications, and information applicable to later models, see Supplement at end of manual

Contents

Specifications

System type
Negative earth, 6V with dynamo (early models) or 12V with dynamo or alternator (later models). Mechanically or solenoid-operated pre-engaged starter motor

Battery capacity

6 volt	45 or 50 Ah
12 volt	25 or 30 Ah

Generator type

6 volt dynamo	Ducellier 7276G or Paris-Rhone G11 R111
12 volt dynamo	Ducellier 7302H
12 volt alternator (type depends on model and year)	Ducellier 7522B, 7532A or B, 7534A, 7542A or G, 8347B or C; Paris-Rhone A11-M4, M6 or M12

Voltage regulator type

With 6 volt dynamo	Ducellier 8325A, Paris-Rhone XT 212 or Cibié D67
With 12 volt dynamo	Ducellier 8243F
With alternator	Ducellier 8347 or Paris-Rhone AYA 213

Starter motor

6V pull knob types	Ducellier 6112A or 6188, Paris-Rhone D8L38, or D8L79, Iskra-Kranj ZC4
12V pull knob types	Ducellier 6134 or 6174, Paris-Rhone D8L67 or 80
12V solenoid types	Ducellier 6202A or B, Paris-Rhone D8E 99 or 116, Iskra ZB4 or AZE 03-05, or Femsa MTA 12-30

Fuses (typical)

	Fuse rating (amps)	Lead colour
2CV4 and 6		
Upper fuse box:		
LH side, tail and number plate lights	10	Green
RH side, tail and number plate lights	10	Red
Stop, interior and hazard warning lights	16	Yellow
Instruments, indicator, wipers, alternator field	16	Blue
Lower fuse box:		
RH dipped beam	16	Green
LH dipped beam	16	Red
RH main beam	16	Yellow
LH main beam	16	Blue

	Fuse rating (amps)	Lead colour
Dyane 4 and 6		
Left-hand fuse box:		
RH side and tail lights	10	Red
LH side and tail and instrument lights	10	Green
Interior light and stoplights	10	Yellow
Instruments, wipers and indicators	16	Blue
Right-hand fuse box:		
LH main beam	16	Blue
RH main beam	16	Yellow
LH dipped beam	16	Red
RH dipped beam	16	Green
Ami 6		
Left-hand fuse box:		
RH main beam	16	Green
LH main beam	16	Red
RH dipped beam	16	Blue
LH dipped beam	16	Yellow
Right-hand fuse box:		
Stoplights, interior light and accessories	10	Yellow
LH parking lights	10	Red
RH parking lights	10	Green
Indicators and wipers	10	Blue
Ami 8		
Left-hand fuse box:		
RH dipped beam	16	Green
LH dipped beam	16	Red
RH main beam	16	Yellow
LH main beam	16	Blue
Right-hand fuse box:		
RH sidelights and number plate light	10	Green
LH sidelights	10	Red
Brake lights and interior light	10	Yellow
Instruments, indicators, windscreen wipers and washer, hazard warning, alternator field	10	Blue
Additional fuse box (when fitted):		
Instrument lights and number plate light	10	White

Bulb wattage (typical)

	6 volt	12 volt
Headlights	36/36	45/40
Sidelights	4	4 or 5
Number plate light	4	4 or 5
Indicators	15 or 21	15 or 21
Stop lights	15 or 21	21
Interior light	7	7
Parking light	2	—
Ignition warning light	1.5, 12V	—
Instrument lights	2	2
Oil pressure and hazard warning lights	—	1.5

Torque wrench setting

	lbf ft	kgf m
Dynamo retaining screws	3.6 to 5.8	0.5 to 0.8

1 General description

The electrical system on all current models is of 12 volt type although certain earlier models were fitted with a 6 volt system. On all models a negative (–) earth system is employed.

Earlier models were fitted with either a 6 volt or 12 volt dynamo, mounted directly in the crankcase, to maintain the battery power. All late models are fitted with an alternator for this function. A separate voltage control regulator is fitted to both dynamo and alternator equipped models.

The battery supplies the power necessary to operate the starter motor. It supplies current to the ignition circuit and also to the lighting and other electrically operated items in the vehicle when their demands exceed the generator output.

Where an alternator is fitted, special care must be taken when working on any part of the electrical circuits. If the battery is to be recharged from an external source, disconnect the battery terminal leads. Whenever work is being carried out on any part of the electrical circuit or associated components requiring the wires to be detached, disconnect the battery earth terminal. For further precautions concerning the alternator refer to Section 8.

The respective circuits are protected by fuses and should a fault occur in any part of the electrical system, first check the circuit fuse concerned. If it has 'blown', find and rectify the cause before installing a replacement fuse (which must be of the correct value).

2 Battery – removal and refitting

1 The battery is housed within the engine compartment. Its exact location depends on the model concerned.

2 To remove the battery, first disconnect the earth terminal lead connector, followed by the positive lead (photo).

3 Pull back the spring-loaded battery retaining clamp on its top edge (photo).

4 Carefully lift the battery from its tray, taking care not to spill any electrolyte.

5 Refitting is a reversal of the removal procedure, but before fitting make sure that the battery is wiped clean and dry, particularly the terminals. Also clean the terminal lead connectors and smear with petroleum jelly (not grease) to prevent corrosion.

6 Check that the battery retaining clamp and the terminals are secure. Do not overtighten the terminal clamps as the terminals are made of lead and easily damaged.

2.2 Detach the battery cables ...

2.3 ... and retaining clamp

3.1 Topping up the battery cells

3 Battery – maintenance and inspection

1 Normal weekly battery maintenance consists of checking the electrolyte level of each cell to ensure that the separators are covered by 1 to 2 cm ($\frac{3}{8}$ to $\frac{3}{4}$ in) of electrolyte. If the level has fallen, top up the battery using distilled water only (photo). Do not overfill. If any electrolyte is spilled, the spillage must be wiped away immediately, as electrolyte attacks and corrodes very quickly any metal with which it comes in contact.

2 As well as keeping the terminals clean and covered with petroleum jelly, the top of the battery, and especially the top of the cells, should be kept clean and dry. This helps prevent corrosion and ensures that the battery does not become partially discharged by leakage through dampness and dirt.

3 Once every three months, remove the battery and inspect the battery tray and battery leads for corrosion (white fluffy deposits on the metal which are brittle to touch). If any corrosion is found, clean off the deposits with ammonia. Paint over the clean metal with an anti-rust/anti-acid paint.

4 At the same time inspect the battery for cracks. If a crack is found, clean and plug it with one of the proprietary compounds. If leakage through the crack has been excessive then it will be necessary to refill the appropriate cell with fresh electrolyte as detailed in Section 4. Cracks are frequently caused in the top of the battery case by topping up with distilled water in the middle of winter *after* instead of *before* a run. This gives the water no chance to mix with the electrolyte and so the former freezes and splits the battery case.

5 If topping-up the battery becomes excessive and the case has been inspected for cracks that could cause leakage, but none are found, the battery is being over-charged and the voltage regulator will have to be checked.

6 With the battery on the bench at the three monthly check, measure the specific gravity with a hydrometer to determine the state of charge and condition of the electrolyte. There should be very little variation between the different cells and if a variation in excess of 0.025 is present it will be due to either:

(a) Loss of electrolyte from the battery at some time caused by spillage or a leak, resulting in a drop in the specific gravity of the electrolyte when the deficiency was replaced with distilled water instead of fresh electrolyte, or

(b) An internal short-circuit caused by buckling of the plates or a similar malady pointing to the likelihood of total battery failure in the near future.

7 The specific gravity of the electrolyte for fully charged and fully discharged conditions at the electrolyte temperature indicated, is listed below.

Fully discharged	Electrolyte temperature	Fully charged
1.098	38°C (100°F)	1.268
1.102	32°C (90°F)	1.272
1.106	27°C (80°F)	1.276
1.110	21°C (70°F)	1.280
1.114	16°C (60°F)	1.284
1.118	10°C (50°F)	1.288
1.122	4°C (40°F)	1.292
1.126	–1.5°C (30°F)	1.296

4 Battery – electrolyte replenishment

1 If the battery is in a fully charged state and one of the cells maintains a specific gravity reading which is 0.025 or more lower than the others, and a check of each cell has been made with a voltage meter to check for short circuits (a four to seven seconds test should give a steady reading of between 1.2 and 1.8 volts), then it is likely that electrolyte has been lost from the cell with the low reading.

2 If a significant quantity of electrolyte has been lost through spillage it will not suffice to merely refill with distilled water. Top up the cell with electrolyte which is a mixture of sulphuric acid and water in the ratio of 2 parts acid to 5 parts water. The ready mixed solution should be obtained from battery specialists or large garages. The 'normal' solution can be added if the battery is in a fully charged state.

If the battery is in a low state of charge, use the normal solution, charge the battery then empty out the electrolyte. Swill the battery out with clean water then refill with a new charge of electrolyte.

5 Battery – charging

1 In winter when a heavy demand is placed on the battery such as when starting from cold, and much electrical equipment is continually in use, it is a good idea to occasionally have the battery fully charged from an external source at a rate of 3.5 to 4 amps.
2 Continue to charge the battery at the rate until no further rise in specific gravity is noted over a four hour period.
3 Alternatively, a trickle charge charging at the rate of 1.5 amps can be safely used overnight.
4 Special rapid 'boost' charges which are claimed to restore the power of the battery in 1 to 2 hours are most dangerous unless they are thermostatically controlled as they can cause serious damage to the battery plates through overheating.
5 While charging the battery ensure that the temperature of the electrolyte never exceeds 37.8°C (100°F).
Caution: *If the battery is being charged from an external power source whilst the battery is fitted in the car, both battery leads must be disconnected to prevent damage to the electrical circuits.*

6 Alternator drivebelt – removal, refitting and adjustment

1 Loosen the three nuts retaining the alternator pulley cover in position and withdraw the cover (photo).
2 Loosen the alternator mounting bolts. One is on the exhaust manifold and one on the slotted adjuster stay.
3 Pivot the alternator towards the engine to slacken the belt and then unhook the belt from the alternator pulley. Disengage the belt from the fan pulley and thread through the fan blades to remove (photo). Remove the front grille panel for access.
4 The new belt is fitted in reverse, threading it through the fan blades onto the fan pulley and up over the alternator pulley. Refit the grille panel.
5 To adjust the belt tension, the alternator mounting bolts must be just loose enough to allow the unit to be pivoted to achieve the correct tension. The tension is correct if the total deflection of the belt at the midway point of its run between the pulleys is 12 mm ($\frac{1}{2}$ in) when a firm thumb pressure is applied.
6 To increase the tension, move the alternator upwards away from the engine, and vice versa to decrease the tension. When the tension is correct, tighten the alternator mounting bolts, then recheck the belt to ensure that the alternator did not move when the bolts were being tightened.
7 Refit the pulley cover, not forgetting the washers, and tighten the nuts to secure. Ensure that the cover is as close to the alternator as possible without touching it.

7 Alternator – general description

1 The use of alternators for generating the current required to operate car electrical systems is now commonplace. Their main advantage over the dynamo type generator is that they provide a higher output for lower revolutions and are lighter in weight/ output ratio.
2 The alternator generates alternating current and this current is rectified by diodes into direct current which is the current needed for battery storage.
3 The voltage regulator is separate from the alternator. If it is suspect, refer to Section 12.

8 Alternator – safety precautions

1 If there are indications that the charging system is malfunctioning in any way, care must be taken to diagnose faults properly, otherwise damage of a serious and expensive nature may occur to parts which are in fact quite serviceable.
2 The following basic requirements must be observed at all times:

(a) All alternator systems use a negative earth. Even the simple mistake of connecting a battery the wrong way round could burn out the alternator diodes in a few seconds
(b) Before disconnecting any wires in the system the engine and ignition circuits should be switched off. This will minimise accidental short circuits
(c) The alternator must never be run with the output wire disconnected
(d) Always disconnect the battery from the car's electrical system if an external charging source is being used
(e) Do not use test wire connections that could move accidentally and short circuit against nearby terminals. Short circuits will not blow fuses – they will blow diodes or transistors
(f) Always disconnect the battery cables and alternator output leads before carrying out any electric welding work on the car
(g) Never lever on the alternator body when adjusting its drivebelt. The casing is easily fractured.

9 Alternator – removal and refitting

1 Disconnect the battery earth lead connection.
2 Disconnect the wire connectors to the alternator, noting their positions (photo).
3 Unscrew the pulley cover retaining nuts and pull the cover clear.
4 Loosen the alternator mounting and adjustment bolts and nuts, pivot the alternator inwards towards the engine and detach the drivebelt from the pulley (photo).

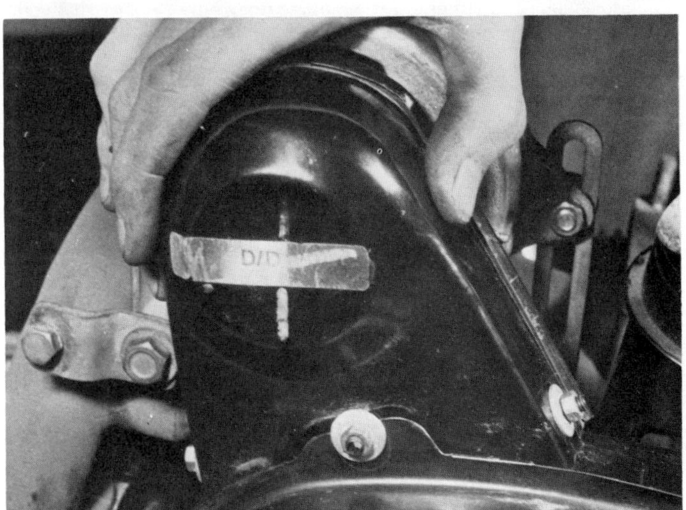

6.1 Remove the pulley cover

6.3 Withdraw the belt through the fan housing

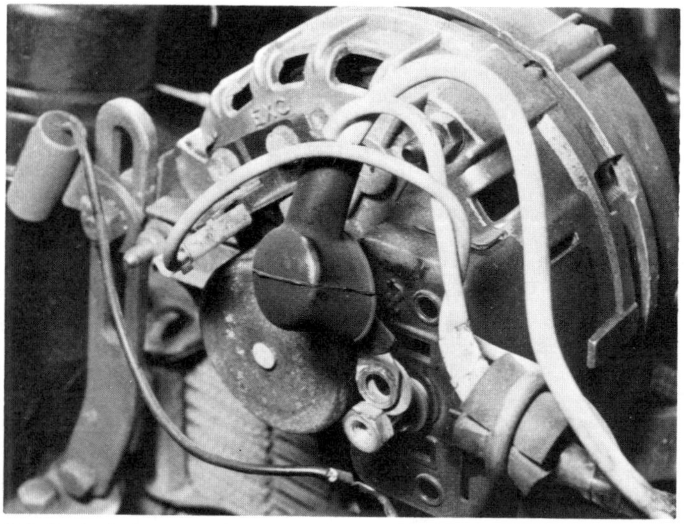

9.2 Typical alternator lead connections

9.4 The alternator mounting bolts (arrowed)

5 Remove the bolts and lift the alternator from the car.
6 Refitting is a reversal of the removal procedure. Retension the drivebelt as described in Section 6.
7 Refit the pulley cover once the belt has been adjusted. Reconnect the wires to the alternator and then the earth lead to the battery.

10 Alternator fuse – renewal

1 If the alternator fuse has blown, a replacement can easily be fitted, but check the cause at the earliest possible convenient time.
2 Detach the battery earth lead connector.
3 Disconnect the output lead from the rear of the alternator. You will have to slide the rubber protector free to gain access to the wire retaining nut and washers.
4 Detach the black plastic cover. On some models this is retained by a wire cable clip, in which case remove this first.
5 The fuse consists of a thin copper segment mounted on plastic. Unscrew and remove the terminal nut in the middle and then the two small screws and washers.
6 Remove the fuse and fit the replacement. A length of 15 amp domestic fuse wire will do temporarily in an emergency.
7 If fitting fuse wire, leave the old fuse in position, wind the wire round the central terminal and bend the wire to the shape of the copper each side. Secure the wire ends to the screws.
8 A length of fuse wire should not be used for long and the correct type fuse must be fitted as soon as possible.
9 Refit the cover and wire assemblies in the reverse order.

11 Alternator brushes – renewal

1 Apart from the fuse mentioned in Section 10, another possible reason for the alternator not to function is worn brushes. To check and if necessary change these proceed as follows.
2 Disconnect the battery earth lead connection.
3 Detach the spade connector from the brush holder unit on the alternator.
4 On the Paris-Rhone alternator you will have to loosen the alternator mounting bolts and swing the unit into a position to get access to the brush holder. It may be easiest to remove the alternator as described in Section 9.
5 On the Ducellier alternator the brush holder unit is on the top and secured in position by two screws. Remove the screws to withdraw the brushes.
6 When fitting new brushes make sure that they can move freely in their holders. The slip rings should be wiped clean with petrol before fitting the brushes.
7 Reassemble in the reverse order and readjust the drivebelt tension if necessary.

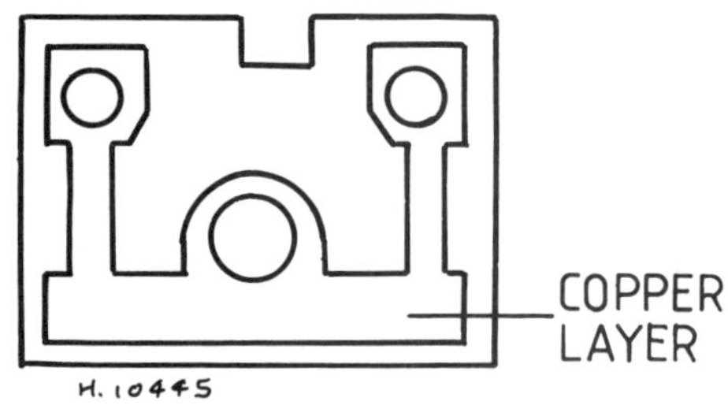

Fig. 10.1 Ducellier alternator output fuse (Sec 10)

12 Voltage regulator (alternator equipped models) – checking and adjustment

1 To check the regulator voltage control you will need a voltmeter and this must be connected across the battery terminals. It should read 12 volts when initially tested (engine not running).
2 Start up the engine and allow it to idle. The voltmeter should increase its reading up to 12.6 volts. Now increase the engine speed progressively until the maximum voltage reading is reached (14 to 15 volts), then allow the engine speed to drop again down to its idle speed and check the voltmeter. If the regulator is in order the voltmeter reading should return to 12.6 volts. If it stabilises at idle speed and gives a reading of around 14 to 14.6 volts then the regulator needs adjustment. If the reading does not rise above 12 volts at any time, the fault may be in the regulator, the wiring or the alternator itself.
3 Turn off the engine, disconnect the battery earth and positive terminals.
4 Detach the regulator cover, on some models the complete unit will have to be removed. Whilst earlier regulator covers were retained by a screw, the later ones are retained by a hollow plastic rivet and this can be removed by pressing the centre pin using a nail or punch and extracting the head with a knife blade. Note the cork gasket round the cover, which must be retained and kept safe during removal.
5 Inspect the regulator contacts. If they are pitted or burnt they can be filed clean using a fine grade wet and dry paper.
6 To check the adjustment of the gap use a feeler gauge. On the Paris-Rhone models the air gap should be 1.5 mm (0.060 in) measured between the coil core at the top and the moving contact arm. The points gap should be between 0.25 and 0.30 mm (0.010 and 0.012 in).
7 Reattach the battery leads (negative last) and, supporting the regulator if it has been removed, recheck the voltage output as described in paragraph 2. Any minor adjustment can be made by turning the cam star wheel using a pair of round-nosed pliers.
8 When refitting the regulator cover be sure to locate the cork gasket. Check that all wiring connections are secure to complete.

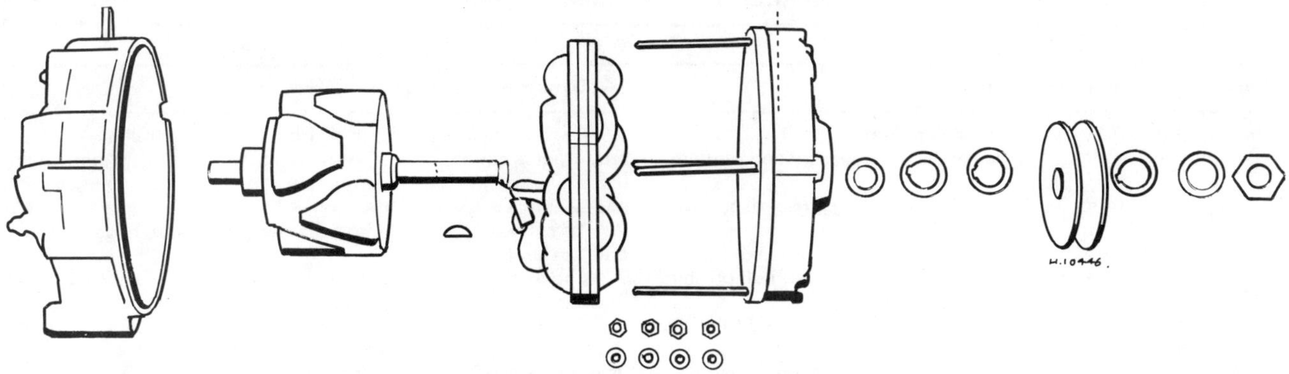

Fig. 10.2 Ducellier 7542A alternator components (Sec 11)

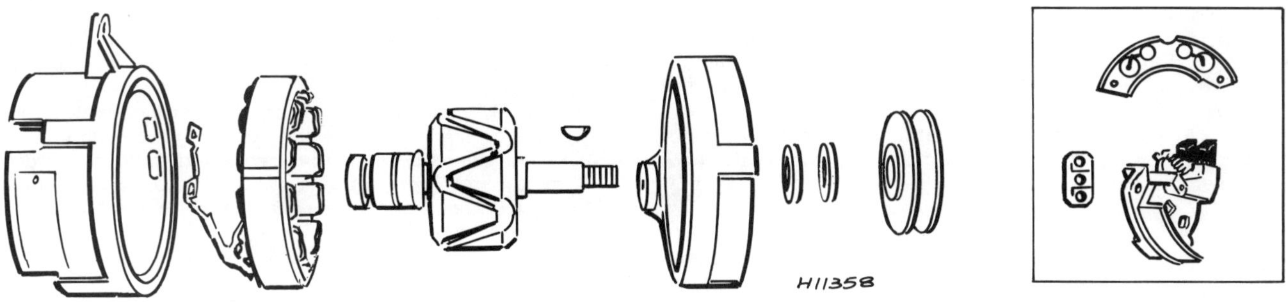

Fig. 10.3 Paris-Rhone A11-M4 alternator components showing (inset, not to same scale) the brush assembly (Sec 11)

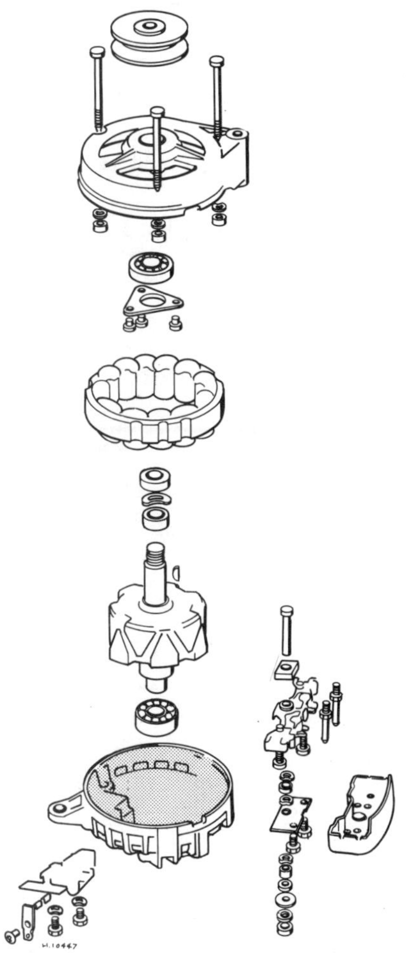

Fig. 10.4 Ducellier 7532 and 7534 alternator components (Sec 11)

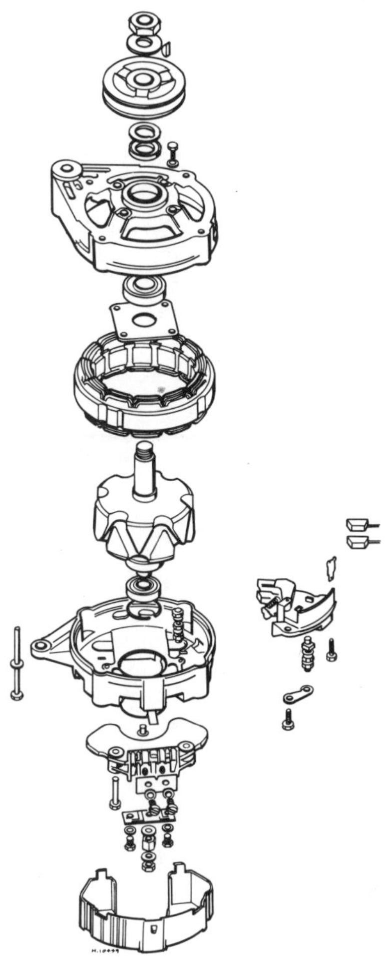

Fig. 10.5 Paris-Rhone A11-M11 or M12 alternator components (Sec 11)

13 Dynamo – removal and refitting

1 Disconnect the battery earth lead connection.
2 Remove the inner and outer grille panels as necessary and remove the cooling fan.
3 Detach the leads from the dynamo unit, noting their respective positions.
4 Unscrew and remove the dynamo retaining screws and withdraw the dynamo body from the crankcase, but take care not to pull on the brush holder as the leads must not be disturbed.
5 To remove the armature from the crankshaft you will need Citroën special tool number 2205-T (Fig. 10.7).
6 Inspect the brushes. If worn down they must be renewed. Unscrew their lead terminal screws to remove them. When fitting check that the brushes can move freely up and down in their guides.
7 Refitting is a reversal of the removal process. Check that the crankcase dynamo aperture is perfectly clean and remove any grease from the tapered bore in the armature and crankshaft journal.
8 With the armature on the crankshaft, pull back the brushes far enough to allow the springs to retain them in the raised position for fitting.
9 Smear some grease in the crankcase bore and fit the dynamo body. Check that the insulation sleeves are in position on the two screws. Tighten the screws, if possible to the specified torque. Do not overtighten.
10 Pull back the brush springs and allow the brushes to slide down the guides to contact the armature and release the springs to secure. The leads must be pressed forwards and retained by the lug.
11 Refit the fan unit and grille panels.

14 Dynamo – testing

1 If a fault develops in the charging circuit first check that all wires are in good condition and securely located between the dynamo and the regulator. The battery terminals and connectors must also be clean and securely attached.
2 To carry out inspection on the dynamo first remove the front grille and fan unit
3 Check the brushes and their wire connections as described in Section 13.
4 Assuming the brushes to be in good condition, a test can be made to check the output of the dynamo. To do this, detach the output and field terminal wires and bridge the terminals with a piece of wire. Now connect a voltmeter to the wire junction and earth.
5 Start the engine and run it at a fast idle speed whilst watching the voltmeter. The reading should increase instantly. A low or possibly no reading suggests faulty brushes or their connections; worse, the field windings or armature may be faulty, in which case the dynamo should be checked and repaired by a competent auto electrician or your Citroën dealer.
6 Do not allow the engine to run at a fast idle for an indefinite period without the cooling fan. The initial increase in speed up to a fast idle should be all that is necessary to see if the dynamo is in order.
7 If the dynamo is proved to be working, reconnect the output and field terminal wires and lease the bridging wire in position. Disconnect the regulator output lead and connect the voltmeter between the lead and earth.
8 Restart the engine and run it at a fast idle. Check the voltage reading which should be the same as that taken when checking the

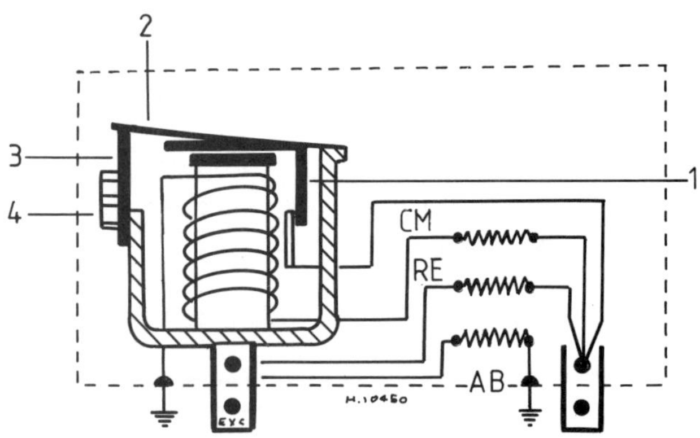

Fig. 10.6 Typical voltage control unit (sec 12)

1 Contacts
2 Leaf spring
3 Cam
4 Star wheel

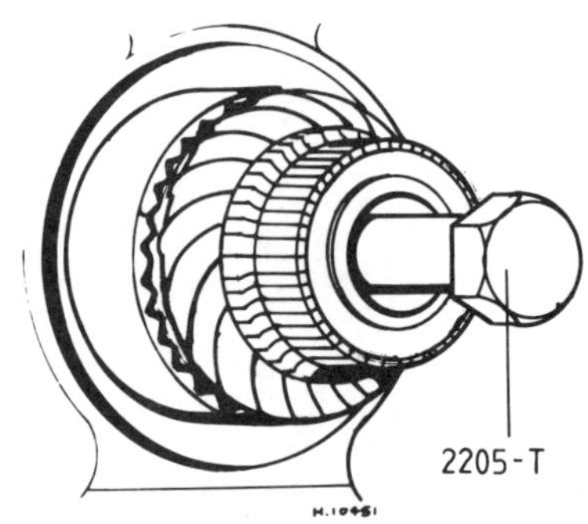

Fig. 10.7 Dynamo armature remover tool 2205-T in position (Sec 13)

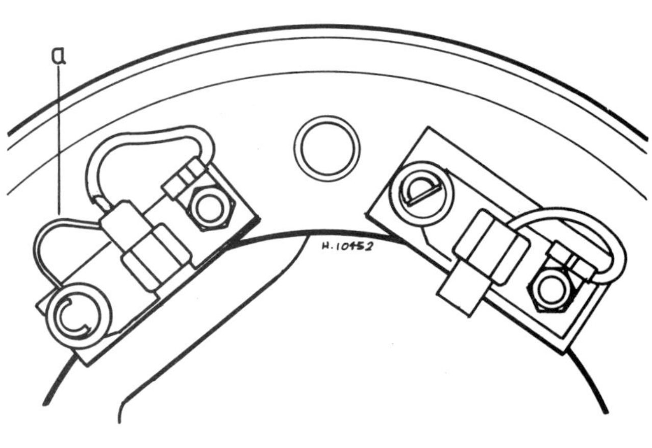

Fig. 10.8 Pull back spring (a) to retain brush in raised position in holder (Sec 13)

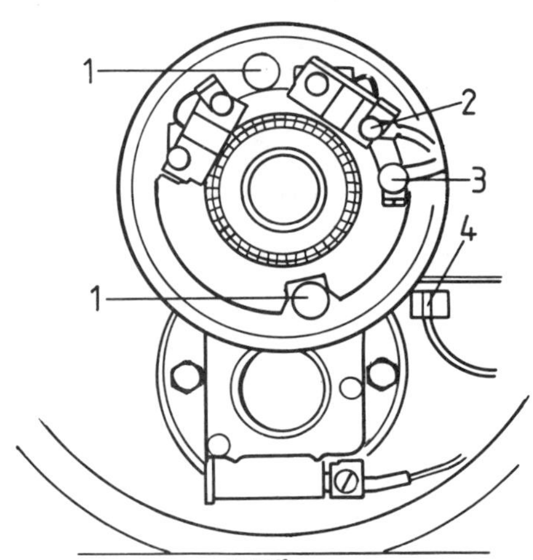

Fig. 10.9 Dynamo front end view (Sec 13)

1 Retaining screws
2 Insulated connection
3 Insulated connection
4 Lug

dynamo. If you are unable to get a reading then the output lead is at fault and must be replaced.

9 A similar test can then be made on the field wire. Remove the bridging wire from the dynamo terminals to complete the test.

10 If the regulator is suspected of being faulty, have it checked by your Citroën dealer or local auto electrician, who will have the necessary equipment to diagnose any malfunction.

15 Starter motor – testing in the car

1 If the starter motor fails to operate then check the condition of the battery by switching on the headlamps. If they glow brightly for several seconds and then gradually dim, the battery is in an uncharged condition.

2 If the headlamps continue to glow brightly and it is obvious that the battery is in good condition, then check the tightness of the battery connections, particularly the earth lead from the battery terminal to its connection on the bodyframe. Check all connections from the battery to the solenoid switch and the cable to the starter for cleanliness and tightness.

3 If the starter motor still fails to turn, check the solenoid by putting a voltmeter or bulb across the main cable connections on the starter side of the solenoid and earth. When the switch is operated there should be a reading or lighted bulb, if not the solenoid switch is faulty. If it is established that the solenoid is not faulty and the battery voltage is getting to the starter then the fault must be in the starter motor.

16 Starter motor – removal and refitting

1 Disconnect the battery earth strap from the negative terminal of the battery. Take note of the connections and disconnect the wiring from the starter motor (photo).

2 Unscrew and remove the starter motor-to-clutch housing retaining bolts and withdraw the starter motor (photo).

3 Refitting is a direct reversal of the removal procedure. Check that the wires are correctly located on completion.

17 Starter motor – dismantling, reassembly and adjustment

1 Such is the inherent reliability and strength of the starter motors fitted that it is very unlikely that a motor will ever need dismantling until it is totally worn out and in need of replacement. It is not a task for the home mechanic because although reasonably easy to undertake, the reassembly and adjustment before refitting is beyond his scope because of the need of specialist equipment. It would under all

16.1 The wiring connections to the starter motor solenoid

16.2 Remove the bolts and withdraw the starter motor

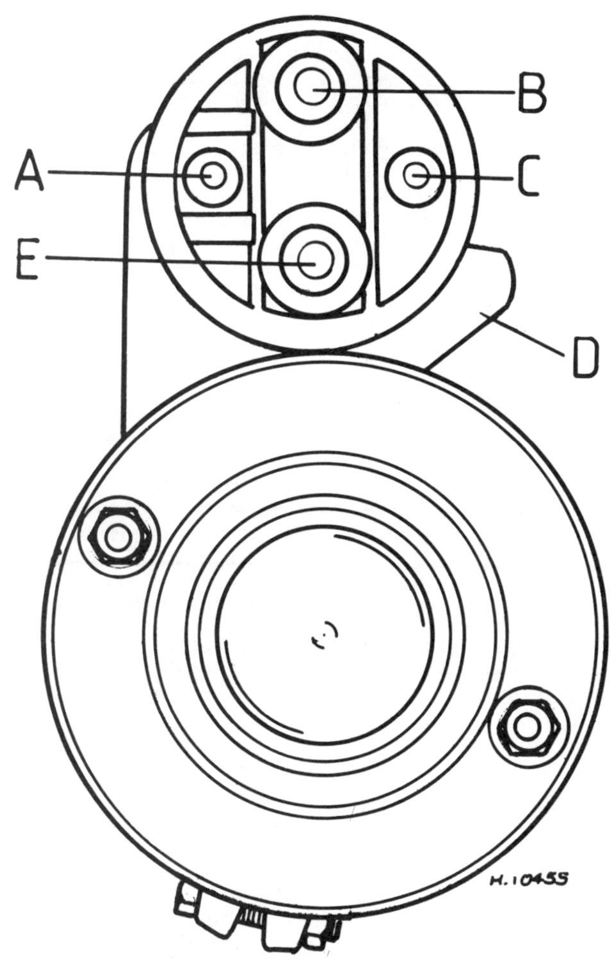

Fig. 10.10 Typical starter solenoid connections (Sec 17)

A To switch
B To battery +
C To earth
D Lead
E To motor

circumstances be realistic for the work to be undertaken by the specialist auto-electrician. It is possible to renew solenoids and brushes on starter motors quite easily.

2 Starter motors should be grouped by manufacture for dismantling rather than by voltage or method of activation.

3 Paris-Rhone starters are easier to work on in terms of replacing solenoids, switches and brushes than Ducellier. On those starters activated manually, remove the switch by undoing the two holding bolts, unhook from the lever and lift away. Check the contacts for wear and always clean before refitting. On solenoid activated starters remove the solenoid by undoing the two holding nuts and unhooking the solenoid plunger from the lever. This may mean pushing out the end locating pin in the plunger. Then lift away.

4 To replace the brushes remove the brush gear band cover and lift out of the brushes from their insulated locations. Inspect and if below the tolerable length renew. This is as far as you should need to go.

5 On Ducellier starters remove the manual activation in the same way and inspect. The solenoid removal is the same too, as is the replacement. To remove the brushes undo the two nuts at the opposite end to the pinion and remove the end cap. Pull off the insulation and spring and ease out the commutator end bracket. On this bracket is located the brushes. Remove and inspect in the same way and renew if necessary. Do not dismantle the rest of the starter motor. Replacement is the direct reversal of removal on all starter motors. Solenoids should always be renewed if they have ceased to function properly – there is little that can be done to them in the way of repair.

6 If the motor has been disassembled down to its component parts the checking of the armature field coils and subsequently bearing bushes should be carried out by a competent auto electrician.

7 Check that the drive pinion moves freely in a spiral movement along the shaft against light spring pressure and returns easily when released. The spiral splines must be completely free of dirt and oil (which collects dirt).

8 Reassembly of a totally dismantled starter motor is easy for the experienced auto electrician but not for the home mechanic if he is to have any measure of success. Each type of starter motor has a different bearing and pinion adjustment which you will find impossible to measure without costly equipment. It is better even at this stage of disassembly to realise, that to pay for the work to be done on this unit is more economic than to do it yourself. The drivegear adjustment is made as follows.

Paris-Rhone D8E99 or D8E 116

9 Refer to Fig. 10.10 and detach lead D from terminal E on the end of the solenoid unit (if attached).

10 Now connect up a cable from the positive (+) terminal on the battery to the solenoid terminal A. Connect a cable from the battery negative (–) terminal to terminal C on the solenoid. With the drivegear now advanced, use feeler gauges and measure the clearance between the end face of the gear and the thrust block (Fig. 10.11). The correct clearance is 1 mm (0.040 in).

11 If necessary adjust the clearance by altering the adjuster screw setting (Fig. 10.12). Remove the plastic plug for access.

12 Disconnect the battery-to-solenoid connections previously made, then check the starter motor body flange-to-drivegear forward face clearance (Fig. 10.13), which should be 21 mm (0.826 in). Where the clearance is found to be incorrect the starter motor is in need of attention.

Ducellier 6202 and Iskra ZB4

13 Remove the plastic plug from the end of the solenoid unit and detach the starter motor-to-solenoid lead.

14 Connect up the battery positive terminal to the supply terminal on the solenoid and the negative terminal to the solenoid terminal marked 'DEM'.

15 With the drivegear advanced, check the gear-to-thrust block clearance which should be 1 mm (0.040 in) (Fig. 10.11).

16 To adjust, rotate the nut in the end of the solenoid in the desired direction.

17 Detach the wires from the battery to the solenoid and with the drivegear fully returned, measure the distance from the drivegear end to the starter end face (clutch flange). This clearance should be 21 mm (0.826 in); if not, the starter motor must be rechecked and if necessary overhauled by your Citroën dealer or automotive electrician.

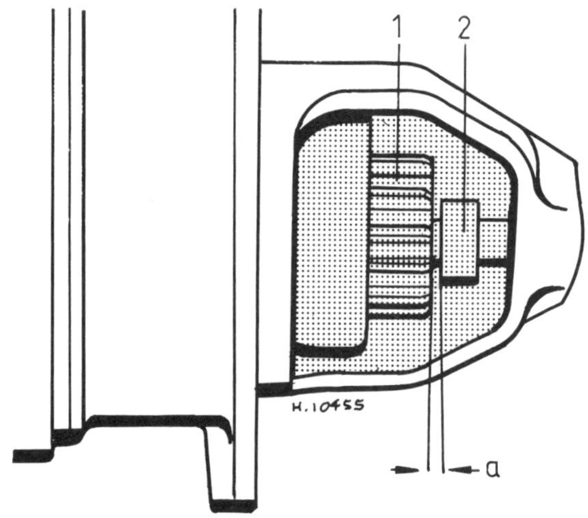

Fig. 10.11 Checking starter operating clearances (Sec 17)

1 Drivegear
2 Thrust block
a 1 mm (0.04 in)

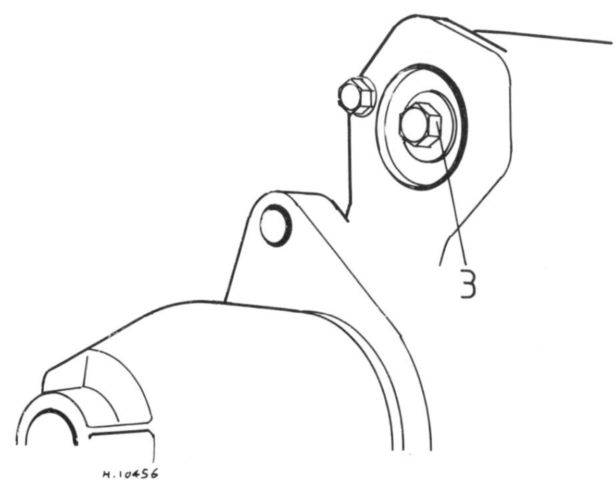

Fig. 10.12 The adjuster screw (3) is in the end of the solenoid (Sec 17)

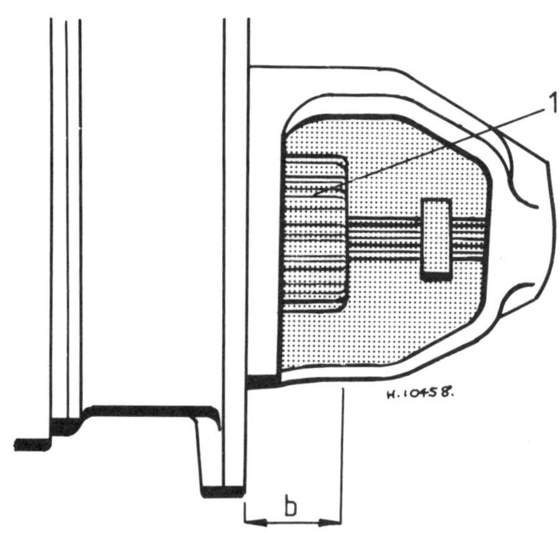

Fig. 10.13 Check clearances between gear (1) and flange (Sec 17)

b 21 mm (0.826 in)

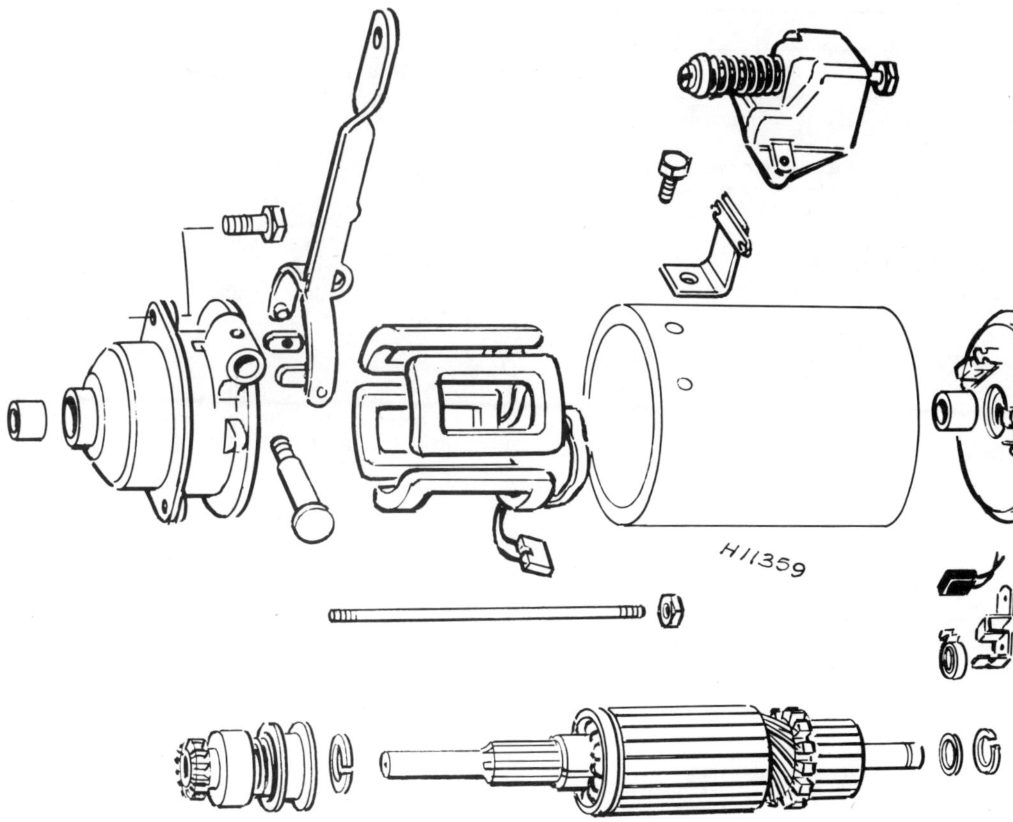

Fig. 10.14 Exploded view of a typical cable-operated starter motor (Sec 17)

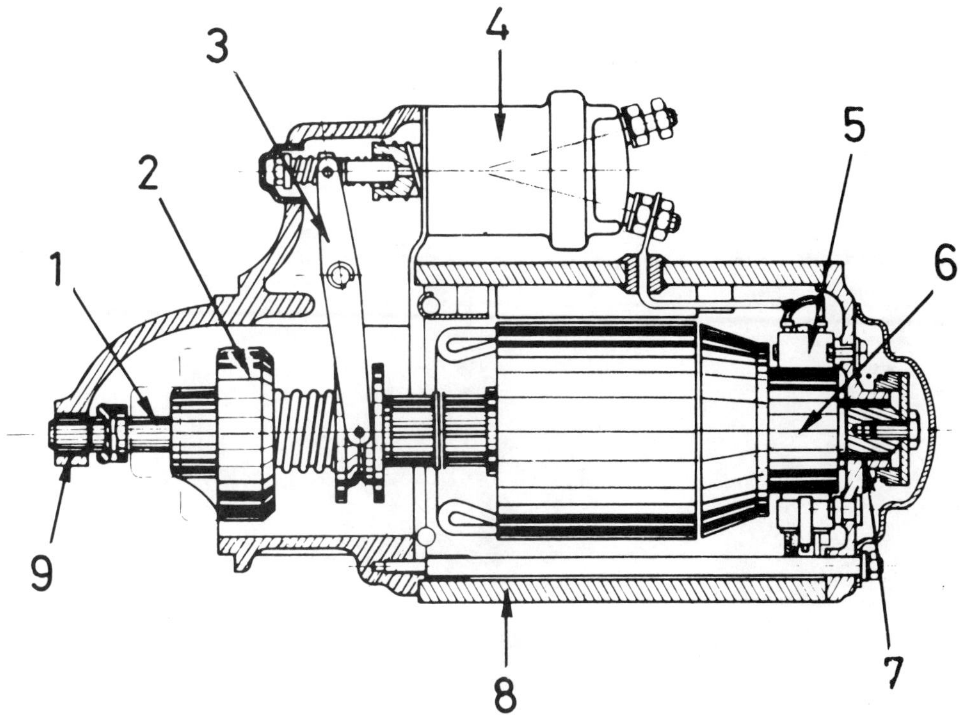

Fig. 10.15 Sectional view of a typical solenoid-operated starter motor (Sec 17)

1 Driveshaft
2 Freewheel
3 Pivot lever
4 Solenoid
5 Brushes
6 Commutator
7 Rear end bearing
8 Field coils and yoke
9 Drive end bearing

18 Fuses – general

1 On most models equipped with 12 volt electrics, there are two fuse boxes.
2 On one box items such as side/tail/interior and warning lights are covered, whilst the second box covers only the headlights main and dipped beams.
3 Some Ami 8 models also have an extra fuse box fitted for the instrument lights and the number plate lights.
4 Details of the respective fuse values are given in the Specifications at the start of this Chapter.
5 If a fuse blows, always replace it with one of the correct value. If a particular fuse persists in blowing there must be a fault in the circuit concerned and this must be found and rectified at the earliest possible moment.
6 Never be tempted to bypass a blown fuse with metal foil or substitute one of a higher value. To do so may cause further damage in the circuit concerned or even cause a fire.
7 Some alternators incorporate their own fuse and this can be renewed. See Section 10 for details.

19 Headlights – adjustment (Dyane models only)

For adjustment procedures on other models refer to Chapter 12.
1 On all models the headlights are adjustable for varying vehicle loads from inside the vehicle by simply rotating the adjuster knob in the desired direction, clockwise to lower the beam and anti-clockwise to raise the beam.
2 The system is operated by a control cable to each headlight unit from the adjuster knob. The cable pivots the headlight unit up or down accordingly.
3 For normal usage the headlight beams should be set to a range of 30 to 50 metres (33 to 55 yards). Do not set the adjustment too high or oncoming drivers will be dazzled.
4 When making any adjustments the vehicle should be parked on a firm flat surface and be normally laden.
5 Any further adjustments should be entrusted to your Citroën dealer who will have the necessary optical testing equipment for accurate alignment adjustments to be made.

20 Headlights – units and bulbs removal and renewal

2CV

1 Unscrew and remove the lens retaining screw and hinge the rim/lens section open. On some models simply press down on the catch at the top of the light to release the lens unit.
2 Disconnect the wiring, prise back the bulb holder clips and extract the bulb (photos). The headlight itself is retained to the pivot bar by a single nut underneath.
3 Reassemble in the reverse order, but check light operation on completion.

Dyane

4 Grip the headlight unit rim and pull it free (photo).
5 To withdraw the light unit, press the retaining spring out of the way. Take care not to alter the position of the retaining/adjustment screws around the rim or the setting will be upset.
6 With the lens removed, detach the lead connector at the rear of the unit and prise the bulb holder springs free to extract the bulb (photo).
7 Refit in the reverse order and on completion check the operation of the lights.

Ami

8 Open the bonnet to gain access to the bulb holders from within the wing panel.
9 Prise free the bulb holder retaining clips and detach the wire connector from the holder unit (photos).
10 Extract the bulb from the holder and insert a new one. Make sure that the flange locating lugs drop into the slot at the bottom of the reflector opening. The position of the slot can be altered by moving the slider to provide LH or RH dipping.
11 Refit in the reverse order and on completion check the headlight operation and adjustment.
12 If the units are to be removed detach the wire connectors, remove the two lens surround retaining screws (photo) and then withdraw the unit.
13 On refitting the unit, locate the lower clip into its slot, fit the pivot pins into the locators each side and fit the spring clip at the top (photos).

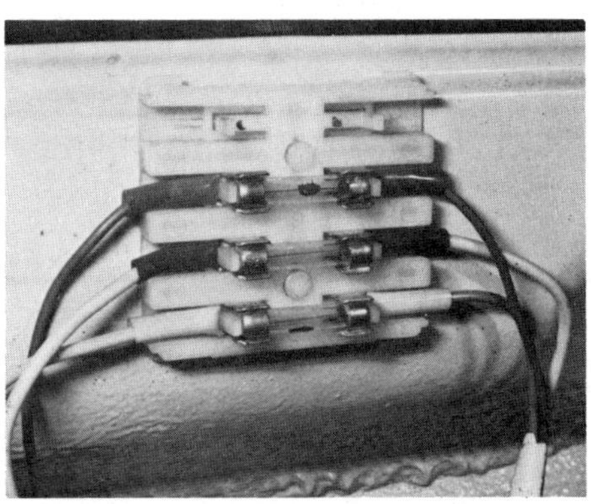

18.2 Typical fuse box

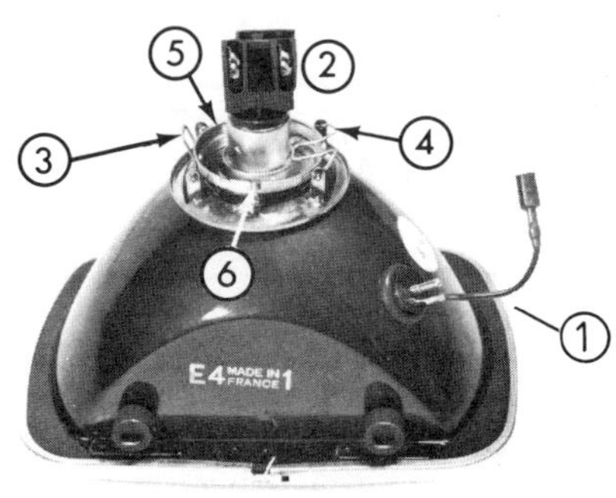

Fig. 10.16 Headlight unit fitted to later 2CV models (Sec 20)

1 *Sidelight bulb holder*
2 *Connector*
3 *Spring clip*
4 *Spring clip*
5 *Bulb holder*
B *Lug*

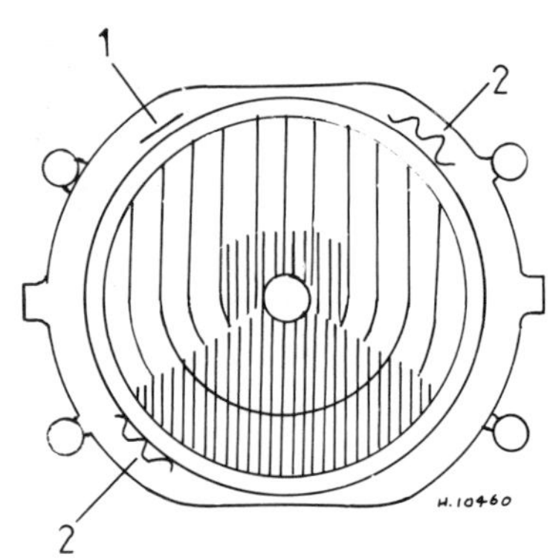

Fig. 10.17 Dyane headlight unit (Sec 20)

1 *Spring clip*
2 *Alignment screws*

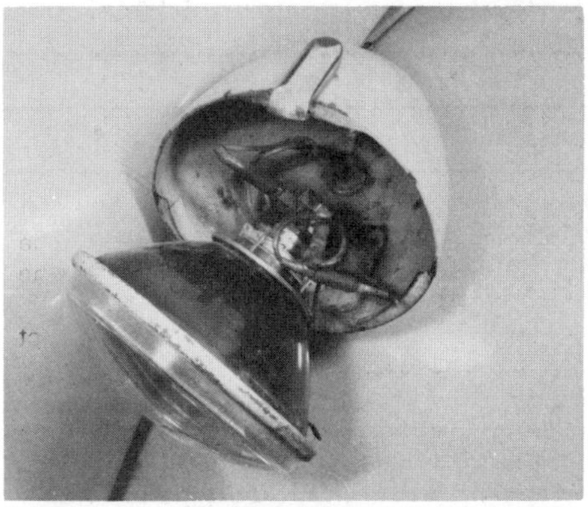

20.2a Remove the lens/reflector unit (2CV) ...

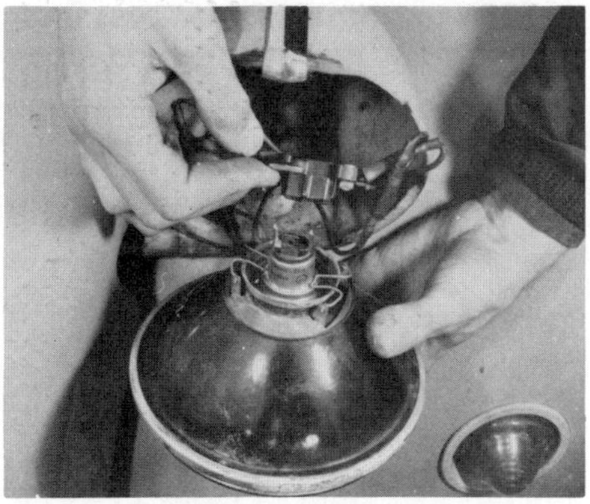

20.2b ... detach the wiring connector ...

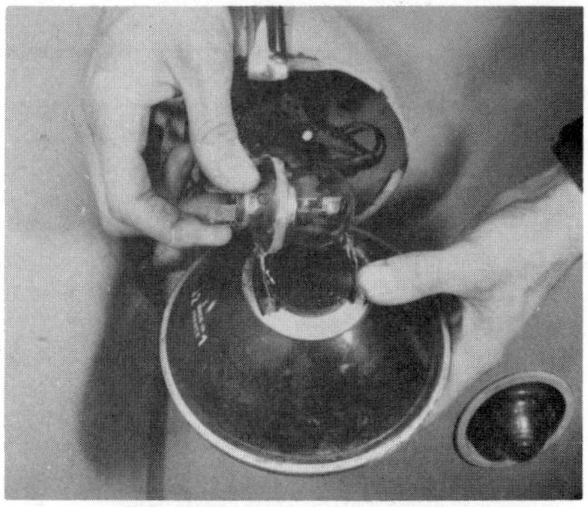

20.2c ... and unclip and remove the bulb

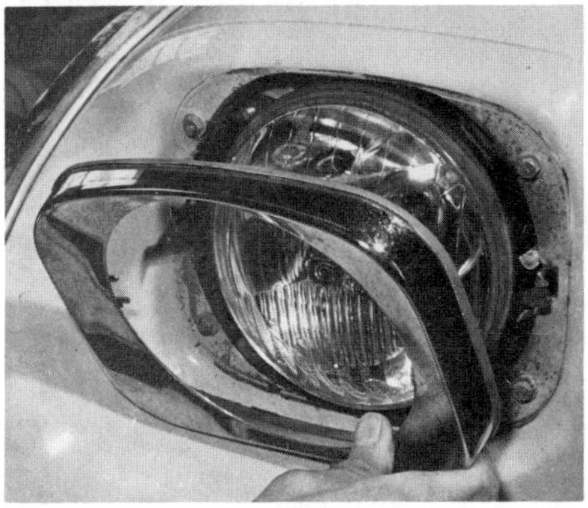

20.4 Remove the rim (Dyane)

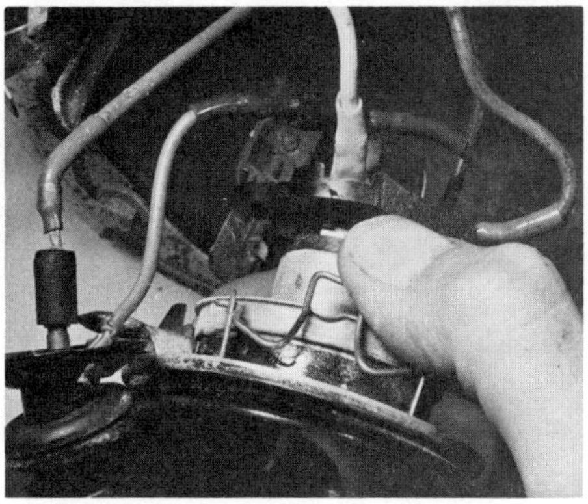

20.6a Bend back clips ...

20.6b ... to remove bulb and holder

20.9a The holder, retaining springs and connector plug shown in position with unit removed (Ami)

20.9b Hinge back springs to release bulb holder (Ami)

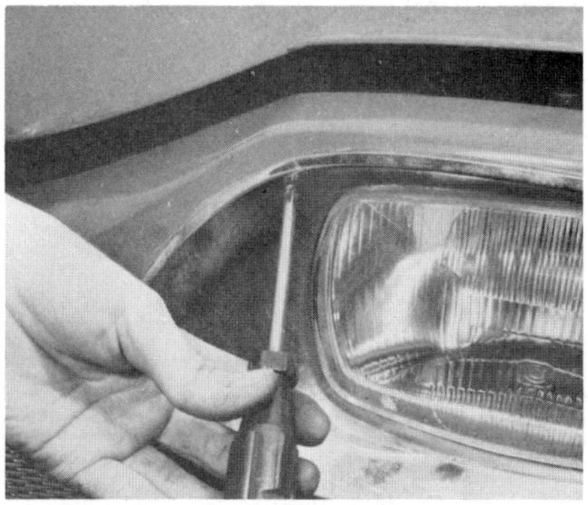

20.12 Remove the surround (Ami)

20.13a Locate into clip at bottom ...

20.13b ... pivot pins at sides ...

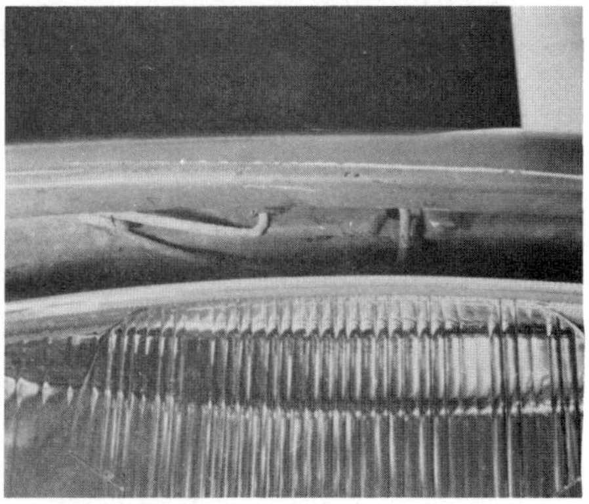

20.13c ... and fit spring at top

21 Front sidelight bulb (2CV and Dyane) – removal and renewal

1 The sidelights are retained in the reflectors of the headlight units. Remove the headlight unit as previously described to gain access to the side-light bulbs.
2 The sidelight bulb holder can be withdrawn from the headlight reflector and the bulb extracted (photo).
3 Refit in the reverse order and check the light operation to complete.

22 Front indicator (2CV and Dyane) – bulb renewal

1 To renew a bulb, unscrew the lens retaining screws, withdraw the lens and remove the bulb (photos).
2 Insert the new bulb, refit the lens and check for correct operation.
3 To remove the indicator unit, work inside the wing panel. Detach the wire at the connector, unscrew the unit retaining bracket nut (photo), withdraw the bracket rearwards and the light unit forwards.
4 Refit in the reverse order.

23 Front combination light (Ami) – bulb renewal

1 Raise and support the bonnet.
2 Working on the light unit from within the front panel, release the clip or springs retaining the unit at the rear (photo).
3 Withdraw the bulb holder and extract the bulb.
4 Refit in the reverse order and check the light operation on completion.

24 Rear number plate light (Ami) – removal and refitting

1 There are two light units located in the top of the rear bumper, both being identical. To remove the unit and/or bulb, unscrew the retaining screws and withdraw the lens from the bumper (photo). Extract the bulb for renewal. To remove the unit complete detach the wire.
2 Refit in the reverse order to removal and check light operation on completion.

25 Rear combination light unit and bulbs – removal and renewal

Bulbs

1 Unscrew the lens retaining screws and carefully remove the lens, taking care not to break the seal. Remove the defective bulb.
2 On some models, the lens is retained in position by a single knurled nut located on the inner panel. In this case first remove the bulb holder protector by pulling it free, then remove the knurled nut and lens (photos).
3 Refit the lens ensuring that the seal is correctly positioned and check the respective light operations to complete.

Light unit

4 Remove the lens as above and then the unit retaining screws or nuts as applicable.
5 Disconnect the wiring to the unit and then withdraw it.
6 Refit the unit in the reverse order to removal, renewing the seal if damaged or defective. Ensure that the wiring connections are securely made and check that all bulbs are operational on completion.

26 Interior light – bulb renewal

1 Compress the lens and remove it from the holder clips (photo). The bulb can now be withdrawn from its holder.
2 Refit in the reverse order.

27 Horn – removal and refitting

1 Disconnect the battery earth terminal.
2 Disconnect the wires at the horn (photo).
3 Unscrew and remove the retaining nut and withdraw the horn from its bracket.
4 Refit in the reverse order and check operation of horn on completion.

28 Windscreen wiper motor – removal and refitting

1 On all models the windscreen wiper motor and linkages are located directly under the facia panel and are accessible from within the car.
2 First remove the wiper arms and blades, pivoting the arms forwards and pulling from the splines of the spindles.
3 Remove the spindle bush retaining nuts and then the bushes and seals. If the seals are perished or defective they must be renewed on assembly.
4 Remove the facia trim panel. This varies according to model and year but in all instances the trim is retained by clips (prise free) and/or screws. Some retaining screws are hidden from view and are only accessible from underneath the dash panel or after removal of facia padding.
5 With the facia trim removed, the windscreen wiper motor and its linkages are readily accessible for inspection and if necessary removal (photo).
6 To remove the motor and linkages, disconnect the wires (note positions) and detach the motor unit from its retaining bracket, then withdraw it through the top.
7 Refit in reverse order, lubricating the linkage pivots. Do not forget to relocate the earth wire under one of the fixing bolts. Check for correct operation prior to refitting the facia panel.

29 Steering column control switches – removal and refitting

1 Various types of switch layouts have been used over the years of production, but they have mainly consisted of individual switches strapped to the steering column or a group of combination switches encased within an upper steering column housing.
2 Before removing any switches, the battery earth terminal must be disconnected.
3 To remove a strap switch, simply unscrew the retaining screw/s and if necessary disconnect the wires at their switch connections.
4 Where the switches are retained in a common housing at the top of the steering column, such as in the Ami models, remove the housing top half by unscrewing the retaining screws from underneath. There are a multitude of screws on show but the cover screws are to be found at the front corners (photo).
5 With the cover removed the respective switches are readily accessible (photo). In most instances the switches are retained in position in the lower housing by screws which are removed from underneath.
6 When refitting a switch, always make sure that it is securely relocated and that the wires are correctly connected.

30 Speedometer and instrument panel – removal and refitting

1 On all models the speedometer and instrument panel are located directly over the steering column and set into the facia assembly.
2 On all types therefore the removal of the instrument panel and speedometer is similar. Unclip, and in some cases unscrew, the facia panel around the instrument panel. Where the panels and trim fittings are clipped into position, carefully prise them free with a flat blade. Avoid damaging the trim or clip.
3 With the trim surround removed, disconnect any wiring connections to instrument panel switches and unscrew or unclip the speedometer and instrument panel to remove (photo). Unscrew the speedometer drive cable to release the speedometer completely.
4 Refitting is a direct reversal of the removal process but check that all wiring connections are correctly and securely made.

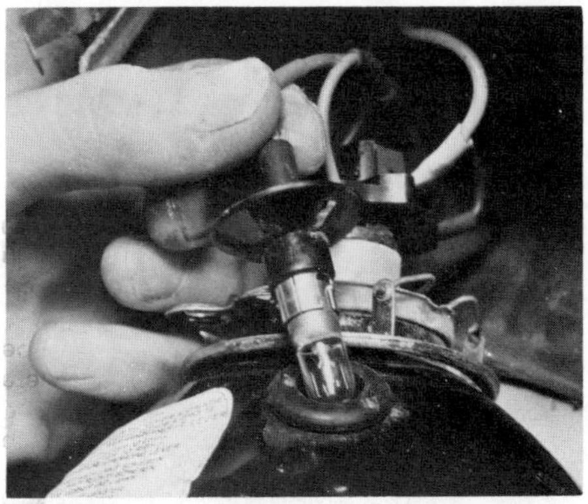
21.2 Removing the sidelight bulb and holder

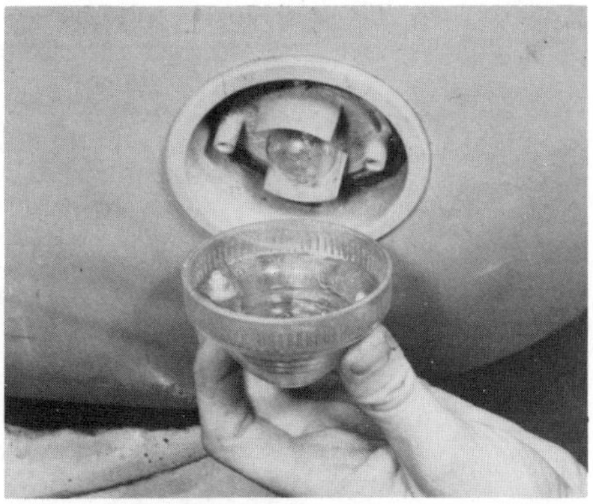
22.1a Removing the lens (2CV)

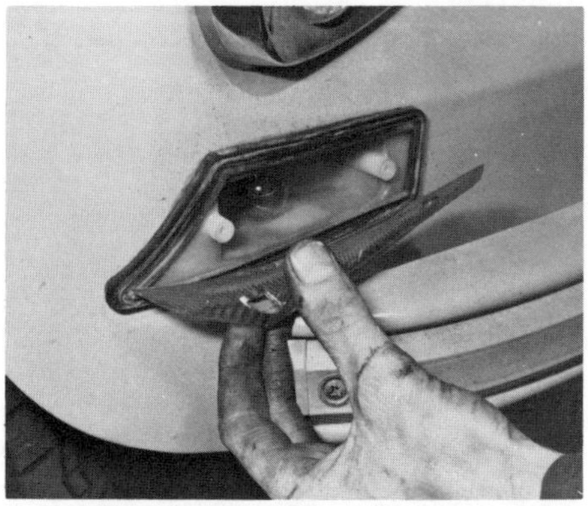
22.1b Removing the lens (Dyane)

22.3 The indicator unit retaining clamp inside the wing

23.2 Release the spring clip (arrowed) to extract the bulb and holder from the combination light (Ami)

24.1 Remove the lens to remove the bulb (Ami)

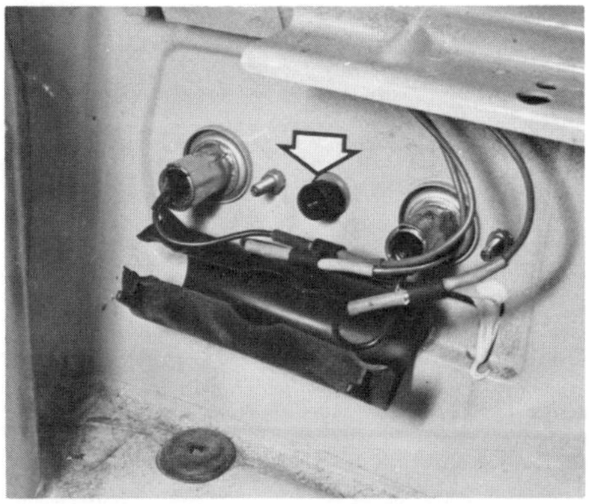
25.2a Removing the rear combination light unit (Dyane). Lens retaining nut is arrowed

25.2b Remove the lens (Dyane)

25.2c Lens removal (Ami)

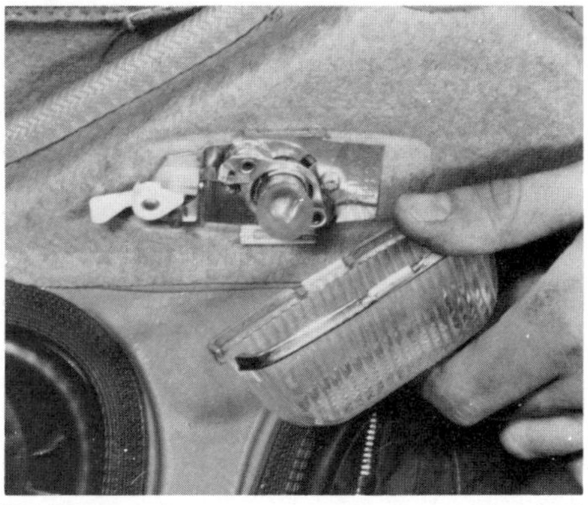
26.1 Removing the interior light lens (typical)

27.2 Disconnect the horn wires

28.5 Wiper motor and linkage shown with facia panels removed (Ami)

29.4 The column control switch housing top section removal (Ami). Note switch retaining screws on underside of lower section

29.5 Remove top cover for access to switches (Ami)

30.3 Withdrawing the speedometer unit (Ami)

31 Fault diagnosis – electrical system

Symptom	Reason(s)
Starter fails to turn engine	Battery discharged Battery terminal leads loose or earth lead not securely attached to body Loose or broken connections in starter motor circuit Starter motor switch or solenoid faulty Starter brushes badly worn, sticking or brush wire connections loose Commutator dirty or worn Starter motor armature faulty Field coils earthed
Starter motor turns engine very slowly	Battery in discharged condition Starter brushes worn, sticking or brush wires loose Loose wires in starter motor circuit
Starter spins but does not turn engine	Pinion or flywheel gear teeth broken or badly worn
Starter motor noisy or excessively rough engagement	Pinion or flywheel gear teeth broken or badly worn Starter motor retaining bolts loose
Battery will not hold charge for more than a few days	Battery defective internally Electrolyte level too low or electrolyte too weak due to leakage Battery terminal connections loose or corroded Generator drivebelt slipping Generator not charging Regulator defective
Ignition light fails to go out	Generator drivebelt loose or broken Regulator faulty No output from generator
Lights do not come on	If engine not running, battery discharged Loose, disconnected or broken connections Light switch faulty Bulb filament burnt out or blown fuse
Lights work erratically	Battery terminal or earth connections loose Lights not earthed properly Lights switch faulty
Horn operates all the time	Horn cable to horn switch earthed Horn switch faulty
Horn fails to operate	Cable connections loose, broken or disconnected Blown fuse Horn faulty
Horn operates intermittently	Loose connections
Windscreen wipers fail to work	Blown fuse Wiring connections loose, disconnected or broken Wiper motor faulty Wiper mechanism jammed or seized
Wiper arms move sluggishly	Wiper motor faulty Wiper mechanism sticking or worn

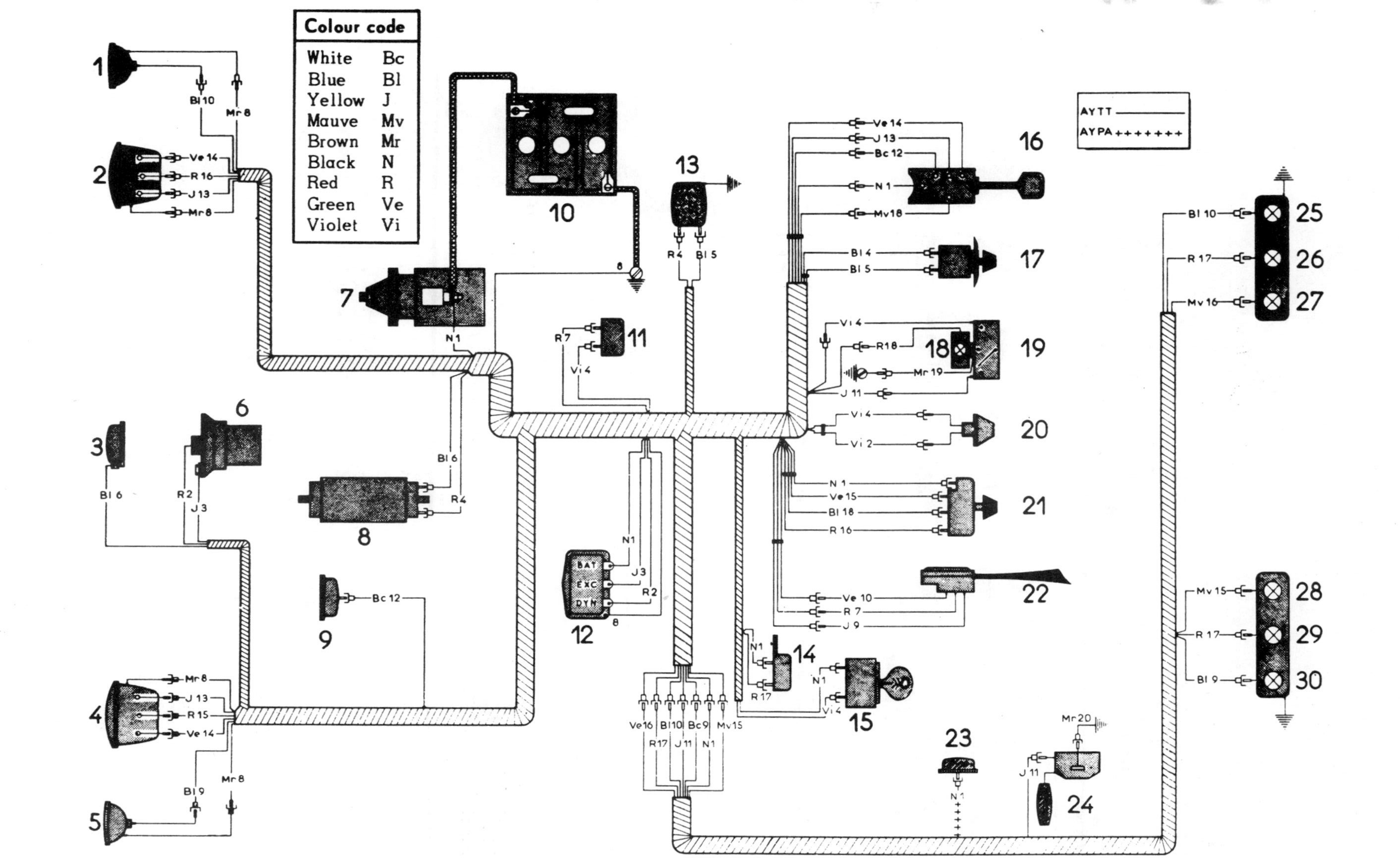

Fig. 10.18 Wiring diagram – Dyane 6 volt

1 Direction indicator, RH front
2 Headlamp unit RH
3 Ignition box
4 Headlamp unit LH
5 Direction indicator, LH front
6 Dynamo
7 Starter motor
8 Coil
9 Horn
10 Battery
11 Flasher unit
12 Voltage regulator
13 Wiper motor
14 Stoplight switch
15 Ignition switch
16 Horn/lighting switch
17 Wiper switch
18 Instrument lighting
19 Fuel gauge
20 Ignition warning light
21 Parking lamp switch
22 Direction indicator switch
23 Interior light
24 Fuel gauge sender
25 Direction indicator, RH rear
26 Stoplight, RH
27 Tail lamp, RH
28 Tail lamp, LH
29 Stoplight, LH
30 Direction indicator, LH

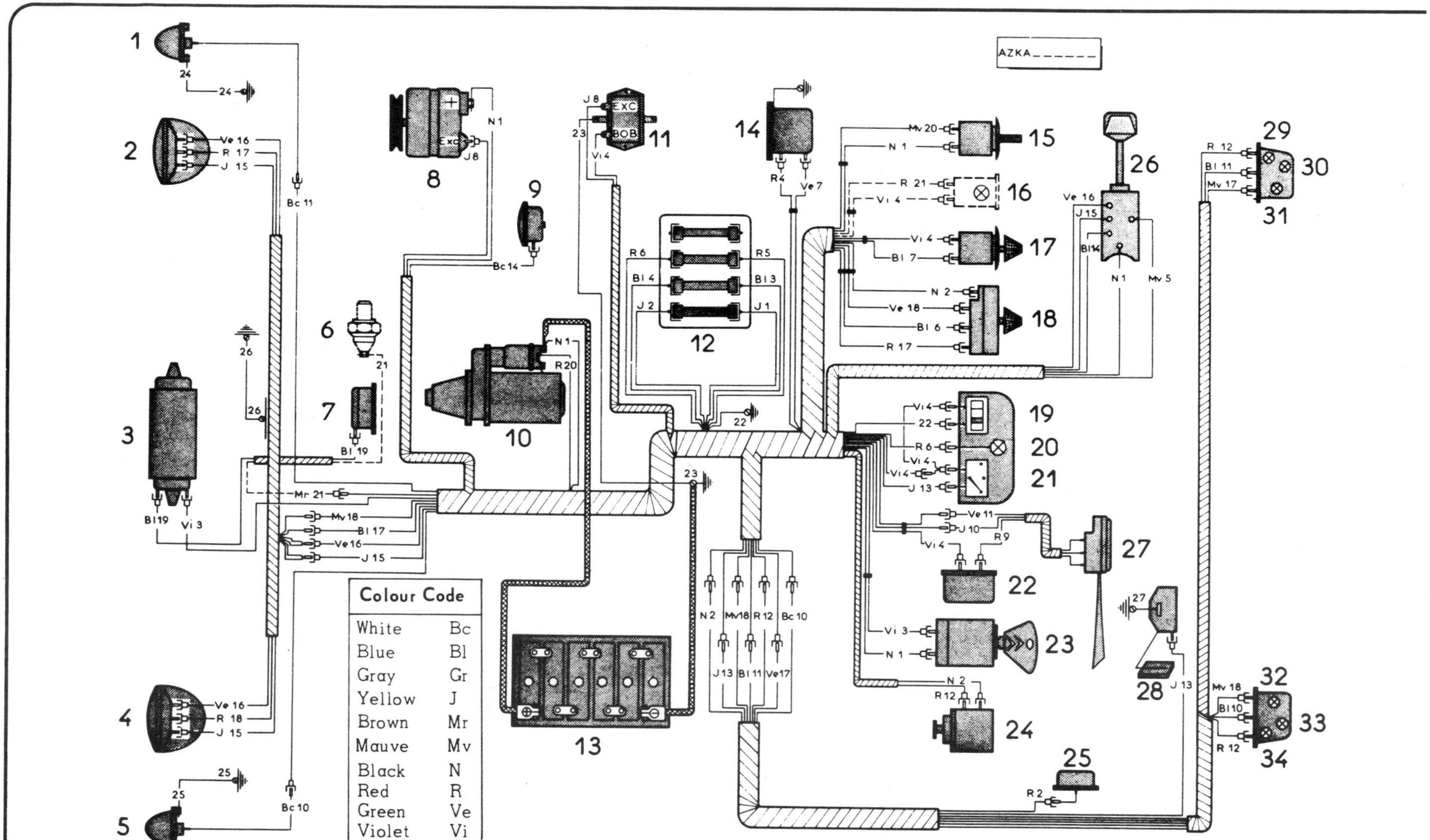

Colour Code	
White	Bc
Blue	Bl
Gray	Gr
Yellow	J
Brown	Mr
Mauve	Mv
Black	N
Red	R
Green	Ve
Violet	Vi

Fig. 10.19 Wiring diagram – 2CV 12 volt, 1970 to 1973

1 Direction indicator, RH front
2 Headlamp unit, RH
3 Coil
4 Headlamp unit, LH
5 Direction indicator, LH front
6 Oil pressure switch (if fitted)
7 Ignition box
8 Alternator
9 Horn
10 Starter motor
11 Voltage regulator
12 Fuse box
13 Battery
14 Wiper motor
15 Starter switch
16 Oil pressure warning lamp (if fitted)
17 Wiper switch
18 Parking light switch
19 Voltmeter
20 Instrument lighting
21 Fuel gauge
22 Flasher unit
23 Ignition switch
24 Stoplight switch
25 Interior light
26 Horn/lighting switch
27 Direction indicator switch
28 Fuel gauge sender
29 Stop and tail light, RH
30 Direction indicator, RH rear
31 Number plate light, RH
32 Number plate light, LH
33 Direction indicator, LH rear
34 Stop and tail light LH

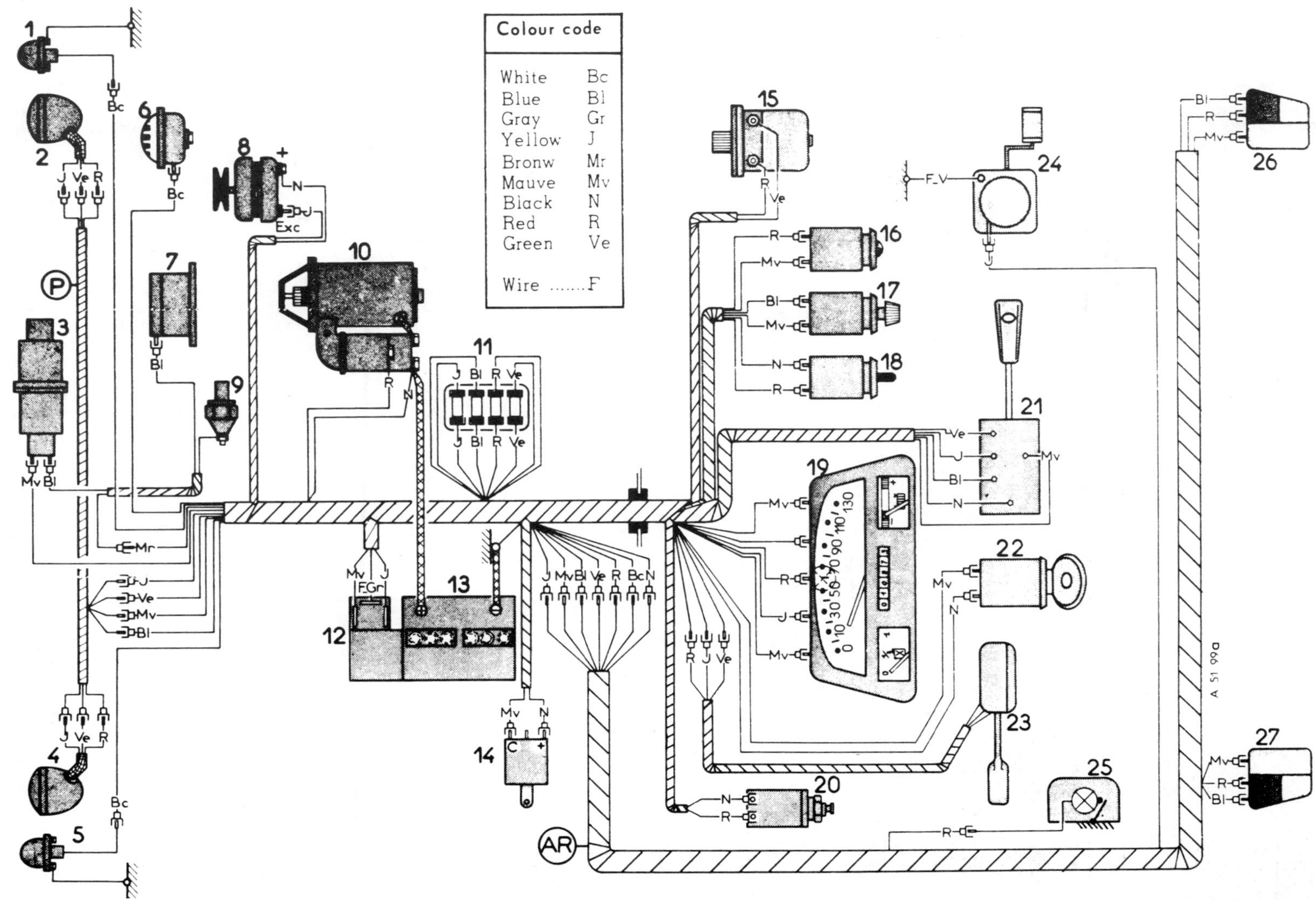

Fig. 10.20 Wiring diagram – 2CV 12 volt, 1974 onwards

1 *Direction indicator, RH front*
2 *Headlamp unit, RH*
3 *Coil*
4 *Headlamp unit, LH*
5 *Direction indicator, LH front*
6 *Horn*
7 *Ignition box*
8 *Alternator*
9 *Oil pressure switch (if fitted)*
10 *Starter motor*
11 *Fuse box*
12 *Voltage regulator*
13 *Battery*
14 *Flasher unit*
15 *Wiper motor*
16 *Oil pressure warning lamp (if fitted)*
17 *Wiper switch*
18 *Starter switch*
19 *Instrument panel*
20 *Stoplight switch*
21 *Horn/lighting switch*
22 *Ignition switch*
23 *Direction indicator switch*
24 *Fuel gauge sender*
25 *Interior lamp*
26 *Rear light cluster, RH*
27 *Rear light cluster, LH*

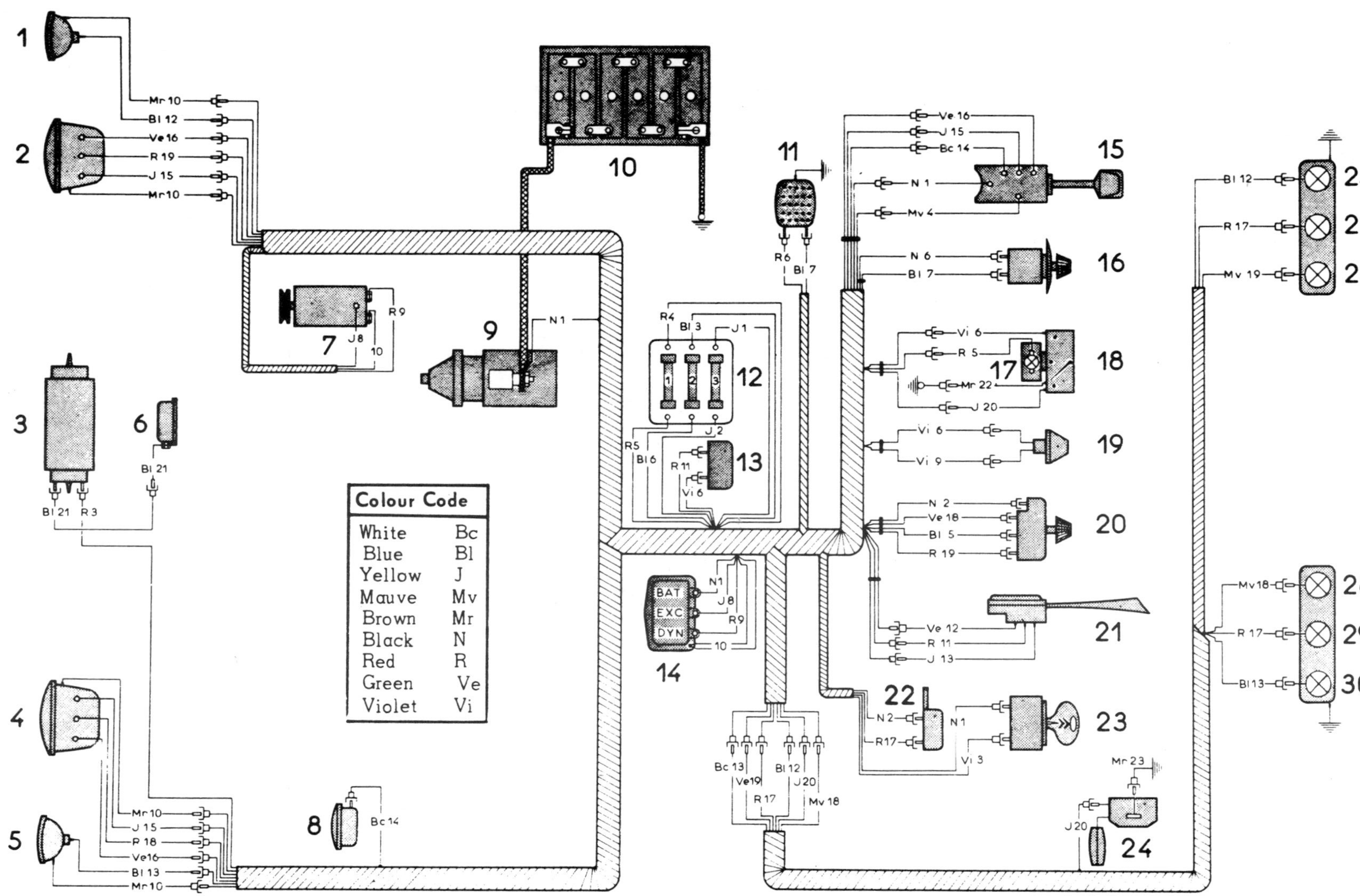

Colour Code	
White	Bc
Blue	Bl
Yellow	J
Mauve	Mv
Brown	Mr
Black	N
Red	R
Green	Ve
Violet	Vi

Fig. 10.21 Wiring diagram – Dyane 12 volt, 1967 to 1968

1 *Direction indicator, RH front*
2 *Headlamp unit, RH*
3 *Coil*
4 *Headlamp unit, LH*
5 *Direction indicator, LH front*
6 *Ignition box*
7 *Dynamo*
8 *Horn*
9 *Starter motor*
10 *Battery*
11 *Wiper motor*
12 *Fuse box*
13 *Flasher unit*
14 *Voltage regulator*
15 *Horn, lighting switch*
16 *Wiper switch*
17 *Instrument illumination*
18 *Fuel gauge*
19 *Ignition warning lamp*
20 *Parking lamp switch*
21 *Direction indicator switch*
22 *Stoplight switch*
23 *Ignition switch*
24 *Fuel gauge sender*
25 *Direction indicator, RH rear*
26 *Stoplight, RH*
27 *Tail lamp, RH*
28 *Tail lamp, LH*
29 *Stoplight, LH*
30 *Direction indicator, LH rear*

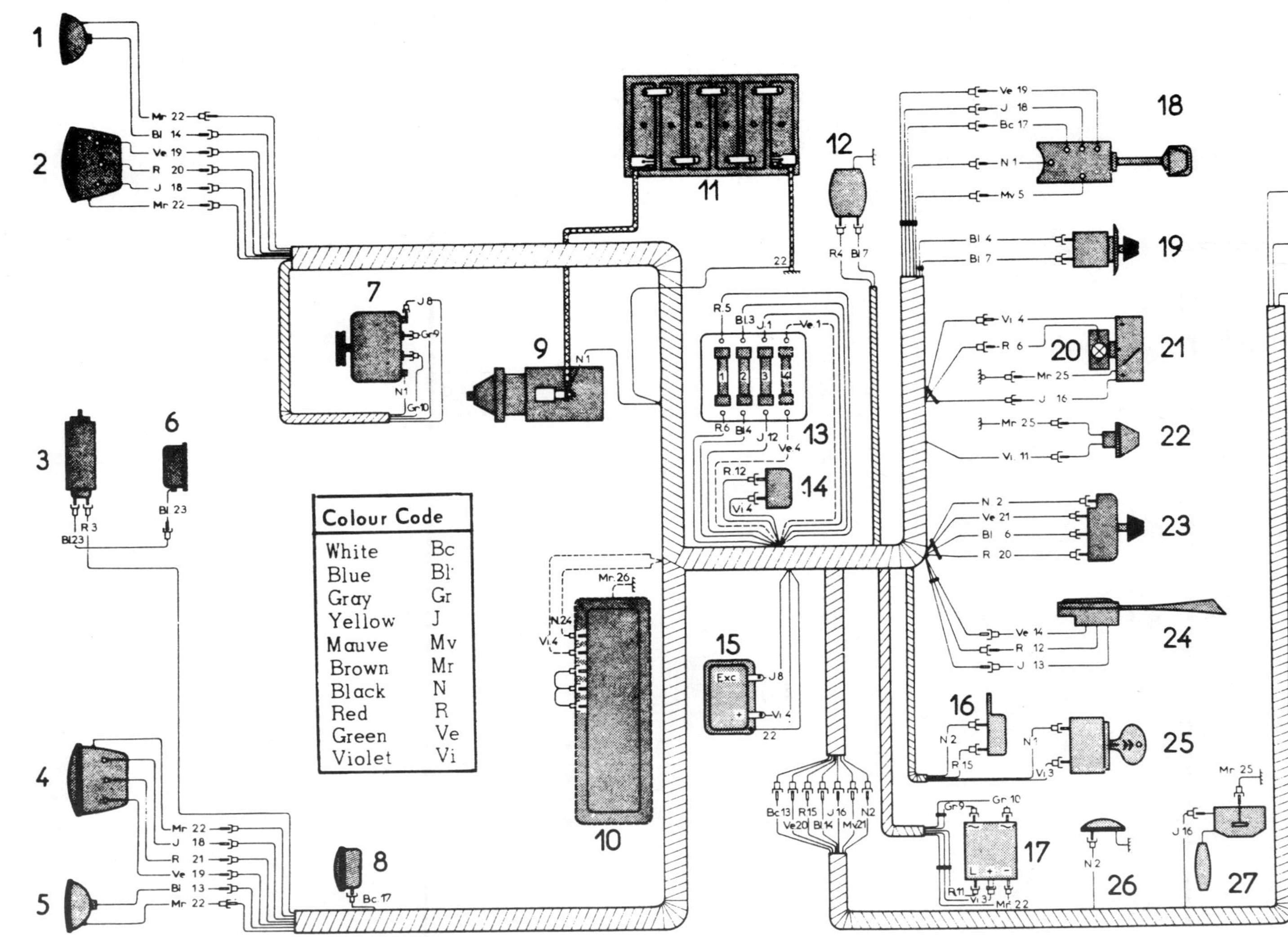

Fig. 10.22 Wiring diagram – Dyane 4, 1968 to 1970, and Dyane 6, 1968 to 1969

1 *Direction indicator, RH front*
2 *Headlamp unit, RH*
3 *Coil*
4 *Headlamp unit, LH*
5 *Direction indicator, LH front*
6 *Ignition box*
7 *Alternator*
8 *Horn*
9 *Starter motor*
10 *Gurtner heating system (optional extra)*
11 *Battery*
12 *Wiper motor*
13 *Fuse box*
14 *Flasher unit*
15 *Voltage regulator*
16 *Stoplight switch*
17 *Ignition warning light relay*
18 *Horn/lighting switch*
19 *Wiper switch*
20 *Instrument illumination*
21 *Fuel gauge*
22 *Ignition warning light*
23 *Parking light switch*
24 *Direction indicator switch*
25 *Ignition switch*
26 *Interior lamp*
27 *Fuel gauge sender*
28 *Direction indicator, RH rear*
29 *Stoplight, RH*
30 *Tail lamp, RH*
31 *Tail lamp, LH*
32 *Stoplight, LH*
33 *Direction indicator, LH rear*

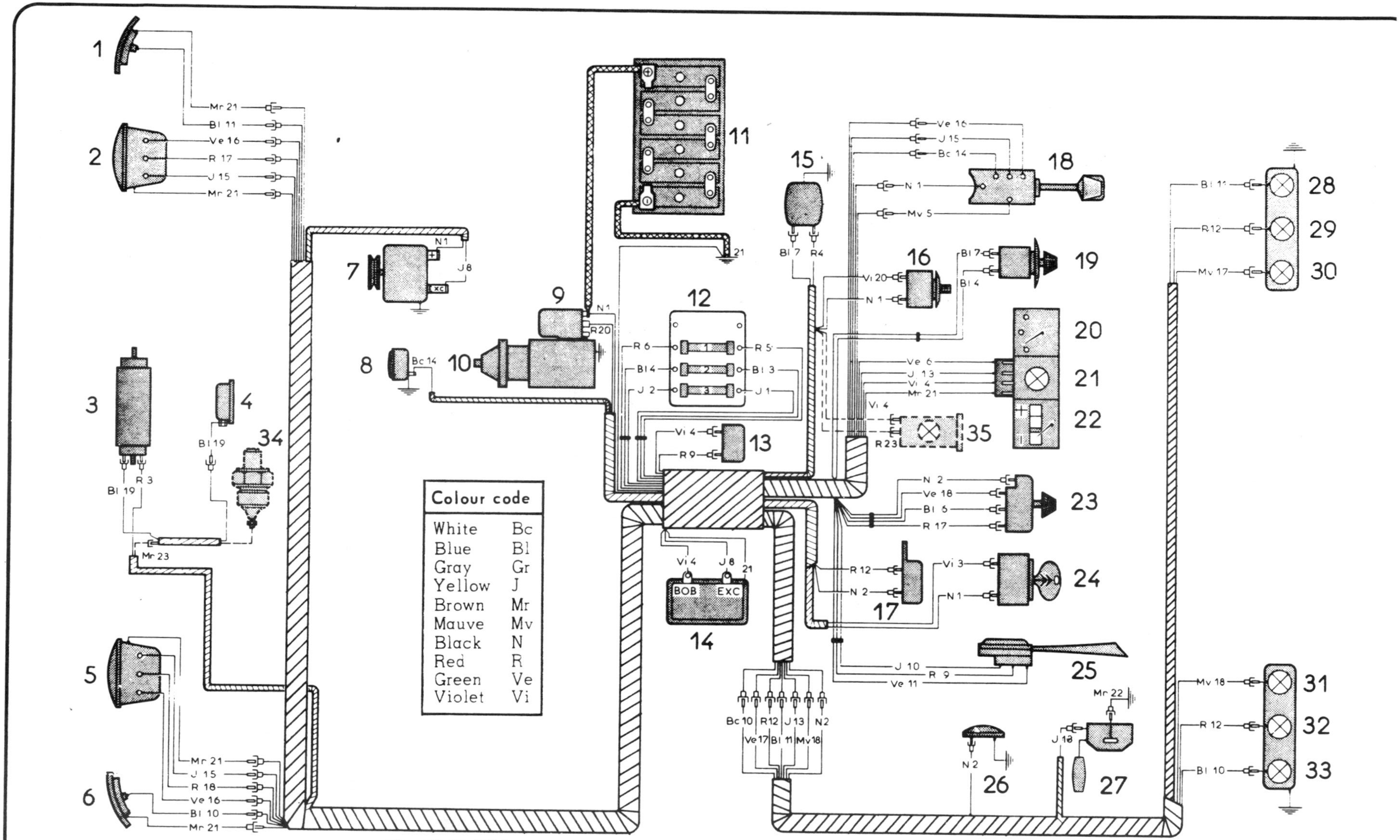

Fig. 10.23 Wiring diagram – Dyane 4, 1970 to 1973, and Dyane 6, 1969 to 1973

1 *Direction indicator, RH front*
2 *Headlight unit, RH*
3 *Coil*
4 *Ignition box*
5 *Headlight unit, LH*
6 *Direction indicator, LH front*
7 *Alternator*
8 *Horn*
9 *Starter solenoid*
10 *Starter motor*
11 *Battery*
12 *Fuse box*
13 *Flasher unit*
14 *Voltage regulator*
15 *Wiper motor*
16 *Starter switch*
17 *Stoplight switch*
18 *Horn/lighting switch*
19 *Wiper switch*
20 *Fuel gauge*
21 *Instrument illumination*
22 *Voltmeter*
23 *Parking lamp switch*
24 *Ignition switch*
25 *Direction indicator switch*
26 *Interior lamp*
27 *Fuel gauge sender*
28 *Direction indicator, RH rear*
29 *Stoplight, RH*
30 *Tail lamp, RH*
31 *Tail lamp, LH*
32 *Stoplight, LH*
33 *Direction indicator, LH rear*
34 *Oil pressure switch (if fitted)*
35 *Oil pressure warning light (if fitted)*

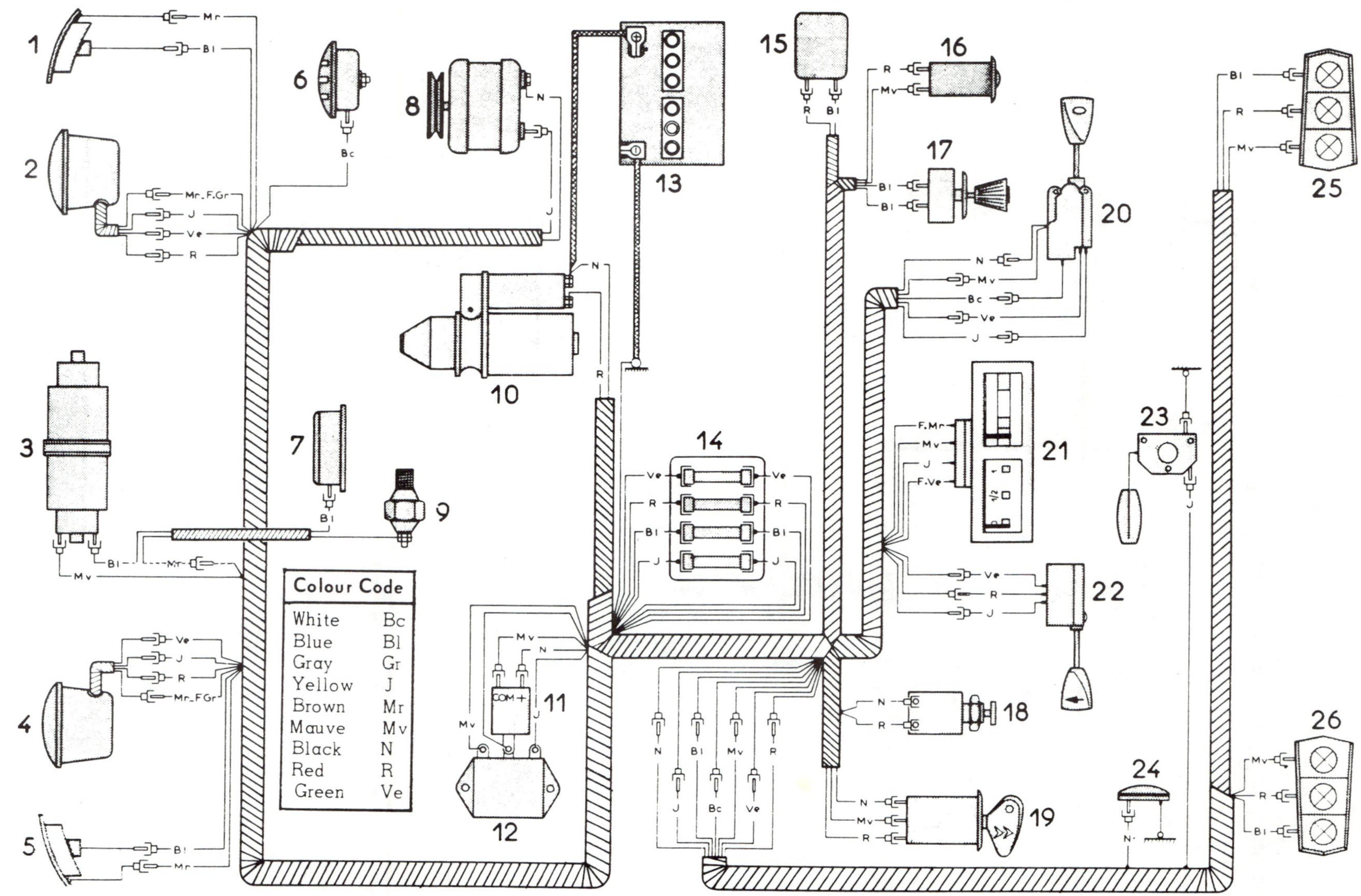

Fig. 10.24 Wiring diagram – Dyane 4 and 6, 1974 onwards

1 *Direction indicator, RH front*
2 *Headlight unit, RH*
3 *Coil*
4 *Headlight unit, LH*
5 *Direction indicator, LH front*
6 *Horn*
7 *Ignition box*
8 *Alternator*
9 *Oil pressure switch (if fitted)*
10 *Starter motor*
11 *Flasher unit*
12 *Voltage regulator*
13 *Battery*
14 *Fuse box*
15 *Wiper motor*
16 *Oil pressure warning light (if fitted)*
17 *Wiper switch*
18 *Stoplight switch*
19 *Ignition/starter switch*
20 *Horn/lighting switch*
21 *Instrument panel*
22 *Direction indicator switch*
23 *Fuel gauge sender*
24 *Interior lamp*
25 *Rear lamp cluster, RH*
26 *Rear lamp cluster, LH*

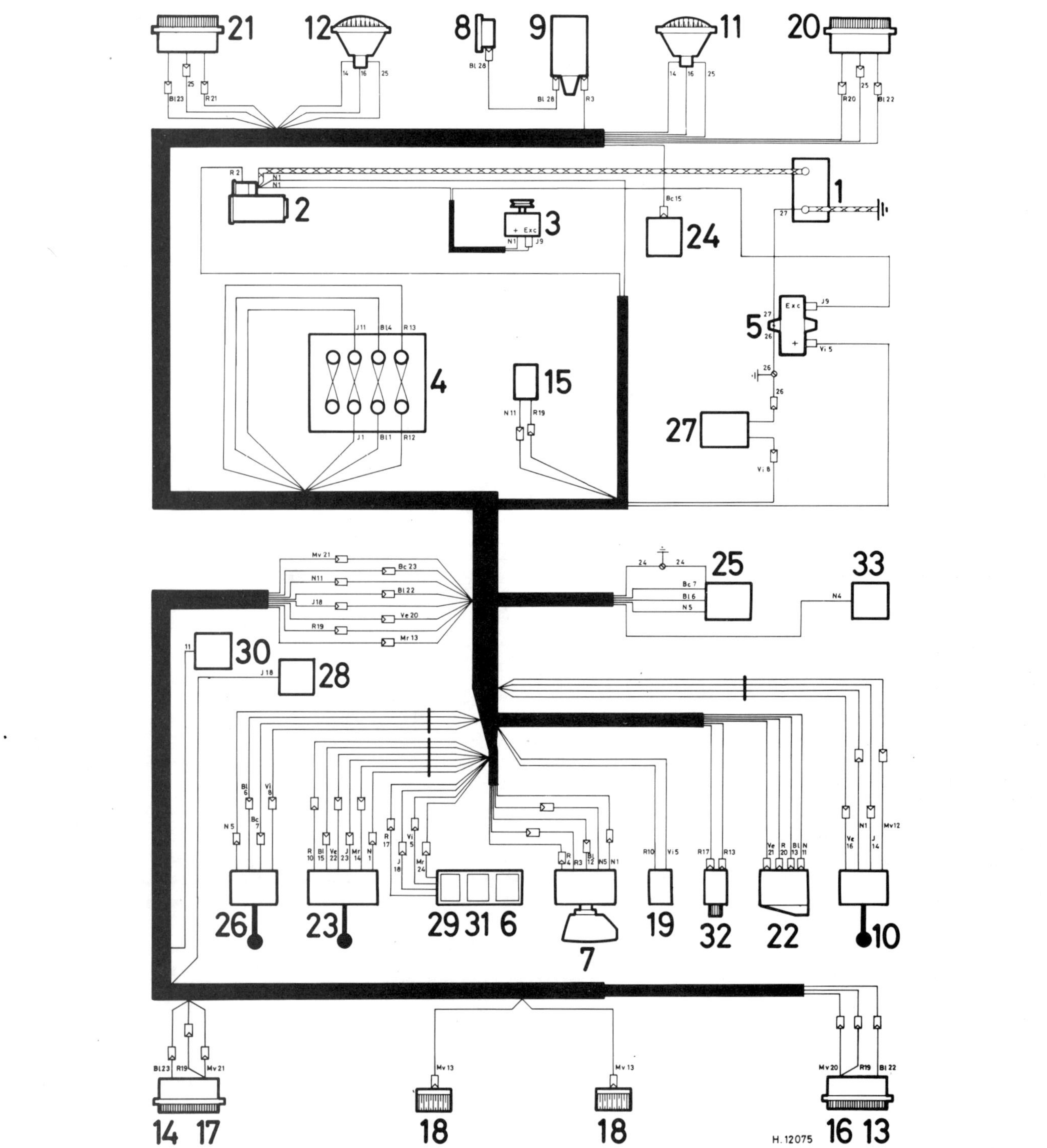

Fig. 10.25 Wiring diagram – Ami 8 to 1973 for colour code see Fig. 10.24

1 Battery
2 Starter motor
3 Alternator
4 Fuse box
5 Voltage regulator
6 Voltmeter
7 Ignition/starter switch
8 Ignition box
9 Coil
10 Lighting switch
11 Headlamp RH
12 Headlamp LH
13 Tail lamp RH
14 Tail lamp LH
15 Stop lamp switch
16 Stop lamp RH
17 Stop lamp LH
18 Number plate lamps
19 Direction indicator flasher
20 Indicator/sidelamp unit, RH front
21 Indicator/sidelamp unit, LH front
22 Hazard warning flasher
23 Horn/direction indicator switch
24 Horn
25 Wiper motor
26 Wiper/washer switch
27 Windscreen washer pump
28 Fuel gauge sender
29 Fuel gauge
30 Interior lamp
31 Instrument illumination
32 Instrument illumination rheostat
33 Accessory terminal

Chapter 11 Bodywork and fittings

For modifications, and information applicable to later models, see Supplement at end of manual

Contents

Specifications

Overall length

2CV Saloon	3.83m (12ft 6.25in)
2CV Van	3.61m (11ft 10in)
Dyane 4 and 6	3.87m (12ft 8in)
Ami	3.99m (13ft 1in)

Width

2CV (Saloon and Van)	1.48m (4ft 10in)
Dyane 4 and 6	1.50m (4ft 11in)
Ami	1.52m (5ft 0in)

Height

2CV Saloon	1.60m (5ft 3in)
2CV Van	1.72m (5ft 8in)
Dyane 4 and 6	1.52m (5ft 0in)
Ami 6	1.47m (4ft 9.5in)
Ami 8	1.49m (4ft 10.75in)

1 General description

The bodywork on all models is mounted on a straight section chassis which has crossmembers to give it substantial strength. A detachable undertray is fitted to some models to give protection from the elements to the engine/transmission unit.

The main body is bolted to the chassis and incorporates floor panels on each side. On all models the front and rear wing panels are secured by bolts and easily removed when necessary. The doors, bonnet and tailgate or boot lid are also easily removed, being retained by bolted or pin hinges.

The 2CV and Dyane models are fitted with a fabric roof section which can be folded back when required for those who prefer open air motoring when the weather permits. The soft-top, although tough and durable, should not be rolled back when wet, but be allowed to dry off first.

All seats are easily removed when required for cleaning, or possibly for carrying awkward loads within the vehicle.

The body panel sections are relatively thin and care must be taken not to dent or damage the panels since they can easily be 'stretched', making repairs more difficult in certain instances. In all other respects the bodywork is practical and requires the minimum of maintenance.

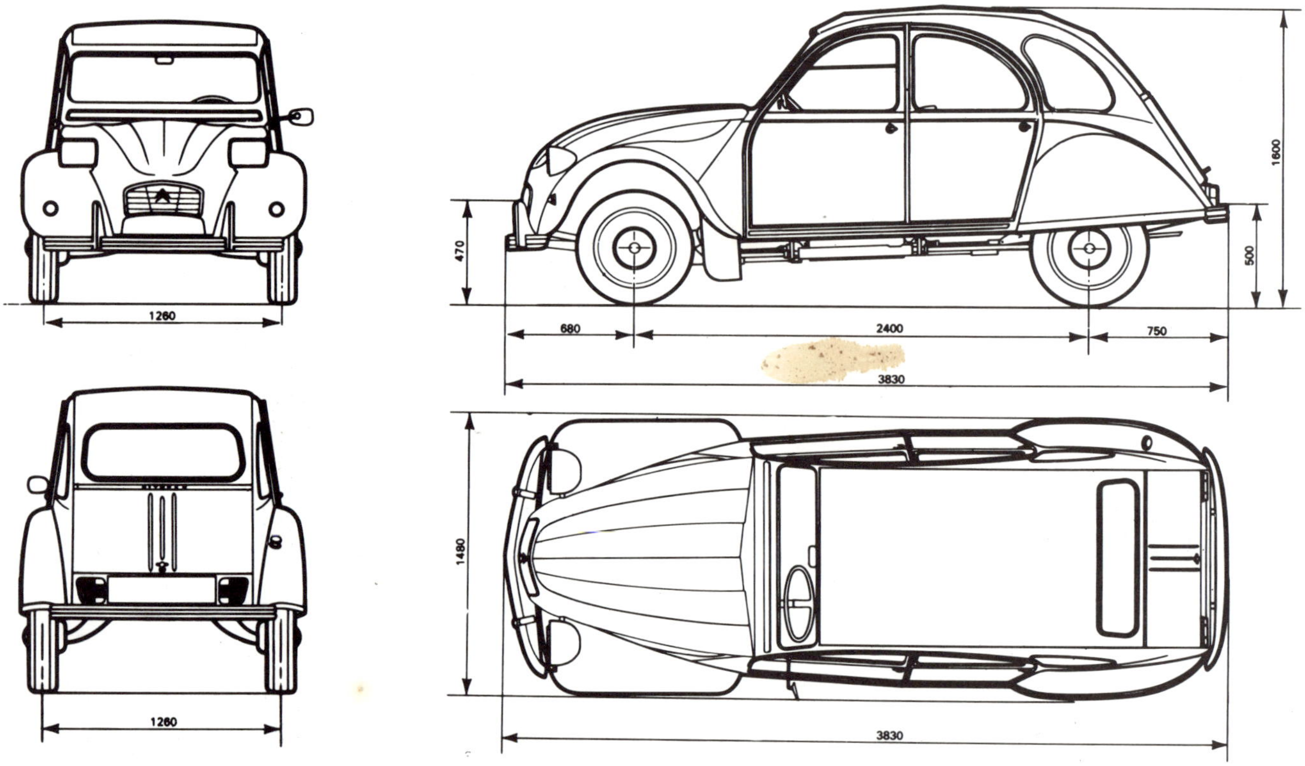

Fig. 11.1 Profile of the 2CV (1978 model). Dimensions in mm (Sec 1)

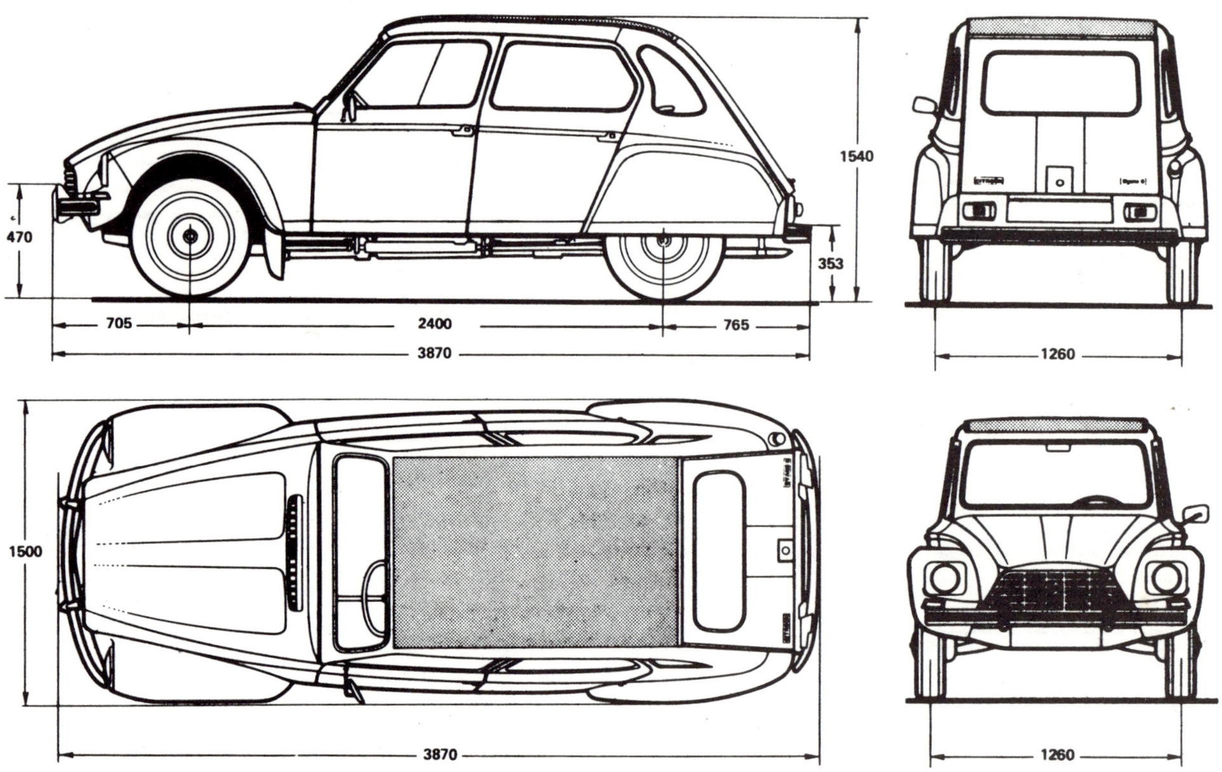

Fig. 11.2 Profile of the Dyane. Dimensions in mm (Sec 1)

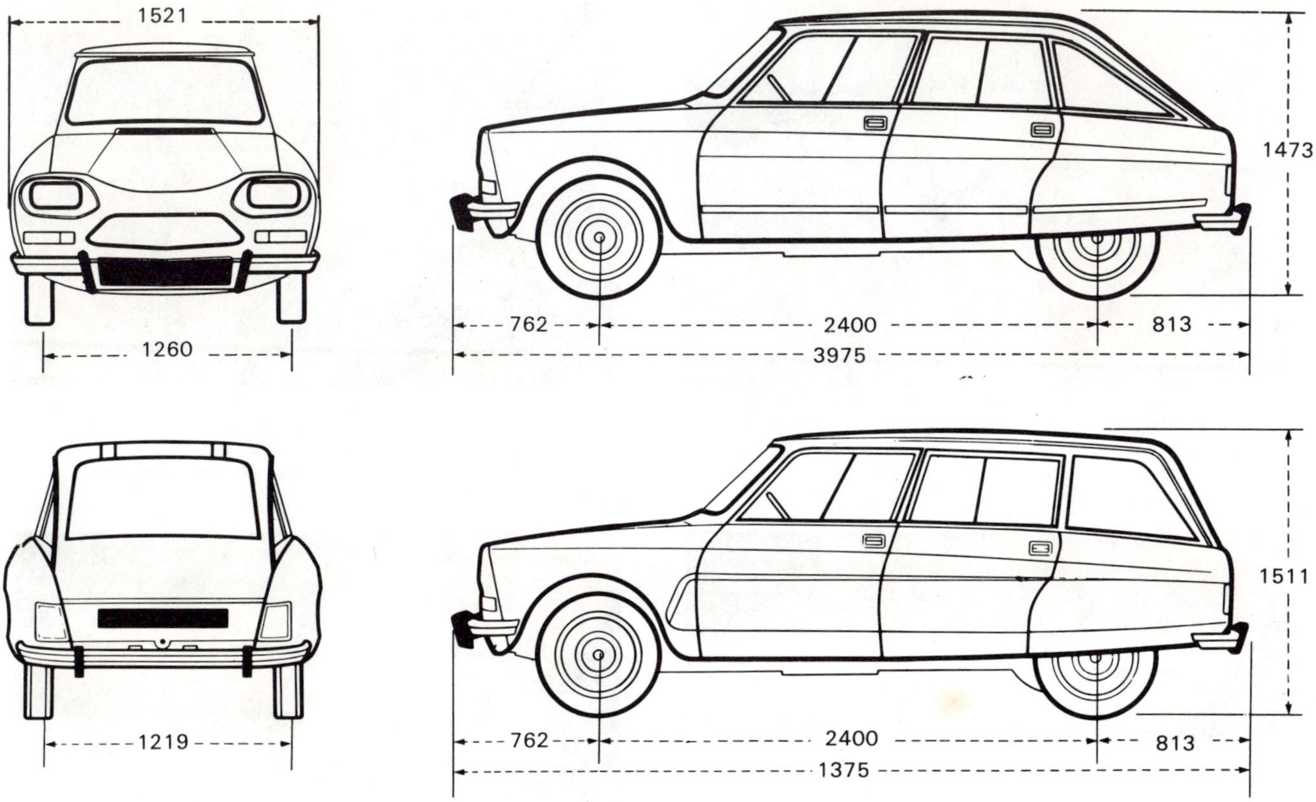

Fig. 11.3 Profile of the Ami. Dimensions in mm (Sec 1)

2 Maintenance – bodywork and underframe

1 The general condition of a car's bodywork is the thing that significantly affects its value. Maintenance is easy but needs to be regular. Neglect, particularly after minor damage, can lead quickly to further deterioration and costly repair bills. It is important also to keep watch on those parts of the car not immediately visible, for instance the underside, inside all the wheel arches and the lower part of the engine compartment.

2 The basic maintenance routine for the bodywork is washing – preferably with a lot of water, from a hose. This will remove all the loose solids which may have stuck to the car. It is important to flush these off in such a way as to prevent grit from scratching the finish. The wheel arches and underframe need washing in the same way to remove any accumulated mud which will retain moisture and tend to encourage rust. Paradoxically enough, the best time to clean the underframe and wheel arches is in wet weather when the mud is thoroughly wet and soft. In very wet weather the underframe is usually cleaned of large accumulations automatically and this is a good time for inspection.

3 Periodically, it is a good idea to have the whole of the underframe of the car steam cleaned, engine compartment included, so that a thorough inspection can be carried out to see what minor repairs and renovations are necessary. Steam cleaning is available at many garages and is necessary for removal of the accumulation of oily grime which sometimes is allowed to become thick in certain areas. If steam cleaning facilities are not available, there are one or two excellent grease solvents available which can be brush applied. The dirt can then be simply hosed off.

4 After washing paintwork, wipe off with a chamois leather to give an unspotted clear finish. A coat of clear protective wax polish will give added protection against chemical pollutants in the air. If the paintwork sheen has dulled or oxidised, use a cleaner/polisher combination to restore the brilliance of the shine. This requires a little effort, but such dulling is usually caused because regular washing has been neglected. Always check that the door and ventilator opening drain holes and pipes are completely clear so that water can be drained out. Bright work should be treated in the same way as paintwork. Windscreens and windows can be kept clear of the smeary film which often appears, by adding a little ammonia to the water. If they are scratched, a good rub with a proprietary metal polish will often clear them. Never use any form of wax or other body or chromium polish on glass.

5 On those models fitted with an opening roof panel, it should be washed using soapy water and then hosed clean and wiped dry. Do not fold the roof back when wet, allow it to dry first.

3 Maintenance – upholstery and carpets

1 Mats and carpets should be brushed or vacuum cleaned regularly to keep them free of grit. If they are badly stained remove them from the car for scrubbing or sponging and make quite sure they are dry before refitting. Seats and interior trim panels can be kept clean by a wipe over with a damp cloth. If they do become stained (which can be more apparent on light coloured upholstery) use a little liquid detergent and a soft nail brush to scour the grime out of the grain of the material. Do not forget to keep the head lining clean in the same way as the upholstery. When using liquid cleaners inside the car do not over-wet the surfaces being cleaned. Excessive damp could get into the seams and padded interior causing stains, offensive odours or even rot. If the inside of the car gets wet accidentally it is worthwhile taking some trouble to dry it out properly, particularly where carpets are involved. *Do not leave oil or electric heaters inside the car for this purpose.*

4 Minor body damage – repair

The photographic sequences on pages 166 and 167 illustrate the operations detailed in the following sub-sections.

Repair of minor scratches in the vehicle's bodywork

If the scratch is very superficial, and does not penetrate to the metal of the bodywork, repair is very simple. Lightly rub the area of the scratch with a paintwork renovator, or a very fine cutting paste, to

This sequence of photographs deals with the repair of the dent and paintwork damage shown in this photo. The procedure will be similar for the repair of a hole. It should be noted that the procedures given here are simplified – more explicit instructions will be found in the text

In the case of a dent the first job – after removing surrounding trim – is to hammer out the dent where access is possible. This will minimise filling. Here, the large dent having been hammered out, the damaged area is being made slightly concave

Now all paint must be removed from the damaged area, by rubbing with coarse abrasive paper. Alternatively, a wire brush or abrasive pad can be used in a power drill. Where the repair area meets good paintwork, the edge of the paintwork should be 'feathered', using a finer grade of abrasive paper

In the case of a hole caused by rusting, all damaged sheet-metal should be cut away before proceeding to this stage. Here, the damaged area is being treated with rust remover and inhibitor before being filled

Mix the body filler according to its manufacturer's instructions. In the case of corrosion damage, it will be necessary to block off any large holes before filling – this can be done with aluminium or plastic mesh, or aluminium tape. Make sure the area is absolutely clean before ...

... applying the filler. Filler should be applied with a flexible applicator, as shown, for best results; the wooden spatula being used for confined areas. Apply thin layers of filler at 20-minute intervals, until the surface of the filler is slightly proud of the surrounding bodywork

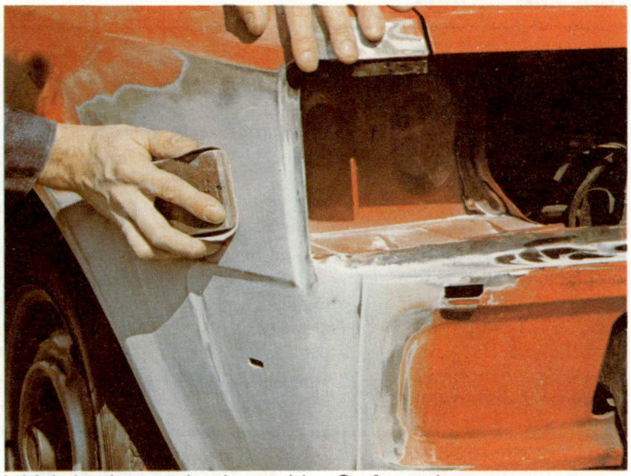

Initial shaping can be done with a Surform plane or Dreadnought file. Then, using progressively finer grades of wet-and-dry paper, wrapped around a sanding block, and copious amounts of clean water, rub down the filler until really smooth and flat. Again, feather the edges of adjoining paintwork

The whole repair area can now be sprayed or brush-painted with primer. If spraying, ensure adjoining areas are protected from over-spray. Note that at least one inch of the surrounding sound paintwork should be coated with primer. Primer has a 'thick' consistency, so will find small imperfections

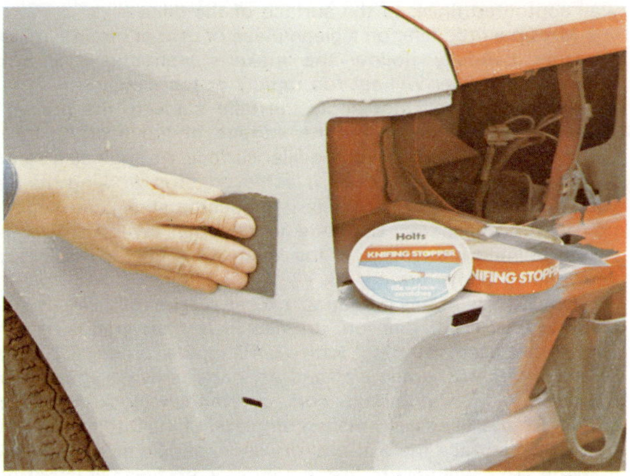

Again, using plenty of water, rub down the primer with a fine grade wet-and-dry paper (400 grade is probably best) until it is really smooth and well blended into the surrounding paintwork. Any remaining imperfections can now be filled by carefully applied knifing stopper paste

When the stopper has hardened, rub down the repair area again before applying the final coat of primer. Before rubbing down this last coat of primer, ensure the repair area is blemish-free – use more stopper if necessary. To ensure that the surface of the primer is really smooth use some finishing compound

The top coat can now be applied. When working out of doors, pick a dry, warm and wind-free day. Ensure surrounding areas are protected from over-spray. Agitate the aerosol thoroughly, then spray the centre of the repair area, working outwards with a circular motion. Apply the paint as several thin coats

After a period of about two weeks, which the paint needs to harden fully, the surface of the repaired area can be 'cut' with a mild cutting compound prior to wax polishing. When carrying out bodywork repairs, remember that the quality of the finished job is proportional to the time and effort expended

remove loose paint from the scratch and to clear the surrounding bodywork of wax polish. Rinse the area with clean water.

Apply touch-up paint to the scratch using a thin paint brush; continue to apply thin layers of paint until the surface of the paint in the scratch is level with the surrounding paintwork. Allow the new paint at least two weeks to harden: then blend it into the surrounding paintwork by rubbing the paintwork, in the scratch area, with a paintwork renovator or a very fine cutting paste. Finally, apply wax polish.

Where the scratch has penetrated right through to the metal of the bodywork, causing the metal to rust, a different repair technique is required. Remove any loose rust from the bottom of the scratch with a penknife, then apply rust inhibiting paint to prevent the formation of rust in the future. Using a rubber or nylon applicator fill the scratch with bodystopper paste. If required, this paste can be mixed with cellulose thinners to provide a very thin paste which is ideal for filling narrow scratches. Before the stopper-paste in the scratch hardens, wrap a piece of smooth cotton rag around the top of a finger. Dip the finger in cellulose thinners and then quickly sweep it across the surface of the stopper-paste in the scratch; this will ensure that the surface of the stopper-paste is slightly hollowed. The scratch can now be painted over as described earlier in this Section.

Repair of dents in the vehicle's bodywork

When deep denting of the vehicle's bodywork has taken place, the first task is to pull the dent out, until the affected bodywork almost attains its original shape. There is little point in trying to restore the original shape completely, as the metal in the damaged area will have stretched on impact and cannot be reshaped fully to its original contour. It is better to bring the level of the dent up to a point which is about $\frac{1}{8}$ in (3 mm) below the level of the surrounding bodywork. In cases where the dent is very shallow anyway, it is not worth trying to pull it out at all. If the underside of the dent is accessible, it can be hammered out gently from behind, using a mallet with a wooden or plastic head. Whilst doing this, hold a suitable block of wood firmly against the outside of the panel to absorb the impact from the hammer blows and thus prevent a large area of the bodywork from being 'belled-out'.

Should the dent be in a section of the bodywork which has double skin or some other factor making it inaccessible from behind, a different technique is called for. Drill several small holes through the metal inside the area – particularly in the deeper section. Then screw long self-tapping screws into the holes just sufficiently for them to gain a good purchase in the metal. Now the dent can be pulled out by pulling on the protruding heads of the screws with a pair of pliers.

The next stage of the repair is the removal of the paint from the damaged area, and from an inch or so of the surrounding 'sound' bodywork. This is accomplished most easily by using a wire brush or abrasive pad on a power drill, although it can be done just as effectively by hand using sheets of abrasive paper. To complete the preparation for filling, score the surface of the bare metal with a screwdriver or the tang of a file, or alternatively, drill small holes in the affected area. This will provide a really good 'key' for the filler paste.

To complete the repair see the Section on filling and re-spraying.

Repair of rust holes or gashes in the vehicle's bodywork

Remove all paint from the affected area and from an inch or so of the surrounding 'sound' bodywork, using an abrasive pad or a wire brush on a power drill. If these are not available a few sheets of abrasive paper will do the job just as effectively. With the paint removed you will be able to gauge the severity of the corrosion and therefore decide whether to renew the whole panel (if this is possible) or to repair the affected area. New body panels are not as expensive as most people think and it is often quicker and more satisfactory to fit a new panel than to attempt to repair large areas of corrosion.

Remove all fittings from the affected area except those which will act as a guide to the original shape of the damaged bodywork (eg headlamp shells etc). Then, using tin snips or a hacksaw blade, remove all loose metal and any other metal badly affected by corrosion. Hammer the edges of the hole inwards in order to create a slight depression for the filler paste.

Wire brush the affected area to remove the powdery rust from the surface of the remaining metal. Paint the affected area with rust inhibiting paint; if the back of the rusted area is accessible treat this also.

Before filling can take place it will be necessary to block the hole in some way. This can be achieved by the use of Zinc gauze or Aluminium tape.

Zinc gauze is probably the best material to use for a large hole. Cut a piece to the approximate size and shape of the hole to be filled, then position it in the hole so that its edges are below the level of the surrounding bodywork. It can be retained in position by several blobs of filler paste around its periphery.

Aluminium tape should be used for small or very narrow holes. Pull a piece off the roll and trim it to the approximate size and shape required, then pull off the backing paper (if used) and stick the tape over the hole; it can be overlapped if the thickness of one piece is insufficient. Burnish down the edges of the tape with the handle of a screwdriver or similar, to ensure that the tape is securely attached to the metal underneath.

Bodywork repairs – filling and re-spraying

Before using this Section, see the Sections on dent, deep scratch, rust holes and gash repairs.

Many types of bodyfiller are available, but generally speaking those proprietary kits which contain a tin of filler paste and a tube of resin hardener are best for this type of repair. A wide, flexible plastic or nylon applicator will be found invaluable for imparting a smooth and well contoured finish to the surface of the filler.

Mix up a little filler on a clean piece of card or board – measure the hardener carefully (follow the maker's instructions on the pack) otherwise the filler will set too rapidly or too slowly.

Using the applicator apply the filler paste to the prepared area; draw the applicator across the surface of the filler to achieve the correct contour and to level the filler surface. As soon as a contour that approximates the correct one is achieved, stop working the paste – if you carry on too long the paste will become sticky and begin to 'pick up' on the applicator. Continue to add thin layers of filler paste at twenty-minute intervals until the level of the filler is just proud of the surrounding bodywork.

Once the filler has hardened, excess can be removed using a metal plane or file. From then on, progressively finer grades of sandpaper should be used, starting with a 40 grade production paper and finishing with 400 grade wet-and-dry paper. Always wrap the abrasive paper around a flat rubber, cork, or wooden block – otherwise the surface of the filler will not be completely flat. During the smoothing of the filler surface the wet-and-dry paper should be periodically rinsed in water. This will ensure that a very smooth finish is imparted to the filler at the final stage.

At this stage the 'repair area' should be surrounded by a ring of bare metal, which in turn should be encircled by the finely 'feathered' edge of the good paintwork. Rinse the repair area with clean water, until all of the dust produced by the rubbing-down operation has gone.

Spray the whole repair area with a light coat of primer – this will show up any imperfections in the surface of the filler. Repair these imperfections with fresh filler paste or bodystopper, and once more smooth the surface with abrasive paper. If bodystopper is used, it can be mixed with cellulose thinners to form a really thin paste which is ideal for filling small holes. Repeat this spray and repair procedure until you are satisfied that the surface of the filler, and the feathered edge of the paintwork are perfect. Clean the repair area with clean water and allow to dry fully.

The repair area is now ready for final spraying. Paint spraying must be carried out in warm, dry, windless and dust free atmosphere. This condition can be created artificially if you have access to a large indoor working area, but if you are forced to work in the open, you will have to pick your day very carefully. If you are working indoors, dousing the floor in the work area with water will help to settle the dust which would otherwise be in the atmosphere. If the repair area is confined to one body panel, mask off the surrounding panels; this will help to minimise the effects of a slight mis-match in paint colours. Bodywork fittings (eg chrome strips, door handles etc) will also need to be masked off. Use genuine masking tape and several thicknesses of newspaper for the masking operations.

Before commencing to spray, agitate the aerosol can thoroughly, then spray a test area (an old tin, or similar) until the technique is mastered. Cover the repair area with a thick coat of primer; the thickness should be built up using several thin layers of paint rather than one thick one. Using 400 grade wet-and-dry paper, rub down the surface of the primer until it is really smooth. While doing this, the work area should be thoroughly doused with water, and the wet-and-dry paper periodically rinsed in water. Allow to dry before spraying on more paint.

Spray on the top coat, again building up the thickness by using several thin layers of paint. Start spraying in the centre of the repair area and then, using a circular motion, work outwards until the whole repair area and about 2 inches of the surrounding original paintwork is covered. Remove all masking material 10 to 15 minutes after spraying on the final coat of paint.

Allow the new paint at least two weeks to harden, then, using a paintwork renovator or a very fine cutting paste, blend the edges of the paint into the existing paintwork. Finally, apply wax polish.

5 Major body damage – repair

Where serious damage has occurred or large areas need renewal due to neglect, it means certainly that completely new sections or panels will need welding in and this is best left to professionals. If the damage is due to impact it will also be necessary to completely check the alignment of the chassis/bodyshell structure. Due to the principle of construction the strength and shape of the whole car can be affected by damage to a critical part. In such instances the services of a Citroën agent with specialist checking jigs are essential. If a chassis is left misaligned it is first of all dangerous as the car will not handle properly and secondly uneven stresses will be imposed on the steering, engine and transmission, causing abnormal wear or complete failure. Tyre wear may also be excessive.

6 Maintenance – hinges and locks

1 Oil the hinges of the bonnet, boot and doors with a drop or two of light oil periodically. A good time is after the car has been washed.
2 Oil the bonnet release catch mechanism and striker pin periodically.
3 Do not over lubricate door latches and strikers. Normally a little oil on the rotary cam spindle is sufficient.
4 On models fitted with a fold-back roof the frame hinges can also be given a small amount of light machine oil, but wipe clean any spillages from the fabric.

7 Door rattles – tracing and rectification

Door rattles are due either to loose hinges, worn or maladjusted catches or loose components of the locking mechanism or window winding assembly inside the door. Loose hinges can be detected by opening the door and trying to lift. Any play will be felt. Worn or badly adjusted catches can be found by pushing and pulling on the outside handle when the door is closed. Once again any play will be felt. Readjust or replace the striker plate as necessary. To check the window winding mechanism (on those models thus equipped), open the door and shake it with the window open and then closed. If rattles are heard the mechanism is loose or worn, rectify as necessary. Where sliding windows are fitted the runner channels may have worn badly and must therefore be renewed as necessary.

8 Front wings – removal and refitting

Dyane

1 Disconnect the battery earth lead. Detach the front light wires at the connectors.
2 Disconnect the headlamp load adjuster cable(s).
3 Unscrew and remove the four bolts at the top and front, also the two bolts at the rear section underneath the panel.
4 Remove the two bolts at the lower front section, also from underneath, and note the bolts that retain the wiring harness clips (photo).
5 The panel can now be removed. If it is wished to remove the wing and small side panel complete, instead of unscrewing the rear wing edge-to-side panel bolts, unscrew the rear panel-to-door pillar screws (photo).
6 Refit in the reverse order, but check alignment before fully tightening the retaining bolts. Check the operation of the lights to complete.

Ami

7 Unscrew and remove the wing-to-front grille panel bolts.
8 Unscrew and remove the wing-to-bumper bolts.
9 Unscrew and remove the wing-to-door pillar bolts and also the top edge bolts to the inner panel. Remove the wing panel.
10 Refit in the reverse order, aligning the panel correctly before fully tightening the bolts.

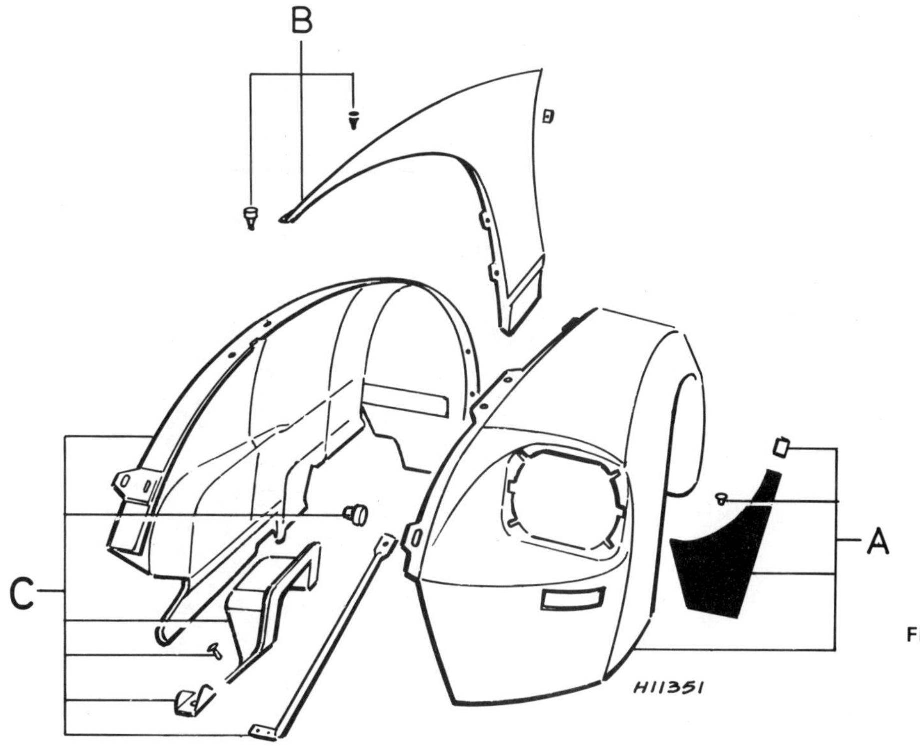

Fig. 11.4 Front wing panels – Dyane (Sec 8)

A Outer wing and mudflap
B Side panel and retaining bolts
C Inner wing assembly and stay

2CV

11 Disconnect the front indicator lead at the inner wing panel. Disconnect the front indicator earth wire. Disconnect the headlamp load adjuster linkage rod.

12 Unscrew and remove the front wing panel retaining nuts and withdraw the panel. The bonnet side panel can be removed with or without the wing panel. It is secured by two screws to the bulkhead at the rear and by one to the wing panel.

13 Refitting the wing panel is a reversal of the removal procedure. Place a rag over the front bumper and around the headlamp to avoid scratching the wing. Align the panel correctly prior to fully tightening the retaining bolts. Reconnect the indicator and check operation.

9 Rear wings – removal and refitting

Dyane

1 Open the tailgate and unscrew the wing retaining bolts and nuts within the spare wheel compartment on the side concerned. At the rear of the wing underneath, disconnect the wing stay strut to body.

2 Open the rear door on the side concerned and unscrew the three retaining bolts from the forward wing section (photo).

3 Unscrew and remove the three bolts above the inner wing panel from the inside, noting that the middle bolt also retains the rear shelf support bracket.

4 On the right-hand rear wing remove the petrol filler cap and rubber seal.

5 Lift the wing clear.

6 Refit in the reverse order, aligning the wing before finally tightening the retaining bolts. Renew the seals if necessary.

Ami

7 Disconnect the battery earth lead.

8 Remove the rear light unit (see Chapter 10).

9 Unscrew the bumper corner stay bolts. These bolts will probably require wire brushing and a spot of penetrating oil to assist removal.

10 From inside the vehicle, prise the trim panel free above the wheel arch and then unscrew the wing panel upper retaining nuts (photo).

11 Open the rear side door on the side concerned and unscrew the forward wing section retaining bolt. Remove the panel.

12 Refit in the reverse order, but check the wing alignment prior to tightening the retaining nuts and bolts fully. Refit the light unit and check operation of lights to complete.

2CV

13 On 2CV models the rear wing removal procedure is similar to that described for the Dyane.

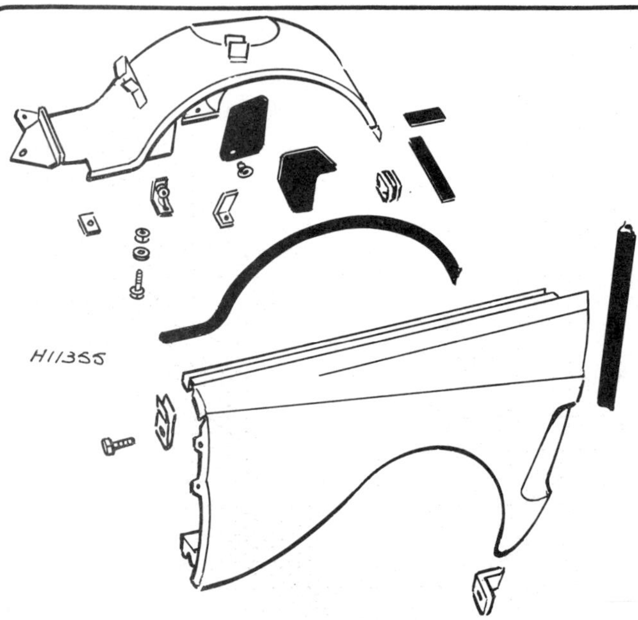

Fig. 11.5 Front wing panels – Ami (Sec 8)

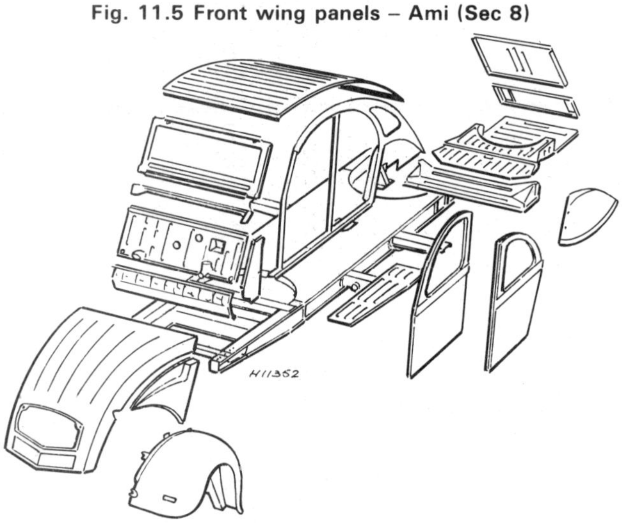

Fig. 11.6 The 2CV body panels (Sec 8)

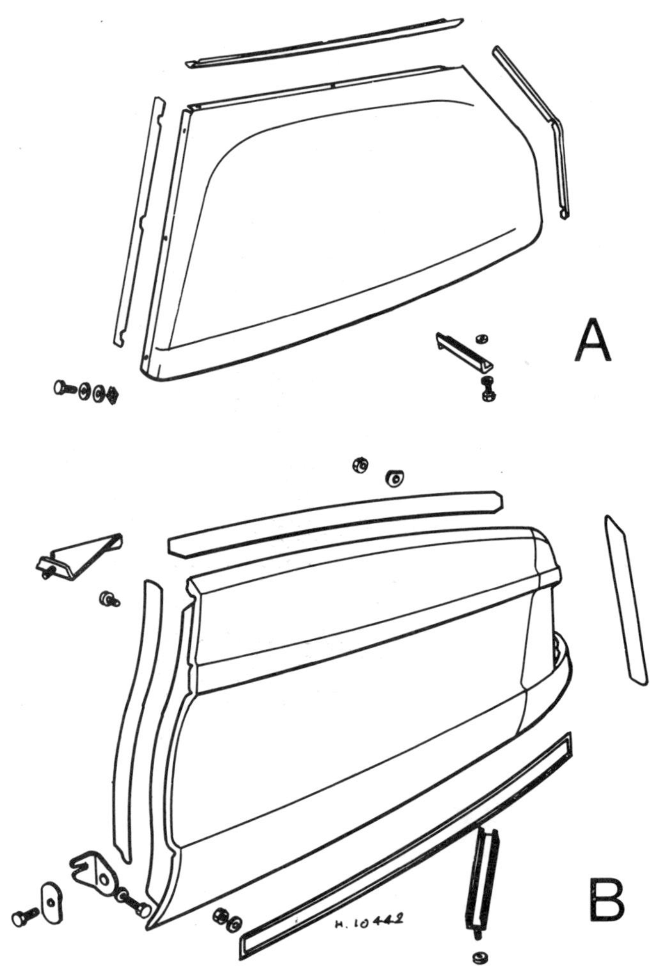

Fig. 11.7 Rear wing panels and fixings (Sec 9)

A Dyane *B Ami*

8.4 Lower front wing panel-to-front panel retaining bolts on the Dyane

8.5 Front wing side panel retaining screws and flat washers

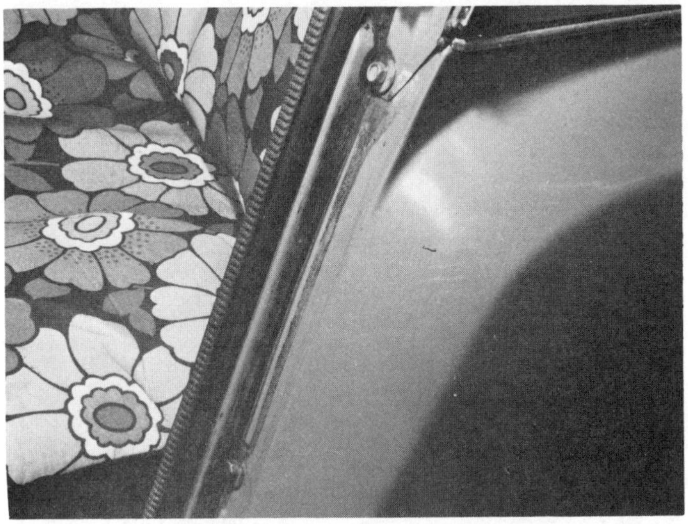

9.2 Rear wing forward mounting bolts (Dyane)

9.10 Rear wing retaining nuts in the Ami boot

10 Tailgate – removal and refitting

Ami

1 Open the tailgate and support it with the aid of an assistant.
2 Extract the strut hinge pin retaining clip at the top (or bottom if the strut is to be removed as well).
3 Unscrew the hinge retaining nuts on the upper inner side of the tailgate and lift it clear to remove.
4 Refit in the reverse order. Check alignment when shut, before fully tightening the hinge bolts.

Dyane

5 Open and support the tailgate with the aid of an assistant.
6 Extract the strut hinge pin (top or bottom as desired). Use pliers or grips to withdraw the tailgate hinge pin.
7 Refit in the reverse order. Check alignment before fully tightening.

11 Boot lid (2CV) – removal and refitting

The boot lid on the 2CV models is removed and refitted in the same manner as the bonnet. Refer to Section 16 for details.

12.1 Boot hinge and support strut (Ami)

12 Boot lid (Ami Saloon) – removal and refitting

1 The removal and refitting instructions for the Ami Saloon boot lid are basically the same as for the tailgate fitted to the Estate version – see Section 10 (photo).

2 The boot lid and its fittings are shown in Fig. 11.10.

13 Doors – removal and refitting

1 Open the door concerned and support it underneath with blocks or a jack.

2 Disconnect the check strap.

3 Mark around the hinge for realignment purposes when refitting. Unscrew and remove the door hinge retaining bolts or Allen screws as applicable and lift the door clear (photo). Note the number of shims to each hinge.

4 On Dyane models the lower hinge can be left in place – simply extract the split pin at the bottom hinge (photo) and the roll pin at the top.

5 Refitting is a reversal of the removal procedure. Refit the correct amount of shims to the respective hinges. Fit new hinge pins and bushes if they have been removed.

6 Check the alignment of the door in the closed position before fully tightening the hinge bolt. If adjustment is necessary, add or remove shims, and if necessary adjust the door catch.

7 On Ami models vertical adjustment can be made at the hinges by loosening the adjuster locknut and screwing the adjustment stud up or down.

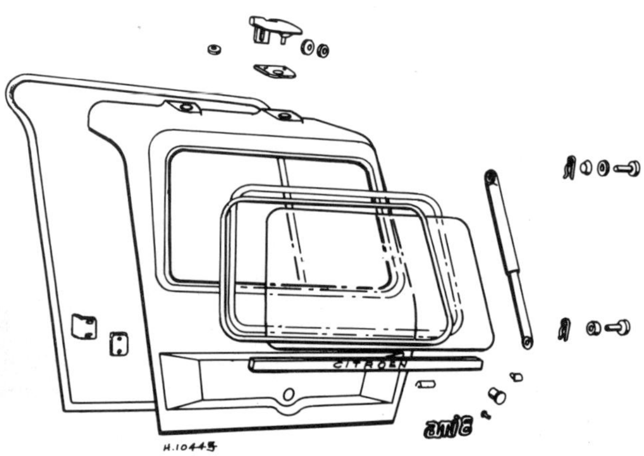

Fig. 11.8 Tailgate assembly – Ami Estate (Sec 10)

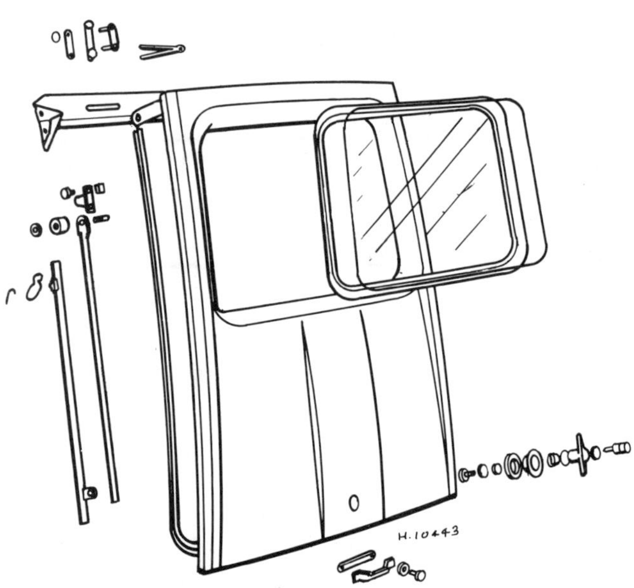

Fig. 11.9 Tailgate assembly – Dyane (Sec 10)

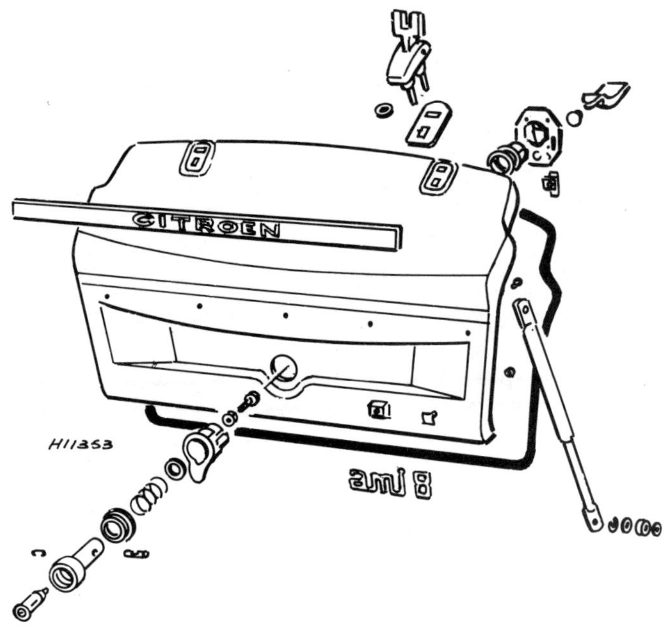

Fig. 11.10 Ami Saloon boot lid and associated components (Sec 12)

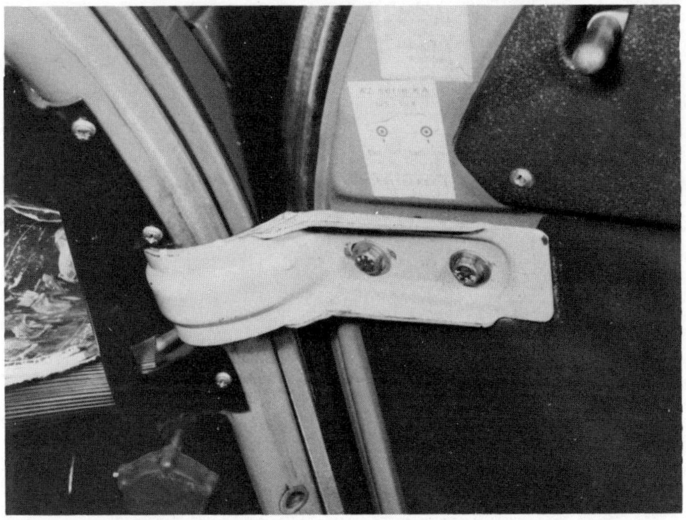

13.3 Door hinge and bolts (2CV)

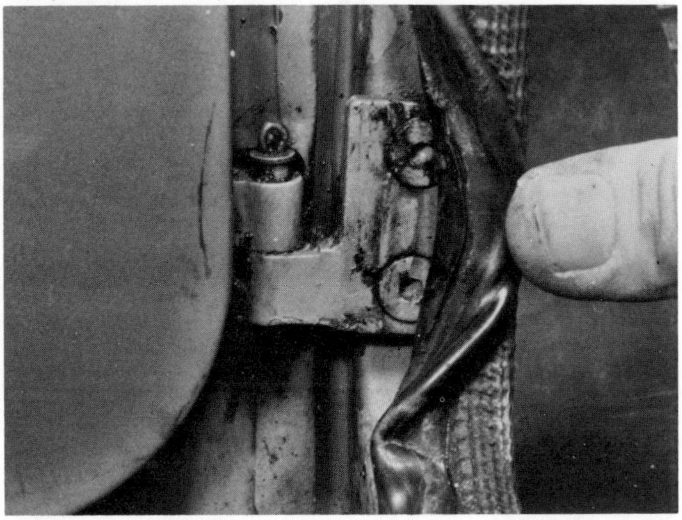

13.4 The lower door hinge on the Dyane showing Allen screws, split hinge pin and bush

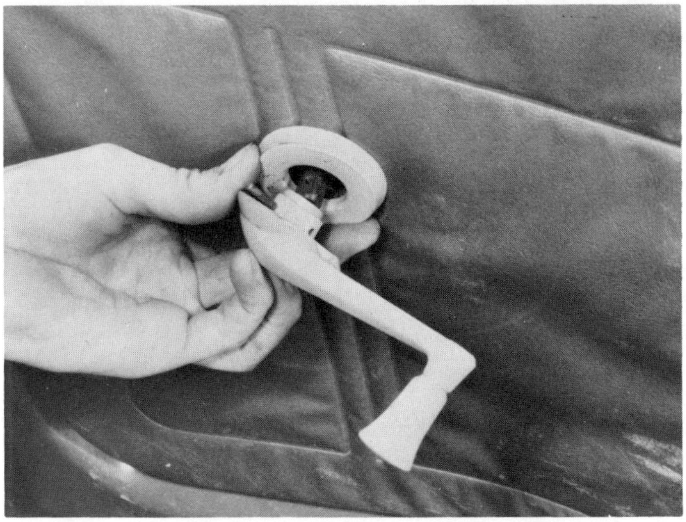

14.2 Window winder, escutcheon and retaining pin (Ami)

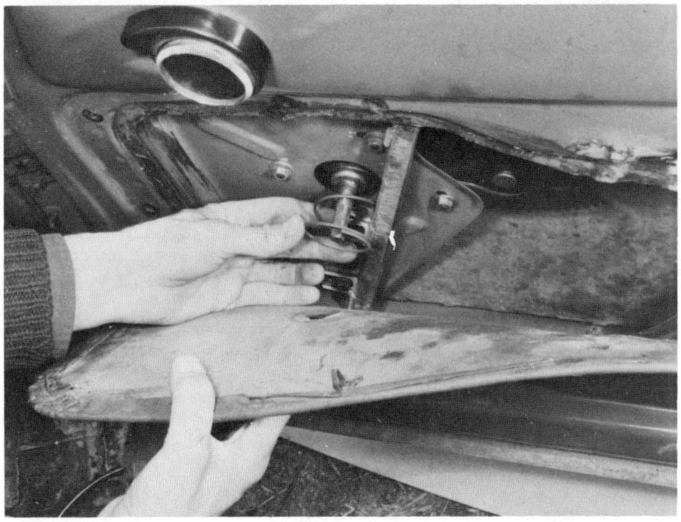

14.3 Removing trim panel and window regulator coil spring on the Ami

14 Door trim panel – removal and refitting

1 Unscrew the armrest/door pull retaining screws and remove the armrest. On some models the armrest is removed by prising it from the trim and then pulling it to the rear and up.

2 On Ami models the window winder handle must now be removed. Press in the escutcheon and extract the handle-to-shaft retaining pin. Push the pin through using a fine punch or a bradawl and needle nose pliers. Remove the winder handle and escutcheon (photo).

3 The trim panel can now be removed by prising free around the outer edges to release it from the securing clips. Some panels are retained by screws also. As the panel is removed on the Ami models, note the tapered coil spring located between the panel and the window regulator unit (photo).

4 Refit in the reverse order to removal.

15 Bumpers – removal and refitting

1 Both front and rear bumpers are attached by brackets which are in turn attached to the chassis member. On some models the bumpers are also braced at each end to the wing panel.

2 Due to their exposed locations the retaining bolts may well be rusty and difficult to remove. This being the case, clean them with a wire brush and soak in penetrating oil for a time before attempting to unscrew them.

3 Note that the nearside rear bumper bracket also retains the exhaust hanger at the rear (photo).

4 Refit in the reverse order and check for alignment.

16 Bonnet – removal and refitting

Ami

1 Raise and support the bonnet. Mark around the hinge-to-bonnet line to give a guide for correct realignment when refitting.

2 Get an assistant to support the bonnet whilst you unscrew the hinge bolts on each side.

3 Detach the windscreen washer tube.

4 Unhook the support stay and remove the bonnet.

5 Refit in the reverse order, adjusting the bonnet alignment as necessary before fully tightening the retaining bolts.

Dyane

6 The bonnet is retained by two hinge pins. The pins are withdrawn from each side by pulling the looped end of each pin and simply withdrawing them. Disconnect the washer pipe.

7 Refit in the reverse order, lubricating the pins prior to assembly.

2CV

8 To remove the 2CV bonnet disconnect the washer pipe, raise the bonnet, support it and slide it sideways from its location channel in the body. Refit in the reverse order.

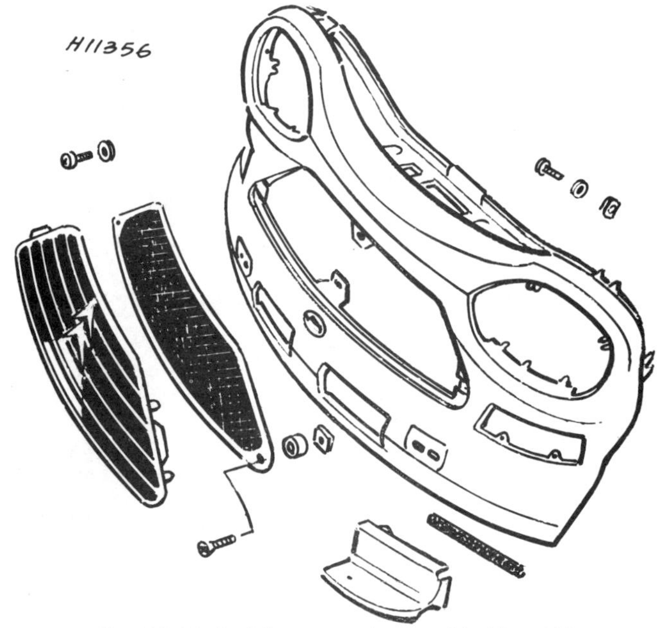

Fig. 11.11 Ami front panel assembly (Sec 17)

17 Front panel – removal and refitting

Ami

1 To remove the grille in the front panel, remove the retaining screws and withdraw the grille unit, leaving the panel in place.
2 To remove the panel, first disconnect the battery earth cable.
3 Unbolt the coil from the middle of the panel and rest it on top of the fan cowl with the wires still attached.
4 Disconnect the bonnet release catch cable.
5 Disconnect the wires from the headlight and front combination lights.
6 Unbolt the bumper assembly from the chassis mounting and withdraw the bumper and bracket. Disconnect the bumper from the front panel at each side corner section.
7 Unbolt the front panel from the front wing on each side and remove the panel.
8 Refit in the reverse order, aligning the panel with the wings prior to fully tightening the bolts. Check the operation of the lights to complete.

Dyane

9 The front grille and lower front panel can be removed complete with bumper assembly. Detach the bonnet release catch.
10 Unscrew and remove the bolts which secure the grille and panel to the wings on each side and the bumper support brackets to cooling fan shroud bolts each side, and remove the complete assembly as shown (photo).
11 Refit in the reverse order to removal.

18 Door lock and control mechanism – removal and refitting

2CV

1 Open the door concerned and remove the inner panel.
2 Unscrew and remove the lock operating finger finishing plate retaining screws (Fig. 11.12).
3 Remove the lock plate housing, which is secured by two screws at the top and one at the bottom. The screws will be tight to unscrew as they were smeared with thread locking compound on assembly.
4 Unhook the spring from the linkage rod.
5 Unscrew and remove the control screw. Remove the control and the rubber seal washers, also the spray.
6 Detach the linkage rod from the inner control lever by unscrewing it. To remove the lever, undo the retaining screw and remove with washers.

15.3 The bumper to-chassis-bracket on the nearside, showing the exhaust retaining strap

16.6 Removing the bonnet hinge pin on one side (Dyane)

17.10 Removing the front panel on the Dyane

18.10a The door external handle retaining nuts (arrowed) (Dyane)

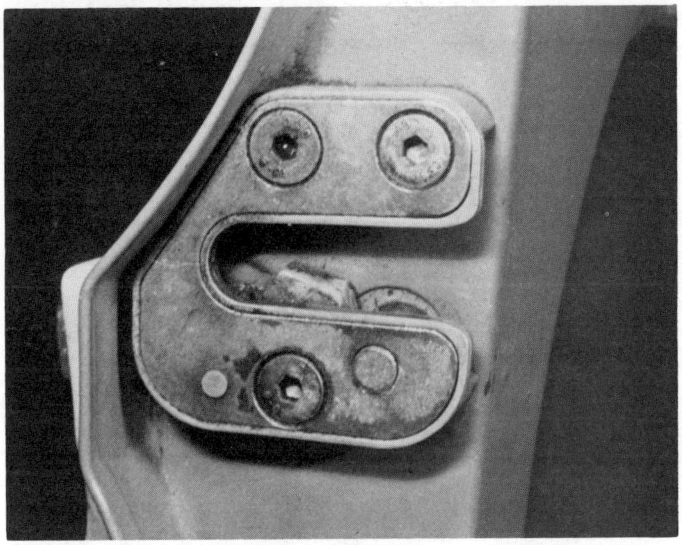

18.10b The lock unit in position (Dyane)

18.13a Remove the two retaining screws

18.13b Withdraw the catch and inner section

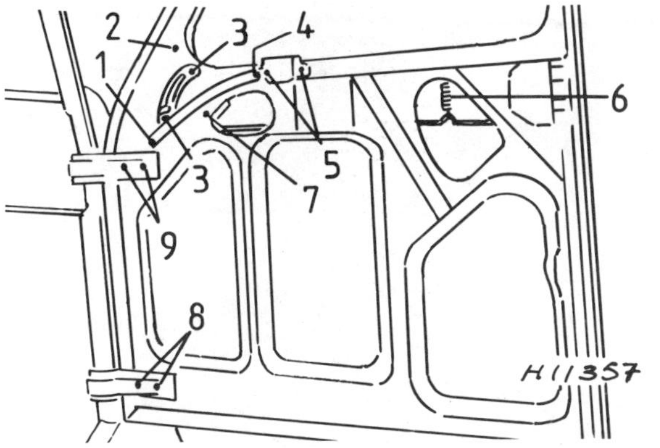

Fig. 11.12 Door inner panel – 2CV from 1972 (Sec 18)

1 Door strap handle screw
2 Mirror screw
3 Finishing plate screws
4 Door strap handle screw
5 Window fastener screws
6 Anti-rattle spring
7 Inner control screw
8 Lower hinge screws
9 Upper hinge screws

Fig. 11.13 2CV door lock (Sec 18)

13 Upper retaining screws
14 Lower retaining screw
15 Control screw

7 Remove the three lock retaining screws and withdraw the lock unit and the linkage rod. Remove the securing plate and rubber seal.
8 Refitting is a reversal of the removal procedure. Smear the threads of the retaining screws with thread lockng compound to ensure security when fitted.
9 When fitting the inner control, screw the connecting rod into position and relocate the anti-rattle spring. Check that a clearance of approximately 2 mm (0.08 in) exists before the lock operates.

Dyane

10 The lock mechanism removal procedure is similar to that for the 2CV (paragraphs 1 to 9), but with the following differences:

(a) When removing the lock outer control, pull the push button outwards and remove the external handle retaining nuts from the inside of the panel (photo).
(b) The lock is retained by three Allen screws (photo). On the front doors only, remove the control bush and then the lock unit

11 The reassembly procedure is a reversal of the removal. Refer to paragraphs 8 and 9 for special instructions.

Ami

12 Remove the door trim.
13 Prise the catch centre section free and then remove the two retaining screws (photo) and the circlip. Withdraw the handle assembly after detaching the control rod (photo).
14 The springs can now be removed from their location slots (photo).
15 Refitting is a reversal of the removal procedure, but check that the circlip is fully located in its groove before refitting the cover.

19 Sliding windows – removal and refitting

1 Slide the windows forwards and use a suitable screwdriver to prise the rear vertical guide free.
2 The rear section of the lower horizontal channel can now be prised upwards and pulled rearwards to disengage it complete with plastic support.
3 Slide the windows rearwards to locate them centrally. The front window can then be removed by pressing it downwards and inwards at the bottom, enabling it to clear the upper horizontal channel for withdrawal.
4 Remove the rear glass in a similar manner.
5 Refitting is a reversal of the removal procedure. When refitting the plastic support, engage the notched side to the lower outer door edge, and push it forwards under the horizontal channel and into position.

20 Winding windows – removal and refitting

1 Remove the door trim as described in Section 14.
2 Unscrew and remove the window regulator retaining nuts (photo). Remove the regulator to the rear, disengaging the rollers from the window channels, and support the glass.
3 Pivot the window forwards, disengage it from the vertical channels and extract it from the outside.
4 Refit in the reverse order. Check that the regulator is in good working order and lubricate it with grease. Clean out the roller channels and smear with grease before assembly.
5 If when reassembled the window binds when raised or lowered, the regulator may need adjustment. To do this simply loosen the retaining screws, reposition the regulator as necessary and retighten the screws. Refit the panel assembly to complete.

21 Windscreen and fixed glass – removal and renewal

1 Windscreen renewal is one of the jobs which the average DIY owner is recommended to leave to the experts. Windscreen specialists usually offer 'free' fitting, and it is unlikely that enough will be saved by doing it yourself to compensate for the time and temper involved. For the owner with enough experience the procedure is given below.

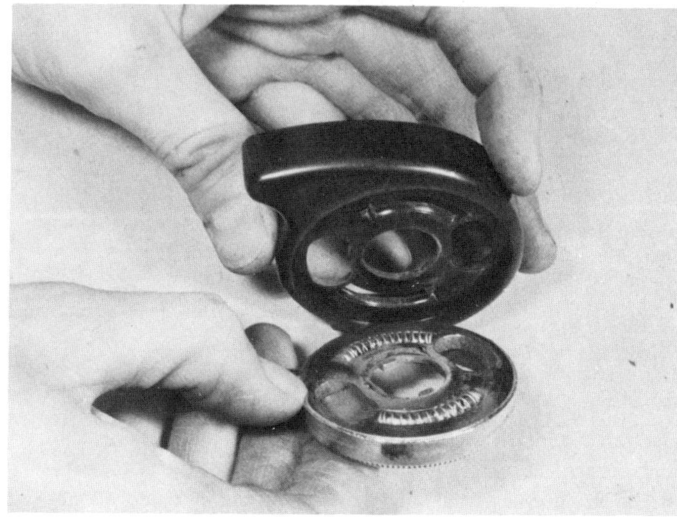

18.14 The springs in their location slots

20.2 Remove the regulator retaining nuts (arrowed)

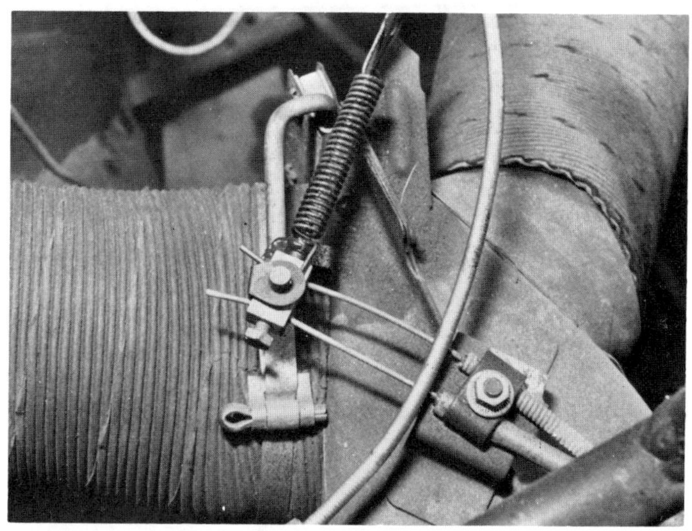

22.5 Detail of heater control cable connections

2 Make sure you know what kind of glass is fitted. Toughened safety glass will stand a certain amount of impact blows without breaking but any other kind will crack at least and only carefully applied sustained pressure may be used with safety. The windscreen is described here, but the rear screen and fixed side windows are removed and replaced in a similar manner.
3 After taking off the windscreen wiper arms, loosen the rubber sealing strip on the inside of the car where it fits over the edge of the window frame. Use a piece of wood for this. Anything sharp may rip the rubber weatherstrip. The screen can be pushed out, weatherstrip attached, if pressure is applied at the top corners. Two people are needed on this to prevent the glass falling out. Push evenly and protect your hands to avoid accidents. Remove the finisher strip from the weatherstrip.
4 When fitting a screen first make sure that the window frame edges are even and smooth. Examine the edges of the screen to see that it is ground smooth and no chips or cracks are visible. Any such cracks could be the source of a much bigger one. The weatherstrip should be perfectly clean. No traces of sealing compound should remain on rubber, glass or metal. If the sealing strip is old, brittle or hard, it is advisable to fit a new one even though they are not cheap.
5 Fit the weatherstrip to the screen first so that the joint comes midway along the top edge.
6 Next fit the decorative moulding into the weatherstrip. This is done by first feeding fine cord into the slot (use a piece of thin tubing as a guide and time saver) and leave the ends overlapping sufficiently to grip later. The two halves of the moulding are then put in place and the cord drawn out so that the edge of the strip locks them into place.
7 Apply suitable sealing compound to the weatherstrip where it will seat onto the metal window frame and also onto the outside faces of the frame at the lower corners.
8 Fit a piece of really strong thin cord into the frame channel of the weatherstrip as already described and then offer up the screen to the aperture. A second person is essential for this.
9 When you are sure that the screen is centrally positioned, pull the cord out so that the lip of the weatherstrip is drawn over the inner edges of the frame flange. One of the most frequent difficulties in this job is that the cord breaks. This is often because of sharp or uneven edges on the frame flange so a little extra time in preparation will pay off.

22 Heating and ventilation system

1 The heating and ventilation system fitted to all models is of a similar design, being of very simple layout.
2 The system comprises a series of cowlings and air ducts which, combined with the engine heat exchangers, supply air at the desired temperature to the vehicle interior.
3 The airflow is controlled by the levers of the facia panel which direct a regulated amount of air at the temperature selected to the windscreen area for demisting or defrosting and/or downwards to the vehicle interior.
4 Because of its simplicity, very little can go wrong with the system. The flexible heating ducts must be in good condition and the respective joints secure. In cold weather, good heater output will not be achieved unless the grille muff is in position.
5 It may be ncessary to adjust the control cables (photo), but normally only if they have been disconnected to gain access to other components in the engine.
6 Cable replacement is self-explanatory on inspection. A small amount of lubricant on the cables occasionally will keep their action smooth and prevent binding.

Chapter 12 Supplement: Revisions and information on later models

Contents

1 Introduction

Over the many years of its production, the 2CV, including its derivatives the Dyane and Ami, has been subjected to a continuing process of development. These have been mostly minor refinements to a very successful design which has remained basically unchanged since its introduction.

Details of these differences together with supplementary maintenance and overhaul information are included in this Supplement.

In order to use the Supplement to best advantage, it is suggested that it is referred to before the main Chapters of the manual; this will ensure that any relevant information can be absorbed into the procedures given in the main Chapters of the manual before commencing work on the vehicle.

2 Specifications

Engine

Application

	Engine plate mark	Engine type	Engine capacity
2CV (AZ)	AZ	A53	425cc
2CV4 (AZ)	AYA2	A79/1	435cc
2CV6 (AZ)	AK2	M28/1	602cc
2CV6 (AZ)	A06/635	M28/1	602cc
2CV van (AZU)	AZ	A53	425cc
2CV van (AZU)	AYA	A79/0	425cc
2CV van (AZU)	AYA2	A79/1	435cc
2CV van (AK)	AYA2	A79/1	435cc
Ami 6 (AM)	AM	M4	602cc
Ami 6 (AMB)	AM	M4	602cc
Ami 6 (AM2)	AM2	M28	602cc
Ami 6 (AMB2)	AM2	M28	602cc
Ami 8 (AM3)	AM2	M28	602cc
Ami 8 (AM)	AM2	M28	602cc
Dyane (AYA)	AYA	A79/0	425cc
Dyane 4 (AYA2)	AYA2	A79/1	435cc
Dyane 6 (AYA3)	AM	M4	602cc
Dyane 6 (AYB)	AK2	M28/1	602cc
Dyane 6 (AY)	AM2	M28	602cc

Electrical system

Fuses – typical (later models)

Circuit covered:	Fuse rating (amps)	Lead colour
Front side and tail lamps	10	Red
Instrument panel illumination	10	Red
Rear number plate	10	Red
Fuel gauge	16	Blue

	Fuse rating (amps)	Lead colour
Windscreen wipers	16	Blue
Direction indicators	16	Blue
Oil pressure warning lamp	16	Blue
Battery condition indicator	16	Blue
Stoplamps	10	Yellow
Interior lamp	10	Yellow
Hazard warning lamp	10	Yellow
Brake fluid low level lamp	10	Yellow

Bodywork

Kerb weight

2CV models:	
Until February 1972	530 kg (1168 lbs)
March 1972 on	560 kg (1235 lbs)
Dyane:	
Until 1968	570 kg (1257 lbs)
1968 on	590 kg (1300 lbs)
Ami 6:	
Saloon	670 kg (1477 lbs)
Estate	690 kg (1521 lbs)
Ami 8:	
Saloon	725 kg (1598 lbs)
Estate	725 kg (1598 lbs)

Maximum towing weight

Trailer without brakes:	
2CV (425cc)	200 kg (441 lbs)
2CV (435cc, 602cc)	270 kg (595 lbs)
Dyane:	
Until 1968	200 kg (441 lbs)
1968 on	270 kg (595 lbs)
Ami 6	340 kg (750 lbs)
Ami 8	360 kg (794 lbs)
Trailer with brakes:	
2CV and Dyane	400 kg (882 lbs)
Ami	500 kg (1102 lbs)

Maximum roof rack load 30 kg (66 lbs)

3 Engine

Fan protective mesh

1 Later models have a protective screen fitted to the fan opening at the front of the engine.

2 The screen can be removed by unbolting the four struts which support the starting handle guide bush.

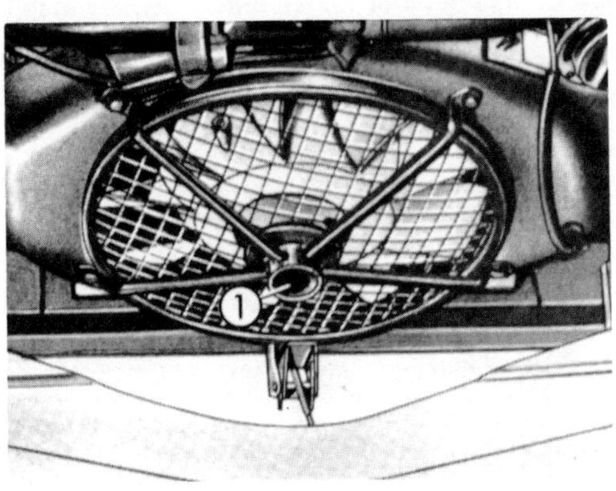

Fig. 12.1 Engine fan protective mesh (Sec 3)

1 Starting handle guide bush

4 Fuel system

Accelerator control cable – Dyane models

1 As from July 1977, the accelerator cable fitted to Dyane models is of new design and operated by a pendant-type foot pedal.

2 To check the cable adjustment, depress the accelerator pedal fully. There should be a clearance between the pedal and the floor of 5.0 mm (0.20 in).

3 To alter the clearance, move the stop clip (A) to another groove in the cable sleeve (B) – see Fig. 12.2.

4 Now check the clearance (J) is at least 2.0 mm (0.08 in) without the coils of the spring being fully compressed.

Choke control warning lamp

5 On models built after September 1980 the choke cable control is fitted with a choke warning lamp switch.

5 Clutch

Diaphragm spring type clutch

1 As from February 1982, the clutch pressure plate is changed from a coil spring type to one incorporating a diaphragm spring.

2 The following parts are also modified when this type of pressure plate is fitted.

Flywheel
Driven plate
Release bearing
Clutch housing
Primary shaft

3 None of the components are interchangeable with previous parts.

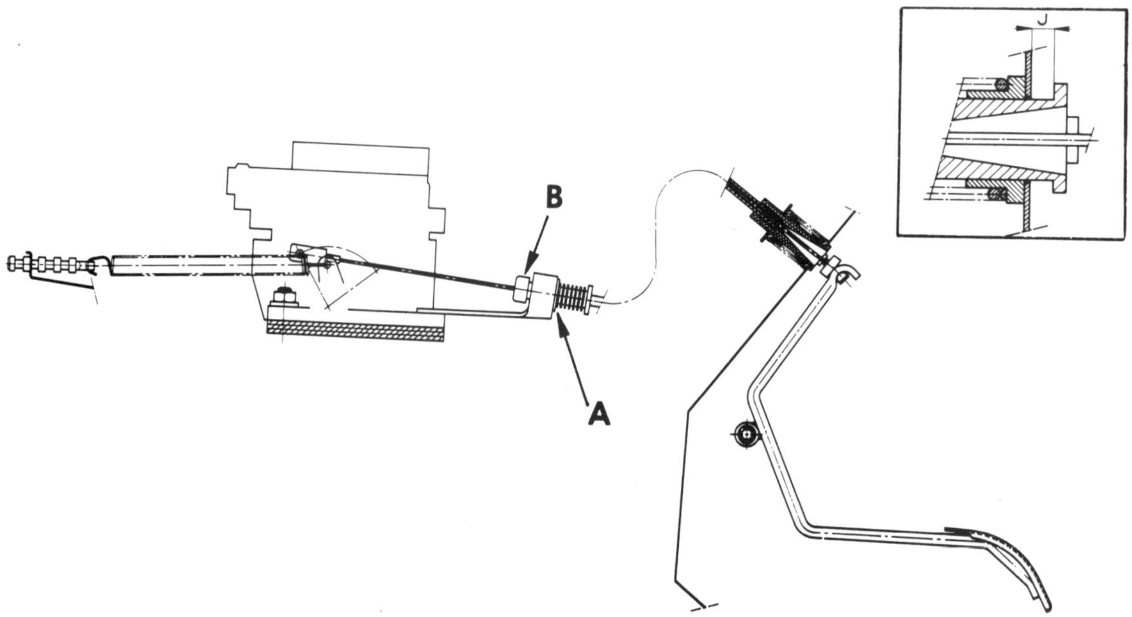

Fig. 12.2 Accelerator control cable – Dyane models (Sec 4)

A Stop clip *B Cable sleeve* *J = 2.0 mm (0.08 in)*

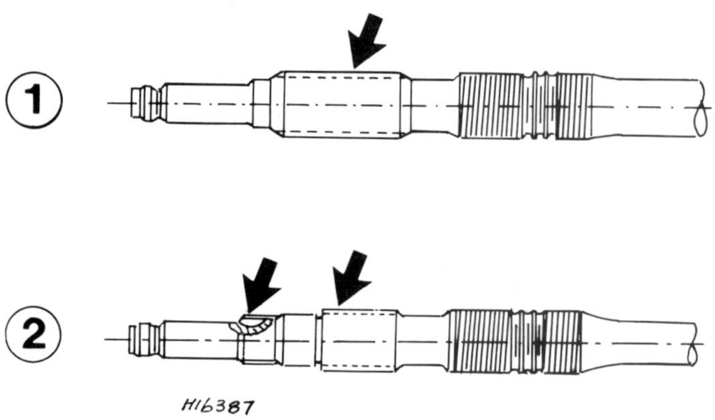

Fig. 12.3 Primary shaft comparison (Sec 5)

1 With diaphragm type clutch
2 With coil spring type clutch

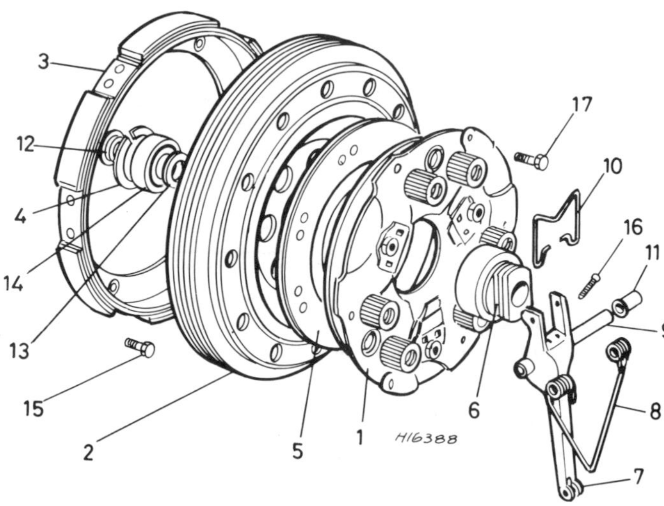

Fig. 12.4 Components of the centrifugal type clutch (Sec 5)

1 Pressure plate
2 Drum
3 Centrifugal friction ring
4 Stop ring
5 Driven plate (friction disc)
6 Ball type release bearing
7 Release fork
8 Spring
9 Pivot shaft
10 Spring
11 Bush
12 Nut
13 Adjustment shim
14 Ball type bearing
15 Screw
16 Screw
17 Screw

Centrifugal clutch

4 Components of this type of clutch are shown in Fig. 12.4.

6 Transmission

Gearchange control linkage

1 The facia-mounted gearchange control lever is connected to the transmission by link rods.

2 The gearchange lever turret is of normal spring-loaded ball and socket type and is mounted either centrally or at the rear of the transmission top cover according to transmission type.

3 Removal of the gearchange linkage is carried out by removing the pinch-bolt at the coupling on the top of the turret, and then unbolting the gearchange lever slide tube brackets from the underside of the facia panel and the engine compartment bulkhead.

4 Provided that the link joints are unworn, positive gear selection should be obtainable in all positions.

5 On 2CV and Dyane models built after February 1980, a modified lever support is fitted. The lever incorporates a shoulder which seats on the coil spring to eliminate any possibility of the ball section of the lever being forced down into the turret.

7 Braking system

Handbrake disc pad – adjustment

1 On 1978 and later models, the eccentric adjusters have hexagonal heads instead of the circular type used previously.

Fig. 12.5 Gearchange link rod coupling (Sec 6)

15 Shaft
16 Pinch-bolt
17 Earth strap

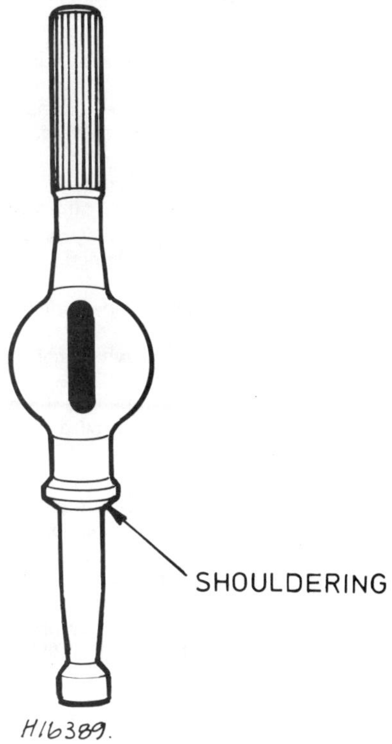

Fig. 12.6 Modified gearchange lever on late models (Sec 6)

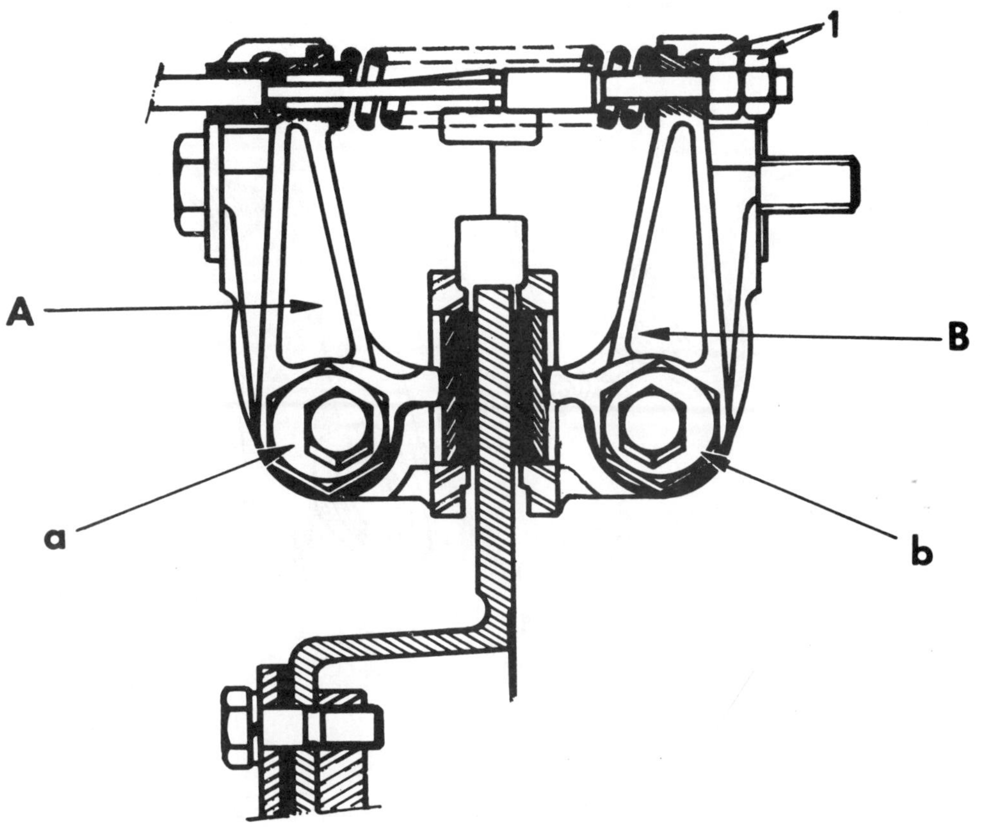

Fig. 12.7 Modified disc pad eccentric adjusters on later models (Sec 7)

1 Handbrake cable adjuster nut and locknut
A Actuating arm
B Actuating arm
a Hexagonal eccentric
b Hexagonal eccentric

Hydraulic unions

2 As from August 1978 all hydraulic pipe unions are of Citroën type.

3 When fitting new components make sure that the original union threads are compatible with those of the new component. Adaptors are available to convert the threads to Citroën type.

Tandem type master cylinder – overhaul

4 The tandem type master cylinder used on later vehicles equipped with dual circuit brakes is overhauled in a similar way to that described in Chapter 6 for single circuit master cylinders, but the following differences must be noted.

5 Two pistons are fitted, the primary one which is nearest the pushrod and the secondary one.

6 The pistons are retained by roll pins which can be extracted as described in Chapter 6, Section 16.

7 When reassembling, depress the pistons into the cylinder using a rod or the special tool so that the retaining roll pins can be inserted.

Pressure bleeding

8 The brake hydraulic system can be pressure bled in the following way as an alternative to the two methods described in Chapter 6.

9 A suitable kit is available from motor accessory shops and is usually operated by air pressure from the spare tyre.

10 By connecting a pressurised container to the master cylinder fluid reservoir, bleeding is then carried out simply by opening each bleed screw in turn and allowing the fluid to run out until no air is visible in the expelled fluid.

11 By using this method, the large reserve of hydraulic fluid provides a safeguard against air being drawn into the master cylinder during bleeding which often occurs if the fluid level in the reservoir is not maintained.

12 Pressure bleeding is of particular value when bleeding the complete system at time of routine fluid renewal.

13 If the vehicle is fitted with a dual circuit braking system bleed the front wheel circuit first.

8 Suspension

Friction dampers – adjustment

1 The friction dampers were fitted before being superseded on later models by telescopic double-acting hydraulic shock absorbers.

2 The need for adjustment of this type of damper is obvious if the car tends to bounce over bumps when being driven or, when the front or rear end is pushed down, bounces up-and-down (oscillates) several times before attaining its normal ride height.

3 Raise the car and remove the roadwheel.

4 Clean away mud and dirt and remove the damper dust cover (3) – see Fig. 12.8.

5 Unscrew the three bolts and remove the cover (7).

6 Make up a tool similar to a pin wrench by drilling two holes in a length of flat metal bar and inserting two short bolts in the holes to engage in the holes or cut-outs in the hub (2).

7 If the hub is now unscrewed to relieve the spring tension between the tongues and the disc plate cut-outs, a screwdriver can be inserted between the suspension arm and the friction unit and the unit prised from its location.

8 With the unit removed, turn the coil spring adjusting nut until five threads are visible above the nut. This should provide the correct friction setting for the discs. Centre punch the thread just above the nut to lock it in position.

9 Align the hub, disc, cup and flange of the unit and refit it to the suspension. The tool used at removal will have to be used again to offset the spring tension while the tongues enter the crescent-shaped apertures of the unit.

10 Refit the cover and dust cover and the roadwheel.

Rear hub bearing – renewal

11 Raise the vehicle, support it safely and remove the wheel. If the reason for removal of the brake drum is to remove and refit the bearings then it will be found easier to release the outer bearing ring

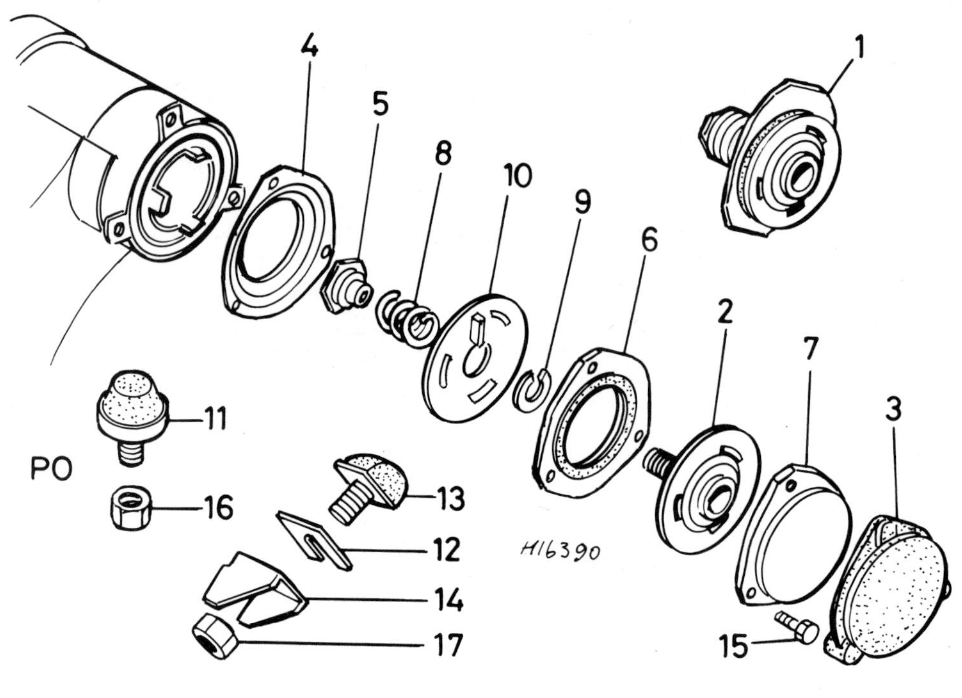

Fig. 12.8 Exploded view of friction damper (Sec 8)

1 Assembled unit	*6 Flange*	*10 Disc plate*	*14 Bracket*
2 Hub	*7 Cover*	*11 Stop*	*15 Screw*
3 Dust cover	*8 Spring*	*12 Packing*	*16 Nut*
4 Cup	*9 Spring washer*	*13 Stop*	*17 Nut*
5 Adjusting nut			

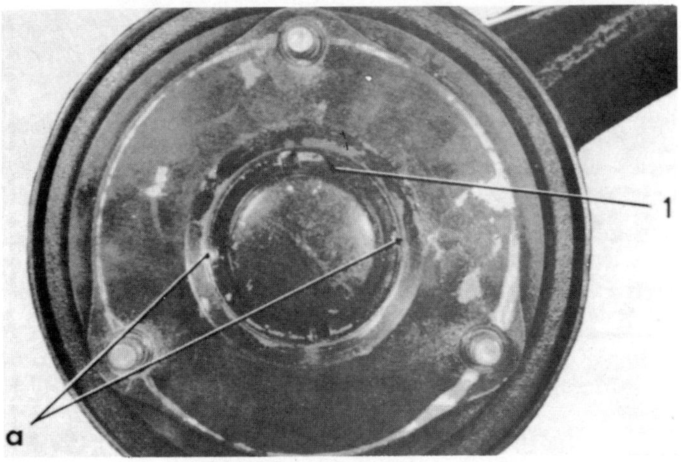

Fig. 12.9 Rear hub (Sec 8)

1 Ring nut *a Cut-outs*

Fig. 12.10 Rear hub (Sec 8)

2 Nut *b Shaft groove*

Fig. 12.11 Rear hub/drum (Sec 8)

1 Oil seal *b Oil seal face*
a Bearing support face

nut before the drum is removed from the vehicle. Remove the grease cap; see Chapter 6, Section 13.
12 Relieve the staking at the ring nut cut-outs, using a drill if necessary.
13 Unscrew the ring nut. If a suitable pin wrench is not available, or the special Citroën tools (3301T and 3304T) cannot be borrowed, it may be possible to unscrew the nut by driving it round with a cold chisel and hammer. Have an assistant apply the brakes hard.
14 Now relieve the staking at the hub nut. Unscrew the nut.
15 Remove the hub/drum. In the absence of a suitable puller, refer to Chapter 6, Section 13 and use one of the alternative methods suggested.
16 It is not unusual for the inner bearing race to remain on the stub axle as the drum is withdrawn.
17 Lever out and discard the oil seal.
18 Press or drive out the bearings and races from the hub/drum assembly.
19 Fit a new oil seal so that there is a gap between the seal and the bearing support shoulder within the hub of between 1.0 and 1.5 mm (0.039 and 0.059 in).
20 Grease the seal lips and the bearing and press, drive or pull the bearing into the hub. A long bolt with suitably sized washers is probably the safest way to draw the bearing into its seat.
21 Refit the drum, as described in Chapter 6, Section 13. Fit a new nut and tighten to the specified torque (see Chapter 6). Stake the nut into the shaft groove.
22 Pack the recess in the ring nut with wheel bearing grease and tighten it to the specified torque if a suitable torque wrench can be borrowed. If it is being tightened by other means, make sure that it is screwed up as tightly as possible using a long handle on the pin wrench. Have an assistant apply the brakes fully while the ring nut is being tightened or use a lever between two wheel studs, but screw on the wheel nuts first to prevent damage to the stud threads.

9 Electrical system

Windscreen washer

1 On early models the windscreen washer is operated by a foot pump, while on later versions the pump plunger is mounted on the facia.
2 The jet pattern varies according to the amount of pressure applied to the pump plunger.
3 The washer fluid reservoir is located on the engine compartment rear bulkhead.
4 Always use a recommended additive in the fluid and, in very cold weather, pour a suitable proprietary preparation or a little methylated spirit into the reservoir fluid to prevent freezing.
5 The jets can be adjusted by inserting a pin into the twin nozzle assembly which is located at the rear of the bonnet.

Headlamp beam load control adjustment – 2CV models

6 The control on 2CV models has rod linkage. Have the car empty with 5.0 litres (1.0 gal) of fuel in the tank, on level ground with the tyres correctly inflated.
7 Check the lateral play of the manual linkage. If necessary insert washers until the clearance between the control lug and the nearest washer is 0.5 mm (0.02 in).
8 Now turn the control knob (1) fully clockwise and then anti-clockwise by $2\frac{1}{2}$ turns. See Fig. 12.14.
9 The headlamp alignment may now be adjusted by moving the headlamp on the top of the wing having released the nut at its ball mounting. It is preferable to have this beam alignment done by your dealer or service station.

Headlamp beam load control adjustment – Ami models

10 Have the car empty, except for 5.0 litres (1.0 gal) of fuel in the tank, on level ground with the tyres correctly inflated. Mask one headlamp.
11 Turn the control knob (1) fully anti-clockwise. See Fig. 12.16.
12 Open the bonnet and screw the beam adjusting screws (2 and 3) in by about half their length. See Fig. 12.17.
13 Switch headlamps to dipped beam and then turn knob (4) to adjust the beam height. The top of the beam must not rise above horizontal.

Fig. 12.12 Foot-operated washer pump (2) (Sec 9)

1 Wiper switch

Fig. 12.13 Facia-mounted wiper switch (1) and washer pump (2) (Sec 9)

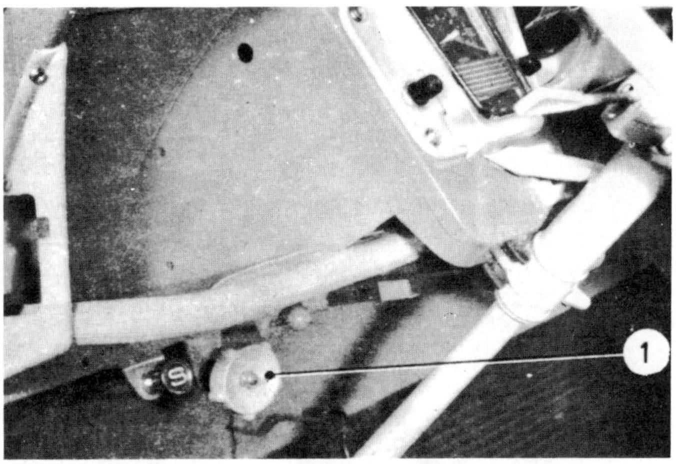

Fig. 12.14 Headlamp control knob (1) – 2CV models (Sec 9)

Fig. 12.15 Headlamp beam (load) adjuster linkage – Ami models (Sec 9)

2 Washers *3 Lug*

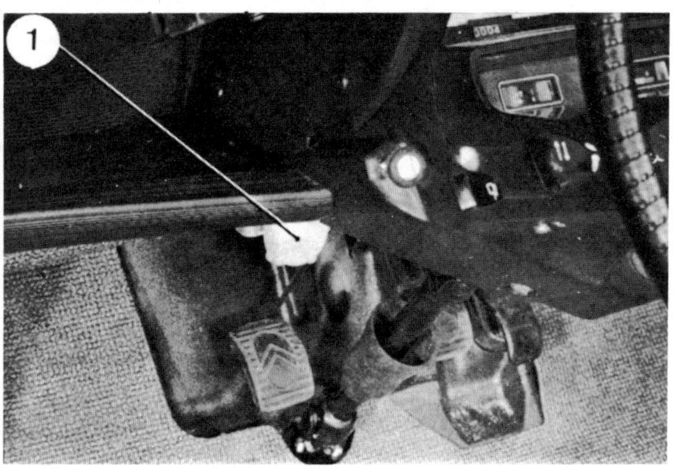

Fig. 12.16 Headlamp control knob (1) – Ami models (Sec 9)

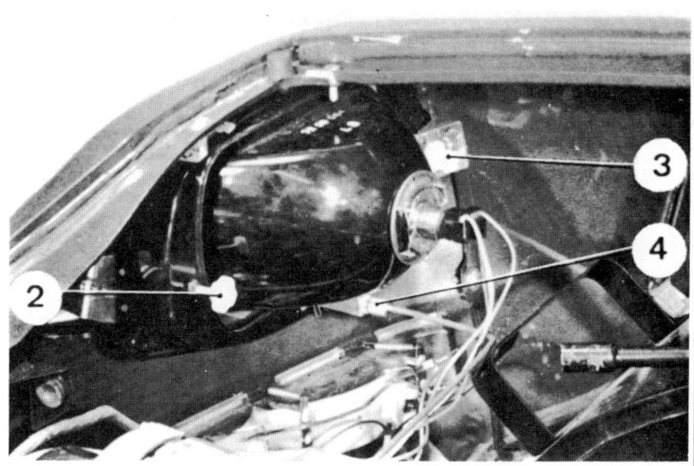

Fig. 12.17 Headlamp adjusters – Ami models (Sec 9)

2 Direction (horizontal) adjuster
3 Direction (horizontal) adjuster
4 Height (vertical) adjuster

14 Now switch to main beam and turn knobs (2) and (3) for directional adjustment.
15 Repeat on the other headlamp.
16 It is emphasised that without proper alignment equipment the beams cannot be really accurate and it is recommended that where possible, the work should be left to your dealer or service station.

Rear lamp cluster

17 There have been modifications to the rear lamp design on 2CV and Dyane models in later years of production, but access to the bulbs remains as described in Chapter 10.

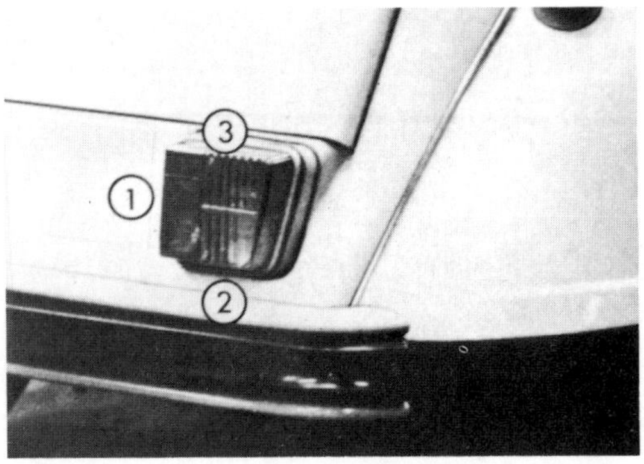

Fig. 12.18 Later 2CV rear lamp cluster (Sec 9)

1 Rear number plate lamp
2 Direction indicator lamp
3 Stoplamp

Fig. 12.19 Later Dyane rear lamp cluster – exterior view (Sec 9)

2 Knurled knob
3 Lens
4 Tail and number plate bulb
5 Stoplamp bulb
6 Direction indicator

Fig. 12.20 Later Dyane rear lamp cluster – interior view (Sec 9)

1 Protective cover
2 Cover retaining knob

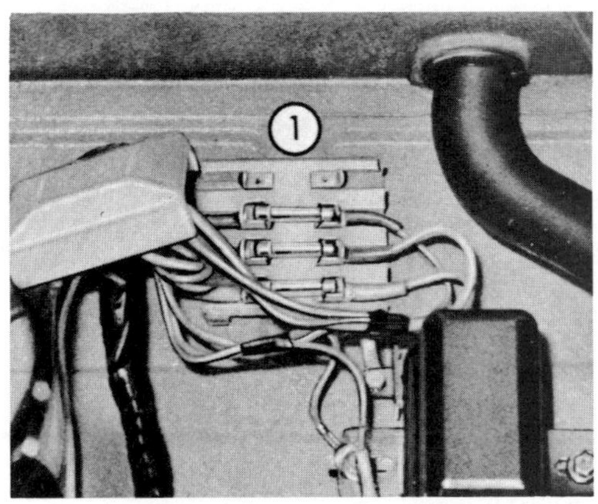

Fig. 12.21 Typical fusebox (1) (Sec 9)

Wiring diagrams commence overleaf

Key to wiring diagram for 2CV models, 1981 onwards

1 Front direction indicator, RH side
2 Headlamp, RH side:
  Main beam
  Dipped beam
  Sidelamp
3 Ignition coil
4 Headlamp, LH side:
  Main beam
  Dipped beam
  Side lamp
5 Front direction indicator, LH side
6 Horn
7 Distributor
8 Alternator
9 Engine oil pressure switch
10 Starter
11 Fusebox
12 Voltage regulator
13 Battery
14 Flasher unit
15 Windscreen wiper motor
16 Oil pressure warning lamp
17 Windscreen wiper switch
18 Switch for hazard warning device
19 Dashboard:
  Lighting
  Voltmeter
  Fuel gauge sender unit
20 Stoplamp switch
21 Lighting switch
22 Anti-theft ignition switch
23 Hazard warning indicator lamp
24 Switch for direction indicator lamps
25 Interior lamp
26 Fuel gauge rheostat
27 Rear lamp cluster, RH side:
  Direction indicator
  Stoplamp
  Taillamp
28 Rear lamp cluster, LH side:
  Direction indicator
  Stoplamp
  Side lamp
29 Level switch on brake fluid reservoir
30 Push-button for checking Nivocode warning lamp
31 Nivocode warning lamp
32 Direction indicator warning lamp
33 Main beam indicator lamp
34 Choke indicator lamp

Identification of harnesses

AR *Rear harness*
AV *Front harness*
PD *Headlamp harness – RH side*
PG *Headlamp harness – LH side*

Not all items are fitted to all models

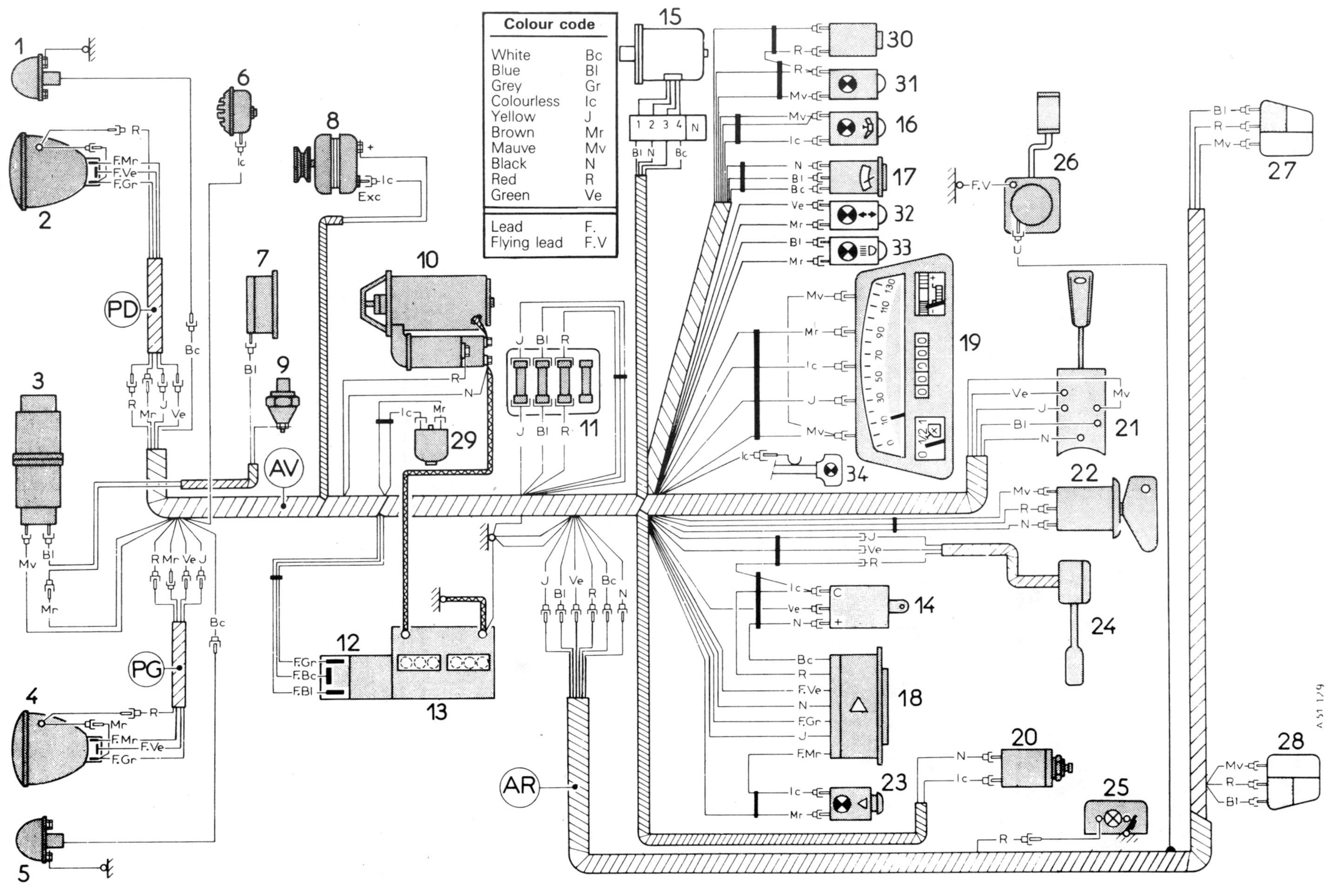

Fig. 12.22 Wiring diagram – 2CV models 1981 onwards (Sec 9)

Key to wiring diagram for Ami 8, 1974 onwards

1 Direction indicator and front sidelamp cluster, RH side:
  Direction indicator
  Front sidelamp
2 Headlamp, RH side:
  Main beam
  Dipped beam
3 Horn
  Headlamp, LH side:
  Main beam
  Dipped beam
5 Direction indicator and front sidelamp, LH side:
  Direction indicator
  Front sidelamp
6 Ignition coil
7 Distributor
10 Alternator
11 Starter
12 Engine oil pressure switch
13 Windscreen washer pump
14 Regulator
15 Battery
18 Fusebox
20 Windscreen wiper motor
21 Accessory terminal, up to 1975
22 Stoplamp switch
23 Door lighting switch
26 Voltmeter-petrol gauge sender unit
28 Oil pressure warning lamp
29 Hazard warning lamp
30 Hazard warning switch
32 Flasher unit
33 Anti-theft ignition switch
34 Windscreen wiper/washer switch
35 Lighting switch
36 Dashboard lighting rheostat, up to 1975
37 Switch for direction indicators, horn and flashers
38 Petrol gauge rheostat
39 Interior lamp
40 Rear direction indicator, RH side
41 Stop and tail lamps, RH side:
  Stoplamp
  Taillamp
42 Number plate lamp
43 Stop and tail lamps, LH side
  Stoplamp
  Taillamp
44 Rear direction indicator, LH side
45 Switch on Nivocode
46 Push-button checking the Nivocode warning lamp
47 Nivocode warning lamp

Identification of harnesses

F *Lead*
FV *Flying lead*
AR *Rear harness*
AV *Front harness*

For a key to the colour coding see Fig. 12.22

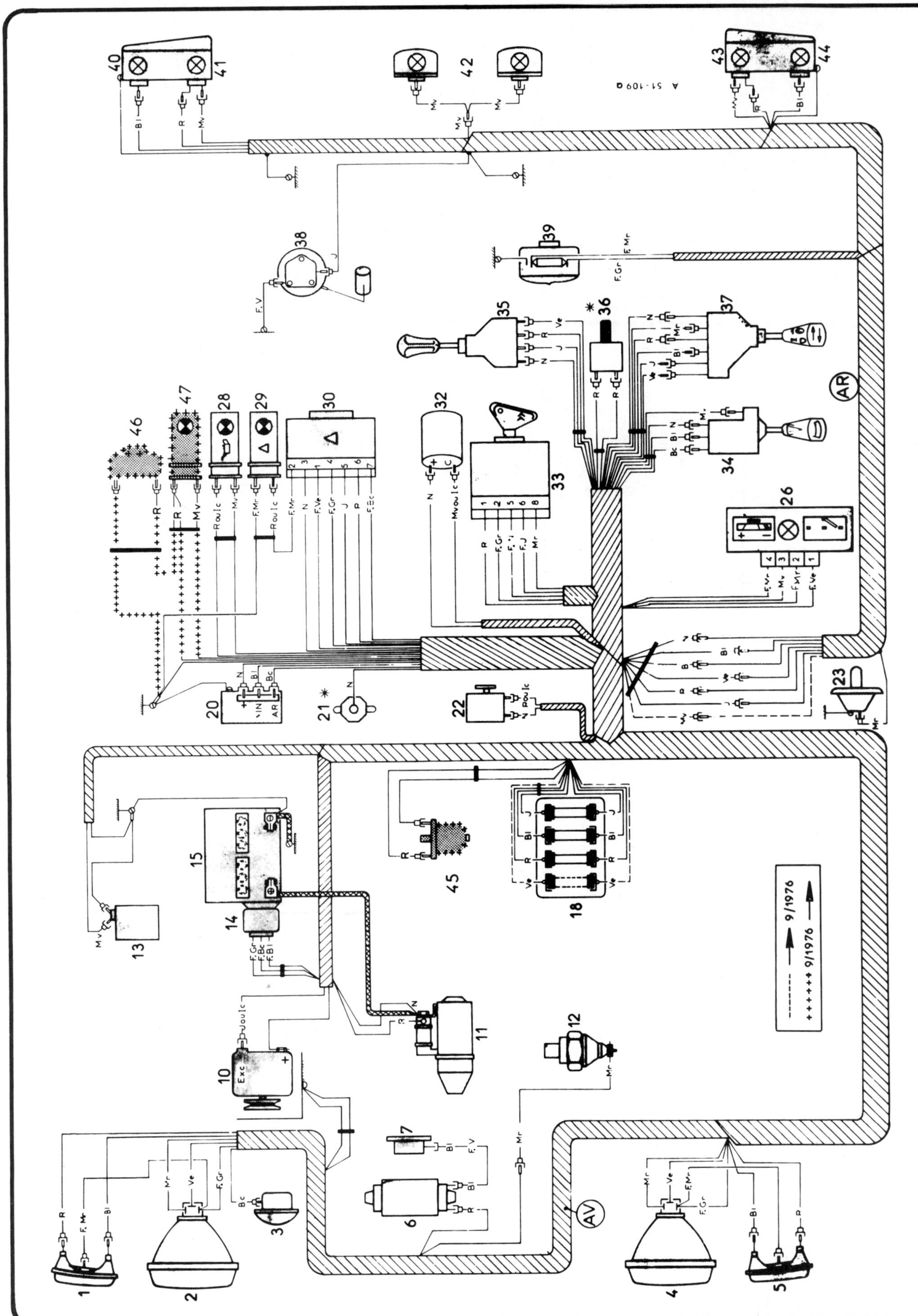

Fig. 12.23 Wiring diagram – Ami 8 1974 onwards (Sec 9)

Key to wiring diagram for Dyane models, 1981 onwards

1 Front headlamp indicator, RH side
2 Headlamp, RH side:
    Main beam
    Dipped beam
    Front sidelamp
3 Ignition coil
4 Headlight, LH side:
    Main beam
    Dipped beam
    Front sidelamp
5 Front direction indicator, LH side
6 Horn
7 Distributor
8 Alternator
9 Engine oil pressure switch
10 Starter
11 Level switch on brake fluid reservoir
12 Voltage regulator
13 Battery
14 Windscreen wiper motor
15 Choke control with built-in indicator lamp
16 Fusebox
17 Switch for hazard warning device
18 Hazard warning indicator lamp
19 Test-button for brake fluid warning lamp
20 Brake fluid level warning lamp
21 Engine oil pressure warning lamp
22 Windscreen wiper switch
23 Main beam indicator lamp
24 Direction indicator warning lamp
25 Dashboard:
    Lighting
    Thermal voltmeter
    Fuel gauge sender unit
26 Stoplamp switch
27 Flasher unit
28 Anti-theft ignition switch
29 Lighting switch and horn
30 Direction indicator switch
31 Petrol gauge rheostat
32 Interior lamp
33 Rear lamp cluster, RH side:
    Stoplamp and sidelamp
    Direction indicator
34 Number plate lighting
35 Rear lamp cluster, LH side
    Stoplamp and tail lamp
    Direction indicator

Identificaton of harnesses

F *Lead*
FV *Flying lead*

Not all items are fitted to all models

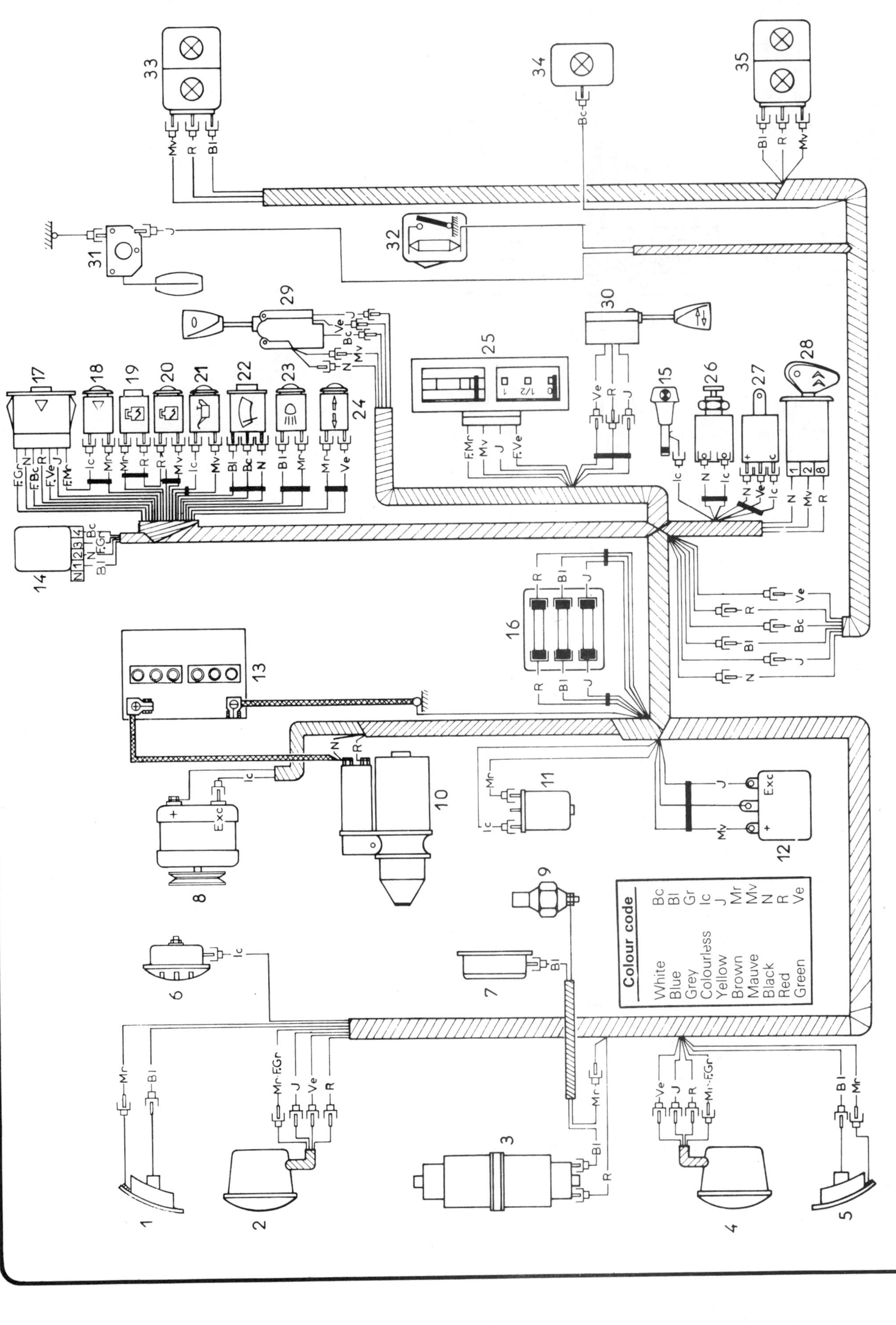

Fig. 12.24 Wiring diagram – Dyane models, 1981 onwards (Sec 9)

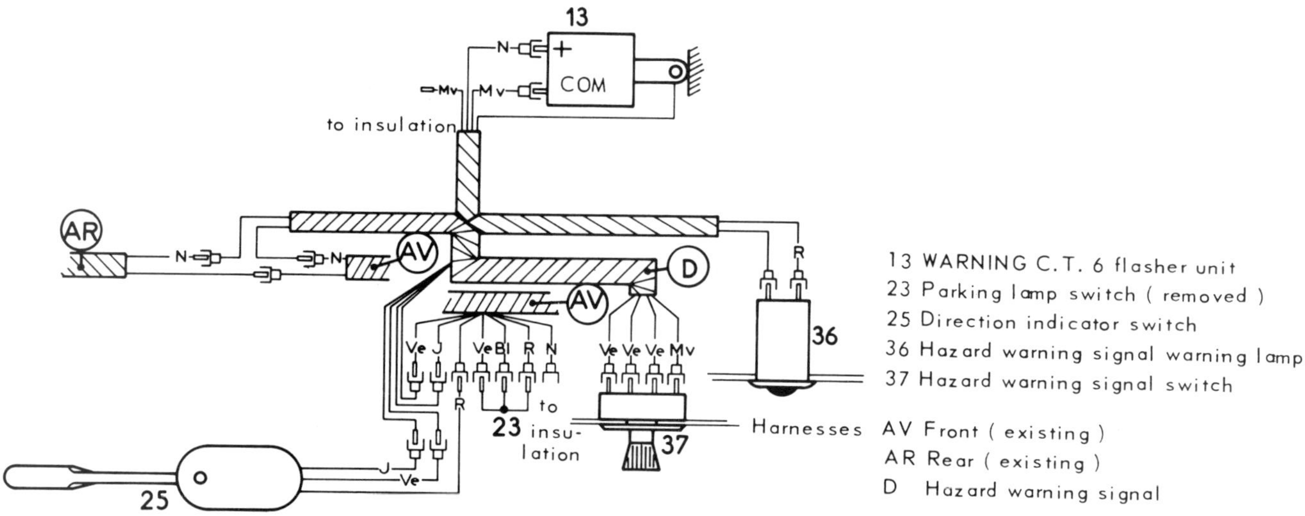

Fig. 12.25 Wiring diagram, hazard warning lights – Dyane up to 1973. Aftermarket fitting (Sec 9)

For colour code see Fig. 12.24

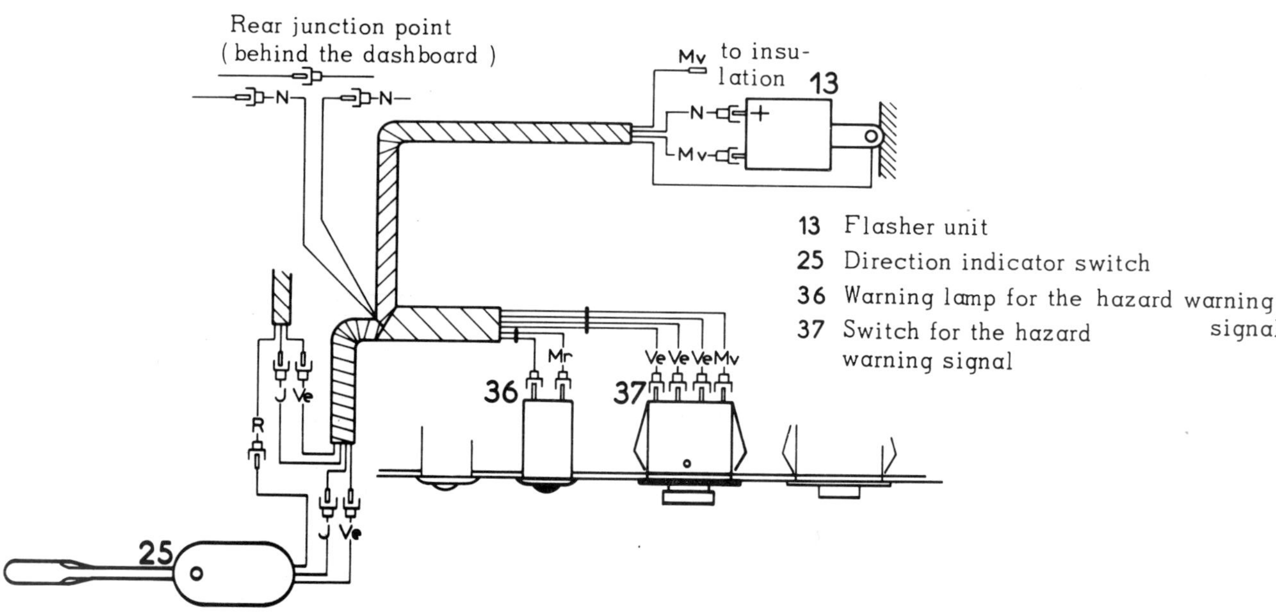

Fig. 12.26 Wiring diagram, hazard warning lights – Dyane 1973 on. Aftermarket fitting (Sec 9)

For colour code see Fig. 12.24

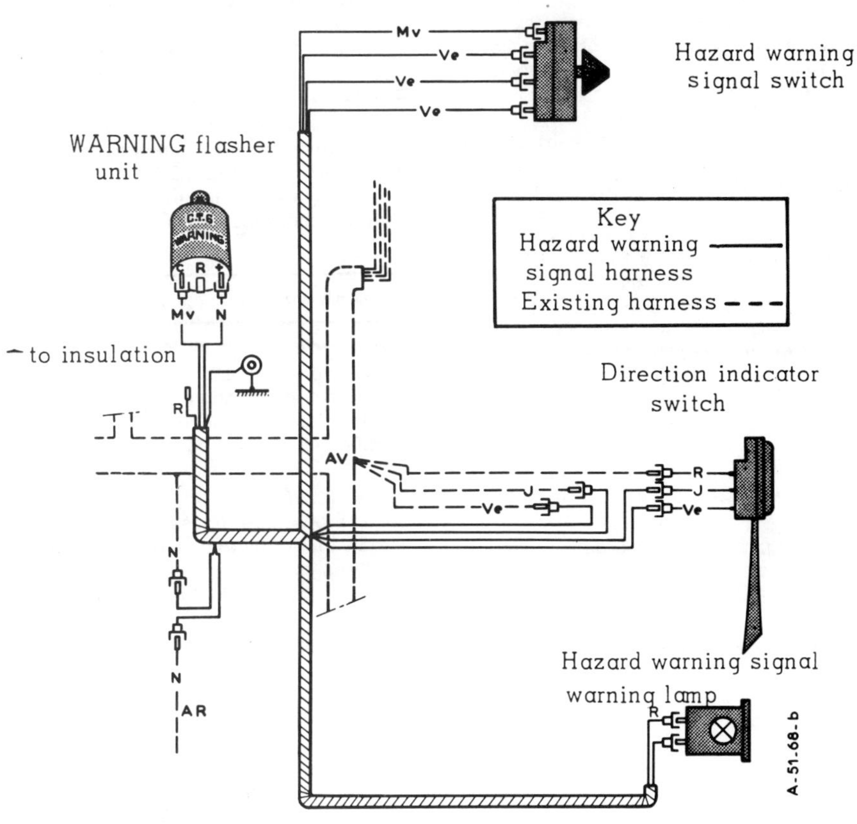

Fig. 12.27 Wiring diagram, hazard warning lights – 2CV models. Aftermarket fitting (Sec 9)

For colour code see Fig. 12.24

Radio

18 A radio or tape player is an expensive item to buy, and will only give its best performance if fitted properly. It is useless to expect concert hall performance from a unit that is suspended from the dashpanel by string with its speaker resting on the back seat. If you do not wish to do the fitting yourself, there are many in-car entertainment specialists who will do the fitting for you.

19 Make sure the unit purchased is of the same polarity as the vehicle. Ensure that units with adjustable polarity are correctly set before commencing the fitting operations.

20 It is difficult to give specific information with regard to fitting, as final positioning of the radio/tape player, speakers and aerial is entirely a matter of personal preference. Space for a radio is very limited in these models and it is probably best to mount the equipment on the facia shelf or by careful cutting of the glove opening backboard.

21 Some radios will have mounting brackets provided, together with instructions; others will need to be fitted using drilled and slotted metal strips, bent to form mounting brackets. These strips are available from most accessory shops. The unit must be properly earthed by fitting a separate earthing lead between the casing of the radio and the vehicle body.

22 Use the radio manufacturers' instructions when wiring the radio into the vehicle's electrical system. A 1 to 2 amp in-line fuse must be fitted in the radio's feed wire; a choke may also be necessary (see below).

23 The type of aerial used and its fitted position, is a matter of personal preference. In general, the taller the aerial the better the reception. It is best to fit a fully retractable aerial; especially if a mechanical car-wash is used or if you live in an area where cars tend to be vandalised. In this respect, electric aerials which are raised and lowered automatically when switching the radio on or off are convenient, but are more likely to give trouble than the manual type.

24 When choosing a position for the aerial, the following points should be considered:

(a) The aerial lead should be as short as possible; this means that the aerial should be mounted at the front of the car

(b) The aerial must be mounted as far away from the distributor and HT leads as possible

(c) The part of the aerial which protrudes beneath the mounting point must not foul the roadwheels, or anything else

(d) If possible, the aerial should be positioned so that the coaxial lead does not have to be routed through the engine compartment

(e) The plane of the panel on which the aerial is mounted should not be so steeply angled that the aerial cannot be mounted vertically (in relation to the end-on aspect of the car). Most aerials have a small amount of adjustment available

25 Having decided on a mounting position, a relatively large hole will have to be made in the panel. The exact size of the hole will depend upon the specific aerial being fitted, although generally, the hole required is of 19 mm ($\frac{3}{4}$ in) diameter. A tank-cutter of the relevant diameter is the best tool to use for making the hole. This tool needs a small diameter pilot hole drilled through the panel, through which the tool clamping bolt is inserted. When the hole has been made the raw edges should be de-burred with a file and then painted to prevent corrosion.

26 Fit the aerial according to the manufacturer's instructions. If the aerial is very tall, or if it protrudes beneath the mounting panel for a considerable distance, it is a good idea to fit a stay beneath the aerial and the vehicle frame. This stay can be manufactured from the slotted and drilled metal strips previously mentioned. The stay should be securely screwed or bolted in place. For best reception, it is advisable to fit an earth lead between the aerial and the vehicle body.
27 It will probably be necessary to drill one or two holes through bodywork panels in order to feed the aerial lead into the interior of the car. Where this is the case, ensure that the holes are fitted with rubber grommets to protect the cable and to stop possible entry of water.
28 Positioning and fitting of the speaker depends mainly on its type.
29 If a pod type speaker was supplied with the radio, this can be secured to the mounting panel with self-tapping screws.
30 When connecting a rear-mounted speaker to the radio, the wires should be routed through the vehicle beneath the carpets or floor mats, preferably along the side of the floorpan where they will not be trodden on by passengers. Make the relevant connections as directed by the radio manufacturer.
31 By now you will have several yards of additional wiring in the car, use PVC tape to secure this wiring out of harm's way. Do not leave electrical leads dangling. Ensure that all new electrical connections are properly made (wires twisted together will not do) and completely secure.
32 The radio should now be working, but before you pack away your tools it will be necessary to trim the radio to the aerial. If specific instuctions are not provided by the radio manufacturer, proceed as follows: Find a station with a low signal strength on the medium-wave band, slowly turn the trim screw of the radio in or out until the loudest reception of the selected station is obtained. The set is then trimmed to the aerial.

Tape players

33 Fitting instructions for cassette stereo tape players are the same, in general, as when fitting a radio. Tape players are not usually prone to electrical interference like radios, so positioning is not so critical. If possible, the player should be mounted on an even keel. Also it must be possible for a driver wearing a seat belt to reach the unit in order to change or turn over tapes.

Suppression of interference

34 To eliminate buzzes and other unwanted noises, costs very little and is not as difficult as sometimes thought. With a modicum of common sense and patience and following the instructions in the following paragraphs, interference can be virtually eliminated.
35 The first cause for concern is the generator. The noise this makes over the radio is like an electric mixer and the noise speeds up when you rev up (if you wish to prove the point, you can remove the drivebelt and try it). The remedy for this is simple; connect a 1.0μF to 3.0μF capacitor between earth, and the *large* (B+) terminal on the generator. This is most important, for if you connect it to the small terminal, you will probably damage the generator permanently.
36 A second common cause of electrical interference is the ignition system. Obtain a suitable capacitor which is compatible with the special Citroen coil. This may stop the tick-tick-tick sound that comes over the speaker. Next comes the spark itself. The ignition HT leads are of suppressed type and no further action is required. Do not fit plug suppressor caps or cut the leads to fit in-line suppressors.
37 At this stage it is advisable to check that the radio is well earthed, also the aerial, and to see that the aerial plug is pushed well into the set and that the radio is properly trimmed. In addition, check that the wire which supplies the power to the set is as short as possible and does not wander all over the car. It is a good idea to check that the fuse is of the correct rating. For most sets this will be about 1 to 2 amps.
38 At this point the more usual causes of interference have been suppressed. If the problem still exists, a look at the causes of interference may help to pinpoint the component generating the stray electrical discharges.
39 The radio picks up electromagnetic waves in the air; now some are made by radio stations and other broadcasters and some, not wanted, are made by the car. The home made signals are produced by stray electrical discharges floating around in the car. Common producers of these signals are electric motors, ie, the windscreen wipers, electric screen washers, heater fan or an electric aerial, if fitted. Other sources of interference are flashing turn signals and instruments. Turn signals are not normally suppressed. In recent years, radio manufacturers have included in the line (live) of the radio, in addition to the fuse, an in-line choke. If your installation lacks one of these, put one in.

Fuses

40 The fusebox on later models is still located on the engine compartment rear bulkhead, but the circuits protected vary from those described in Chapter 10 (see Specifications).
41 The spare position in the fusebox can be used for the wiring circuit if extra accessories are fitted.

10 Bodywork

Front grille

1 As from July 1977, the air intake grille on the front of the car is removable independently of the front panel.
2 The grille is secured by eight self-tapping screws and the modification makes access to the front of the engine much easier.

Bonnet release

3 The bonnet is released by a remote control cable from inside the car (Dyane) or by means of a lever mounted below the bumper (2CV).
4 Keep the bonnet latch and safety catch well lubricated.
5 Adjustments to alignment can be made by moving the position of the hinges, latch or striker as necessary within the tolerance provided by their bolt holes.

Fig. 12.28 Bonnet release catch – Dyane (Sec 10)

2 *Safety lever*

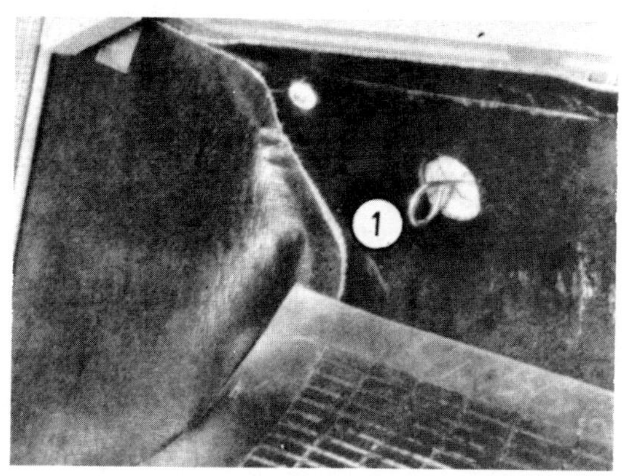

Fig. 12.29 Bonnet release handle (1) – Dyane (Sec 10)

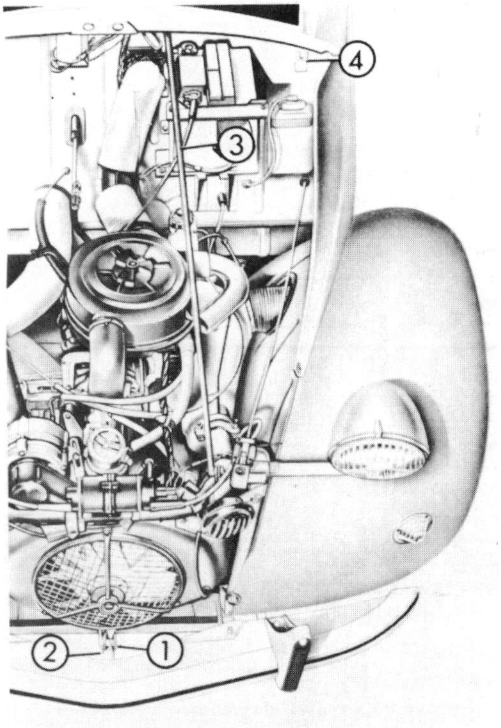

Fig. 12.30 Bonnet release – 2CV models (Sec 10)

1 *Release lever* 3 *Stay*
2 *Safety catch* 4 *Stay locating notch*

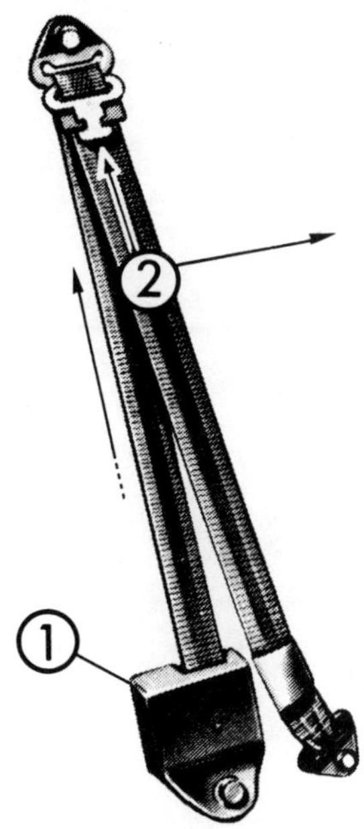

Fig. 12.31 Inertia reel seat belt (Sec 10)

1 *Reel casing* 2 *Catch tongue*

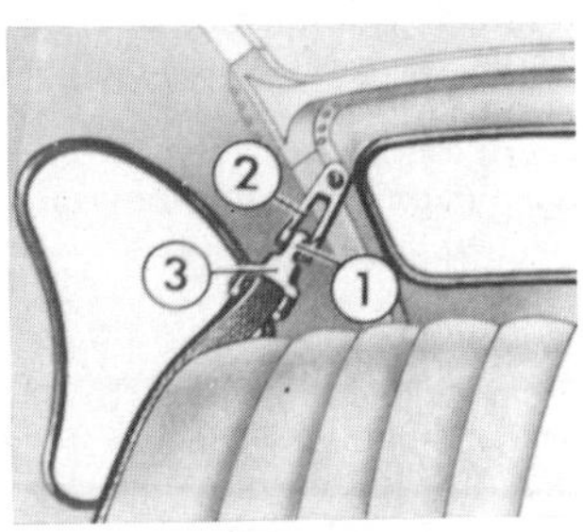

Fig. 12.32 Rear seat belt anchorage (Sec 10)

1 *Catch* 3 *Catch tongue*
2 *Holder*

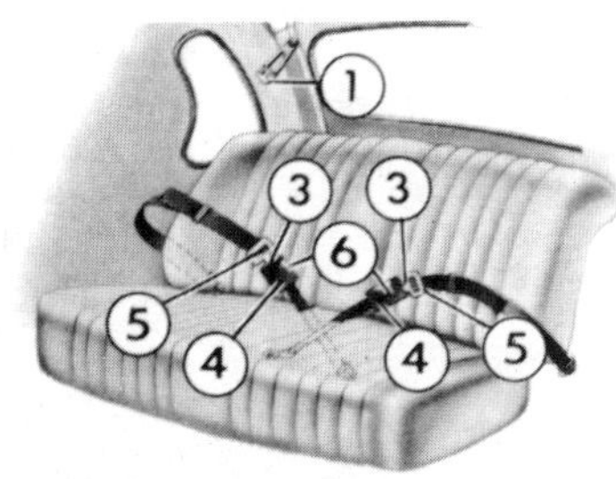

Fig. 12.33 Rear seat belt routing (Sec 10)

1 *Catch* 5 *Adjuster buckle*
3 *Catch tongue* 6 *Release button*
4 *Buckle*

Safety belts

6 Front safety belts may be of static or inertia reel type according to model and date of production.

7 Clean the belts with warm water and detergent – nothing else.

8 Never alter the location of the seat belt anchorages and, if the belts are disconnected, make sure that the sequence of the anchor components (washers, spacer and anchor plate) is as originally fitted.

9 If the belts become frayed or have been subjected to strain due to a front end collision they must be renewed.

10 Rear seat belts are available for later models.

General repair procedures

Whenever servicing, repair or overhaul work is carried out on the car or its components, it is necessary to observe the following procedures and instructions. This will assist in carrying out the operation efficiently and to a professional standard of workmanship.

Joint mating faces and gaskets

Where a gasket is used between the mating faces of two components, ensure that it is renewed on reassembly, and fit it dry unless otherwise stated in the repair procedure. Make sure that the mating faces are clean and dry with all traces of old gasket removed. When cleaning a joint face, use a tool which is not likely to score or damage the face, and remove any burrs or nicks with an oilstone or fine file.

Make sure that tapped holes are cleaned with a pipe cleaner, and keep them free of jointing compound if this is being used unless specifically instructed otherwise.

Ensure that all orifices, channels or pipes are clear and blow through them, preferably using compressed air.

Oil seals

Whenever an oil seal is removed from its working location, either individually or as part of an assembly, it should be renewed.

The very fine sealing lip of the seal is easily damaged and will not seal if the surface it contacts is not completely clean and free from scratches, nicks or grooves. If the original sealing surface of the component cannot be restored, the component should be renewed.

Protect the lips of the seal from any surface which may damage them in the course of fitting. Use tape or a conical sleeve where possible. Lubricate the seal lips with oil before fitting and, on dual lipped seals, fill the space between the lips with grease.

Unless otherwise stated, oil seals must be fitted with their sealing lips toward the lubricant to be sealed.

Use a tubular drift or block of wood of the appropriate size to install the seal and, if the seal housing is shouldered, drive the seal down to the shoulder. If the seal housing is unshouldered, the seal should be fitted with its face flush with the housing top face.

Screw threads and fastenings

Always ensure that a blind tapped hole is completely free from oil, grease, water or other fluid before installing the bolt or stud. Failure to do this could cause the housing to crack due to the hydraulic action of the bolt or stud as it is screwed in.

When tightening a castellated nut to accept a split pin, tighten the nut to the specified torque, where applicable, and then tighten further to the next split pin hole. Never slacken the nut to align a split pin hole unless stated in the repair procedure.

When checking or retightening a nut or bolt to a specified torque setting, slacken the nut or bolt by a quarter of a turn, and then retighten to the specified setting.

Locknuts, locktabs and washers

Any fastening which will rotate against a component or housing in the course of tightening should always have a washer between it and the relevant component or housing.

Spring or split washers should always be renewed when they are used to lock a critical component such as a big-end bearing retaining nut or bolt.

Locktabs which are folded over to retain a nut or bolt should always be renewed.

Self-locking nuts can be reused in non-critical areas, providing resistance can be felt when the locking portion passes over the bolt or stud thread.

Split pins must always be replaced with new ones of the correct size for the hole.

Special tools

Some repair procedures in this manual entail the use of special tools such as a press, two or three-legged pullers, spring compressors etc. Wherever possible, suitable readily available alternatives to the manufacturer's special tools are described, and are shown in use. In some instances, where no alternative is possible, it has been necessary to resort to the use of a manufacturer's tool and this has been done for reasons of safety as well as the efficient completion of the repair operation. Unless you are highly skilled and have a thorough understanding of the procedure described, never attempt to bypass the use of any special tool when the procedure described specifies its use. Not only is there a very great risk of personal injury, but expensive damage could be caused to the components involved.

Index

Printed by
Haynes Publishing Group
Sparkford Yeovil Somerset
England